KEY TO THE B

W9-AUS-720

LIST OF BOXES

 **KEY POINTS BOXES**

LANGUAGE AND CULTURE BOXES

For **ESL Note** and **Tech Note** listings see pages viii–ix.

KEYS FOR WRITERS

FOURTH EDITION

ANN RAIMES

Hunter College, City University of New York

Houghton Mifflin Company
Boston   New York

Publisher: Patricia Coryell
Executive Editor: Suzanne Phelps Weir
Senior Development Editor: Martha Bustin
Editorial Assistant: Anne Leung
Senior Project Editor: Rosemary Winfield
Editorial Assistant: Jake Perry
Art and Design Coordinator: Jill Huber
Photo Editor: Jennifer Meyer Dare
Composition Buyer: Sarah Ambrose
Designer: Henry Rachlin
Manufacturing Manager: Florence Cadran
Marketing Manager: Cindy Graff Cohen
Marketing Assistant: Wendy Thayer

Credits continue on page 514, which constitutes an extension of the copyright page.

Printed in China   Library of Congress Catalog Card Number 2003108482

7 8 9 10 11-SDP-10 09 08 07 06 05

Instructor's exam copy ISBN 0-618-49650-5
For orders use student text ISBN 0-618-43785-1

book of writing instruction, practice exercises, examples, diagnostic tests, KeyTabs® for bookmarking, and hotlinks. When students look up a topic, they have two choices: they can read a brief explanation, or they can click a button for more detailed explanation and annotated examples. From either the brief screen or the detailed explanation screens, students can instantly access exercises and models.

- **Digital Keys Online passkey**   Students receive a 12-month subscription to a Web version of the CD-ROM (without diagnostic tests).

- **WriteSpace online writing environment registration code**   An easy-to-use Web-based writing program, WriteSpace delivers writing tutorials, interactive exercises, diagnostic tests, assignments, models, and more. Built within our new Eduspace® platform and powered by Blackboard, the program can be used in online, distance learning courses, in "wired" classrooms, and as an easily integrated enhancement to traditional courses.

- **SMARTHINKING™ online writing tutoring program**   Embedded in the WriteSpace program, Smarthinking links students to a Web-based writing center, staffed by experienced composition instructors. Tutors interact with students in real-time during afternoon and evening homework hours, five days a week, and answer questions and offer helpful feedback on drafts.

For more information about these HelpDesk for Writers technology tools, please contact your local Houghton Mifflin sales representative; call toll free 800-733-1717, ex. 4020; or go to <college_English@hmco.com>.

Other Technology Tools

In addition to the above HelpDesk for Writers (new technology writing tools that can be packaged together with the print handbook), students can also access other resources on the free, non-password-protected Houghton Mifflin English Student Web site.

Keys for Writers **Student Website**   can be accessed at <http://college.hmco.com/keys.html>. The Web site features research templates for keeping track of one's sources, flashcards for a quick review of usage issues, ESL information, interactive exercises, updated live links to Sources in 27 Subject Areas, and more.

e-Exercises   This rich e-library of enjoyable self-quizzes lets students hone their grammar skills, go at their own pace, and work wherever is convenient for them—home, computer lab, or classroom.

Adverb Placement, 368
Relative vs. Personal Pronouns, 376
Number before *Hundred, Thousand,* and *Million,* 415

Helpful tips for using the Internet TechNotes appear throughout the handbook on the following topics:

TechNotes
Web Sites for Generating Ideas and Planning, 7
Using Web Directories to Find Topics, 12
Using Word in Collaborative Writing, 20
Useful Web Sites for Writing Arguments, 45
Logical Fallacies on the Web, 58
Students' Writing in Service Learning Courses, 73
Useful Sites for Writing across the Curriculum, 76
Links from the Web Site for *Keys for Writers,* 102
A Web Site on Plagiarism, 116
Keeping a Bookmark or Favorites File on the Internet, 119
Indentation Online, 152
Underlining versus Italics, 152
Using Outline View, 234
ESL Web Sites, 428

Coverage of writing across the curriculum and writing in the workplace, making this a handbook to keep *Keys for Writers* prepares students for a range of writing tasks they may meet in their college career and beyond. Part 1 looks at genres common within the humanities, social sciences, and sciences, and discusses the art of writing well under pressure. With many model documents and practical tips, Part 5 covers job-related writing, such as résumés (print and electronic).

A COMPLETE SUPPORT PACKAGE

New Technology Tools for Student Writers

The multimedia edition of *Keys for Writers* — the print textbook packaged with the new **HelpDesk for Writers** ensemble of technology products—provides four convenient and powerful electronic aids for self-paced and personalized writing instruction on the computer.

- **Digital Keys 4.0 student CD-ROM** This new CD-ROM has a host of interactive tools and resources to help students work on all aspects of their writing, including grammar, punctuation, mechanics, and style. The core of this writing aid is an easily navigated hand-

Bracketed labels on selected sample citations in all styles These show at a glance what types of information to include and how to format, arrange, and punctuate that information.

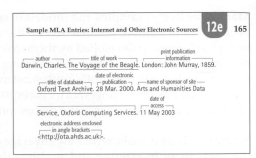

Whole part on Style, including the Five C's of Style   *Keys for Writers* devotes a full part (Part 6) to the important area of style, covering sentence- and word-related style issues in a unified presentation. Part 6 retains the distinctive and popular Five C's of Style, which advises students in a straightforward, memorable way to Cut, Check for Action, Connect, Commit, and Choose Your Words.

Thorough and clear coverage of grammar, in one convenient part Part 7, Common Sentence Problems, gives students one central place to turn to when they have grammar questions. Grammar coverage is not split confusingly over several parts, as in other handbooks. Handy sections on students' frequently asked grammar questions and top ten sentence problems begin Part 7.

Distinctive and thorough help for ESL/Multilingual Writers   *Keys for Writers* features clear coverage of ESL grammar points and a unique opening segment that places this instruction within a supportive framework. It includes a section on English and Englishes, a Language Guide to Transfer Errors (now with edited example sentences), and a section on False Friends (confusing cognates). ESL Notes appear throughout the handbook on the following topics:

ESL Notes
Writing in Different Languages and Cultures, 16
The Dangers of Grammar-Check Programs, 37
Evidence Used to Support an Argument, 51
Be, Been, and *Being,* 332
Verbs Not Followed by *-ing* Forms, 334
No *Will* in Time Clause, 334
Passive Voice with Transitive Verbs, 342
Base Form after a Modal, 345
Singular Verb after *It,* 347
No Plural Form for Adjectives, 365

Many more lively examples and models of student writing *Keys for Writers*, Fourth Edition, is enlivened by the work of student writers, on topics chosen and developed by them in writing classes around the country. For example, in Part 1, The Writing Process, a full paper on uniforms is shown in two drafts, with substantial content revision and with annotations. Numerous shorter excerpts provide helpful models and bring students' voices into the discussion.

An emphasis on visuals, with new coverage on writing and presenting ideas in an interactive and multimedia environment An increased art program and a new section on document design address some of the many ways that visuals now enhance the power of the written word. This edition contains an abundance of new model documents, visuals, screen captures, charts, graphs, art, and photos.

 More Key Points boxes This helpful feature provides easy-to-review summaries, tips, and checklists. For example, the handbook now includes new boxes on critical thinking, using italics, posting an academic paper online, and avoiding plagiarism.

HELPFUL CONTENTS DESIGNED FOR EASY ACCESS

Two rows of color-coded divider tabs The simplicity and clarity of two rows of tabs (the first row—red, for whole-paper issues; the second row—gold, for sentence-level issues) make it easy to find information quickly. Students do not have to follow three or more color threads through several layers or banks of tabs or puzzle over what category, from an overly large assortment of similarly named categories, will hold the information they are looking for.

Unique KeyTabs® Found in the back of the handbook, the five moveable, custom-fit KeyTabs® serve as bookmarks, extended margins, and note cards. Students and instructors simply insert these locator cards into the binding, with the top of the KeyTab® extending from the top of the book, to gain quick access to information that is often consulted.

Starting points for research in a range of disciplines A newly updated and expanded list, Sources in 27 Subject Areas, contains frequently used reference works in print, print and electronic indexes, and Web sites. This extensive time-saving research source list, compiled with the aid of college reference librarians, remains a tool that students can use throughout their college career as they work on papers across the disciplines. Live and regularly updated links are also available at the *Keys for Writers* Web site.

So when friends ask me why I'm working on a new edition, I can answer that it's because we are lucky enough to live in a world where things are not static and bound by tradition, where new traditions are forged daily and the numbers of questions grow. Other Englishes exist alongside Standard English, challenging and extending its boundaries. The excitement of keeping up is thrilling. I hope it is contagious.

NEW TO THE FOURTH EDITION

Expanded and updated MLA, APA, and *Chicago Manual of Style* guidelines   Parts 3 and 4 reflect the changes found in the *MLA Handbook for Writers of Research Papers*, Sixth Edition (2003), the *Publication Manual of the American Psychological Association*, Fifth Edition (2001), and the Fifteenth Edition of *The Chicago Manual of Style* (2003).

Keys now covers in greater detail, with more examples, how to document sources from electronic resources, including full-text online databases, online encyclopedias, and Web sites. A new sample student MLA paper on "Safety First: Women and Men in Police and Fire Departments" provides a fresh, timely model.

Expanded coverage of argument   Students need to know how to plan, develop, and write strong arguments. This expanded section now gives them more practical, comprehensive guidance. New sections include formulating a good argument, choosing a topic, deductive and inductive reasoning, visual arguments, and a complete sample student argument paper.

New section on avoiding plagiarism, with a Key Points box that stresses the essential points   No-nonsense instruction on this crucial academic topic gives clear guidance, presenting the definition of plagiarism, how to avoid even the suspicion of plagiarism, how to keep track of sources to forestall any inadvertent plagiarism, and how to summarize, paraphrase, and give full credit to all sources. A unique section also covers a related topic: indicating the boundaries of a citation.

Expanded and updated coverage of using search engines, keyword searches, online indexes, and databases, and more on evaluating sources   Thoroughly updated to reflect current developments, Part 2 presents the latest approaches to doing effective, substantial online searches. It includes the search done by the student author of the new MLA paper in Part 3, with screen shots of a Web page from a full-text article subscription database and from two popular search engines.

Preface

When I tell friends and students I am working on the fourth edition of a handbook, they wonder—often out loud—what I could possibly find new to say about grammar and commas. Fellow teachers, however, know exactly what goes into a new edition. Writing instructors shift their approaches as they keep trying different ways to help their students learn to be good writers. In the changing technological world, information is increasingly conveyed by sound and images as well as by the written word. Writing is also seen as extending beyond one required college course. The cross-curricular and cross-cultural perspective takes over, as students write in all their courses, in their communities, and around the globe using e-mail. Style changes, conventions change, readers' expectations change. And handbooks inevitably change.

Students change, too. Those entering colleges and universities today often far outshine their faculty instructors in their facility with computers, the Internet, and rapid exchange of information. They write more than they did before the age of instant messaging, acquiring not just print literacy but also visual literacy as they navigate complex Web sites and design their own.

In addition, the nature of research is in a constant state of flux, with more and more academic material available online, with the attendant challenges of how to access, use, cite, integrate, and present that material effectively. As if all this were not enough to call for a new edition, professional organizations that establish the conventions for documenting research publish new editions that put their old recommendations to rest as they, too, grapple with this exciting changing world of unlimited information at our fingertips.

I continue to believe that the best handbook is the one that students will use, as well as the one that keeps pace with their changing needs. The success of the previous editions of *Keys for Writers* tells me to keep this handbook's distinctive navigation and clearly labeled rows of tabs, the coaching tone that students see as lively but respectful, and the concise explanations of grammar and style that have delighted many users. Yet *Keys for Writers* has also changed because both teachers and students have conveyed in person, sent, and e-mailed invaluable suggestions to help the book keep pace with current trends in writing and be as accurate and timely as a handbook should be. I am grateful for those shared ideas and delighted to incorporate them.

Exercises cover thirty areas within the broad categories of punctuation, mechanics, parts of speech, spelling, and sentence problems.

Internet Research Guide This online guide by Jason Snart of College of DuPage presents six extended learning modules with practice exercises (tutorials) for using the Internet as a research tool. Topics include evaluating Web information, building an argument with Web research, and plagiarism and documentation.

Print Supplements for Students

Raimes and Flanagan, *Exercise Booklet*, **Fourth Edition** This well-regarded print booklet contains eighty-two well-crafted editing exercises. It has been carefully revised to match *Keys for Writers*, Fourth Edition, and make a good companion to it.

THEA (formerly TASP) and CLAST Preparation Manuals These exercise and review booklets include practice tests to help students pass the Texas Higher Education Assessment Test and Florida's College Level Academic Skills Test.

The American Heritage College Dictionary, **Fourth Edition** This best-selling reference is an indispensable tool and desk reference.

The American Heritage English as a Second Language Dictionary This reference is specially designed with additional sample sentences to suit the needs of intermediate to advanced ESL students.

Technology Tools for Instructors

WriteSpace online writing environment WriteSpace includes a complete classroom management system, giving instructors the ability to send or post papers; diagnostic skills tests; Virtual Classroom tools that include online chat functions, interactive whiteboards, synchronous and asynchronous class discussions, and online office hours; and flexible tools for building customized grade books, syllabi, bulletin boards, assignments, and more.

Blackboard Course Cartridge and Web/CT e-Pack This first-year college composition course was designed by Joel A. English, Coordinator of Professional Writing at Old Dominion University, to be used with *Keys* and its ancillary media. It provides all of the writing projects, quizzes, daily work, readings, multimedia components, and teaching objectives for a full first-year college composition course. The course objectives can guide teachers in what to teach during class sessions yet remain adaptable to a full range of teaching styles.

Print Supplements for Instructors

Instructor's Support Package   In a convenient $8\frac{1}{2}$" x 11", three-hole-punched format, this packet is designed to slip into a binder; instructors can then add or take out information as needed. In five parts, this packet provides an overview of the handbook and transparency masters on how to use it; a section on teaching composition to ESL and multilingual students; a section on using the Internet in the composition classroom, with student tutorials; diagnostic tests on five main areas of grammar; answers to numbered items in the *Exercise Booklet*; and approximately sixty-five transparency masters.

Three new books by writing instructors for writing instructors and tutors provide a wealth of practical ideas and support. These complimentary books are available on request by instructors adopting *Keys for Writers*, Fourth Edition. For more information about these books, please contact your local Houghton Mifflin sales representative; call toll free 800-733-1717, ex. 4020; or go to <college _English@hmco.com>.

Teaching Writing with Computers: An Introduction   Edited with an introduction by Pamela Takayoshi and Brian Huot, both of the University of Louisville, this book is an up-to-date resource on integrating technology into writing instruction. Essays cover: (1) Writing Technologies for Composition Pedagogies; (2) Learning to Teach with Technology; (3) Teaching Beyond Physical Boundaries; (4) Teaching and Learning New Media; and (5) Assigning and Assessing Student Writing.

Finding Our Way: A Writing Teacher's Sourcebook   Edited with an introduction by Wendy Bishop and Deborah Coxwell Teague of Florida State University in Tallahassee, this collection of essays is a unique and powerful guide for new or relatively new composition teachers. It addresses many of the unvoiced questions, challenges, and seldom-discussed, yet crucial, issues that arise for writing teachers.

The Essentials of Tutoring: Helping College Students Develop Their Writing Skills   Paul Gary Phillips and Joyce B. Phillips of Grossmont College have written this supportive and comprehensive guide for writing tutors. Covering the general guidelines of how to tutor and the specifics of both sentence-level and essay-level tutoring, it can be used as a self-paced training program, in a classroom setting, in a formal tutor training class, or as a reference tool during the course of a tutoring session.

Exercises to Accompany *Keys for Writers*

Exercises to accompany *Keys for Writers*, Fourth Edition, may be

Katherine Green, Albuquerque Technical-Vocational Institute
John Gregorian, Contra Costa Community College
Claudia Gresham-Shelton, Stanly Community College
Jane E. Hardy, Cornell University
Beth L. Hewett, Community College of Baltimore County—Essex
Christopher Z. Hobson, State University of New York, College at
    Old Westbury
Franklin E. Horowitz, Columbia University
Michael Hricik, Westmoreland City Community College
Margaret Hughes, Butte College
Mary L. Hurst, Cuyahoga Community College
John Hyman, American University
Ernest H. Johansson, Ohio University
Mary Kaye Jordan, Ohio University
Ann Judd, Seward County Community College
Susan Kincaid, Lakeland Community College
Sally Kurtzman, Arapahoe Community College
Joseph LaBriola, Sinclair Community College
Lindsay Lewan, Arapahoe Community College
Daniel Lowe, Community College of Allegheny County
Kelly Lowe, Mount Union College
Dianne Luce, Midlands Technical Community College
Mike MacKey, Community College of Denver
Mary Sue MacNealy, The University of Memphis
Louis Martin, Elizabethtown College
Ann Maxham-Kastrinos, Washington State University
Michael G. Moran, University of Georgia
Marie Nigro, Lincoln University, PA
Carolyn O'Hearn, Pittsburgh State University
Liz Parker, Nashville State Technical Institute
Sally Parr, Ithaca College
Kathy Parrish, Southwestern College
Jane Peterson, Richland College
Lillian Polak, Nassau Community College
Nelljean M. Rice, Coastal Carolina University
Kenneth Risdon, University of Minnesota at Duluth
Mark Rollins, Ohio University
Cheryl W. Ruggiero, Virginia Polytechnic Institute
Kristin L. Snoddy, Indiana University at Kokomo
Ellen Sostarich, Hocking College
Jami M. Taylor, ECPI College of Technology
Amy Ulmer, Pasadena City College
Jane Mueller Ungari, Robert Morris College

Margaret Urie, University of Nevada
Thomas Villano, Boston University
Colleen Weldele, Palomar College
Barbara Whitehead, Hampton University
Stephen Wilhoit, University of Dayton
James D. Williams, University of North Carolina, Chapel Hill
James Wilson, LaGuardia Community College, CUNY
Sallie Wolf, Arapahoe Community College
Randell Wolff, Murray State
Martin Wood, University of Wisconsin at Eau Claire
Randal Woodland, University of Michigan—Dearborn
Laura W. Zlogar, University of Wisconsin—River Falls

My colleagues at Houghton Mifflin have been a pleasure to work with. They are warm, supportive, responsive, and incredibly knowledgeable about textbook publishing. Special thanks go to Pat Coryell, Vice President, and Suzanne Phelps Weir, Executive Editor, for their leadership, energy, and enthusiasm for the project; to Martha Bustin, Senior Development Editor, for her keen editorial eye, contributions to the manuscript, and unfailing grace under pressure—she surely must be a textbook writer's perfect editor; to Rosemary Winfield, Senior Project Editor, for coping with challenging deadlines during the production process; and to Cindy Graff Cohen, Marketing Manager, for keeping me attuned to market needs and adding to the fun of my trips to colleges across the United States. I also gratefully acknowledge the help and professionalism of others on the large *Keys* team: Jill Haber, Henry Rachlin, Florence Cadran, Sarah and Iris Bishins, Diana Coe, Sarah Helyar Smith, Anne Leung, Janet Edmonds, Jake Perry, Janet Young, Carolyn Lengel, Bruce Carson, Michael Farmer, Ellen Whalen, Pat Cabeza, Marianne L'Abbate, Lisa Wehrle, Bernice Eisen, Leoni McVey, Sam Davison, and the miracle workers at New England Typographic Service.

Warmest thanks to my friends in Brooklyn and in Chatham, New York, for making sure I took time to play tennis, go to movies, eat out, and have fun. Above all, thanks go to my daughters, Emily and Lucy, and to my husband, James Raimes, who helped with research, typed, edited, offered advice, and cooked great meals. If I hadn't known before that writing was a collaborative effort, I would surely know it now.

Ann Raimes
Hunter College, City University of New York

Through writing, you do not just *display* what you know; you can also *discover* what you know and think. The process of writing helps you have ideas, make connections, and raise questions, whether you are working on an e-mail message or a research report. Use the time and solitude that the writing process affords to discover as well as to present, to learn as well as to fulfill an assignment. Expect writing to be not a linear or step-by-step procedure, but a messy adventure, one that you control but that often surprises you with your own insights.

Though virtually no one marches neatly through the steps in this order, the writing process does involve several steps:

planning
- critical thinking and reading
- determining your purpose and audience
- generating ideas
- establishing a topic and thesis
- gathering information and support

drafting
- organizing and developing ideas
- writing drafts (preliminary versions)

revising
- revising and checking for clarity, coherence, and unity
- editing and proofreading

1 Getting Started and Finding a Focus

Getting started can be hard if you think of a piece of writing as a permanent document. A blank page or an empty screen with its blinking cursor can be daunting, but the act of writing offers an advantage over speaking: you can go back and make changes. You are not locked into what you have written—not until you decide to turn your finished work over to readers. You can also present whatever image of yourself you choose. You have the freedom to invent yourself anew. As journalist Adam Gopnik says fondly of writing, "It's you there, but not quite you."

1a Reading, thinking, writing

"I wonder where she gets that from? I don't understand that point. She hasn't convinced me at all." Just as we think critically about what we read, readers think critically when they read what we write, sometimes making comments like these. Thinking is inextricably tied to reading and writing, so much so that thinking critically is essential to being a good reader and a good writer.

Thinking critically is what we all do when we ask questions about what we see, hear, or read, when we don't accept something at face value just because someone else has thought it and expressed it and someone has seen fit to publish it. Thinking critically does not mean thinking negatively in order to criticize—though if what you read is badly written, that could well be the result. Instead, it means questioning, discussing, and looking at an issue from a number of sides.

KEY POINTS

Critical Thinking

1. *Do close readings.* Read more than once; read slowly and carefully, immersing yourself in the text.

2. *Question and challenge.* Take on the role of a debater. Ask, for example, where an idea comes from, what biases the writer reveals, whether the writer provides you with enough information in an interesting way, what evidence a writer provides, whether the writer's logic is sound, and whether opposing views are taken into account.

3. *Write as you read.* Interact with a text by highlighting points. Write comments and questions in the margins of a page or between the lines in an online document saved to your word processor. In this way, you start a conversation with anything you read. The text you are reading will look messy—but that is a good sign.

4. *Keep reading journals and write summaries and reactions.* See **1c** for how to keep a double-entry journal.

5. *Remember that readers will read critically what you write.* It is not enough to read critically. Be aware that your own writing has to stand up to readers' careful scrutiny and challenge, too.

1b   Defining purpose and audience

Before you begin writing, consider the question "What is the main purpose of this piece of writing?" The following questions will help guide you to an answer.

KEY POINTS

Asking about Purpose

1. Is your main purpose to explain an idea or provide information? Writing with this purpose is called *expository writing*.

2. Is your main purpose to persuade readers to see things your way or move readers to action? This aim leads to *persuasive writing* or *argumentation*.

3. Is your main purpose to describe an experiment or a detailed process or to report on laboratory results? Writing with this purpose is frequently referred to as *scientific* or *technical writing*.

4. Is your main purpose to record and express your own experience, observations, ideas, and feelings? In the humanities, such accounts are known as *expressive, autobiographical,* or *personal writing*.

5. Is your main purpose to create an original work of art, such as a poem, story, play, or novel? Writing with this purpose is called *creative writing*.

The first three items listed in the Key Points box (on expository, persuasive, and scientific or technical writing) are generally the main purposes of writing across the college curriculum. Among these categories, however, the overlap can be considerable. Some assignments may require you to explore and test concepts and opinions against what you already know. Other assignments may ask you to blend explanation with persuasion. Creative nonfiction, which includes memoir, biography, and travel writing, crosses categories to present information in a literary and original way, adding the art of storytelling to the reporting of information. Whatever you determine to be the main purpose or purposes of a given assignment should guide you as you begin writing.

Audience and discourse community A good writer connects with his or her audience and keeps readers in mind at all times, as if in a face-to-face communication. Achieving this connection, however, often proves challenging, because not all readers have the same characteristics. Readers come from different discourse communities— that is, from different regions, communities, ethnic groups, organizations, and academic disciplines, all with their own linguistic and rhetorical conventions (see 4f). Ask yourself the following questions about your readers.

LANGUAGE AND CULTURE
Assessing Your Readers' Expectations

- Who will read your piece of writing? What will readers expect in terms of length, format, date of delivery, and content?
- What kinds of texts do your readers usually read and write, and what are the conventions of those texts? For example, if you are writing a business letter to a company in another country, consult a business communications book to find out what readers there expect in a business letter.
- Will readers expect formal or informal language? The expectations of teenagers online and college professors, for example, differ greatly.
- Will readers expect you to use technical terms? If so, which terms are in common use?
- What characteristics do you and your readers have in common: nationality, language, culture, race, class, ethnicity, gender? Consider what limitations writing for these readers places on your use of dialect, punctuation, vocabulary, and political and cultural expectations. Cultivate common ground, and try not to alienate readers.
- Is your instructor your main reader? If so, what do you know about the expectations of a reader in his or her academic discipline? Be sure to ask what background information you should include and what you can safely omit. Ask to see a model paper. In most cases, regard your instructor as a stand-in for an audience of general readers, not as an individual expert.

1c   Exploring ideas for writing

Whether you have to generate your own idea for a topic or you already have a clear sense of purpose and topic, you need strategies other than staring at the ceiling or waiting for inspiration to fly in through the window. Professional writers use a variety of techniques to generate ideas at various stages of the process. In her article "Oh Muse! You Do Make Things Difficult!" Diane Ackerman reports that the poet Dame Edith Sitwell used to lie in an open coffin, French novelist Colette picked fleas from her cat, statesman Benjamin Franklin soaked in the bathtub, and German dramatist Friedrich Schiller sniffed rotten apples stored in his desk.

Perhaps you have developed your own original approach to generating ideas. Perhaps you were taught a more formal way to begin a writing project, such as by constructing an outline. If what you do now does not seem to produce good results, or if you are ready for a change, try some of the following methods and see how they work. Not every method works equally well for every project or for every writer. Experimenting is a good idea.

 TechNote Web Sites for Generating Ideas and Planning

The *Purdue University Online Writing Lab* at <http://owl.english .purdue.edu> and the *Paradigm Online Writing Assistant* at <http://www.powa.org/discover/index.html> include information on generating ideas and planning. ■

Keeping a journal A *journal* can be far more than a personal diary. Many writers carry a notebook and write in it every day. Journal entries can be observations, references, quotations, questions for research, notes on events, and ideas about assigned texts or topics, as well as specific pieces of writing in progress. A journal can also serve as a review for final examinations or essay tests, reminding you of areas of special interest or subjects you did not understand.

The *double-entry* or *dialectical journal* provides a formalized way for you to think critically about readings and lectures. Two pages or two columns or open windows in your word processor provide the space for interaction. On the left-hand side, write summaries, quotations, and accounts of readings, lectures, and class discussions— that is, record as exactly and concisely as you can what you read or heard. The left-hand side, in short, is reserved for information about the material. On the right-hand side, record your own comments, reactions, and questions about the material. (See **4c** on critical thinking.)

Freewriting If you do not know what to write about or how to approach a broad subject, try doing five to ten minutes of *freewriting* either on paper or on the computer. When you freewrite, you let one idea lead to another in free association, without concern for correctness. The important thing is to keep writing. If you cannot think of a word or phrase while you are freewriting, simply write a note to yourself inside square brackets, or put in a symbol such as #, as Zhe Chen does when she questions her use of the word *puttering* and can't remember the word *windowpanes*. On a computer, use the Search command to find your symbol later, when you can spend more time thinking about the word.

Zhe Chen did some freewriting on the topic "name and identity," which led her eventually to an essay topic examining the effects of the Cultural Revolution on family identity.

> I have a unusual name, Zhe. My friends in China say it's a boys name. My friends in America think it has only one letter. Most of my American friends have difficulty pronouncing my name.
>
> Some people ask me why don't I Americanize my name so it would be easier to pronounce. But I say if I change my name, it will not be me any more. What else can I write? When I was seven years old, I asked my mother what my name meant. "Ask your father," she said as she washed dishes. It was raining outside, and the room was so quiet that I could hear the rain puttering [? Look this up] on the #. My father's thoughts returned to another rainy day in 1967 when the Cultural Revolution just begun. Thousands of people had been banished to countryside and all the schools were closed. My grandparents fled to Hong Kong but my father and aunt stayed in China. Life was difficult. Gangs sent them to the countryside to work. It was here that my parents met.
>
> Back to name again. My father named me Zhe. In Chinese my name means remember and hope. He wanted me remember the Cultural Revolution and he wanted me to finish college. He didn't have that chance.

Brainstorming Another way to generate ideas is by *brainstorming*—making a freewheeling list of ideas as you think of them. Brainstorming is enhanced if you do it collaboratively in a group, discussing and then listing your ideas. (See also **1h**, Writing collaboratively.) You can then, by yourself or with the group, scrutinize the ideas, arrange them, reorganize them, and add to or eliminate them.

One group of students working collaboratively made the following brainstorming list on the topic "changing a name":

> voluntary changes—hate name
> escape from family and parents
> show business
> George Eliot (Mary Ann Evans)
> Woody Allen (Allen Stewart Konigsberg)

P. Diddy (Sean Combs aka Puff Daddy)
writers and their pseudonyms
married women
writers and their pseudonyms—who?
some keep own name, some change, some use both names and
  hyphenate
Hillary Clinton/Hillary Rodham Clinton
immigrants
Ellis Island
forced name changes
political name changes
name changes because of racism or oppression
criminals?

Once the students had made the list, they reviewed it, rejected some items, expanded on others, and grouped items. Thus, they developed a range of subcategories that led them to possibilities for further exploration and essay organization:

Voluntary Name Changes

authors: George Eliot, Mark Twain, Isak Dinesen
show business and stage names: Woody Allen, Bob Dylan, Ringo Starr,
    P. Diddy, Eminem, Pink
ethnic and religious identification: Malcolm X, Muhammad Ali

Name Changes upon Marriage

reasons for changing or not changing
Hillary Clinton
problem of children's names
alternative: hyphenated name

Forced Name Changes

immigrants on Ellis Island
wartime oppression
slavery

E-mail conversations   Network with others on a course bulletin board, in a chat room, or in a newsgroup (see **22c**), or set up your own group of students who want to work together to brainstorm over cyberspace. Daniel Kies at the College of DuPage in Glen Ellyn, Illinois, set up an "eForum" for his students in English 101. Here are some of their communications (used with permission) about an essay assignment on the "techno-future":

By Rick Waters on Thursday, April 27 - 04:09 pm:

I don't know how far along all of you are, but I wanted to offer some ideas for Essay 3. We're supposed to describe the techno-future as we see it, and I figured I would give you a reminder on what's been in the works and what's been accomplished lately.

"Smart Homes" are being built. Bill Gates' is probably the extreme (more info at www.usnews.com/usnews/nycut/tech/billgate/gates.htm)
Microchips are being implanted in brains to reverse the effects of blindness and deafness.
The genetics industry is booming.
There's a pill for just about everything nowadays.
There are (3) cars that can actually fly.
"Lawnmower Man Technology" (the effects of virtual teaching - facts being fed into the brain via multiple stimuli at once) has been testing since 1992.
Materials (not unlike clothing) are being developed to display video images.
Digital phones are being "blended" with Palmtop computers.
    And there's a TON more!

By Jennifer Thomas on Thursday, April 27 - 10:55 pm:

Sadly enough, I haven't heard of half the things that Rick mentioned! Am I behind or what! I think that we are far more technologically advanced than the government wants us to know. I am sitting below two skylights in my livingroom, and I'm pretty sure if "Big Brother" wanted to, he could probably interrupt this transmission. Scary as it is, technology is far beyond our realm. And we will be left in the dark, until the government decides we are privy to the information. The laptop I write on, although sufficient for my purposes, is an ancient artifact compared to the laptops on the market today. And my laptop can do a lot of stuff. It's far better than my parents' desktop! But yet, still outdated. Technology scares me in certain ways. Did you also know that the purchases you make at stores are tracked by certain barcodes present on coupons? Every credit card in the country is linked to a profile. I am hesitant to call it a technological age, but more of an information age. The President could probably find out how often you buy peanut butter, what brand, and whether you use a coupon for it. SCARY! There's food for thought.

Mapping   *Mapping,* also called *clustering,* is a visual way of generating and connecting ideas and can be done individually or in a group. Write your topic in a circle at the center of a page, think of ideas related to the topic, and write those ideas on the page around the central topic. Draw lines from the topic to the related ideas. Then add details under each of the ideas you noted. For a writing assignment that asked students to respond to something they had read, a student created the following map. She saw that it indicated several possibilities for topics, such as the increasing casualness of American society and the power of uniforms to both camouflage and identify their wearers. (See the drafts of her essay in **3e**.)

Using journalists' questions Journalists check the coverage of their stories by making sure that they answer six questions—Who? What? When? Where? Why? How?—though not in any set order. A report on a public transit strike, for example, would include details about the union leaders (who they were), the issue of working conditions and benefits (what the situation was), the date and time of the confrontation (when the strike occurred), the place (where it occurred), what caused the confrontation (why it happened), and how the people involved behaved and resolved the strike (how it evolved and ended). If you are telling the story of an event, either as a complete essay or as an example in an essay, asking the journalists' six questions will help you think comprehensively about your topic. If you are writing creative nonfiction, you will move beyond the objective reporting of facts to the inclusion of dramatic and poetic details and language.

Using formal sets of prompts   Sometimes you might find it helpful to use a formal set of directions (known as *prompts*) to suggest new avenues of inquiry. Write down responses to any of the prompts that apply to your topic, and note possibilities for further exploration.

DEFINE YOUR TERMS   Look up key words in your topic (like *success, identity, ambition,* and *ethnicity*) in the dictionary, and write down the definition you want to use. Consider synonyms, too.

INCLUDE DESCRIPTIONS   Whatever your topic, make your writing more vivid with details about color, light, location, movement, size, shape, sound, taste, and smell. Help your reader "see" your topic, such as a person, place, object, or scientific experiment, exactly as you see it.

MAKE COMPARISONS   Help your reader understand a topic by describing what it might be similar to and different from. For example, how is learning to write like learning to juggle?

ASSESS CAUSE AND EFFECT   Convey information on what causes or produces your topic and what effects or results emerge from it. For example, what are the causes and effects of dyslexia? inflation? acid rain? hurricanes? asthma?

CONSIDER WHAT OTHERS HAVE SAID   Give your reader information, facts, and statistics on what others say about your topic in interviews, surveys, reading, and research.

Doing research   Sometimes you will find that discussing your topic with others, conducting an interview, administering a questionnaire or survey, or doing research can produce good ideas for writing (see **6–8**).

 TECHNOTE   Using Web Directories to Find Topics

Internet search engines and directories such as Google at <http://www.google.com>, Yahoo! at <http://www.yahoo.com>, and AltaVista at <http://www.altavista.com> offer subject categories that you can explore and successively narrow down to find a topic suitable for a short essay. For example, a Yahoo! search beginning with "Education" produced more than thirty different categories, such as *bilingual, distance learning, financial aid, organizations, special education,* and *reform.* Clicking on *reform* produced links to eighteen sites (such as *multicultural education reform programs, computers as tutors, guide to math and science reform,* and *about school choice*). Many of the sites included Web pages on topics such as "voucher programs" and "charter schools," as well as links to many other sites, some with bibliographies with further online links. Such directories can suggest a wide range of interesting topics for you to explore. ■

1d Finding a topic and focus

You might be given any of the following types of assignments for an essay, arranged here from the broadest in scope to the narrowest:

- a free choice of subject
- a broad subject area, such as "genetic engineering" or "affirmative action"
- a focused and specific topic, such as "the city's plans to build apartments on landfill" or "the treatment of welfare recipients in California"
- an actual question to answer, such as "In what ways is age an issue in cases of driving accidents?"

If you are given a free choice of subject, you will need to move through all the points in the continuum to narrow your focus to specific subject area, to topic, to question. After that, still more narrowing is necessary. You will need a thesis. Your thesis, or claim, is your statement of opinion, main idea, or message that unifies your piece of writing, makes a connection between you and the subject area, lets your reader know where you stand in relation to the topic, and answers the question posed.

 KEY POINTS

Subject, Topic, Question, Thesis: A Continuum

Level 1: Broad *subject area*
↓
Level 2: *Topic* for exploration within that subject area
↓
Level 3: *Key question* that concerns you
↓
Level 4: Your *thesis* (your claim or statement of opinion or your main idea in answer to the question). Often you need to do a great deal of reading and writing before you get to this point.

Here is one student's movement from subject to thesis over several days of reading, discussion, freewriting, and note-taking:

Subject: College admissions policies
Topic: Affirmative action in college admissions
Question: How do people react to students who are accepted by colleges under affirmative action policies?

Thesis: The public and the press often unjustly question the abilities of students accepted into colleges under affirmative action policies.

If you choose a topic and a question that are too broad, you will find it difficult to generate a thesis with focused ideas and examples. Whenever you find yourself thinking, for instance, "There's so much to say about affirmative action—its history, goals, practice, criticisms, successes—that I don't know where to start," narrow your topic. If you begin by choosing a topic and a question that are too narrow, you probably will not find enough material and will end up being repetitive. Whenever you feel you have enough material to fill only a page and can't imagine how you will find more ("What else can I say about how my cousin got into college?"), broaden your topic. Above all, stay flexible: you may want to change your topic or your question as you discover more information.

What if you are assigned a topic that you are not interested in? That can happen, but do not despair. Read as much as you can on the topic until something strikes you and captures your interest. You can try taking the opposite point of view from one of your sources, challenging the point of view. Or you can set yourself the task of showing readers exactly why the topic has not grabbed people's interest— maybe the literature and the research have been just too technical or inaccessible? If you can, find a human angle.

1e Formulating a working thesis—and why you need one

Suppose someone were to ask you, "What is the main idea that you want to communicate to your reader in your piece of writing?" The sentence you would give in reply is your *thesis statement*, also known as a *claim*. Your claim tells readers what stand you are going to take. It is not enough to say, "I am writing about bilingual education." Are you going to address bilingual education in elementary, secondary, or higher education? Which readers do you regard as your primary audience? Which geographical areas will you discuss? Will you be concerned with the past or with the present? What do you intend to propose about the area of bilingual education you have selected? In short, what point do you want to make about which aspect of bilingual education—for which readers? You don't have to know exactly where to put your thesis statement in your essay right now, but having a thesis will focus your thoughts as you read and write. See **4d** for more on the thesis in an argument paper.

A good thesis statement may be one or more of the following:

1. a strong, thought-provoking, or controversial statement

   ▶ **Bilingual education has not fulfilled its early promise.**

2. a call to action

   ▶ **Inner-city schools should set up bilingual programs.**

3. a question that will be answered in detail in the essay

   ▶ **What can bilingual education accomplish for a child? It can lead to academic and personal development.**

4. a preview or reflection of the structure of the essay

   ▶ **Bilingual education suffers from two main problems: a shortage of trained teachers and a lack of parental involvement.**

After you have formulated your thesis statement, write it on a self-stick note or an index card and keep it near you as you write. The note or card will remind you to stick to the point. If you still digress as you write, you may need to consider changing your thesis.

 KEY POINTS

Thesis Checklist

You should be able to put a checkmark next to each quality as you examine your draft. Your thesis

1. is worth presenting and is the answer to a question that could be debated (is not an obvious truism or vague generalization)

2. narrows your topic to the main idea that you want to communicate

3. makes a claim or states your view about your topic

4. can be supported by details, facts, and examples within the assigned limitations of time and space

5. stimulates curiosity and interest in readers and prompts them to think "Why do you say that?" and then to read on and be convinced by what you have written

6. forecasts and unifies all that follows in your essay; does not include ideas or points that you do not intend to discuss in your essay

7. is expressed concisely in one or two complete sentences (though you will come across many variations as you read)

Stating your thesis in your paper   In most academic writing in the humanities and social sciences, a thesis is stated clearly in the essay, usually near the beginning. See your thesis statement as a signpost— both for you as you write your draft and, later, for readers as they read your essay. A clear thesis prepares readers well for the rest of the essay. If you use key words from your thesis as you write, you will keep readers focused on your main idea.

Sometimes, though, particularly in descriptive, narrative, and informative writing, you may choose to imply your thesis and not explicitly state it. In such a case, you make your thesis clear by the examples, details, and information you include. You may also choose to state your thesis at the end of your essay instead of the beginning, presenting all the evidence to build a case and then making the thesis act as a climax and logical statement about the outcome of the evidence.

On not falling in love with your thesis   A good thesis often takes so long to develop that you might be reluctant to change it. Be willing, however, to refine and change your thesis as you find more information and work with your material. Many writers begin with a tentative working thesis and then find that they come to a new conclusion at the end of the first draft. If that happens to you, start your second draft by focusing on the thesis that emerged during the writing of the first draft. Be flexible: it's easier to change a thesis statement to fit new ideas and newly discovered evidence than to find new evidence to fit a thesis. Note that your final thesis statement should take a firm stand on the issue. Flexibility during the writing process is not the same as indecision in the final product.

 ESL Note   Writing in Different Languages and Cultures

Often writers who have developed their writing skills in one language notice distinct differences in the conventions of writing in another, particularly with respect to the explicit statement of opinion in the thesis. It is difficult to determine how much of a role one's culture plays in the way one writes and to separate culture's role from the roles of gender, socioeconomic status, family background, and education. However, always consider what approaches your readers are likely to be familiar with and to value.   ■

1f   Preparing outlines

A *scratch outline* is a rough list of numbered points that you intend to cover in your essay. A scratch outline lets you see what ideas you already have, how they connect, what you can do to support and develop them, and what further planning or research you still need to do. One student in the group that made the brainstorming list on pages 8–9 developed the following scratch outline and formulated a tentative thesis:

Topic: Changing a name
Question: Why do people change their names?
Tentative thesis: People change their names because they either have to or want to.
Points:

1. Some are forced to make name changes in a new country or a new school.
2. Some change a name to avoid discrimination or persecution.
3. Some (women only?) change a name upon marriage.
4. Show business personalities often change their names.
5. Some people change a name to avoid recognition.
   a. Criminals—witness protection program
   b. Writers

When this student began to write his draft, however, he changed direction and unified some of his points, developing a more focused thesis (see the formal outline below).

A *formal outline* spells out, in order, what points and supportive details you will use to develop your thesis and arranges them to show the overall form and structure of the essay. You may produce a formal outline before you begin to write, but you are likely to find that making an outline with a high level of detail is more feasible after you have written a draft. Done at this later point, the outline serves as a check on the logic and completeness of what you have written, revealing any gaps, repetition, or illogical steps in the development of your essay.

The student who did the brainstorming (1c) and made the scratch outline finally settled on a thesis and made this formal topic outline of an essay draft.

Thesis: A voluntary name change is usually motivated by a desire to avoid or gain recognition.

I. The desire to avoid recognition by others is one motive for a name change.
   A. Criminals
   B. Writers
      1. Women writers adopt men's names.
         a. George Eliot (Mary Ann Evans)
         b. George Sand (Amandine Aurore Lucie Dupin)
         c. Isak Dinesen (Karen Blixen)

2. Some writers adopt a pseudonym.
   a. Mark Twain (Samuel Clemens)
   b. Lewis Carroll (Charles Dodgson)
   c. Amanda Cross (Carolyn Heilbrun)
C. Some change a name to avoid ethnic identification.
II. Married women and entertainers may change a name to join a group and gain recognition.
   A. Married women mark membership in a family.
      1. They want to indicate married status.
      2. They want the same name as their children.
   B. Entertainers choose eye-catching names.
      1. Marilyn Monroe (Norma Jean Baker)
      2. Woody Allen (Allen Stewart Konigsberg)
      3. Ringo Starr (Richard Starkey)
      4. P. Diddy (Sean Combs) and Eminem (Marshall Mathers)

Making this outline allowed the student to see that his draft was basically well structured but that he needed to find out more about criminals and their aliases (I.A.) and about people who change a name to avoid ethnic identification (I.C.). See also **6f** for purpose statements and proposals.

1g Overcoming writer's block

Most of us, even if we write a great deal or profess to like writing, have at some time or another felt that dreaded block. We sit and stare at the blank screen or a messy draft and keep going to the refrigerator or vending machine for solace. If you feel overwhelmed with the task of organizing your research findings, frustrated because your writing doesn't seem to "sound right," or blocked for any reason, consider the following questions and strategies.

KEY POINTS

Overcoming Writer's Block

1. Do you have a set of rules that you try to follow in your writing process, such as "Always begin by writing a good introduction" or "Always have a complete outline before starting to write"? If you do, consider whether your rules are too rigid or even unhelpful. As you gather ideas and do your

(Continued)

(Continued)

preparatory drafting, try ignoring any self-imposed rules that hinder you.

2. Do you edit as soon as you write, and do you edit often? If you answer yes, your desire to write correctly might be preventing you from thinking about ideas and moving forward. Try journal writing, freewriting, brainstorming, or mapping (see **1c**).

3. Do you feel anxious about writing, even though you have knowledge of and interest in your topic? If you do, try using some of the freewriting and brainstorming strategies in **1c**, or begin writing as if you were talking about your topic with a friend.

4. Do you feel that you do not yet know enough about your topic to start writing, even though you may have done a great deal of research? If so, try freewriting or try drafting the sections you know most about. Writing will help show you what you know and what you need to know.

5. Do you find you need more information, insight, or background knowledge than you have so far gathered? If so, set aside more time and devote yourself to reading, interpreting, taking notes, and critical thinking. What you think is writer's block may miraculously disappear once you feel in control of your topic.

1h Writing collaboratively

Writing is not necessarily a solitary process. In the academic or business world, you will often have to work collaboratively with one or more classmates or colleagues. You might be part of a group, team, or committee assigned to draft a proposal or a report. You might be expected to produce a document reflecting the consensus of your section or group. Or you might need to draft and circulate a document and then incorporate into it the comments of many people, as was the case with the student drafts in **3e** and **35**.

In group settings in college, make sure that every member of the group has the opportunity to contribute and does contribute. You can do this by assigning each person a set of specific tasks, such as making lists of ideas, drafting, analyzing the draft, revising, editing, assembling visuals, and preparing the final document. Schedule regular meetings, and expect everyone to come with a completed written assignment. Build on strengths within the group. For example, ask the member skilled in document design and computer graphics to prepare the visual features of a business report (**21**).

However, make sure that you work collaboratively only when doing so is expected. An instructor who assigns an essay will not always expect you to work on it with your sister, classmate, or tutor. If collaborative peer groups are encouraged, you may find the peer response form in **3b** useful.

 TechNote   Using Word in Collaborative Writing

Microsoft Word provides useful tools for collaboration. Click Tools and then Revisions or Track Changes. You can work on a text, highlight changes, and attach the revised text to an e-mail message to a colleague, who can then Accept or Reject the changes and compare the original with the revised version (Compare Documents). ▪

1i   Writing drafts: Six tips

Writing provides what speech can never provide: the opportunity to revise your ideas and the way you present them. The drafting process lets you make substantive changes as you progress through drafts. You can add, delete, and reorganize sections of your paper. You can rethink your thesis and support. You can change your approach to parts or all of the paper. Writing drafts allows you to work on a piece of writing until it meets your goals.

 KEY POINTS

Tips for Drafting

1. Plan the steps and set a schedule. Work backward from the deadline, and assign time in days or hours for each of the following: deciding on a topic, brainstorming ideas, making a scratch outline, writing a draft, getting feedback, analyzing the draft, making large-scale revisions, finding additional material, editing, proofreading, formatting, and printing. The *Keys* Web site provides a sample schedule for you to use at <http://college.hmco.com/keys.html>.

2. Begin by writing the essay parts for which you already have some specific material. You do not need to begin at the beginning.

(Continued)

(Continued)

3. Write in increments of twenty to thirty minutes to take advantage of momentum.

4. Write your first draft as quickly and fluently as you can. Write notes to yourself in capitals or surrounded by asterisks to remind yourself to add or change something or to do further research. Some word processing programs have a Comment function that allows you to type notes that appear only on the screen, not in a printout. These notes are easily deleted from later drafts. In addition, if you use a term frequently (for example, the phrase "bilingual education"), abbreviate it (as "b.e.") and use a tool like AutoCorrect to substitute the whole phrase throughout your draft as you type.

5. Avoid obvious, vague, or empty generalizations (such as "All people have feelings"). Be specific, and include interesting supporting details.

6. Save all your notes and drafts until your writing is completed and until the course is over. Print out and save a copy of each new draft so that if something happens to the computer or the disk, you have a copy of your work.

2 Developing Paragraphs and Essays

Sentences make up paragraphs, and paragraphs are the building blocks of essays.

2a Writing a paragraph: The basics

The first line of a paragraph is indented five spaces from the left margin or, in business and online documents, begins after a blank line. A good paragraph makes a clear point, supports your main idea, and keeps to one topic.

Some paragraphs have more to do with function than with content. They serve to take readers from one point to another, making a connection and offering a smooth transition from one idea to the next. These transitional paragraphs are often short.

For introductory and concluding paragraphs, see **2e**.

When to Begin a New Paragraph

1. to introduce a new point (one that supports the claim or main idea of your essay)

2. to expand on a point already made by offering new examples or evidence

3. to break up a long discussion or description into manageable chunks that readers can assimilate

Both logic and aesthetics dictate when it is time to begin a new paragraph. Think of a paragraph as something that gathers together in one place ideas that connect to each other and to the main purpose of the piece of writing.

2b Composing a unified paragraph

A *unified paragraph,* in academic writing, includes one main idea that the rest of the piece of writing (paragraph or essay) explains, supports, and develops. Just as a thesis statement helps readers of an essay keep your main idea in mind, a *topic sentence* in a body paragraph lets readers know what the main idea of the paragraph is. Readers should notice a logical flow of ideas as they read through a paragraph and as they move from one paragraph to another through an essay.

When you write a paragraph, imagine a reader saying, "Look, I don't have time to read all this. Just tell me in one sentence (or two) what point you are making here." Your reply would express your main point. Each paragraph in an academic essay generally contains a controlling idea expressed in a sentence (a topic sentence) and does not digress or switch topics in midstream. Its content is unified.

The following paragraph is devoted to one topic—tennis—but does not follow through on the promise of the topic sentence to discuss the *trouble* that the *backhand* causes *average* players (the key words are italicized).

> The backhand in tennis causes average weekend players more trouble than other strokes. Even though the swing is natural and free-flowing, many players feel intimidated and try to avoid it. Serena Williams, however, has a great backhand and she often wins difficult points with it. Her serve is a powerful weapon, too. When faced by a backhand

coming at them across the net, mid-level players can't seem to get their feet and body in the best position. They tend to run around the ball or forget the swing and give the ball a little poke, praying that it will not only reach but also go over the net.

What is Grand Slam winner Serena Williams doing in a paragraph about average players? What relevance does her powerful serve have to the average player's problems with a backhand? The student revised by cutting out the two sentences about Serena Williams.

Serena Williams

When placed first, as it is in the paragraph on the troublesome backhand, a topic sentence makes a generalization and serves as a reference point for the rest of the information in the paragraph (*deductive organization*). When placed after one or two other sentences, the topic sentence focuses the details and directs readers' attention to the main idea. When placed at the end of the paragraph, the topic sentence serves to summarize or draw conclusions from the details that precede it (*inductive organization*).

Some paragraphs, such as the short ones typical of newspaper writing or the one-sentence paragraphs that make a quick transition, do not always contain a topic sentence. Sometimes, too, a paragraph contains such clear details that the point is obvious and does not need to be explicitly stated. However, in academic essays, a paragraph in support of your essay's claim or thesis (main point) will usually be unified and focused on one clear topic, whether or not you state it in a topic sentence.

2c Developing ideas

Whether you are writing a paragraph or an essay, you will do well to keep in mind the image of a skeptical reader always inclined to say something challenging, such as "Why on earth do you think that?" or "What could possibly lead you to that conclusion?" Show your reader that your opinion is well founded and supported by experience, knowledge, logical arguments, the work of experts, or reasoned examples, and provide vital, unique details.

Give examples. Examples make writing more interesting and informative. The paragraph that follows begins with a topic sentence that announces the controlling idea: "Ant queens . . . enjoy exceptionally long lives." The authors could have stopped there, expecting us to assume that they were right. We might wonder, however, what "exceptionally long" means about the life of an ant (a month? a year? seven years?). Instead of letting us wonder, the authors develop and support the controlling idea with five examples, organized to build to a convincing climax. Beginning with a generalization and supporting it with specific illustrative details is a common method of organizing a paragraph, known as *deductive organization.*

> Ant queens, hidden in the fastness of well-built nests and protected by zealous daughters, enjoy exceptionally long lives. Barring accidents, those of most species last 5 years or longer. A few exceed in natural longevity anything known in the millions of species of other insects, including even the legendary 17-year-old cicadas. One mother queen of an Australian carpenter ant kept in a laboratory nest flourished for 23 years, producing thousands of offspring before she faltered in her reproduction and died, apparently of old age. Several queens of *Lasius flavus,* the little yellow mound-building ant of European meadows, have lived 18 to 22 years in captivity. The world record for ants, and hence for insects generally, is held by a queen of *Lasius niger,* the European black sidewalk ant, which also lives in forests. Lovingly attended in a laboratory nest by a Swiss entomologist, she lasted 29 years.
>
> —Bert Hölldobler and Edward O. Wilson, *Journey to the Ants*

Tell a story. Choose a pattern of organization that readers will easily grasp. Organize the events in a story chronologically so that readers can follow the sequence. In the following paragraph, a writer tells a story that leads to the point that people with disabilities often face ignorance and insensitivity. Note that she uses *inductive organization,* beginning with background information and the specific details of the story in chronological order and ending with a generalization.

> Jonathan is an articulate, intelligent, thirty-five-year-old man who has used a wheelchair since he became a paraplegic when he was twenty years old. He recalls taking an ablebodied woman out to dinner at a nice restaurant. When the waitress came to take their order, she patronizingly asked his date, "And what would he like to eat for dinner?" At the end of the meal, the waitress presented Jonathan's date with the check and thanked her for her patronage. Although it may be hard to believe the insensitivity of the waitress,

this incident is not an isolated one. Rather, such an experience is a common one for persons with disabilities.

—Dawn O. Braithwaite, "Viewing Persons with Disabilities as a Culture"

Describe with details appealing to the senses. To help readers see and experience what you feel and experience, describe people, places, scenes, and objects by using sensory details that recreate those people, places, scenes, or objects for your readers. In the following paragraph from a memoir about growing up to love food, Ruth Reichl tells how she spent days working at a summer camp in France and thinking about eating. However, she does much more than say, "The food was always delicious" and much more than "I looked forward to the delicious bread, coffee, and morning snacks." Reichl appeals to our senses of sight, smell, touch, and taste.

When we woke up in the morning the smell of baking bread was wafting through the trees. By the time we had gotten our campers out of bed, their faces washed and their shirts tucked in, the aroma had become maddeningly seductive. We walked into the dining room to devour hot bread slathered with country butter and topped with homemade plum jam so filled with fruit it made each slice look like a tart. We stuck our faces into the bowls of café au lait, inhaling the sweet, bitter, peculiarly French fragrance, and Georges or Jean or one of the other male counselors would say, for the hundredth time, "*On mange pas comme ça à Paris.*" Two hours later we had a "*gouter,*" a snack of chocolate bars stuffed into fresh, crusty rolls. And two hours later there was lunch. The eating went on all day.

—Ruth Reichl, *Tender at the Bone: Growing Up at the Table*

Develop a point by providing facts and statistics. The following paragraph supports with facts and statistics the assertion made in its first sentence (the topic sentence) that the North grew more than the South in the years before the Civil War.

While southerners tended their fields, the North grew. In 1800, half the nation's five million people lived in the South. By 1850, only a third lived there. Of the nine largest cities, only New Orleans was located in the lower South. Meanwhile, a tenth of the goods manufactured in America came from southern mills and factories. There were one hundred piano makers in New York alone in 1852. In 1846, there was not a single book publisher in New Orleans; even the city guidebook was printed in Manhattan.

—Geoffrey C. Ward, *The Civil War: An Illustrated History*

Define key terms. Sometimes writers clarify and develop a topic by defining a key term, even if it is not an unusual term. Often they will explain what class something fits into and how it differs from others in its class: for example, "A duckbilled platypus is a mammal that has webbed feet and lays eggs." In his book on diaries, Thomas Mallon begins by providing an extended definition of his basic terms. He does not want readers to misunderstand him because they wonder what the differences between a diary and a journal might be.

> The first thing we should try to get straight is what to call them. "What's the difference between a diary and a journal?" is one of the questions people interested in these books ask. The two terms are in fact hopelessly muddled. They're both rooted in the idea of dailiness, but perhaps because of *journal*'s links to the newspaper trade and *diary*'s to *dear*, the latter seems more intimate than the former. (The French blur even this discrepancy by using no word recognizable like *diary*; they just say *journal intime*, which is sexy, but a bit of a mouthful.) One can go back as far as Dr. Johnson's *Dictionary* and find him making the two more or less equal. To him a diary was "an account of the transactions, accidents, and observations of every day; a journal." Well, if synonymity was good enough for Johnson, we'll let it be good enough for us.
>
> —Thomas Mallon, *A Book of One's Own: People and Their Diaries*

Analyze component parts. Large, complex topics sometimes become more manageable to writers (and readers) when they are broken down for analysis. The *Columbia Encyclopedia* online helps readers understand the vast concept of life itself by breaking it down into six component parts (at <http://www.bartleby.com/65/li/life.html>).

> Although there is no universal agreement as to a definition of life, its biological manifestations are generally considered to be organization, metabolism, growth, irritability, adaptation, and reproduction. . . . Organization is found in the basic living unit, the cell, and in the organized groupings of cells into organs and organisms. Metabolism includes the conversion of nonliving material into cellular components (synthesis) and the decomposition of organic matter (catalysis), producing energy. Growth in living matter is an increase in size of all parts, as distinguished from simple addition of material; it results from a higher rate of synthesis than catalysis. Irritability, or response to stimuli, takes many forms, from the contraction of a unicellular organism when touched to complex reactions involving all the senses of higher animals; in plants response is usually much different than in animals but is nonetheless present. Adaptation, the accommodation of a living

organism to its present or to a new environment, is fundamental to the process of evolution and is determined by the individual's heredity. The division of one cell to form two new cells is reproduction; usually the term is applied to the production of a new individual (either asexually, from a single parent organism, or sexually, from two differing parent organisms), although strictly speaking it also describes the production of new cells in the process of growth.

Classify into groups.   Dividing people or objects into the classes or groups that make up the whole gives readers a new way to look at the topic. In the following paragraphs, the writer develops his essay on cell phones by classifying users into three types and devoting one paragraph to each.

Cell phone use has far exceeded practicality. For many, it's even a bit of an addiction, a prop—like a cigarette or a beer bottle—that you can hold up to your mouth. And each person is meeting a different psychological need by clinging to it.

As I see it, the pack breaks down something like this: Some users can't tolerate being alone and have to register on someone, somewhere, all of the time. That walk down [the street] can be pretty lonely without a loved one shouting sweet nothings in your ear.

Others are efficiency freaks and can't bear to lose 10 minutes standing in line at Starbucks. They have to conduct business while their milk is being steamed, or they will implode. The dividing line between work and home has already become permeable with the growth of telecommuting; cell phones contribute significantly to that boundary breakdown.

Then there are those who like to believe they are so very important to the people in their personal and professional lives that they must be in constant touch. "Puffed up" is one way to describe them; "insecure" is another.

—Matthew Gilbert, "All Talk, All the Time"

Compare and contrast.   When you examine similarities and differences among people, objects, or concepts, different types of development achieve different purposes.

1. You can deal with each subject one at a time in a block style of organization, perhaps summarizing the similarities and differences at the end. This organization works well when each section is short and readers can easily remember the points made about each subject.

2. You can select and organize the important points of similarity or difference in a point-by-point style of organization, referring within each point to both subjects.

The following example uses the second approach in comparing John Stuart Mill, a British philosopher and economist, and Harriet Taylor, a woman with whom Mill had a close intellectual relationship. The author, Phyllis Rose, organizes the contrast by points of difference, referring to her subjects' facial features, physical behavior, ways of thinking and speaking, and intellectual style. A block organization would deal first with the characteristics of Taylor, followed by the characteristics of Mill.

John Stuart Mill

> You could see how they complemented each other by the way they looked. What people noticed first about Harriet were her eyes—flashing—and a suggestion in her body of mobility, whereas his features, variously described as chiseled and classical, expressed an inner rigidity. He shook hands from the shoulder. He spoke carefully. Give him facts, and he would sift them, weigh them, articulate possible interpretations, reach a conclusion. Where he was careful, she was daring. Where he was disinterested and balanced, she was intuitive, partial, and sure of herself. She concerned herself with goals and assumptions; he concerned himself with arguments. She was quick to judge and to generalize, and because he was not, he valued her intellectual style as bold and vigorous where another person, more like her, might have found her hasty and simplistic.
>
> —Phyllis Rose, *Parallel Lives: Five Victorian Marriages*

Harriet Taylor

2d Using transitions and links for coherence

However you develop your individual paragraphs, readers expect to move with ease from one sentence to the next and from one paragraph to the next, following a clear flow of argument and logic. When you construct an essay or paragraph, do not force readers to grapple with "grasshopper prose," which jumps suddenly from one idea to another without obvious connections. Instead, make your writing *coherent*, with all the parts connecting clearly to one another with transitional expressions, context links, and word links. (See also **40j** for examples of the contribution of parallel structures to coherence.)

Transitional words and expressions Make clear connections between sentences and between paragraphs either by using explicit connecting words like *this, that, these,* and *those* to refer to something mentioned at the end of the previous sentence or paragraph or by using transitional expressions.

TRANSITIONAL EXPRESSIONS

adding an idea: also, in addition, further, furthermore, moreover

contrasting: however, nevertheless, nonetheless, on the other hand, in contrast, still, on the contrary, rather, conversely

providing an alternative: instead, alternatively, otherwise

showing similarity: similarly, likewise

showing order of time or order of ideas: first, second, third (and so on), then, next, later, subsequently, meanwhile, previously, finally

showing result: as a result, consequently, therefore, thus, hence, accordingly, for this reason

affirming: of course, in fact, certainly, obviously, to be sure, undoubtedly, indeed

giving examples: for example, for instance

explaining: in other words, that is

adding an aside: incidentally, by the way, besides

summarizing: in short, generally, overall, all in all, in conclusion

For punctuation with transitional expressions, see **47e**.

Though transitional expressions are useful to connect one sentence to another or one paragraph to another, do not overuse these expressions. Too many of them, used too often, give writing a heavy and mechanical flavor.

Context links   A new paragraph introduces a new topic, but that topic should not be entirely separate from what has gone before. Let readers know the context of the big picture. If you are writing about the expense of exploring Mars and then switch abruptly to the hazards of climbing Everest, readers will be puzzled. You need to state clearly the connection with the thesis: "Exploration on our own planet can be as hazardous and as financially risky as space exploration."

Word links   You can also provide coherence by using repeated words or connected words, such as pronouns linked to nouns; words with the same, similar, or opposite meaning; or words linked by context. Note how Deborah Tannen maintains coherence: not only by using transitional expressions (*for example, furthermore*), but also by repeating words and phrases (italicized) and using certain pronouns (boldface)—*she* and *her* to refer to *wife,* and *they* to refer to *Greeks.*

> Entire cultures operate on elaborate systems of *indirectness.* For example, I discovered in a small research project that most Greeks assumed that a wife who asked, "Would you like to go to the party?" was hinting that **she** *wanted to go.* **They** *felt* that **she** wouldn't bring it up if **she** didn't *want to go.* Furthermore, **they** *felt,* **she** would not state **her** *preference* outright because **that** would sound like a demand. *Indirectness* was the appropriate means for communicating **her** *preference.*
>
> —Deborah Tannen, *You Just Don't Understand*

2e   Writing introductions and conclusions

Introduction   Imagine a scene at a party. Someone you have never met before comes up to you and says, "Capital punishment should be abolished immediately." You're surprised. You wonder where this position came from and why you are being challenged with it. You probably think this person rather strange and pushy. Imagine readers picking up a piece of your writing. Just like people at a party, readers need to know why a topic is being discussed before hearing what you have to say about the issue. In your introduction, establish a context for the forthcoming discussion, capture your readers' interest, and lead into your thesis. If you find it difficult to write an introduction because you are not yet clear about your thesis or how you will support it, wait until you have written the body of your essay. You may find something concrete easier to introduce than something you have not yet written.

When you write an essay in the humanities, keep the following points in mind. (For other disciplines, see **4i**, **5d**, and **5e**.)

KEY POINTS

How to Write a Good Introduction

Options

1. Do not assume that your reader knows your assigned question.
2. Provide context and background information to set up your thesis. Lead readers to expect a statement of your point of view.
3. Define key terms that are pertinent to the discussion.
4. Establish the tone of the paper: informative, persuasive, serious, humorous, personal, impersonal, formal, informal.
5. Engage readers' interest; provide a hook (attention grabber) that will make readers want to continue reading.

What to Avoid

6. Avoid being overly general and telling readers the obvious, such as "Crime is a big problem" or "In this fast-paced world, TV is a popular form of entertainment" or "Since the beginning of time, the sexes have been in conflict."
7. Do not refer to your writing intentions—"In this essay, I will. . . ." Do not make extravagant claims, such as "This essay will prove that bilingual education works for every student."
8. Do not restate the assigned essay question.

To provide a hook for your reader, an introduction might include any of the following:

surprising statistics   a challenging question

a pithy quotation   interesting background details

an unusual fact   an intriguing opinion statement

a relevant anecdote

Examine the hook in the following example:

> On the day before Memorial Day, 1983, a poet called me to describe a city he had just visited. He said that one section included mosques, built by the Islamic people who dwelled there. Attending his reading, he said, were large numbers of Hispanic people, forty thousand of whom lived in the same city. He was not talking about a fabled city located in some mysterious region of the world. The city he'd visited was Detroit.
>
> —Ishmael Reed, "America: The Multinational Society"

Reed introduces the theme of multinationalism in the United States with a hook, an anecdote that leads readers to expect the city he describes to be in an unfamiliar part of the world. Then he surprises them in the last sentence—the city is Detroit—and prepares them for his discussion of a multinational continent.

Conclusion   Think of your conclusion as completing a circle. You have taken readers on a journey from presentation of the topic in your introduction, to your thesis, to supporting evidence and discussion, with specific examples and illustrations. Remind readers of the purpose of the journey. Recall the main idea of the paper, and make a strong statement about it that will stay in their minds. Readers should leave your document feeling satisfied, not turning the page and looking for more.

KEY POINTS

How to Write a Good Conclusion

Options

1. Include a summary of the points you have made, but keep it short and use fresh wording.
2. Frame your essay by reminding the reader of something you referred to in your introduction and by reminding the reader of your thesis.
3. End on a strong note: a quotation, a question, a suggestion, a reference to an anecdote in the introduction, a humorous and insightful comment, a call to action, or a look to the future.

What to Avoid

4. Do not apologize for the inadequacy of your argument ("I do not know much about this problem") or for holding your opinions ("I am sorry if you do not agree with me, but . . .").
5. Do not use the identical wording you used in your introduction.
6. Do not introduce totally new ideas. If you raise a new point at the end, your reader might expect more details.
7. Do not contradict what you said previously.
8. Do not be too sweeping in your conclusions. Do not condemn the whole medical profession, for example, because one person you know had a bad time in one hospital.

A chapter on designing a home page includes examples and illustrations, and its concluding paragraph succinctly presents some parting advice and reminders.

In summary, a home page should offer three features: a directory of the site's main content areas (navigation), a summary of the most important news or promotions, and a search feature. If done well, directory and news will help answer the first-time user's need to find out what the site is about in the first place. Even so, always look at the page with an eye to asking, "What can this site do for me?" And remember the name and logo.

—Jakob Nielsen, *Designing Web Usability*

3   Revising, Editing, and Formatting

Always allow time in your writing schedule for putting a draft away for a while before you look at it with a critical eye.

Revising—making changes to improve a piece of writing—is an essential part of the writing process. It is not a punishment inflicted on inexperienced writers. Good finished products are the result of careful revision. Even Leo Tolstoy, author of the monumental Russian novel *War and Peace,* commented: "I cannot understand how anyone can write without rewriting everything over and over again."

As you revise and edit, address both "big-picture" and "little-picture" concerns. Big-picture revising involves making changes in content and organization. When you revise, you may add or delete details, sections, or paragraphs; alter your thesis statement; vary or strengthen your use of transitions; move material from one position to another; and improve clarity, logic, flow, and style. Little-picture editing involves making adjustments to improve sentence variety; vary sentence length; and correct errors in grammar, spelling, word choice, mechanics, and punctuation. Both are necessary, but most people like to focus first on the big picture and then on the details.

3a   Developing strategies for revising

For college essays and important business documents, always allow time in your schedule for a second draft, and more drafts if possible. Develop systematic strategies for examining the drafts and revising.

- Print out a draft triple-spaced so that you can easily write in changes and comments. Revise for ideas, interest, and logic; do not merely fix errors. It is often tempting just to correct errors in spelling and grammar and see the result as a new draft. Revising entails more than that. You need to look at what you have written, imagine a reader's reaction to your thesis and title, and rethink your approach to the topic.

- Create distance and space. Put a draft away for a day or two, and then read it again with fresher, more critical eyes.
- Highlight key words in the assignment. Mark passages in your draft that address the words. If you fail to find any, that could signal where you need to revise.
- Read your draft aloud. Mark any places where you hesitate and have to struggle to understand the point. Go back to them later. Alternatively, ask somebody else to read a copy of the draft and to note where he or she hesitates or feels unsure about the meaning.
- Copy and paste first sentences. Select the first sentence of each paragraph, and use the Copy and Paste features to move the sequence of sentences into a new file. Then examine these first sentences: see if they provide a logical progression of ideas; check for repetition or omission.
- Make an outline of what you have written (see **1f**).
- Save every draft under a separate file name, one that clearly labels the topic and the draft. Some people prefer to save deleted sections in a separate "dump" file and retrieve deleted parts from there.
- Use the Tools/Track Changes/Compare Documents features in Microsoft Word to highlight and examine the differences between drafts.
- Use the "Triggers for Revision" Key Points box to alert yourself to things to look for as you read your draft.

KEY POINTS

Triggers for Revision

Any of the following should alert you to a need for revision:

1. a weak or boring introductory paragraph
2. a worried frown, a pause, or a thought of "Huh? Something is wrong here" in any spot as you read your draft
3. a paragraph that never makes a point
4. a paragraph that seems unrelated to the thesis of the essay
5. a phrase, sentence, or passage that you cannot immediately understand (if you have trouble grasping your own ideas, readers surely will have trouble, too)

(Continued)

(Continued)

6. excessive use of generalizations—*everyone, most people, all human beings, all students/lawyers/politicians,* and so on (use specific examples: *the students in my political science course this semester*)

7. a feeling that you would have difficulty summarizing your draft (maybe it is too vague?)

8. an awareness that you have just read the same point earlier in the draft

9. failure to find a definite conclusion

3b Giving and getting feedback

Ask a friend, colleague, or tutor to read your draft with a pencil in hand, placing a checkmark next to the passages that work well and a question mark next to those that do not. Ask your reader to tell you what main point you made and how you supported and developed it. This process might reveal any lack of clarity or indicate gaps in the logic of your draft. Your reader does not have to be an expert English teacher to give you good feedback. If you notice worried frowns (or worse, yawns) as the person reads, you will know that something in your text is puzzling, disconcerting, or boring. Even that simple level of feedback can be valuable. See **3e** and **35** for examples of student writing revised after feedback.

If you are asked to give feedback to a classmate or colleague, use the following guidelines.

KEY POINTS

Giving Feedback to Others

1. When you are asked to give feedback to a classmate, don't think of yourself as an English teacher armed with a red pen.

2. Read for positive reactions to ideas and clarity. Look for parts that make you think "I agree," " I like this," or "This is well done."

3. As you read, put a light pencil mark next to one or two passages that make you pause and send you back to reread.

4. Try to avoid comments that sound like accusations ("You were too vague in paragraph 3"). Instead, use *I* to emphasize your reaction as a reader ("I had a hard time visualizing the scene in paragraph 3").

Here is a sample peer response form that can be used to provide feedback. This form is also available online for downloading and printing at <http://college.hmco.com/keys.html>.

Draft by _____   Date _____

Response by _____   Date _____

1. What do you see as the writer's main point in this draft?
2. What part of the draft interests you the most? Why?
3. Where do you feel you would like more detail or explanation? Where do you need less?
4. Do you find any parts unclear, confusing, or undeveloped? Mark each such spot with a pencil question mark in the margin. Then write a note to the writer with questions and comments about the parts you have marked.
5. Give the writer one suggestion about one change that you think would improve the draft.

3c   Writing and revising a title

You might have a useful working title as you write, but after you finish writing, brainstorm several titles and pick the one you like best. If titles occur to you as you write, be sure to make a note of them. A good title captures the reader's attention, makes the reader want to read on, and lets the reader know what to expect in a piece of writing.

WORKING TITLE **The Benefits of Travel**

REVISED TITLE **From Katmandu to Kuala Lumpur: A Real Education**

3d   Editing, proofreading, and using computer tools

Examine your draft for grammar, punctuation, and spelling errors. Often, reading your essay aloud will help you find sentences that are tangled, poorly constructed, or not connected. Looking carefully at every word and its function in a sentence will alert you to grammatical problem areas. Turn to **37a–37c** for help with Standard English and methods for correcting common errors.

Computer tools for editing   Use your word processor's spelling-check feature on your draft. The spelling checker will flag any word it does not recognize, and it is very good at catching typographical errors such as *teh* for *the* or *responsability* for *responsibility*. However, it will not identify grammatical errors that affect only spelling, such as missing plural or *-ed* endings. Nor will it flag an omitted word or find a misspelled word that forms another word, such as *then* for *than*, *their* for *there*, or *affect* for *effect*.

The Word Count feature under Tools in Microsoft Word is handy when you are given a word limit; it provides an immediate, accurate count.

Grammar-check programs such as MLA Editor and the program with Microsoft Word will analyze your sentences and make suggestions about what might need to be fixed, tightened, or polished. These programs provide observations about simple mechanical matters, advising, for instance, that commas and periods go inside quotation marks, or they indicate a problem with a sentence like "Can the mayor wins?" Be aware, though, that these programs cannot take context or meaning into account, so their capabilities are limited. Some errors they cannot recognize because they do not "understand" the context. For example, if you wrote "The actors were boring" but meant to write "The actors were bored," the grammar-check programs would not reveal your mistake. Use these programs with great care.

 ESL NOTE   The Dangers of Grammar-Check Programs

Never make a change in your draft at the suggestion of a grammar-check program before verifying that the change is really necessary. A student from Ukraine wrote the grammatically acceptable sentence "What he has is pride." Then, at the suggestion of a grammar-check program, he changed the sentence to "What he has been pride." The program had not recognized the sequence "has is." ■

Proofreading   Even after editing carefully and getting as much help from computer tools as you can, you still need to proofread your final draft to make sure no errors remain.

KEY POINTS

Proofreading Tips

1. Do not try to proofread on the computer screen. Print out hard copy.
2. Make another copy of your manuscript, and read it aloud while a friend examines the original as you read.
3. Use proofreading marks to mark typographical and other errors (see last page of book).
4. Put a piece of paper under the first line of your text. Move it down line by line as you read, focusing your attention on one line at a time.
5. Read the last sentence first, and work backward through your text. This strategy will not help you check for meaning, logic, pronoun reference, fragments, or consistency of verb tenses; but it will focus your attention on the spelling, punctuation, and grammatical correctness of one sentence at a time.
6. Put your manuscript away for a day or two after you have finished it. Proofread it when the content is not so familiar.

3e   Revising an essay: A student's drafts

With her class, student Catherine Turnbull was assigned to read a portion of an assigned book and respond to it. After she wrote a first draft, she read it aloud to a group of classmates and took note of their comments. She also received feedback from her instructor in a conference. Here you see Turnbull's first rough draft with her notes and annotations for revision. Following that is her second draft, in which she moved material from the end to the beginning for a clearer thesis statement; fine-tuned her style, sentence structure, word choice, and accuracy; and cited her source.

FIRST DRAFT

Shift emphasis from self to topic

Reader Response Essay: Non-Military Uniforms *Think up title*

I read the wedding gown chapter from Paul Fussell's assigned book. This chapter covered the history of the white tradition, cost, fanciness, and ~~saving~~ *Storing* the dress afterwards, etc. This chapter and the idea of the book made me look at the uniforms of people around me. While wedding dresses are intended to be incredibly (special) *say how* and are

Move to end ~~basically~~ heavy, tight, and uncomfortable, *In contrast* many "real" uniforms are ~~*Expand*~~
intended to be comfortable, *and* casual, and are team- or job- related.

For example, my brother is on his high school basketball team, and
he of course has a uniform. *It is royal blue and white with* ~~Actually, two—one for home games (white)~~
Wordy ~~and one for away games (blue). In contrast to those old pictures of~~
~~basketball players from the past, the~~ *great, baggy long* trunks ~~on this uniform are~~
~~ridiculously baggy and long in style and look to me~~ *that look* almost more like
skirts than boxers. ~~Be that as it may, his uniform symbolizes Team and~~
~~School—he represents the school through the colors of it, name, logo,~~
~~matching sneakers, warm-up suits, jackets, and duffle bags.~~ The*se*
uniform*s* ~~itself is~~ *are* functional, ~~in that it has to be something that will~~ not
overly be ~~too~~ hot or restricting as ~~they~~ *the players* pound up and down the courts and,
~~with the~~ numbers on the backs, ~~it~~ help*s* the umpires and scorekeepers
to know who is who. ~~The shoes have to be comfortable, that's for sure,~~ *high-tech sneakers give maximum comfort.*
The uniforms are ~~to avoid blisters. But it~~ also ~~has to be~~ "cool" looking, ~~and~~ *as well as practical;* every school
competes a little to have the coolest-~~looking,~~ most intimidating athletic
wear. He says that to him the uniform means "_____" [Fill in later.]

The conductor on my train to school every day wears an official
black uniform, a suit with tie, big pockets, and hat with a gold ~~label~~ *badge*
on the front and a short bill. The suit has a loose cut and appears ~~just~~ *neat*
~~plain~~ functional and comfortable, both the summer and winter versions.
~~Of course comfortable~~ *The* shoes ~~are a must because he puts~~ *obviously have* a lot
of mileage on them. ~~When I had to move last year, it was a hard~~
~~process. One of the things that helped me get more settled was this~~
~~conductor.~~ Every morning ~~he~~ *this man* is remarkably friendly and cheery to
all his passengers ~~everyone, in a nice way, not an obnoxious, put-on way.~~ He punches *show, don't tell*
tickets, greets people, puts the stairs up and down, *and* calls out station
names, ~~everything smooth and efficient, and~~ generally *he* is a testament
to the difference one person can make, doing a good job. ~~Also, if~~
~~someone makes trouble, he barks at them sternly, for safety reasons.~~
~~He has to keep order.~~ His uniform ~~says,~~ *signals,* "I am part of the train team
and am ~~the official person in charge~~ *a reliable authority.*"
Used "official" before
too mechanical ~~The third example is~~ My aunt, a nurse at a hospital, ~~She~~ wears
colorful, baggy, easy-wash scrubs ~~most days,~~ like pajamas with pockets

Add more detail and a badge. Her name and credentials (RN) are on her badge. She wears ~~super~~ comfortable shoes because she has to walk miles in the course of making her rounds, day or night. Her uniform says," I am part of the hospital team and am ^{here} ~~hear~~ to help you. "

Move this idea to 1st ¶ — states thesis ~~In sum,~~ Paul Fussell writes on wedding dresses in his uniform book, but they are not really uniforms in the sense most working people mean the term. More commonly, uniforms are functional and comfortable garments, symbolizing an active day-to-day role played for ^a ~~the~~ larger good. They make you one with your team and also stand out from the rest of the general populace. Unlike a

Add material from ¶1 and expand wedding dress, an average uniform is not so ^{valuable} ~~special~~ that it needs to be preserved in a special garment bag. ~~special storage.~~ It is what people do and their role _{in their uniforms} ~~in society that they have taken on~~ ~~are special.~~ within their larger community that has special value.

SECOND DRAFT

<u>Comfortable Shoes: Everyday Uniforms</u>
and Three People Who Fill Them

In one chapter of <u>Uniforms: Why We Are What We Wear</u>, Paul Fussell looks at the history, cost, and traditions associated with the formal wedding gown, particularly the way it is often stored carefully away for future generations. While Fussell considers wedding dresses to be uniforms, they are not uniforms in the sense that most people mean the term. More commonly, uniforms are functional and comfortable garments, symbolizing an active day-to-day role played for a larger good.

For example, my brother is on his high school basketball team, and he of course has a uniform. It is royal blue and white, with baggy, long trunks that look almost more like a skirt than boxers, as is the style these days. These uniforms are functional, not overly hot or restricting as players pound up and down the court, and the high-tech sneakers give maximum comfort. The large numbers help the umpires and scorekeepers. The uniforms are also "cool" looking, as well as practical. Every school competes a little to have the coolest, most intimidating athletic wear. When I asked my brother what this uniform meant to him, he said, "Pride in representing my school's team."

The conductor on the train I take to school wears an official black uniform, a suit with big pockets, a tie, and a hat with a gold badge on the front. The suit has a loose cut and appears neat, comfortable, and functional, both the warmer winter version and the lighter-weight summer version. The shoes obviously have a lot of mileage on them from traveling up and down the aisles. Every morning this man plays the role his uniform requires by remaining remarkably friendly and cheery to all his passengers, but efficient and businesslike at the same time. He greets people, punches tickets, puts the stairs up and down, and calls out station names. If someone makes trouble, he can bark sternly, for safety reasons. He has to keep order. But he generally brightens people's days with his manner. He is a testament to the difference one person can make by doing a good job. His uniform signals, "I am part of the train team and am a reliable authority."

Nurses' uniforms aim for comfort, too. My aunt, a hospital nurse, wears colorful, baggy, cotton medical scrubs to work, like pajamas with pockets. She says this outfit is easy to wash, which is important in the hygienic hospital setting. She wears the most comfortable rubber-soled shoes she can find since her job involves a lot of walking in the course of a day, making her rounds. Her name and credentials (RN) are on her badge, letting people know her official status and role as well-trained caregiver. In the past, nurses might have had to dress in white or wear more formal outfits and caps, but today the code is relaxed, with an emphasis on comfort and ease of laundering. Still, no matter how casual, her uniform definitely communicates the message, "I am an experienced member of the hospital team. I am here to help you."

Paul Fussell stretches the definition of uniform to include wedding gowns. He makes the point that wedding dresses conform to many set features even though they are intended to be as out of the ordinary and beautiful as possible. They are usually expensive, heavy, snugly fitting, and made with impractical fabrics and beads. In contrast, many everyday uniforms are loose and comfortable. They identify wearers as part of a particular team with a particular mission. Unlike a wedding dress, an average uniform is not so valuable that it needs to be preserved in a special garment bag. It is what people do in their uniforms--the role they have taken on within their larger community--that has special value.

Works Cited

Fussell, Paul. Uniforms: Why We Are What We Wear. Boston: Houghton, 2002.

3f Formatting a college essay (print)

Once you have written, revised, and edited your document, you need to prepare it for presentation to readers. Guides are available for presenting essays in specific disciplines and media. Frequently used style guides are those published by the MLA (Modern Language Association), APA (American Psychological Association), and CSE (Council of Science Editors), in addition to *The Chicago Manual of Style* and *The Columbia Guide to Online Style*. The features of these guides are covered in this handbook. However, there are commonalities among the differences. Here are basic guidelines for preparing your essay on paper, whichever style guide you follow. For preparing and formatting a paper for presentation online, see **24**.

KEY POINTS

Guidelines for College Essay Format

Paper   White bond, unlined, $8^{1}/_{2}"$ × 11"; not erasable or onionskin paper. Clip or staple the pages.

Print   Dark black printing ink—an inkjet or laser printer if possible.

Margins   One inch all around. In some styles, one and one-half inches may be acceptable. Lines should not be justified (aligned on the right). In Microsoft Word, go to Format/Paragraph to adjust alignment.

Space between lines   Uniformly double-spaced for the whole paper, including any list of works cited. Footnotes (in *Chicago* style) may be single-spaced.

Spaces after a period, question mark, or exclamation point   One space, as suggested by most style manuals. Your instructor may prefer two in the text of your essay.

Type font and size   Standard type font (such as Times New Roman or Arial), not a font that looks like handwriting. Select a regular size of 10 to 12 points.

Page numbers   In the top right margin. (In MLA style, put your last name before the page number. In APA style, put a short version of the running head before the page number.) Use Arabic numerals with no period (see p. 43). See **20a** for the header formatting tools available in Word.

(Continued)

(Continued)

Paragraphing   Indent one-half inch (5 spaces) from the left.

Title and identification   On the first page or on a separate title page. See the examples that follow.

Parentheses around a source citation   MLA and APA style, for any written source you refer to or quote, including the textbook for your course (for an electronic source, give author only); then add at the end an alphabetical list of works cited.

Your instructor may prefer a separate title page or ask you to include the identification material on the first page of the essay.

Title and identification on the first page   The following sample of part of a first page shows one format for identifying a paper and giving it a title. The MLA recommends this format for papers in the humanities.

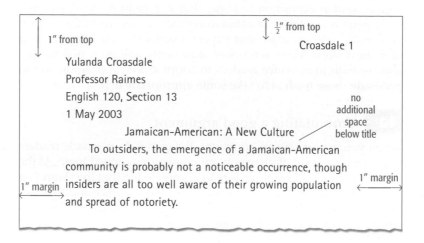

At the top of subsequent pages, write the page number in the upper right corner, preceded by your last name (**20a** shows you how to make this header). No period or parentheses accompany the page number.

Title and identification on a separate title page   In the humanities, include a title page only if your instructor requires one or if you include an outline. On the title page include the following, all double-spaced:

Title: Centered, about one-third of the way down the page. Do not enclose the title in quotation marks, do not underline it, and do not put a period at the end.

Name: Centered, after the word *by,* on a separate line.

Course information: Course and section, instructor, and date, each centered on a new line, either directly below your name or at the bottom of the title page.

With a title page, you do not need the title and identification on your first page.

4   Writing an Argument

An argument in the academic sense is a reasoned, logical piece of writing designed to persuade an audience to pay attention to significant points you raise. For example, you could construct a reasoned, logical written exposition to argue that as a fashion trend, piercing body parts is a potentially dangerous practice, not worth the risk. Or you could write an argument paper to support your interpretation of a short story. Many writers of arguments will go a step further and try both to convince readers to adopt a certain position and to persuade those readers to take some appropriate action.

4a   Formulating a good argument

When you are writing an argument, the goal is to persuade readers to adopt your point of view on your chosen or assigned topic. At the very least, you will want readers to acknowledge that the claim you make about your topic rests on solid, reliable evidence and that you provide a fair, unbiased approach to this evidence. Let readers discover that you have good reasons for your position.

KEY POINTS

The Features of a Good Argument

A good argument

- deals with an arguable issue (**4b**)
- is not based solely on strong "knee-jerk" feelings or beliefs, unsubstantiated by evidence (**4b**)

(Continued)

(Continued)

- stands up to a critical reading (**4c**)
- takes a position on and makes a clear claim about the topic (**4d**)
- supports that position with detailed and specific evidence (such as reasons, facts, examples, descriptions, and stories) (**4e**)
- establishes common ground with listeners or readers and avoids confrontation (**4f**)
- takes opposing views into account and either refutes them or shows why they may be unimportant or irrelevant (**4g**)
- presents reasons logically (**4h, 4i, 4j**)
- is engaged and vital, a reflection of your thinking rather than just a marshaling of others' opinions

 TECHNOTE Useful Web Sites for Writing Arguments

Try the following sites for help with writing arguments.

- *Paradigm Online Writing Assistant,* a site that began at Boise State University, at <http://www.powa.org/argument/index.html>
- The Capital Community College site on writing arguments at <http://ccc.commnet.edu/grammar/composition/argument.htm> with a sample annotated argument paper ■

4b Selecting a topic

If you are not assigned a topic from class discussion or reading, choose one that will be interesting for you to write about and for readers to read about. The topic you choose should be one that is significant and can be debated—"Standardized testing should not begin until the fifth grade"—rather than a fact, such as "Standardized testing is administered in many states."

If the choice of topic for a written argument is up to you, choose one that is fresh. Unless personal involvement, experience, and thorough, wide-ranging research drive you to explore topics like the death penalty, prayer in public schools, drug laws, and abortion, it is best to avoid them; they have been written about so often that original or interesting arguments are hard to find. Brainstorming, reading (books, magazines, and newspapers), and browsing on the Internet in search directories, informational sites, or online discussion groups (see **7e, 7f,** and **22**) can help you discover novel and timely issues. When you find an interesting topic and your instructor has approved it (if necessary), begin by writing a question about it. Then make lists of the arguments on both (or all) sides.

Because her family had been plagued by a spate of intrusive telephone marketing calls, Jennifer Hopper decided to tackle the topic of telemarketing and its impact on society. She began by thinking she would claim that telemarketing is more harmful than beneficial. Here are her initial research question and her brainstormed scratch outline (**1f**) before she began doing research and formulating her claim.

Topic: The impact of telemarketing on our society

Question: Does telemarketing have more harmful than beneficial effects on our daily lives?

HARMFUL EFFECTS

Telemarketing intrudes on our privacy.

Some telemarketers prey on the elderly.

Some of their offers are scams.

Telemarketing takes business away from retail stores.

BENEFICIAL EFFECTS

Telemarketing provides jobs, especially for women, students, retirees, and minorities.

It promotes the economy in rural areas.

It provides buying opportunities for people who are elderly, disabled, and homebound.

See **4d** for Hopper's thesis and **4m** for a draft of her essay.

4c Thinking critically about arguments

Whatever your topic, approach it by thinking critically as you read and do research and as you write (see **1a**). Thinking critically means keeping an open mind and asking probing questions. It is a good habit to step back and read an argument critically, whether it is your own or somebody else's, in order to identify its merits and faults. Be aware, too, that readers will use the same care when they read an argument that *you* write.

Develop a system of inquiry. Do not assume that because something is in print, it is accurate. Here are questions to ask while reading an argument:

1. What am I reading? a statement of fact, an opinion, an exaggeration, an attack, an emotional belief?

2. Where does the information come from? Are the sources trustworthy?

3. How reliable are the writer's statements? Are they measured, accurate, fair, and to the point?

4. Can I ascertain the writer's background, audience, and purpose? What biases does the writer reveal?

5. What assumptions does the writer make? If a writer argues for a college education for everyone, would I accept the underlying assumption that a college education automatically leads to happiness and success? (For more on assumptions, see **4h**.)

6. Does the writer present ideas in a convincing way, relying on rational presentation of evidence rather than on emotional language or name-calling?

For critical reading of visual texts, see **4l**. For critical reading of literary texts, see **5b**.

4d Formulating an arguable claim (thesis)

The position you take on a topic constitutes your claim or your thesis. Jennifer Hopper knew that the claim in her argument paper should be debatable. Two claims she considered were "Telemarketing provides jobs and benefits the economy" and "Telemarketers seek out the elderly and the gullible," both of which would be debatable. Avoid using any of the following as claims, as they are not debatable:

- a neutral statement, which gives no hint of the writer's position
- an announcement of the paper's broad subject
- a fact, which is not arguable
- a truism (statement that is obviously true)
- a personal or religious conviction that cannot be logically debated
- an opinion based only on your own feelings
- a sweeping generalization

Here are some examples of nondebatable claims, each with a revision.

NEUTRAL STATEMENT	**There are unstated standards of beauty in the workplace.**
REVISED	**The way we look affects the way we are treated at work and the size of our paychecks.**

TOO BROAD	This paper is about violence on TV.
REVISED	TV violence has to take its share of blame for the violence in our society.

FACT	*Plessy v. Ferguson*, a Supreme Court case that supported racial segregation, was overturned in 1954 by *Brown v. Board of Education*.
REVISED	The overturning of *Plessy v. Ferguson* by *Brown v. Board of Education* has not led to significant advances in integrated education.

TRUISM	Bilingual education has advantages and disadvantages.
REVISED	A bilingual program is more effective than an immersion program at helping students grasp the basics of science and mathematics.

PERSONAL CONVICTION	Racism is the worst kind of prejudice.
REVISED	The best weapon against racism is primary and secondary education.

OPINION BASED ONLY ON FEELING	I think water-skiing is a dumb sport.
REVISED	Water-skiing should be banned from public beaches.

SWEEPING GENERALIZATION	Women understand housework.
REVISED	The publication of a lengthy guide to housekeeping and its success among both men and women suggest a renewed interest in the domestic arts.

Avoiding loaded terms In your claim, avoid sweeping and judgmental words, for instance, *bad, good, right, wrong, stupid, ridiculous, moral, immoral, dumb, smart.*

Modifying or changing your claim Sometimes you will have an instant reaction to an issue and immediately decide which position you want to take. At other times, you will need to reflect and do research before you take a stand. Whenever you decide what your position is, formulate a position statement that will serve as your working thesis—for example, "Undocumented aliens should (or should not) have to pay higher college tuition fees than citizens or other immigrants." However, keep an open mind. Be prepared to find out more about an issue so that you can make an educated claim with concrete support, and be prepared to modify, qualify, or even change your original claim as you do your research.

Jennifer Hopper began her argument paper expecting to make a case for one side of the telemarketing debate (telemarketing takes trade away from retail stores, deceives the elderly, and invades everyone's privacy), only to find that her research produced enough evidence to persuade her to look at the situation from a different angle (telemarketing is a valuable source of American dollars and provider of goods and services).

You can read a draft of her essay in **4m**.

LANGUAGE AND CULTURE
Arguments across Cultures: Making a Claim and Staking a Position

The types of arguments described in this section are those common in academic and business settings in North America and the Western world. Writers state their views directly, arguing for their viewpoints. The success of their arguments lies in the credibility and strength of the evidence they produce in support. But such an approach is not universal. Other cultures may prefer a less direct approach, one that begins by exploring and evaluating all options rather than by issuing a direct claim. One of the basic principles of writing well—know your audience's expectations—is especially relevant to writing arguments in cultures different from your own.

4e Supporting the claim with reasons and concrete evidence

Supporting your claim means telling your readers what reasons, statistics, facts, examples, and expert testimony bolster and explain your point of view. If a reader asks, "Why do you think that?" about your claim, then the support you offer answers that question in detail.

Reasons Imagine someone saying to you, "OK. I know your position on this issue, but I disagree with you. What led you to your position?" This is asking you to provide the reasons for your conviction. To begin to answer the question, add at least one "because clause" to your claim.

Claim: Colleges should stop using SAT scores to determine admissions.
Reason: (because) High school grades predict college success with more accuracy.

Once you have formulated a tentative claim, make a scratch outline listing the claim and your reasons for supporting it. As you work more on your argument, you will need to find specific and concrete evidence to explain and support each reason. Here is an example of a scratch outline (see **1f**) for an argument against building a cement factory in a rural scenic region.

Claim: Although a large cement factory on the Hudson River would satisfy the increased demand for building materials and might help boost the local economy, it would not only pollute air and water but also threaten the wildlife and the natural beauty of the area.

Reasons:
1. Drilling, blasting, and mining pose dangers to the local aquifer and to the nearby city's water supply.
2. A 1,800-acre coal-burning plant with a 406-foot stack would emit just under 20 million pounds of pollution a year, including arsenic, lead, and mercury.
3. Smokestack emissions could affect birds; barge traffic and discharge into the river could affect fish.
4. Views portrayed by the Hudson River school of painters would be spoiled.

A view of the Hudson River

Concrete evidence You need reasons, but reasons are not enough. You also need to include specific evidence that supports, illustrates, and explains your reasons. Imagine a reader saying, after you give one of your reasons, "Tell me even more about why you say that." The details you provide are what will make your essay vivid and persuasive.

Add to the outline any items of concrete evidence you will include to illustrate and explain your reasoning. What counts as evidence? Facts, statistics, stories, examples, and testimony from experts can all be used as evidence in support of your reasons.

 ESL Note Evidence Used to Support an Argument

The way arguments are structured, the concept of *expertise,* and the nature of evidence regarded as convincing may vary from one culture to another. In some cultures, for example, the opinions of religious or political leaders may carry more weight than the opinions of a scholar in the field. Be sure to consider the readers you will be writing for and the type of evidence they will expect. ∎

 Appealing to the audience and establishing common ground

Ask who your readers are. Consider the readers you are writing for. Assess what they might know, what assumptions they hold, what they need to know, how they can best be convinced to accept your position, and what strategies will persuade them to respect or accept your views.

If you are writing for readers with no specific prior knowledge, biases, or expertise—a *general audience*—remember to include background information: the place, the time, the context, the issues. Do not assume that a general reader knows a great deal more than you do. For more on audience, see **1b**.

Appeal to readers. Your profile of readers will help you decide what types of appeal to use in arguments. See examples in **4m**.

> *Rational appeal* A rational appeal bases an argument's conclusion on logical reasoning from evidence. Such an appeal is appropriate for academic readers and useful when readers are uninformed or hostile.
>
> *Ethical appeal* You make an ethical appeal to readers when you represent yourself or any experts you refer to as knowledgeable,

reliable, reasonable, and evenhanded. Such an appeal is appropriate for formal situations in business and academic worlds. In advertising, ethical appeals are often adapted to include testimony from famous people, whether they are experts or not—for example, Buick's using Tiger Woods to sell cars.

Emotional appeal You make an emotional appeal when you try to gain the empathy and sympathy of your readers by assessing their values and using stories and language to appeal to those values. Such an appeal is less common in academic writing than in journalism and the other media. It is also appropriate when readers are regarded as either already favorable to particular ideas or apathetic toward them.

Within one extended argument, you will probably find it necessary to use all types of argument to reach the maximum number of readers, each with individual expectations, preferences, and quirks.

Establish common ground. Remember that readers turned off by exaggerations or extreme language have the ultimate power to stop reading and ignore what you have to say.

KEY POINTS

Ways to Establish Common Ground with Readers

1. Avoid extreme views or language. Do not label someone's views as *ridiculous, ignorant, immoral, fascist,* or *crooked,* for example.

2. Write to convince, not to confront. Recognize shared concerns, and consider the inclusive use of *we.*

3. Steer clear of sarcastic remarks, such as "They have come up with the amazingly splendid idea of building a gigantic cement factory right in the middle of a natural beauty spot."

4. Use clear, everyday words that sound as if you are speaking directly to your readers.

5. Acknowledge when your opponents' arguments *are* valid, and work to show why the arguments on your side carry more weight.

6. If possible, propose a solution with long-term benefits for everyone.

4g Refuting opposing views

It is not enough to present your own reasons and evidence for your claim. You need also to take into account any opposing arguments and the reasons and evidence that support those arguments. Examine those arguments; describe the most common or convincing ones; evaluate their validity, applicability, and limitations; and explain what motivates people to take those positions. Then discuss the ways in which your reasons and evidence are more pertinent and convincing than those in opposing arguments.

Be careful to argue logically and rationally without insulting your opponents—for instance, do not call opposing views *immoral, ridiculous,* or *stupid.* Take pains to explain rationally why your views differ from theirs. You might choose to do this by following each one of your own points with a discussion of an opposing view. Or you may prefer to devote a section of your essay to dealing with opposing views.

4h Asking Toulmin's four questions

The four questions in the Key Points box, derived from Stephen Toulmin's *The Uses of Argument,* will provide you with a systematic way to construct a logical argument.

KEY POINTS

Four Questions to Ask about Your Argument

1. What is your point? (What are you claiming?)

2. What do you have to go on? (What support do you have for your claim, in the form of reasons, data, and evidence?)

3. How do you get there? (What assumptions—Toulmin calls them *warrants*—do you take for granted and expect readers to take for granted, too?)

4. What could prevent you from getting there? (What qualifications do you need to include, using *but, unless,* or *if* or adding words such as *usually, often, several, mostly,* or *sometimes* to provide exceptions to your assumptions?)

Here is an example showing how the Toulmin questions can be used to develop the claim and supporting reason introduced in **4e**:

CLAIM   **Colleges should stop using SAT scores in their admissions process.**

SUPPORT   **(because) High school grades and recommendations predict college success with more accuracy.**

ASSUMPTION/ WARRANT   **Colleges use SAT scores to predict success in college.**

QUALIFIER   **. . . unless the colleges use the scores only to indicate the level of knowledge acquired in high school.**

REVISED CLAIM   **Colleges that use SAT scores to predict college success should use high school grades and recommendations instead.**

Examine your assumptions.   Pay special attention to examining assumptions that link a claim to the reasons and evidence you provide. Consider whether readers will share those assumptions or whether you need to explain, discuss, and defend them. For example, the claim "Telemarketing should be monitored because it preys on the elderly and the gullible" operates on the assumption that monitoring will catch and reduce abuses. The claim "Telemarketing should be encouraged because it benefits the economy" operates on the assumption that benefiting the economy is an important goal. These different assumptions will appeal to different readers, and some may need to be persuaded of the assumptions before they attempt to accept your claim or the reasons you give for it.

Note that if your claim is "Telemarketing should be encouraged because it is useful," you are saying little more than "Telemarketing is good because it is good." Your reader is certain to object to and reject such circular reasoning. That is why it is important to ask question 3 on page 53. That question leads you to examine how you get from your evidence to your claim and what assumptions your claim is based on.

4i   Reasoning deductively and inductively

Another way to check the logic of your arguments is to assess that they are valid examples of deductive or inductive reasoning.

Deductive reasoning   A deductive argument draws a valid conclusion from true statements. This classical Aristotelian method of constructing an argument is based on a reasoning process known as a syllogism. A valid syllogism first presents a major premise that is true, then moves to a minor premise, and finally arrives at a certain and true conclusion. Here is an example:

PREMISE 1   **Editors for *XXL* magazine know the hip-hop music world.**

PREMISE 2   **Dave Bry is an editor for *XXL*.**

TRUE
CONCLUSION   **Dave Bry knows the hip-hop music world.**

This argument is both valid (the chain of logical reasoning works) and true (nobody would question the truth of either of the premises). We learn something about all *XXL* editors; then we learn the identity of one of the editors and make the deduction accordingly.

Always check the logic of an argument by testing for any assumptions or unstated premises that may make a deductive argument untrue or invalid. The following is an invalid argument. The major term in premise 1 (*writers*) does not appear in premise 2 in either its singular or its plural form.

PREMISE 1   **Writers for *XXL* magazine know the hip-hop music world.**

PREMISE 2   **Georgia Winston knows the hip-hop music world.**

UNTRUE
CONCLUSION   **Georgia Winston is a writer for *XXL* magazine.**

The problem here is that there could be many explanations for why Georgia Winston knows about hip-hop music: she could collect CDs, go to performances, and read *XXL* regularly, for example. The conclusion does not follow from the premises. The argument is invalid. (In fact, Georgia Winston is a lawyer, not a writer.)

In contrast, in the following syllogism, the conclusion follows logically from the premises. The first premise, however, is not true; many or most of the editors are *not* performers. Therefore the conclusion is not true.

PREMISE 1
(UNTRUE)   **Editors for *XXL* magazine are professional hip-hop performers.**

PREMISE 2   **Dave Bry is an editor for *XXL*.**

CONCLUSION
(UNTRUE)   **Dave Bry is a professional hip-hop performer.**

Inductive reasoning A deductive argument begins with a generalization and leads to a *certain* conclusion, but an inductive argument begins with details that lead to a *probable* conclusion.

Inductive arguments are used often in the sciences and social sciences. Researchers begin with a tentative hypothesis. They conduct studies and perform experiments; they collect and tabulate data; they examine the evidence of other studies. Then they draw a conclusion to support, reject, or modify the hypothesis. The conclusion, however, is not necessarily certain. It is based on the circumstances of the evidence. Different evidence at a different time could lead to a different conclusion. Conclusions drawn in the medical field change with the experiments and the sophistication of the techniques—eggs are called good for you one year, bad the next. That is because the nature of the evidence changes.

4j Recognizing flaws in logic

Faulty logic can make readers mistrust you as a writer. Watch out for these flaws as you write and check your drafts.

Sweeping generalization Generalizations can sometimes be so broad that they fall into stereotyping. Avoid them.

> All British people are stiff and formal.

> The only thing that concerns students is grades.

The reader will be right to wonder what evidence has led to these conclusions. Without any explanation or evidence, they will simply be dismissed. Beware, then, of the trap of words like *all, every, only, never,* and *always.*

Hasty conclusion with inadequate support To convince readers of the validity of a generalization, you need to offer enough evidence—usually more than just one personal observation. Thoughtful readers can easily spot a conclusion that is too hastily drawn from flimsy support.

> My friend Arecelis had a terrible time in a bilingual school. It is clear that bilingual education has failed.

> Bilingual education is a success story, as the school in Chinatown has clearly shown.

> A conclusion that can be contradicted by any evidence is not a sound conclusion.

Non sequitur *Non sequitur* is Latin for "It does not follow." Supporting a claim with evidence that is illogical or irrelevant causes a non sequitur fallacy.

Maureen Dowd writes so well that she would make a good teacher.

The writer does not establish a connection between good writing and good teaching.

Studying economics is a waste of time. Money does not make people happy.

Here the writer does not help us see any relationship between happiness and the study of a subject.

Causal fallacy You are guilty of a causal fallacy if you assume that one event causes another merely because the second event happens after the first. (The Latin name for this logical flaw is *post hoc, ergo propter hoc:* "after this, therefore because of this.")

The economy collapsed because a new president was elected.

Was the election the reason? Or did it simply occur before the economy collapsed?

The number of A's given in college courses has increased. This clearly shows that faculty members are inflating grades.

But does the number of A's clearly show any such thing? Or could the cause be that students are better prepared in high school? Examine carefully any statements you make about cause and effect.

Ad hominem attack *Ad hominem* (Latin for "to the person") refers to appeals to personal considerations rather than to logic or reason. Avoid using arguments that seek to discredit an opinion through criticizing a person's character or lifestyle.

The new curriculum should not be adopted because the administrators who favor it have never even taught a college course.

The student who is urging the increase in student fees for social events is a partygoer and a big drinker.

Argue a point by showing either the logic of the argument or the lack of it, not by pointing to flaws in character. However, personal considerations may be valid if they pertain directly to the issue, as in "The two women who favor the abolition of the bar own property on the same block."

Circular reasoning In an argument based on circular reasoning, the evidence and the conclusion restate each other, thus proving nothing.

> Credit card companies should be banned on campus because companies should not be allowed to solicit business from students.

> That rich man is smart because wealthy people are intelligent.

Neither of these statements moves the argument forward. They both beg the question—that is, they argue in a circular way.

False dichotomy or false dilemma Either/or arguments reduce complex problems to two simplistic alternatives without exploring them in depth or considering other alternatives.

> After September 11, New York can do one of two things: increase airport security or screen immigrants.

This proposal presents a false dichotomy. These are not the only two options for dealing with potential terrorism. Posing a false dilemma like this will annoy readers.

 TechNote Logical Fallacies on the Web

Go to *Stephen's Guide to the Logical Fallacies* at <http://datanation.com/fallacies/> for lists of many more types of logical fallacies, all with explanations and examples. ■

 4k Structuring an argument essay

General to specific The general-to-specific structure, used frequently in the humanities and arts, moves from the thesis to support and evidence.

 KEY POINTS

Basic Structure for a General-to-Specific Argument

- *Introduction:* Provide background information on the issue, why it is an issue, and what the controversies are. After you have introduced your readers to the nature and importance of the issue, announce your position in a claim or thesis statement, perhaps at the end of the first paragraph or in a prominent posi-

(Continued)

(Continued)

tion within the second paragraph, depending on the length and complexity of your essay.

- *Body*: Provide evidence in the form of supporting points for your thesis, with concrete and specific details. For each new point, start a new paragraph.

- *Acknowledgment of opposing views:* Use evidence and specific details to describe and logically refute the opposing views. You could also deal with opposing views one by one as you deal with your own points of support.

- *Conclusion:* Return to the topic as a whole and your specific claim. Without repeating whole phrases and sentences, reiterate the point you want to make. End on a strong note.

Specific to general   Alternatively, you might choose to begin with data and points of evidence first and then draw a conclusion from that evidence, providing that the evidence is relevant and convincing. A basic specific-to-general argument on the topic of driving with a cell phone looks like this:

Introduction: background, statement of problem and controversy

Data:

1. Cell phone users admit to being distracted while driving (cite statistics).

2. Many accidents are attributable to cell phone use (cite statistics).

3. Several states have passed a law against using a handheld cell phone while driving.

4. NPR talk show hosts Click and Clack (Tom and Ray Magliozzi) criticize the small sample size used by the AAA (only forty-two cases) to claim that only very few (8.3 percent) car crashes are caused by driver distraction, with even fewer of those distractions (1.5 percent of 8.3 percent) attributable to cell phone use (<http://www.newsfactor.com/perl/story/12502.html>).

Conclusion: Discussion of data and presentation of thesis (generalization formed from analysis of the data): All states should pass laws prohibiting handheld cell phones while driving.

In an argument in the sciences or social sciences (as in the APA paper in **16**), writers often begin with a hypothesis that they can test: they list their findings from experimentation, surveys, facts, and statistics. Then, from the data they have collected, they draw conclusions to support, modify, or reject the hypothesis.

Problem and solution If your topic offers solutions to a problem, you probably will find it useful to present the details of the problem first and then offer solutions. Consider where the strongest position for the solution you consider most desirable would be: at the beginning of your solutions section, or at the end? Do you want to make your strong point early, or would you rather lead up to it gradually?

4l ▸ Using visual arguments

We commonly think of arguments as being spoken or written, and **4a–4k** deal largely with the features of written arguments. However, another type of argument is widespread—an argument that is presented visually. Think, for example, of arguments made in cartoons, advertisements, and works of art. The famous 1976 *New Yorker* magazine cover by Saul Steinberg called "View of the World from Ninth Avenue" shows New York City in the foreground, with cars on Ninth Avenue, gradually giving way to New Jersey, Kansas, the Pacific Ocean, and Japan in the background. The argument? That New York City is the center of the world to New Yorkers.

© Reuters NewMedia Inc./CORBIS

Pictures that tell a story You can supplement your written arguments with visual arguments: maps, superimposed images, photographs, charts and graphs, political cartoons—vivid images that will say more than many words to your readers. An argument essay on animal preservation in the wild, for example, would make a strong emotional impact if its argument included the picture above. This photograph shows a young chimpanzee confiscated from poachers by Kenya Wildlife Service officials in 2003.

Visual arguments make their appeals in ways similar to written arguments, appealing to logic, showcasing the character and credentials of the author, or appealing to viewers' emotions.

Interactive multimedia: The language of words, sound, and images
Present-day technology allows for a new way to express ideas. No longer limited to using type on a page, writers now can use screens to

present an interaction of words, color, music, sound, images, and movies to tell a story and make a point.

In preparing a multimedia presentation, consider, then, the effectiveness of juxtaposing images and conveying emotion and meaning through colors and pictures, as well as using words. If you use media imaginatively, you can do what writing teachers have long advised: Show, don't just tell.

For an example of a multimedia visual argument, see <http://www.iml.annenberg.edu/projects>. This project on the ancient city of Troy was created by undergraduates at the University of Southern California for a course in Near Eastern and Mediterranean Archeology. Using excavation records, archaelogical findings, and Homer's texts (as well as architectural modeling software, audio, and virtual reality techniques), the students reconstructed "the citadel as it may have appeared at the time of the Trojan War in the 13th Century B.C."

4m Sample argument essay

Here is the second draft of Jennifer Hopper's argument paper on telemarketing, developed from her brainstormed notes and further research (**4b** and **4d**).

Why Telemarketing Is a Real Job:

The Ongoing War between the Right to Privacy and Telemarketing

Just a few years ago, when we wanted to shop, we had to leave our homes to go to the store or mall. The alternative was to order from catalogs. But the initiative remained with us, and for couch potatoes, that was not always easy. Now, however, we do not have to leave our house or dial a number. We can wait for goods and services to come to us. And come they will. Telemarketing involves millions of telephone calls every day from company representatives to households across America, with over 100 million calls projected for 2003 (Bacon and Roston 56). The demand for workers to make those calls and the billions of dollars' worth of goods and services sold via the calls have created a booming business for telemarketers, with revenues increasing 250% in twelve years, reaching a total of $295 billion in 2002 (Bacon and Roston 56).

> Background context and statistics

Yet every silver lining has its cloud. There has been a substantial outcry from the American public about the irritation of receiving sales calls at home, especially at meal times and during family gatherings. These objections have led to several attempts at solutions: the creation of anti-telemarketing Web sites, legislation, the proliferation of caller-ID plans, phone company services to protect

> Presentation of problem

telephone privacy, and court battles. Training programs remind telemarketers that if a prospective client does not need their services, no one will benefit from a forced sale (Allen 101). These developments center around the issue of Americans' right to privacy at home and whether telephone solicitations are an intrusion on that privacy.

Of course, this ugly side of telemarketing is accompanied by a bright side. Telemarketing has proven itself substantially important to both American workers and consumers. It increasingly provides millions of jobs to Americans (growing from 175,000 jobs to 5 million in ten years) and has sparked the growth and development of many declining U.S. cities (Greenwald). Therefore, if some individuals find that telephone solicitations do them more harm than good, they can address the problem without compromising the rights of the consumers and workers who benefit from the industry. In short, telemarketing

Claim (thesis)

cannot be written off as a public nuisance when it is such a valuable source of American dollars and provider of goods and services.

Support 1: importance to business (rational appeal)

Although it is difficult to find a person with a listed phone number who has never received a telemarketing call, consumers are not the main target of phone solicitations. Greenwald reports that "pitches to other businesses generate more than 80% of the revenues of telemarketing

Concrete evidence

and account for some 90% of its jobs." Just as companies have found it cheaper to use phone calls rather than mail to gain customers, they have also found telemarketing to be a cheaper means of promoting business than sending sales teams (Greenwald).

Support 2: Creation of jobs in rural areas (rational and ethical appeal)

In some parts of the country, the impact of telemarketing industries is especially beneficial. Omaha, Nebraska, is a prime example. In 1995, there were as few as thirty telemarketing companies located there, and yet "20,000 or so Omahans—about 5% of the resident population—work for them dialing out more than one million quality calls per week" (Singer). Omaha proved to be a very profitable site for the industry, from the viewpoints of both company owners and Omaha residents. Located right in the middle of the United States, the town lends itself to "easy access" to all corners of the country and its four time zones (Singer). Not only that, but the majority of Omahan laborers are reasonably well-educated, another advantage in the telemarketing field. According to <u>New York Times</u> correspondent James Brooke, a

Concrete evidence

Concrete evidence

similar situation has developed in North Dakota, where Native Americans have been able to take telemarketing jobs near their reservations. In fact, Native Americans, usually vastly overlooked by

American employers, are catching the interest of telemarketers. It may not be the exhibition of social consciousness on the part of telemarketing companies, but it still provides opportunities for a group of people not known for their earning power.

An important point to note is not just the number of jobs that telemarketing provides but the significant economic changes those jobs make in the lives of the people who hold them. In both Omaha and North Dakota, farming used to be the way of life (Brooke). As it became more and more difficult to subsist on crops and cattle in the United States of the late twentieth century, the need arose for another way for locals to supplement their earnings and gain security. Telemarketing provided a means for people to keep their homes and farms by working part-time in a booming industry. Telemarketing also provided part-time jobs that were stable and relatively easy. When asked about the rigors of her job, Omahan telemarketer Erin Kline responded, "Stressful? More tiring. But to sit here and get paid over 10, 11 bucks an hour to sit on your butt, basically, and make phone calls . . . that's a really good job" (qtd. in Singer). Telemarketing jobs continue to be held by housewives, college students, and retired persons.

Support 3: economic benefit and security (emotional appeal)

Yet we can hardly forget the millions of people receiving these phone calls. Many Americans express distaste for the entire industry, united in the belief that people's homes should be a safe haven from the rabid commercialism that has permeated all corners of society. Some believe that telemarketing preys on so-called "nice guys" and older people, who are loath to be rude and reject the sale offered, which may even be a scam. Legislation is helping, too. Thirty states have initiated a "Do Not Call" list that informs companies of homes that request no more calls, with more than 15 million people signing the lists (Bacon and Roston 58). In addition, a national "Do Not Call" list was signed into law on 11 March 2003, legislating fines for violators ("House Passes"). However, even with legislation and penalties, consumers often take matters into their own hands.

Use of we to establish common ground

Presentation of opposing view of telemarketing as a nuisance

Concrete evidence

Two different approaches have been used by aggravated consumers to fight the telemarketing industry. One method is used most notably by a man named Robert Bulmash, of Private Citizen, Inc., whose name is practically synonymous with anti-telemarketing. Mr. Bulmash took his grievances straight to the American legal system, suing a telemarketing company that had especially plagued him (Sharkey). He has channeled his efforts into heading a group that

Ethical and emotional appeal in opposition to telemarketing

helps cut down on unwelcome telephone solicitations. Its members' names are given to telemarketing companies who are then informed there is a "service charge" for calling them. If calls continue, Mr. Bulmash helps members take legal action against the companies (Raisfield). Mr. Bulmash's approach was unique in that he brought his objections to the owners and operators of the company, who would have to deal with the lawsuit.

Other people use less noble tactics. Many screen calls or simply hang up, as shown in Fig. 1. Some are rude or irritating to telemarketers in order to make them hang up and/or stop calling permanently. One proponent of this technique is Vince Nestico, who has even created a Web site to provide ideas to other exasperated people on how to "torture" telemarketers. He sells tapes that offer such extreme retorts to solicitors as, "Shhh . . . Wait a minute. I'm here robbing the house. Whoa! I think the owners just got home. Can you hold?" (qtd. in Sharkey). Unlike Mr. Bulmash, Mr. Nestico has decided that the best way to obtain phone lines free of solicitors is to take up his grievances with the employees, not the heads of the telemarketing companies. It is understandable that Mr. Nestico is tired of receiving telemarketing calls, but it may be more difficult to comprehend his motivations for trying to capitalize on the sale of goods like the "Telemarketer Torture Tape" he has created.

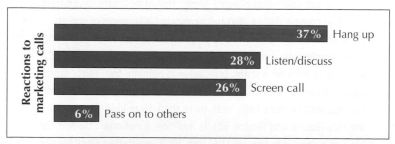

Fig. 1. Gerda Gallop-Goodman, "Please Don't Hang Up," American Demographics 23.5 (2001): 28. Source: Pitney Bowes.

Are such tapes the mature, responsible way to handle an onslaught of telemarketing calls? Just as the consumer has a right to privacy, the telemarketer has the right to hold a job and not be tormented in the process. If people have a problem with telemarketing as a selling strategy, then they need to add their names to the "Do Not Call" lists and take up any violations with the heads of companies or the government, as many of them already have. The Federal Trade

Visual to augment the point about consumers' resistance

Refutation of opposing views (rational appeal) with solution to problem

Commission also has a useful Web site on consumer protection at
<http://www.ftc.gov/bcp/menu-tmark.htm>. Better reforms such as
recent legislated penalties are certainly viable options, which will put
no dent in the thriving telemarketing industry, because the people
who want to be placed on a "Do Not Call" list are not likely to be
interested in buying the telemarketer's wares anyway.

After learning the industry's employment numbers and sales   Conclusion
revenues, we can no longer write off telemarketing as unnecessary
and dispensable. It has become important and necessary to places like
Omaha and North Dakota, where jobs were badly needed. Telemarketing
industries are selling billions of dollars' worth of goods and services to
American consumers every year. Not all these sales, or even a majority of   Reiteration of
them, can be the result of telemarketers supposedly deceiving consumers.   claim and
                                                                             main points
Americans who may not agree with telemarketing techniques can fight   of argument
the industry legally. But telemarketers have as much a right to hold down
a job without interference as other Americans. Linda Scobee, an Omahan
telemarketer, had this in mind when a man attacked her for doing her
job. "He said, 'Why don't you get a real job?' and I wanted to say, 'If
you'd like to send me a check every month to take care of my kids, I'll
stop.' But I didn't. You know, company policy" (qtd. in Singer 69).

Works Cited   New page

Allen, Margaret. Direct Marketing. London: Kagan Page, 1997.

Bacon, Perry, Jr., and Eric Roston. "Stop Calling Us." Time
    28 Apr. 2003: 56–58.

Brooke, James. "Telemarketing Finds a Ready Labor Market in Hard-
    Pressed North Dakota." New York Times 3 Feb. 1997:
    A10. Academic Universe: News. LexisNexis. City U of New York
    Lib. 23 Apr. 2003 <http://web.lexis-nexis.com/>.

Greenwald, John. "Sorry, Right Number." Time 13 Sept. 1993: 66.
    Academic Search Premier. EBSCO. City U of New York Lib.
    18 Apr. 2003 <http://search.epnet.com/direct.asp?an=
    9309080045&db=aph>.

"House Passes 'Do Not Call' Legislation." Association Management
    Apr. 2003: 7. Business Source Premier. EBSCO.
    City U of New York Lib. 29 Apr. 2003 <http://search.epnet.com/
    direct.asp?an+9376434&db=buh>.

Raisfield, Robin. "Telenuisances." <u>New York Magazine</u> 31 Jan. 1994: 31.

Sharkey, Joe. "Answering the Phone as an Act of Revenge."
    <u>New York Times</u> 22 June 1997, sec. 4: 3. <u>Academic
    Universe: News</u>. LexisNexis. City U of New York Lib. 24 Apr.
    2003 <http://web.lexis-nexis.com/>.

Singer, Barry. "It's 7 P.M. and 5 Percent of Omaha Is Calling. Want 28
    Steaks and a Radio?" <u>New York Times Magazine</u> 3 Dec. 1995:
    68– . <u>Academic Universe: News</u>. LexisNexis. City U of New York
    Lib. 1 May 2003 <http://web.lexis-nexis.com/>.

5   Writing in All Your Courses

5a   Writing under pressure: Essay exams and short-answer tests

In an examination setting, you have to write quickly and on an
assigned topic. Learn how to cope with these tests so that you can
choose the facts and ideas you need and present them clearly.

KEY POINTS

How to Approach an Essay Exam

1. For a content-based essay test, review assigned materials and
   notes; assemble facts; underline, annotate, and summarize significant information in your textbooks and other assigned materials;
   predict questions on the basis of the material your instructor has
   covered in detail in class; and draft some answers.

2. Highlight or underline key terms in the assigned questions (see
   the list on p. 67).

3. Think positively about what you know. Work out a way to
   emphasize the details you know most about. Stretch and relax.

4. Plan your time. Jot down a rough schedule; allow the most time
   for the questions that are worth the most points. To increase
   your confidence, answer the easiest question first.

5. Make a scratch outline (see **1f**) to organize your thoughts. Jot
   down specific details as evidence for your thesis.

(Continued)

(Continued)

6. Focus on providing detailed support for your thesis. In an exam, this is more important than an elaborate introduction or conclusion.

7. Check your essay for content, logic, and clarity. Make sure you answered the question.

In *short-answer tests,* use your time wisely. So that you know how long you should spend on each question, count the number of questions and divide the number of minutes you have for taking the test by the number of questions (add 1 or 2 to the number you divide by, to give yourself time for editing and proofreading). Then for each answer decide which points are the most important ones to cover in the time you have available. You cannot afford to ramble or waffle in short-answer tests. Get to the point fast, and show what you know.

For essay exams and short-answer tests, always read the questions carefully, and make sure you understand what each question asks you to do. Test writers often use the following verbs:

analyze: divide into parts and discuss each part

argue: make a claim and point out your reasons

classify: organize people, objects, or concepts into groups

compare: point out similarities

contrast: point out differences

define: give the meaning of

discuss: state important characteristics and main points

evaluate: define criteria for judgment and examine good and bad points, strengths and weaknesses

explain: give reasons or make clear by analyzing, defining, contrasting, illustrating, and so on

illustrate: give examples from experience and reading

relate: point out and discuss connections

5b Writing about literature

Before you begin writing, pay careful attention to the content and form of the work of literature by reading the work more than once and highlighting significant passages. Then use the Key Points box to analyze the work systematically.

Here are some guidelines for writing about literature, followed by more specific guidelines for analyzing fiction, creative nonfiction, poetry, and drama.

- Be aware of the distinction between author and narrator. The narrator is the person telling the story or serving as the voice of the poem, not necessarily the author. Often the author has invented the narrator.

- Assume a larger audience than your instructor. Think of your readers as people who have read the work but not thought of the issues you did.

- Make sure that you formulate a thesis. Do not devote a large part of your essay to summary; assume that readers have read the work. Occasionally, though, you may need to include a brief summary of the whole or of parts to orient readers. Make sure you tell them not just what is in the work but how you perceive and interpret important aspects of the work.

- Turn to the text for evidence, and do so often. Text references, in the form of paraphrase or quotation, provide convincing evidence to support your thesis. But do not let your essay turn into a string of quotations.

KEY POINTS

Ten Ways to Analyze a Work of Literature

1. *Plot or sequence of events*   What happens, and in what order? What stands out as important?

2. *Theme*   What is the message of the work, the generalization that readers can draw from it? A work may, for example, focus on making a statement about romantic love, jealousy, sexual repression, courage, ambition, revenge, dedication, treachery, honor, lust, greed, envy, social inequality, or generosity.

3. *Characters*   Who are the people portrayed? What do you learn about them? Do one or more of them change, and what effect does that have on the plot or theme?

4. *Genre*   What type of writing does the work fit into—parody, tragedy, love story, epic, sonnet, haiku, melodrama, comedy of manners, mystery novel, for example? What do you know about the features of the genre, and what do you need to know? How does this work compare with other works in the

(Continued)

(Continued)

same genre? What conventions does the author observe, violate, or creatively vary?

5. *Structure*   How is the work organized? What are its major parts? How do the parts relate to each other?

6. *Point of view*   Whose voice speaks to the reader and tells the story? Is the speaker or narrator involved in the action or an observer of it? How objective, truthful, and reliable is the speaker/narrator? What would be gained or lost if the point of view were changed?

7. *Setting*   Where does the action take place? How are the details of the setting portrayed? What role, if any, does the setting play? What would happen if the setting were changed?

8. *Tone*   From the way the work is written, what can you learn about the way the author feels about the subject matter and the theme? Can you, for example, detect a serious, informative tone, or is there evidence of humor, sarcasm, or irony?

9. *Language*   What effects do the following have on the way you read and interpret the work: word choice, style, imagery, symbols, and figurative language?

10. *Author*   What do you know, or what can you discover through research, about the author and his or her time and that author's other works—and does what you discover illuminate this work?

Writing about prose fiction or creative nonfiction   As you read novels, short stories, memoirs, and biographies or autobiographies, consider these basic questions for thinking about what you read: What happened? When and where did it happen? Who did what? How were things done? Why? Then extend your inquiry by considering all or some of the following factors in detail:

plot: sequence of events in the work

character and character development: main characters, who they are, how they interact, and if and how they change

theme: main message of the work

setting: time and place of the action and cultural/social context

point of view: position from which the events are described, such as first or third person narrator (*I/we* or *he/she/they*), biased or reliable, limited or omniscient *author:* relationship to narrator (same or different person?); relevant facts of author's life

tone: attitudes expressed directly or indirectly by the author or narrator

style: word choice, sentence length and structure, significant features

imagery: effect of figures of speech, such as similes and metaphors (see p. 71 and **33e**)

symbols: objects or events with special significance or with hidden meanings

narrative devices: foreshadowing, flashback, leitmotif (a recurring theme), alternating points of view, turning point, and dénouement (outcome of plot)

Writing about poetry   In addition to using some of the suggestions relating to prose, you can consider the following factors when you analyze a poem.

stanza: lines set off as a unit of a poem

rhyme scheme: system of end-of-line rhymes that you can identify by assigning letters to similar final sounds—for example, a rhyme scheme for couplets (two-line stanzas), *aa bb cc;* and a rhyme scheme for a sestet (a six-line stanza), *ababcc*

meter: number and pattern of stressed and unstressed syllables (or *metric feet*) in a line. Common meters are trimeter, tetrameter, and pentameter (three, four, and five metric feet). The following line is written in iambic tetrameter (four metric feet, each with one unstressed and one stressed syllable):

Whŏse woóds / thĕse aŕe / Ĭ thínk / Ĭ knów.   —Robert Frost

foot: unit (of meter) made up of a specific number of stressed and unstressed syllables

Writing about drama   As you prepare to write about a play, use any of the relevant points listed for fiction, creative nonfiction, and poetry, and in addition focus on the following dramatic conventions:

structure of the play: acts and scenes

plot: episodes, simultaneous events, chronological sequence, causality, climax, turning point

characters: analysis of psychology, social status, relationships

setting: time, place, and description

time: real time depicted (all action takes place in two hours or so of the play) or passage of time

stage directions: details about clothing, sets, actors' movements, expressions, and voices, information given to actors

scenery, costumes, music, lighting, props, and *special effects:* purpose and effectiveness

presentation of information: recognition of whether the characters in the play know things that the audience does not or whether the audience is informed of plot developments that are kept from the characters

Figurative language   The writers of literary works often use figures of speech to create images and intensify effects.

simile: a comparison, with two sides stated.

> Like as the waves make towards the pebbled shore,
> So do our minutes hasten to their end.   —William Shakespeare

> The weather is like the government, always in the wrong.
> —Jerome K. Jerome

> A pretty girl is like a melody.   —Irving Berlin

> A woman without a man is like a fish without a bicycle.
> —Attributed to Gloria Steinem

metaphor: an implied comparison, with no *like* or *as*

> The still, sad music of humanity   —William Wordsworth
> The quicksand of racial injustice   —Martin Luther King, Jr.

alliteration: repetition of consonant sounds

> He bravely breach'd his boiling bloody breast.
> —William Shakespeare

assonance: repetition of vowel sounds

> And feed deep, deep upon her peerless eyes   —John Keats

onomatopoeia: sound of word associated with meaning

> murmuring of innumerable bees   —Alfred, Lord Tennyson

personification: description of a thing as a person

> rosy-fingered dawn   —Homer

zeugma: use of a word with two or more other words, forming different and often humorous logical connections

> The art dealer departed in anger and a Mercedes.

For more on using figurative language, see **33e**.

KEY POINTS

Common Conventions in Writing about Literature

Tense Use the present tense to discuss works of literature even when the author is no longer alive (**41e**).

Authors' Names Use an author's full name the first time you mention it: "Stephen King." Thereafter, and always in parenthetical citations, use only the last name: "King," not "Stephen," and certainly not "Steve."

Titles of Works Underline or italicize the titles of books, journals, and other works published as an entity and not as part of a larger work. Use quotation marks to enclose the title of a work forming part of a larger published work: short stories, essays, articles, songs, and short poems.

Quotations Integrate quotations into your text, and use them for help in making your point (**10e**). Avoid a mere listing and stringing together: "Walker goes on to say. . . . Then Walker states. . . ." When quoting two or three lines of poetry, separate lines by using a slash (/). When using long quotations (more than three lines of poetry or four typed lines of prose), indent one inch. Do not add quotation marks; the indentation signals a quotation (**10f**).

Citations Supply specific references to the literary text under discussion to support your opinions, and cite any references to the work or to secondary sources. (See **9g** for advice on what to cite.) Cite author and page number within your essay for all quotations and references to the work of others; at the end of your paper, attach an alphabetical list of works cited. Follow the MLA style of documentation (**11–13**).

5c Writing about community service

Service learning projects link a college to the community. For such projects, students volunteer for community service, often related to the content of a discipline or a particular course. They then must demonstrate to the college instructor what they learned from the service experience. There are three main types of writing for community service projects:

1. writing done initially with the site supervisor to outline the goals, activities, and desired outcomes of the service project

2. writing done during the service work, such as reports to a supervisor, daily records, and summaries of work completed

3. writing done for the college course—usually reflective reports describing the service objectives and the writer's experiences and assessing the success of the project

To reflect fully on the work you do, keep an ongoing journal of your activities, so that you can provide background about the setting and the work and give specific details about the problems you encounter and their solutions. Link your comments to the goals of the project.

The following paragraph is from Joanne L. Soriano's reflective journal. While enrolled in a microbiology course at Kapi'olani Community College in Hawaii, Soriano worked at an arboretum (a place to study trees) propagating endangered plant species.

> Through Service Learning, I am able to contribute to the Lyon Arboretum's efforts. I made my first visit on February 5th, and was taken to their micropropagation lab. In it, my supervisor, Greg Koob, showed me racks and racks of test tubes filled with plantlets. They were either endangered or native Hawaiian, or both. The endangered ones were clones; in some cases they were derived from only a few remaining individuals. A major function of the lab is to perpetuate these species by growing them in the test tubes and then splitting each individual into more test tubes as they grow. Thus one specimen can become hundreds, under the right conditions. They can be planted on the Arboretum's grounds, or sent to various labs to be studied. I am thrilled to be given the opportunity to participate in the process.

Source: Excerpt from KCC Service Learning at the Lyon Arboretum.

 TechNote Students' Writing in Service Learning Courses

For samples of student writing, go to *The Writing Center: Michigan State University* site at <http://writing.msu.edu/content/wipi/10.pdf> and to the *Virginia Tech Service-Learning Center* at <http://www.majbill.vt.edu/SL/>. ■

5d Writing laboratory reports

Students write laboratory reports to describe their experiments in social science and science courses. Instructors may provide detailed directions on the format they expect for a lab report. If they do not, use the following guidelines for reports in introductory courses.

The *Publication Manual of the American Psychological Association* (APA) describes a report format that generally is acceptable to college instructors in the sciences as well as the social sciences, especially since the APA author/year style closely resembles the author/year style described in the CBE/CSE manual (see **17**) as one of its recommended styles of documentation. (You will find an example of a typical APA-style report of an experimental procedure in **16**.)

For an APA-style lab report, include a title page, a page header on every page, and an abstract (see p. 202). Divide the report into headed sections: Introduction, including the purpose and background of the experiment, your hypothesis, and a review of similar experiments; Materials and Methods (with subheadings such as Apparatus, Participants, and Procedure); Results (include statistical data and explain your tables and figures); Discussion; and Conclusion(s). Include a list of references (**15–16**) and notes, on separate pages. Finally, attach any tables and figures, such as graphs, drawings, and photographs, on separate pages at the end of your report (see p. 209).

The following passage is from Natasha Williams's lab report on microbial genetics conjugation, written for a college cell biology course. This excerpt shows part of the Discussion section, annotated to point out various conventions of science writing.

Discussion

Conjugation involves transfer by appropriate mating types. F+ and Hfr are donor cells with respectively low and high rates of genetic transfer. F- cells are recipients. Contact between the cell types is made by a conjugation bridge called an F pilus extending from the Hfr cell. The donor chromosome appears to be linearly passed through the connecting bridge. Sometimes this transfer is interrupted. The higher the frequency of recombination, the closer the gene is to the beginning of the circular DNA. In this way one can determine the sequence of genes on the chromosome.

Table 1 shows consistently that histidine is the last amino acid coded with the smallest number of recombinants, and arginine is the second to last coded with the next smallest number of recombinants. However, the results obtained for proline and leucine/threonine vary.

Major section heading is centered.

Passive construction, common in lab reports

Note the use of one *for general reference*

Researcher places Table 1 at end of report and here discusses its details.

5e Writing in the disciplines

In a biology course, you might be expected to write scientific laboratory reports and to use a style of documentation different from one you learned in an English course. In a music course, another format and still another documentation style might be required.

LANGUAGE AND CULTURE
The Culture of the Academic Disciplines

Each discipline has its own culture and its own expectations of the people who practice in the discipline and write about it. When you take a course in a new discipline, use the following strategies to get acquainted with its ways of thinking and operating.

1. Listen carefully to lectures and discussion; note any specialized vocabulary. Make lists of new terms and definitions.
2. Read the assigned textbook, and note the conventions that apply to writing about the field.
3. Use subject-specific dictionaries and encyclopedias to learn about the field. Examples include the *Encyclopedia of Religion* and *Encyclopedia of Sociology.*
4. Subscribe to e-mail discussion lists (**22b**) in the field so that you can see what issues people are concerned about.
5. When given a writing assignment, make sure you read samples of similar types of writing in that discipline.
6. Talk with your instructor about the field, its literature, and readers' expectations.

Find out what way of writing and documenting is expected in each of your courses. Although each course may call for some adaptation of the writing process and for awareness of specific conventions, in general you will engage in familiar activities—planning, drafting, revising, and editing.

You will be aware of the biggest differences when you come to do research and write research papers or accounts of experiments. Follow the conventions of the discipline you are writing in. Consider the following:

- types of data to gather—from primary or secondary sources? (**6d**)

- sources to consult (**7a–7e**)
- methods of presenting papers (**3f, 13, 16**)
- documentation style to use (**11–19**)
- terminology specific to the field (**33d**)
- type of language in common use: subjective or objective? (**10g**)

This book contains several samples of or from student papers written in different disciplines: humanities (**3e, 4m, 13, 18h**), social sciences (**16**), and sciences (**5d**).

 TECHNOTE Useful Sites for Writing across the Curriculum

Try these Web sites for useful advice on writing in all your courses and for more links to other sites. The Dartmouth University site offers advice to nonmajors on writing science: <http://www.dartmouth.edu/~compose/student/sciences/write.html>. The Dartmouth University site also offers advice to nonmajors on writing in the social sciences: <http://www.dartmouth.edu/~compose/student/soc_sciences/write.html>. The *Research QuickStart* site at the University of Minnesota Libraries provides links to many resources in subjects and topics across the curriculum: <http://research.lib.umn.edu>. ▪

Doing Research/
Evaluating Sources

PART 2   Doing Research/Evaluating Sources

6 Beginning a Research Project

You think you might have West Nile virus, and you try to find out what the symptoms are and the best way to treat them. That's research. You want to buy a digital camera, but you don't know anything about the features, brands, and prices. You order catalogs, talk to salespeople, go to stores, try out cameras, ask friends what they recommend, read consumer magazines, and roam the Web. That's research, too. And when your English professor asks you to write a paper on the impact of shopping malls on town centers, research helps you do that. Doing research is finding out as much as possible about an issue, finding good questions to ask, formulating one major research question, and then attempting to find answers to that question. It is a vital part of daily life as well as an essential part of academic and scholarly work.

6a A guide to writing a research paper

1. Know the requirements, and set a realistic schedule. Find out what the demands of the assignment are, such as length, due date, information you should include, number and types of sources, documentation style, and manuscript format. Set a week-by-week or day-by-day schedule for the steps in the process (see **6b**).

2. Assemble the tools you will need. Have on hand a research notebook, disks, printer cartridges, index cards, highlighting pens, folders, paper clips, a stapler, self-stick notes, and a card for the library copier. Set up computer folders for all your research files, such as "Drafts," "Notes from Sources," and "Works Cited."

3. Do preliminary research to establish your topic. Make sure you understand and answer the assigned question or address the assigned topic. If you select your own topic, check with your instructor to make sure it is appropriate. Narrow the topic so that it is manageable for the number of pages you intend to write. You may have to do a great deal of background reading before you settle on a narrow enough topic (**1d**). The more you know about a topic, the easier it will be for you to find good questions to ask. Make sure, too, to choose a topic that will engage and sustain not only readers' interests but your own. Connect your topic to your own experience whenever possible.

Readers recognize a bored writer who is simply going through the motions of writing a paper. If your topic is assigned, make sure you understand the terms used in the assignment (**5a**).

4. Develop your research question. For a full-scale research paper, design a research question that gets at the heart of what you want to discover. The answer you find as you do research is likely to become your thesis. See **6c**.

5. Write a statement of purpose, proposal, or scratch outline. See **6f** for how to do this.

6. Determine types of sources and how to find them. Decide which types of primary and secondary sources will give you the best results (**6d, 7**); then draw up a plan of action. Allow large blocks of time for research. This work cannot be done in just an hour or two.

7. Evaluate sources, make copies, and keep full and accurate records. Select only reliable sources (**8**). Record full bibliographical information for every source you consult. For the essential information to record, see **9d**. Download, print, or make photocopies of your source material whenever possible, so that you can annotate and make notes later.

8. Make precise notes. Paraphrase and summarize as often as possible while taking notes (**9f**). Be sure to use your own words and write down why the information is useful or how you might integrate it into your paper (**10e**). Make sure you copy quotations exactly as they are written (**10f**), with quotation marks or in a colored font. In your notes, record all page numbers of print sources. Copy and save Web addresses.

9. Establish your thesis or hypothesis. Digest your material, and determine your focus. Your paper should not string together what others have said, with no commentary from you. Especially in the humanities, use your research to help yourself form opinions and arrive at conclusions about your topic. Readers want to find *you* and your ideas in your paper (**10c**). Develop a working thesis as soon as you can, and make lists of supporting evidence and specific details from what you know and what you read. In the sciences and social sciences, it is more usual to form a hypothesis, present the evidence, and draw conclusions (**10g**).

10. Write drafts. Write more than one draft. As with almost all writing for college and beyond, revision is an essential step in the writing process. You should not expect to produce a perfect first draft. Make an outline of each draft to check on the logic of your argument (**3a, 10a**).

11. Acknowledge all your sources. Avoid plagiarism by providing information in your text every time you not only quote but also refer to the ideas you find in a source (**9f, 10f**).

12. Prepare a list of works cited. Follow a clear and consistent set of conventions (spacing, indentation, names, order, and punctuation of entries) when you prepare a list of works cited (see **12–13** and **15–19**). Then compare your citations with your list. Make sure that every item on your list appears in your paper and that every work referred to in your paper appears in your list. Use a system of checkmarks in both places as you read a draft.

6b Setting a schedule

Get started as early as you can. As soon as a project is assigned, set a tentative schedule, working backward from the date the paper is due and splitting your time so that you know when you absolutely must move on to the next step. On page 82 and on the *Keys for Writers* Web site is a sample time block schedule that you can use and adapt. You will find that in reality, several tasks overlap and the divisions are not neat. If you finish a block before the deadline, move on and give yourself more time for the later blocks.

6c Establishing a research question

Establish a research question as soon as you can, but be prepared to refine it and change it. For instance, if you find huge amounts of material on your question and realize that you would have to write a book (or two) to cover it, narrow your question.

QUESTIONS NEEDING FOCUS

a. How important are families? (too broad—important to whom and for what?)

b. What problems does the Internet cause? (too broad—what types of problems? what aspects of the Internet?)

RESEARCH SCHEDULE

Starting date:
Date final draft is due:

Block 1: Getting started
Understand the requirements.
Select a topic or narrow a given topic.
Determine the preliminary types of sources to use.
Do preliminary research to discover the important issues.
Organize research findings in computer files.
Write a purpose statement or proposal.

Complete by _____

Block 2: Reading, researching, and evaluating sources
Find and copy print and online sources.
Annotate and evaluate the sources.
Write summaries and paraphrases and make notes.
Set up a working bibliography.

Complete by _____

Block 3: Planning and drafting
Formulate a working thesis.
Make a scratch outline.
Write a first draft.

Complete by _____

Block 4: Evaluating the draft and getting feedback
Put the draft away for a day or two—but continue collecting useful sources.
Outline the draft and evaluate its logic and completeness.
Plan more research as necessary to fill any gaps.
Get feedback from instructor and classmates.

Complete by _____

Block 5: Revising, preparing list of works cited, editing, presenting
Revise the draft.
Prepare a list of works cited.
Design the format of the paper.
Edit.
Proofread the final draft.

Complete by _____
(final deadline for handing in)

QUESTIONS REVISED TO HAVE GREATER FOCUS

a. In what ways does a stable family environment contribute to an individual's future success?

b. Should Internet controls be established to protect individual privacy?

A research question will give you a sense of direction. Frequently, as you read and take notes, you will have in mind a tentative response to your question. Sometimes that hypothesis will be confirmed. Sometimes, though, your research will reveal issues you did not consider and facts that are new to you, so you will refine, adapt, or even totally change your question. If after a few days of research you either cannot find enough material on your topic or discover that all the information is dated, flimsy, or biased, waste no more time. Turn immediately to another topic, and formulate a new research question. (See **8** on evaluating sources.)

6d Exploring primary and secondary sources

PRIMARY SOURCES Primary sources are the firsthand, raw, or original materials that researchers study and analyze. You can consult historical documents, people's journals and letters, autobiographies, memoirs, government statistics and studies, speeches, and news reports. You can examine works of art, literature, and architecture or watch or listen to performances and programs. You can conduct your own observations or scientific experiments and take extensive field notes. You can also conduct interviews and use questionnaires. The use of such primary sources can bring an original note to your research and new information to your readers.

Interviews Interview people who have expert knowledge of your topic. Plan a set of interview questions, but do not stick so closely to your script that you fail to follow up on good leads in your respondent's replies. Ask permission to tape-record the interview; otherwise, you will have to take quick and accurate notes, particularly if you want to quote. Check the functioning of your tape recorder beforehand. Make note of the date, time, and place of the interview.

Questionnaires Designing useful questionnaires is tricky, since much depends on the number and sample of respondents you use, the types of questions you ask, and the methods you employ to analyze the data. Embark on questionnaire research only if you have been introduced to the necessary techniques in a college course or have consulted experts in this area.

SECONDARY SOURCES   Secondary sources are analytical works that comment on and interpret other works, such as primary sources. Examples include reviews, discussions, biographies, critical studies, analyses of literary or artistic works or events, commentaries on current and historical events, class lectures, and electronic discussions.

6e Setting up a working thesis

As you do your preliminary work of examining the task, planning which types of sources to use, and moving toward a topic, you will probably have in mind the point you want to make in your paper. If your research question is "Should Internet controls be established to protect individual privacy?", you probably favor either a "yes" or "no" answer to your question. At this point, you will formulate a working thesis in the form of a statement of opinion, which will help drive the organization of your paper. See also **1e**.

> Internet controls to protect individual privacy should be established.

Or Internet controls to protect individual privacy should not be established.

KEY POINTS

Writing a Working Thesis

1. Make sure the thesis is a statement. A phrase or a question is not a thesis: "Internet controls" is a topic, not a thesis statement. "Are Internet controls needed?" is a question, not a thesis statement.

2. Make sure the thesis statement is not merely a statement of fact: "NUA Internet Surveys estimate that 513.41 million people were online as of August 2001" is a statement that cannot be developed and argued. A statement of fact does not let readers feel the need to read on to see what you have to say.

3. Make sure the thesis statement does more than announce the topic: "This paper will discuss Internet controls." Instead, your thesis statement should give information about or express an

(Continued)

(Continued)

opinion on the topic: "Service providers, online retailers, and parents share the responsibility of establishing Internet controls to protect an individual's privacy."

4. Above all, be prepared to change and refine your thesis as you do your research and discover what your topic entails.

6f Writing a purpose statement, proposal, and outline

A purpose statement is useful to focus your ideas and give yourself something to work with. Write a simple statement of purpose after you have done some preliminary research. This statement may become more developed or later even change completely, but it will serve to guide your first steps in the process. Here is an example:

> The purpose of this documented paper is to persuade general adult readers that historical films—such as Amadeus—should give precedence to a good story over historical accuracy because readers expect entertainment rather than education when they go to the movies.

Your instructor may also ask for a fuller proposal with a working bibliography attached (9d), or an outline (1f). In either case, a brief purpose statement will serve well to get you started.

7 Finding Sources

The Internet provides access to reference works, complete texts, and reliable sources such as databanks of scholarly articles. It can be seen as a virtual library, available at the click of a mouse. It also provides a means of access to what were once seen as traditional print sources and to information that exists only online.

Using the Internet as a means to access information can lead you to many sources once viewed as traditional—reference works, books, scholarly articles, newspaper reports, government documents, and other traditional reference works, as well as to many reputable sources available only online, such as scholarly online journals and professional sites. Check at your library reference desk and on your library's Web page to find out which scholarly reference works and databases are available to you online and which Web sites might be particularly pertinent to your topic.

However, not everything you need is going to be available to you from your home computer. Your search will not be comprehensive if you limit yourself to generally available online sources. Do not neglect the print and online resources provided by your library. Apart from giving you access to the world of books, the library can extend your search choices for other resources, too. Get to know your library, its layout, and what its holdings include: What online databases and indexes does it subscribe to? Does it provide online access to the full text of scholarly articles? The greatest resource of all is the reference librarian, who can direct you to valuable sources, a service not available from America Online (AOL). Never be afraid to ask for a librarian's help.

7a Basic reference works

The reference section of your college or local library is a good place to gather basic information. Reference books cannot be taken home, so they are in the library at all times. Also, more and more reference works are being made generally available online, so the accessibility of material from a library or home computer increases.

Reference works provide basic factual information and lead to other sources. However, use reference works only to get started with basic information; then quickly move beyond them. See **7b–7e** for details on finding sources other than basic reference works.

Encyclopedias   Encyclopedias can help you choose or focus a topic. They provide an overview of the issues involved in a complex topic. Some may also provide extensive bibliographies of other useful sources, so they can also help you develop your research and formulate a research proposal if you are asked to provide one.

Caution: Use encyclopedias only as a way to start investigating your subject, but do not rely on them for most of your project.

Here are some basic tools for initial explorations. Some, such as the first one listed, are available to everyone online. Others may be available free online only through your local library, your college library system, or your Internet service provider.

General   *Columbia Encyclopedia*
                  Encyclopaedia Britannica

Art   *Encyclopedia of World Art*

Biology	*Encyclopedia of the Biological Sciences*
Business	*International Encyclopedia of Business and Management*
Chemistry	*Encyclopaedia of Chemistry*
Communications	*International Encyclopedia of Communications*
Computer science	*Encyclopedia of Computer Science* *McGraw-Hill Circuit Encyclopedia*
Economics	*Encyclopedia of American Economic History*
Education	*Encyclopedia of Educational Research*
Engineering	*McGraw-Hill Encyclopedia of Engineering*
English literature	*Oxford Companion to English Literature*
Environmental science	*Encyclopedia of the Environment*
Ethnic studies	*Gale Encyclopedia of Multicultural America*
Film	*International Encyclopedia of Film*
Geography	*Encyclopedia of World Geography*
Geology	*Encyclopedia of Earth System Science*
History	*Encyclopedia of American History*
Linguistics	*Cambridge Encyclopedia of Language*
Mathematics	*CRC Concise Encyclopedia of Mathematics*
Music	*New Grove Dictionary of Music and Musicians*
Nursing	*Encyclopedia of Nursing Research*
Philosophy	*Encyclopedia of Philosophy*
Physics	*Encyclopedia of Physics*
Political science	*International Handbook of Political Science*
Psychology	*Encyclopedia of Psychology*
Religion	*Encyclopedia of Religion*
Sciences	*McGraw-Hill Encyclopedia of Science and Technology*
Sociology	*Encyclopedia of Sociology*
Women's studies	*Women's Studies Encyclopedia*

For sources beyond encyclopedias, see **7g**.

Bibliographies (guides to the literature)   You can find lists of books and articles on a subject in bibliographies such as *Books in Print, Foreign Affairs Bibliography, Political Science Bibliographies, MLA*

International Bibliography of Books and Articles on the Modern Languages and Literature, Bibliographies in American History, Science and Engineering Literature, and specialized bibliographies on topics of interest, such as *Homelessness: An Annotated Bibliography.*

Biographies Read accounts of people's lives in biographical works such as *Who's Who, Dictionary of American Biography, Biography Index: A Cumulative Index to Biographic Material in Books and Magazines, Contemporary Authors, Dictionary of Literary Biography, African American Biographies, Chicano Scholars and Writers, Lives of the Painters,* and *American Men and Women of Science.*

Critical works Read what scholars have to say about works of art and literature in *Contemporary Literary Criticism* and in *Oxford Companion* volumes (such as *Oxford Companion to Art* and *Oxford Companion to African American Literature*).

Statistics and government documents Among many useful sources are *Statistical Abstract of the United States, Current Index to Statistics, Handbook of Labor Statistics, Occupational Outlook Handbook,* U.S. Census Bureau publications, *Digest of Educational Statistics, UN Demographic Yearbook,* and *Population Index.*

Almanacs, atlases, and gazetteers For population statistics and boundary changes, see *The World Almanac, Countries of the World,* or *Information Please.* For locations, descriptions, pronunciation of place names, climate, demography, languages, natural resources, and industry, consult *Columbia-Lippincott Gazetteer of the World* and the CIA *World Factbook,* both available in print and online.

Dictionaries For etymologies, definitions, and spelling, consult *American Heritage Dictionary of the English Language,* 4th edition (one volume), *Oxford English Dictionary* (multiple volumes—useful for detailed etymologies and usage discussions and examples), *Facts on File* specialized dictionaries, and other specialized dictionaries such as *Dictionary of Literary Terms* and *Dictionary of the Social Sciences.*

Collections of articles of topical interest and news summaries *CQ (Congressional Quarterly)* weekly reports, *Facts on File* publications, and *CQ Almanac* are available in print and online by subscription. *Newsbank* provides periodical articles on microfiche, classified under topics such as "Law" and "Education," and *SIRS (Social Issues Resources Series)* appears in print and online.

7b Indexes and databases

Indexes Indexes of articles appearing in periodicals will start you off in your search for an article on a specific topic. Print indexes, such as *Readers' Guide to Periodical Literature,* will list works published before 1980. More recent publications are listed in online indexes, such as *Applied Science and Technology Index, Engineering Index,* and *Art Index.* An index will provide a complete citation: author, title, periodical, volume, date, and page numbers, often with an abstract. That information will narrow your search. Then you have to locate the periodical in a library and find the actual article.

Online databases Online databases provide a variety of types of data based on a variety of time periods. *PsycINFO,* for example, lists article abstracts from 1887 to the present; other databases are far less comprehensive in their time span. An online library or museum catalog is a database, providing information about the institution's collection. Some databases (such as *Wilson Readers' Guide Abstracts, Wilson Business Abstracts, General Science Abstracts, ERIC, Humanities Abstracts, Sociological Abstracts*) function as an online index, providing only basic bibliographic information about where and when a source was published, along with an abstract. Others, known as full-text databases (such as *EBSCO Academic Search Premier, Dialog, InfoTrac,* and *Lexis-Nexis*), provide the publication information along with the full text of the article, available for downloading, printing, or e-mailing to yourself right from your computer. *Netlibrary* provides the full text of books. You can also access databases devoted to statistics (such as Bureau of Labor Statistics Data at <http://www.bls.gov/data/home.htm> or Census Bureau figures at <http://www.census.gov/>) or to images, such as works of art, at <http://www.getty.edu/>.

For basic information on authors and literary works, turn to *InfoTrac Literature Resource Center.* Try *J-Stor* for pre-1980 sources; the database is not as vast as others but it does provide access to older materials. For ethnic magazines and newspapers, *Ethnic Newswatch* is the database to turn to. Frequently, access to databases in university library Web sites is limited to enrolled students who have been assigned a password. Check with your college library to see which databases are available online in the library only and which are available on the Web.

7c Online searching

Keyword searches Use keywords to search for any material stored electronically. Keyword searching is especially effective for finding material in journal and newspaper articles in databases such as *EBSCO, InfoTrac, LexisNexis,* and specialized subject-area databases because a computer can search not only titles but also abstracts (when available) or full articles.

Keywords are vital for your Web searches. Spend time thinking of the keywords that best describe what you are looking for. If a search yields thousands of hits, try requiring or prohibiting terms and making terms into phrases (see the Key Points box on pages **92–93**). If a search yields few hits, try different keywords or combinations, or try another search engine. In addition, try out variant spellings for names of people and places: *Chaikovsky, Tchaikovsky, Tschaikovsky.*

Use the results to help tailor and refine your search. If your search produces only one useful source, look at the terms used in that one source and its subject headings and search again, using those terms maybe with a different search engine. Above all, be flexible. Each search engine indexes only a portion of what is available on the Web. Once you find a promising reference to a source that is not available online in full text, check whether your library owns the book or journal. If your search yields a source available only on microfilm or microfiche, you might need a librarian's help to learn how to use the reading machines and how to make copies.

URLs If you already know the Web address (the uniform resource locator or URL) of a useful site, type it exactly, paying attention to spaces (or, more often, lack of spaces), dots, symbols, and capital or lowercase letters. Just one small slip can prevent access. Whenever you can, copy and paste a URL from a Web source so that you do not make mistakes in typing. If you ever get a message saying "site not found," check your use of capitals and lowercase letters (and avoid inserting spaces as you type an address), and try again. You may find that the site is no longer available. See **22a** for more on e-mail and Web addresses.

Search engines If you do not know the exact Web site you want, you need to use search tools. Some search the whole Web for you; some search selected sites; some search only the first few pages of a document; still others search only a specific site, such as a university library system or a noncommercial organization; or they search other search engines (these are called *meta search engines*). Make sure you try all types to find information on your topic.

Your Web browser, probably Netscape, Internet Explorer, or AOL, will give you access to search engines and other resources that do for you most of the work of rapidly searching Web sites. Whichever browser you use, spending time searching (and playing) is the best way to become familiar with reliable search tools, the types of searches they do best, and the system they use for searching. Google and AltaVista are popular search tools. Try them both and others listed here.

- AltaVista <http://www.altavista.com> is a comprehensive search tool using keywords. It is a good tool for serious academic research. Its database is huge, more than 500 million Web pages and Usenet groups, so you need to be precise with your search terms. It can also search for images and for audio and video files. AltaVista allows you to check the reliability of a site by doing a reverse search to find out who else is linking to it. It can also provide translations.

- Argus Clearinghouse <http://www.clearinghouse.net> provides links to virtual (that is, online) libraries, subject guides, and search engines.

- Google <http://www.google.com> (the favorite of many academics) searches more than three billion Web pages and other search engines. It organizes and ranks results by the numbers of links to a site. A tilde (~) typed in front of a search term will search for synonyms.

- iLOR <http://www.ilor.com> has results similar to Google's but offers different options and a listing of findings that Google does not offer.

- INFOMINE <http://infomine.ucr.edu/> provides scholarly resources in social sciences, humanities, and general reference, selected and annotated.

- Internet Public Library <http://www.ipl.org> is run by librarians. It includes a guide to home pages and a Reference Center, which allows you to e-mail a question about a research project to librarians for evaluation and possible response.

- MetaCrawler <http://www.metacrawler.com> provides a subject directory, and it searches many of the best search engines: AltaVista, Excite, Lycos, Infoseek, Google, WebCrawler, and others.

- WWW Virtual Library <http://vlib.org> is useful for finding sources in a large number of academic disciplines.

- Yahoo! <http://www.yahoo.com> is a subject index and directory of the Web, organized hierarchically. You can keep narrowing down your subjects, or you can use specific key-words. Such a tool is particularly useful when you are trying to decide what to write about.

KEY POINTS

Doing a Keyword Search

1. *Know the search engine's system.* Use the Search Tips or Help link to find out how to conduct a search. Search engines vary. Some search for any or all of the words you type in, some need you to indicate whether the words make up a phrase, and some allow you to exclude words or search for alternatives.

2. *Use Boolean terms to narrow or expand a search.* Some advanced searches operate on the Boolean principle, which means that you use the "operators" *AND*, *OR*, and *NOT* in combination with keywords to define what you want the search to include and exclude. Imagine that you want to find out if and how music can affect intelligence. Using only the term *music* would produce vast numbers of hits. Using *AND* narrows the search. The term *music AND intelligence* would find sources in the database that include both the word *music* and the word *intelligence* (the overlap in the circles below).

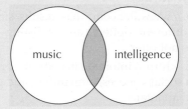

Parentheses can aid in searches, too. The search term *music AND (intelligence OR learning)* would expand the previous search. You would find sources in the database that include both the word *music* and either the word *intelligence* or the word *learning.*

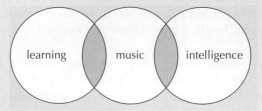

(Continued)

(Continued)

In Boolean searches, *AND* and *NOT* narrow the search: *chicken AND salmonella; dolphins NOT Miami*. The operator *OR* expands the search: *angiogram OR angioplasty*. Not all databases and search engines use this system. In Google, for instance, you simply add words to narrow or refine a search. And MetaCrawler asks simply if you want to include *any* or *all* of the search terms, or use *all* the terms as a phrase. Always check the instructions with each search engine or database—for its basic search and the advanced search.

3. *Use a wildcard character to truncate a term and expand the search.* A wildcard allows you to use at the end of a phrase a character that indicates that more letters can be attached. Common wildcard characters are * and ?. The truncated search term *addict** will produce references to *addict, addicts, addiction, addictive*, and so on. (Google does not provide this feature.)

4. *Narrow a search by grouping words into phrases.* Often, you can use double quotation marks—"Michael Jackson"—or parentheses—(Michael Jackson)—to surround a search term and group the words into a phrase. *Michael Jackson* entered as a term without such quotation marks or parentheses would produce references to other Michaels—Johnson and Jordan, for instance—and to other Jacksons—Stonewall Jackson, Jackson Pollock, and so on.

5. *Learn how to require or prohibit a term to narrow a search.* Many search engines allow you to use a symbol such as + (plus) before a term that must be included in the document indexed; a – (minus) symbol prohibits a term: + "Civil War" – Gettysburg. Some search engines use these symbols in place of the *AND* and *NOT* of Boolean searching.

6. *Take advantage of the "proximity" search feature if available.* Some search engines—AltaVista is one—let you indicate when you want your search terms to occur close to each other in the text. Check in the Help or Tips file to determine whether the engine you are using has this feature. Proximity is indicated in various ways in various search engines. *NEAR* or *ADJ* (adjacent) are common: "Virginia Woolf" *NEAR* "Bloomsbury group" would search for the two phrases near each other in the text.

7. *Be flexible.* If the word *hog* does not produce good hits, try *swine, pig*, and *pork*.

7d   Print sources: Books and periodical articles

Types of search   For library catalogs and periodical databases, decide whether to search under *T* (title), *A* (author), *S* (subject), or *K* (keyword). Exact wording and exact spelling are essential for all these searches.

Use keyword searching (**7c**) when searching for material that is electronically stored, whether in a library catalog, on a CD-ROM, in a database, or on a Web page. For subject searching, you need to know the specific subject headings the catalogers used to identify and classify material. Consult a reference source such as *Library of Congress Subject Headings,* or ask a librarian for help. For example, you won't find *cultural identity* or *social identity* in *Library of Congress Subject Headings,* but you can look up *culture* and find a list of thirty-two associated headings, such as "language and culture" and "personality and culture." In addition, these subject headings show related terms, which can suggest ways to narrow or broaden a topic and can help you in other subject searches, particularly in electronic keyword searches. *Bilingualism,* for example, takes you to topics such as "air traffic control," "code-switching," and "language attrition." An entry in a library catalog will appear with the subject descriptors, so if you find one good source, use its subject classifications to search further. A search in a library online catalog using the keywords *bilingual, education,* and *politics* finds thirty-three records. One of these (on page 95) provides some subject terms to help with further searching: *education and state, educational change,* and *educational evaluation.* Similarly, a keyword search of an online database of full-text articles will produce articles with subject descriptors attached, as in the screenshot on page 100.

If your college library does not own a book or periodical you want, ask a librarian about interlibrary loan. This option is helpful, of course, only if you begin your search early.

Books

CALL NUMBER   Most college libraries use the Library of Congress classification system, which arranges books according to subject area and often the initial of the author's last name and the date of publication. The call number tells you where a book is located in the library stacks (the area where books are shelved). Write this number down immediately if a book looks promising, along with the book's title and author(s) and publication information (**9d**). If a library has open stacks, you will be able to browse through books on a similar topic on the same shelf or on one nearby.

INFORMATION IN THE CATALOG   The screens of electronic catalogs vary from one system to another, but most screens contain the name of the system you are using; the details of your search request and of the search, such as the number of records found; and detailed bibliographical information.

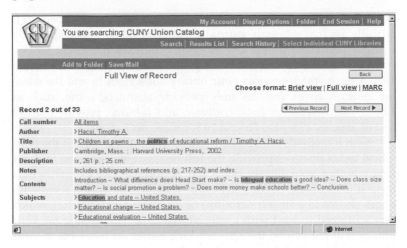

The screen shown here with its links to the call number (LC89.H215202) and the locations of the holdings (colleges where the book is housed) provides all the essential information you will need to document the source at the end of your paper: author, title, place of publication, publisher, and date of publication. In addition, it lets you know the number of pages in the book and shows that the book contains a bibliography and an index—useful research tools. The subject search terms shown can help structure further searches.

Once you find a book that seems to be related to your topic, you do not have to read the whole book to use it for your paper. Learn what you can from the catalog entry; then skim the table of contents, chapter headings, and bibliography. Your best time-saver here is the index. Turn to it immediately, and look up some key words for your topic. Read the section of the book in which references to your topic appear; take notes; annotate a photocopy of the relevant pages (**9e**). A book's bibliography and references are useful, too. The author has done research, and this can help you in your search. It is a good idea to make a copy of the title page and the page on which the copyright notice appears. If you find nothing remotely connected to your research question, do not cite the book as a resource, even though you looked at it.

BOOKS IN PRINT AND ALTERNATIVES If you want to find a book or to check on bibliographical details, use *Books in Print* (available in print and online). If your library does not subscribe to the online version, you can use the Amazon.com site at <http://www.amazon.com> or any other large commercial online bookseller to look up the details of a book—free.

Periodical articles Find articles in periodicals (works issued periodically, such as scholarly journals, magazines, and newspapers) by using a periodical index. Use electronic indexes for recent works, print indexes for earlier works—especially for works written before 1980. Check which services your library subscribes to and the dates the indexes cover. Indexes may provide abstracts; some, such as *EBSCO, LexisNexis Academic Universe,* and *InfoTrac,* provide the full text of articles. (See also **7b** and **7e** for more on indexes.)

Search methods are similar to those in book searches. If the periodical index does not provide the full text, you will need to find out first whether your library owns the periodical and then in which form it is available: in files, in bound volumes, or in film form with pages shown in a strip (microfilm) or on a sheet (microfiche), which you will need to read with a special machine. The catalog for your library will tell you on the screen which issues are available in your library and in which format and location.

7e Online sources

The Internet can take you to many sources formerly accessible only if you went to a library and dug through shelves and bound volumes of periodicals. Newspaper and magazine articles from ten or more years ago, scholarly journal articles, news commentary, statistical information from government agencies—all are available. However, the democratic nature of the Internet means that many Web pages have no editorial control, so although you might find considerable material, much of it could be mindless and inaccurate (**8d**). On the plus side, you will find vast resources, current material, and frequent updates—all without leaving your computer. As you plan your research, consider which of the following Internet resources might be the most appropriate for your topic. A reference librarian can help you decide.

Online indexes and databases Online databases of journal articles are a wonderful resource for researchers. Start with these. They are comprehensive and easy to use. They also provide sources that have been previously published and referred to by experts. See **7b** for details.

Online library catalogs and home pages of libraries and universities The Web gives you access to the online resources of many libraries (actual and virtual) and universities, which are good browsing sites. Some useful sites follow:

- *Library of Congress* at <http://lcweb.loc.gov> provides lists of links (with descriptions) of Internet search tools, as well as access to subject guides, government resources, online library catalogs, and Internet tutorials.
- *LibWeb* at <http://sunsite.berkeley.edu/Libweb> offers information on library holdings in over 100 countries.
- *New York Public Library* at <http://www.nypl.org/index.html> allows searching of its vast online catalog.
- *Smithsonian Institution Libraries* at <http://www.sil.si.edu> provides a catalog and links to databases and e-journals.

Online magazines and journals   Some of the articles you can find online are conventional print sources with Web access (often only for the current issue unless you or your library subscribes). Others, such as the following, are journals published only online:

- *Slate* <http://slate.msn.com>
- *Salon* <http://www.salon.com>
- *Early Modern Literary Studies* <http://www.shu.ac.uk/emls/emlshome.html>
- *Postmodern Culture* <http://jefferson.village.virginia.edu/pmc>
- *Sociological Research Online* <http://www.socresonline.org.uk>

Some online journals are available free or allow you to view only the current issue at no cost. Many, however, require a subscription through your library network or a personal subscription.

Online texts   Literary texts that are out of copyright and in the public domain are increasingly available online for downloading. The following are useful sites to consult, although the versions of texts you see may not always be authoritative:

- *Project Bartleby* <http://www.bartleby.com>
- *Project Gutenberg* <http://www.promo.net/pg/index.html>
- *University of Virginia's Electronic Text Center* <http://etext.lib.virginia.edu>

EBooks   Many books are becoming available as eBooks, either to be read online at a computer or downloaded and read in an eBook reader. NetLibrary.com is one of the companies offering eBooks. If your library subscribes to its database, make sure you check its offerings when you are looking for a book.

Online news sites   The Web sites of major newspapers, magazines, and television networks provide up-to-date news information; some offer archived information but often only to subscribers. See, for example, *The New York Times on the Web* <http://www.nytimes.com> and CNN Interactive <http://www.cnn.com>.

Nonprofit research sites   Many nonprofit sites offer valuable and objective information. For example, see *Public Agenda Online* <http://www.publicagenda.org>, *American Film Institute* <http://www.afi.com>, and *San Francisco Bay Bird Observatory* <http://www.sfbbo.org>.

Web pages and hypertext links   Many universities and research institutes provide information through their own Web home pages, with hypertext links that take you with one click to many other sources. Try, for example, <http://www.refdesk.com> for more than twenty thousand links to reference works and informational sites. Individual Web pages can provide useful information, too, but need careful evaluation, since anyone can publish anything on the Web (**8d**).

E-mail discussion lists   With e-mail, you have access to many discussion groups. Messages go out to a list of people interested in specific topics. Without charge, you can join a list devoted to a topic of interest (see **22b** for how to join and participate in a list). However, most of the lists are not refereed or monitored, so you have to evaluate carefully any information you find. The *HyperNews* site at <http://www.hypernews .org> sponsors independent Web discussions on specific themes (threads) and allows you to read and contribute to the discussions.

Other interactive sources   For academic research, Usenet newsgroups and chat rooms provide little that is substantive. Evaluating the reliability of a contributor's comments can be difficult. See **22c** for more on these interactive sources.

7f   A student's search

To do research for a documented paper in MLA style assigned in her required first-semester writing course, Lindsay Camp used print and online sources. She chose as her broad subject the physical exams for police and fire department recruits. Her complete paper is in **13**.

Step 1: Topic and schedule   Camp was interested in this topic because she was planning to become a police officer, was studying for the New York Police Department exams, and felt strongly that women should be required to attain the same physical standards as men. She had five weeks to do the research and produce a proposal and two drafts, before including her final draft in her portfolio; she made a schedule (**6b**) to plan her time.

Step 2: Research question and plan for resources   She thought it might not be easy to find evidence to support the claim that women needed to be held to equal standards, but in a preliminary search in an online database, she found several sources with references to further sources. She therefore assessed that she would be able to find supporting evidence, made a plan of the types of secondary sources she would try to find, and decided to include an interview to introduce a primary source and a real-life situation into her paper. She also formulated her research question: "Should women be held to the same physical standards as men for recruitment into police and fire departments?"

Step 3: Library online catalog   Camp's instructor (the author of this book) had asked for sources to include books and scholarly articles. Camp owned a police preparation study guide by Fred M. Rafilson but wanted some scholarly sources, so she searched the library catalog of her university system. She used the keywords *police* and *women* and got 203 hits, most of which were available not at her college but at another college in the university system. With catalog printouts and call numbers (HV 8023) in hand, she went across town to that library and browsed the stacks. Several of the recently published books she had hoped to find were not available on the shelves, but to her relief she found three relevant sources (Heidensohn, Horne, and Wexler), all with extensive bibliographies.

Step 4: Working thesis   Camp formulated a working thesis, expanding the idea of equality to include the issue of safety: "For reasons of equality and safety, women should take and pass the same physical tests as men." She eventually refined the wording of the thesis but retained the claim.

Step 5: Online subscription databases   Camp then ran a search on EBSCOhost Academic Search Premier, a database her library subscribed to. Her first search term, *fire department,* produced 1,603 hits, so she knew she had to refine and limit her search. She then tried the search terms *fire department, police department,* and *women,* which produced only one source. When Camp accessed the article and the link to the citation details, she noted that although the URL for the article on the screen was impossibly long, the citation page provided a persistent link, which she knew she should use. She marked this as a relevant article and e-mailed it to herself. The citation link on the article site included bibliographical details necessary for a works-cited list and subject terms useful for further searching (see the screenshot on p. 100).

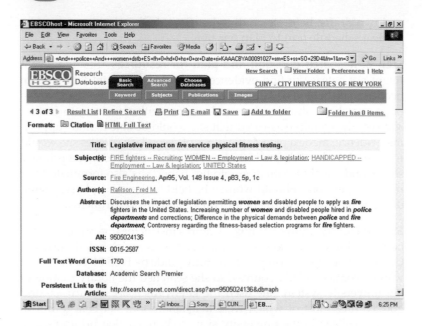

Still in *EBSCO,* Camp then used *fire fighters* and *recruiting* as subject search terms, not keywords, and found more articles. However, one by Baker that she thought would be particularly relevant was not available in *EBSCO* in full text (see screenshot below).

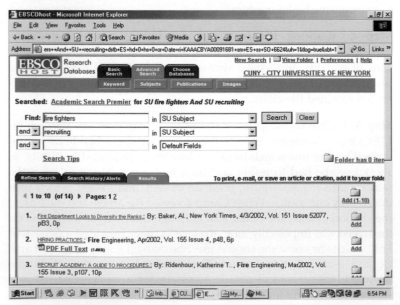

Camp then went to the *LexisNexis* database, a good place to find full-text newspaper articles, and used the Guided News Search feature to search the *New York Times* with the search terms *Baker* as author and *fire department* as a general search term (information taken from the *EBSCO* listing). There she found Baker's article in full text. The screenshot below shows the first screen of the article.

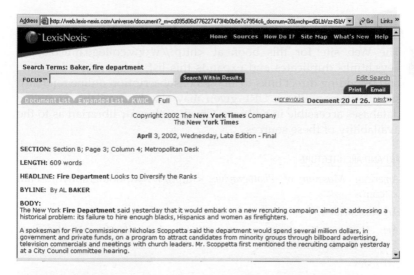

Step 6: A Web search Camp's next step was a Web search on Google, with the very first hit taking her to a scholarly article with endnotes, which she used as a source for her paper.

Throughout her searches, Camp made print copies or saved all online materials, kept a working bibliography (**9d**), and took careful notes, distinguishing her own ideas and words from those of her sources by using different fonts, quotation marks, and names of authors of sources. She found enough evidence to support her thesis but also came across sources that presented opposing views, which she tried to address and refute in her paper. She reworded her thesis, made a scratch outline, and drafted and revised her paper several times. Her final draft is in section **13**.

7g Sources in 27 subject areas

This selective list of frequently used reference works in print, print and electronic indexes, and Web sites was compiled with the help of twenty-one college librarians from eighteen colleges in thirteen states. For encyclopedias in these disciplines, see **7a**.

 TechNote Links from the Web Site for *Keys for Writers*

 The Web site for this book at <http://www.college.hmco.com/ keys.html> duplicates and expands this list, keeping it up-to-date and providing direct links to all the nonsubscription online reference sites. Sources with no URL given may also be available in online databases accessible in a library. Check with your librarian as to the availability of these sources. ■

ART AND ARCHITECTURE

American Museum of Photography: <http://www.photographymuseum .com>

Art Abstracts

Art History Resources on the Web: <http://witcombe.sbc.edu/ ARTHLinks.html>

Art Index

Arts and Humanities Citation Index

Avery Index to Architectural Periodicals

Bibliography of the History of Art

Contemporary Artists

Dictionary of Art (known as *Grove's*)

Getty Institute: <http://www.getty.edu>

Lives of the Painters

Metropolitan Museum of Art Time Line: <http://www.metmuseum .org/toah/splash.htm>

Mother of All Art and Art History Links: <http://www.art-design .umich.edu/mother/>

Oxford Companion to Art

World Wide Arts Resources: <http://wwar.com>

BIOLOGY

Bio Network: <http://www.pasteur.fr/recherche/BNB/bnb-en.html>

Biological Abstracts: BIOSIS (print and online)

Biological and Agricultural Index (print and online)

Biology Browser: <http://www.biologybrowser.org>

BioView.com: <http://www.biolinks.com>

Cell and Molecular Biology Online: <http://cellbio.com>

Gray's Anatomy

Henderson's Dictionary of Biological Terms

Tufts University Biology Research Guide: <http://ase.tufts.edu/biology/bio14v2>

WWW Virtual Library: Biosciences: <http://mcb.harvard.edu/Biolinks.html>

BUSINESS

ABI Inform Index (online)

Bureau of Labor Statistics: <http://www.bls.gov>

Business Abstracts (online, full text)

Business and Industry (database with full texts of articles): <http://library.dialog.com/bluesheets/html/bl0009.html>

Business Dateline (database of full-text articles from business journals)

Business Periodicals Index (print and online)

Gale Business and Company Resource Center: <http://www.galegroup.com>

Hoover's Handbook of World Business

Monthly Labor Review

MSU-Ciber International Business Resources on the WWW (Michigan State University): <http://ciber.bus.msu.edu>

Prentice Hall Encyclopedic Dictionary of Business Terms

Ward's Business Directory of U.S. Private and Public Companies

CHEMISTRY

American Chemical Society Website: <http://www.chemistry.org>

Beilstein Handbook of Organic Chemistry

Chemical Abstracts (online from the American Chemical Society)

Chemicool Periodic Table: <http://www-tech.mit.edu/Chemicool/index.html>

ChemInfo (Chemical Information Sources): <http://www.indiana.edu/~cheminfo>

Chemistry Virtual Library Resources: Links for Chemists: <http://www.liv.ac.uk/Chemistry/Links/links.html>

CRC Handbook of Chemistry and Physics

Kirk-Othmer Encyclopedia of Chemical Technology

NIST (National Institute of Standards and Technology) *Webbook* (physical properties for thousands of substances): <http://webbook.nist.gov>

Ullman's Encyclopedia of Industrial Chemistry

CLASSICS

Chronology of the Ancient World

Classical Scholarship: An Annotated Bibliography

Concise Oxford Companion to Classical Literature

DCB: Database of Classical Bibliography

Internet Classics Archive: <http://classics.mit.edu>

Library of Congress Websites for Classical and Medieval History: <http://www.loc.gov/rr/main/alcove9/classics.html>

Perseus Digital Library: <http://www.perseus.tufts.edu>

COMMUNICATIONS AND MEDIA

ABC-CLIO Companion to the Media in America

American Communication Association: <http://www.uark.edu/~aca>

Argus Clearinghouse: Communications and Media Studies: <http://www.clearinghouse.net>

ComAbstracts (print and online)

ComIndex (print and CD-ROM index of articles)

Encyclopedia of Rhetoric and Composition

International Women's Media Foundation: <http://www.iwmf.org>

Kidon Media-Link: <http://www.kidon.com/media-link/index.shtml>

Webster's New World Dictionary of Media and Communications

WWW Virtual Library: Communications and Media: <http://vlib.org/Communication.html>

COMPUTER SCIENCE

ACM Guide to Computing Literature (print and online)

Association for Computing Machinery: <http://www.acm.org>

Computer Abstracts

History of the Internet: A Chronology, 1843 to the Present (ed. Christos Moschovitis)

Information Resources for Computer Science: <http://www.library.ucsb.edu/subj/computer.html>

Microcomputer Abstracts (online by subscription)

MIT Laboratory for Computer Science: <http://www.lcs.mit.edu>

Virtual Computer Library: <http://www.utexas.edu/computer/vcl>

WWW Virtual Library: Computing: <http://vlib.org/Computing.html>

ECONOMICS

Dictionary of Economics

Econlit (online by subscription)

Gale Encyclopedia of U.S. Economic History (ed. Thomas Carson)

PAIS (Public Affairs Information Service) database (print and online)

Prentice Hall Encyclopedic Dictionary of Business Terms

Social Sciences Citation Index: <http://www.hwwilson.com>

WWW Virtual Library: Economics: <http://hkkk.fi/EconVLib.html>

EDUCATION

Ask ERIC (Educational Resources Information Center; supplies indexes such as *Current Index to Journals in Education* and *Resources in Education*): <http://www.askeric.org/>

Dictionary of Education

Education Index: <http://www.educationindex.com>

Education Virtual Library: <http://www.csu.edu.au/education/library.html>

Higher Education Research Institute, UCLA: <http://www.gseis.ucla.edu/heri/heri.html>

Michigan Electronic Library: Education: <http://mel.lib.mi.us/education/education-index.html>

National Center for Education Statistics: <http://nces.ed.gov>

U.S. Department of Education: Other Educational Resources: <http://www.ed.gov/about/contacts/gen/othersites/index.html>

ENGINEERING

Applied Science and Technology Index (print and online)

Compendex/Engineering Index (online by subscription)

Engineering Library at Cornell University: <http://www.englib.cornell.edu>

WWW Virtual Library: Engineering: <http://vlib.org/Engineering.html>

ENVIRONMENTAL STUDIES

Environmental Science: Working with the Earth

Facts on File Dictionary of Environmental Science

National Library for the Environment: <http://www.cnie.org/nle>

Scripps Institution of Oceanography: <http://www.sio.ucsd.edu>

Sourcebook on the Environment: A Guide to the Literature

Toxic Air Pollution Handbook

United Nations Environment Programme: <http://www.unep.org>

U.S. Environmental Protection Agency: <http://www.epa.gov/>

WWW Virtual Library: Earth Science: <http://vlib.org/EarthScience .html>

ETHNIC STUDIES

Chicano Scholars and Writers

Encyclopedia of Asian History

Harvard Encyclopedia of American Ethnic Groups

Historical and Cultural Atlas of African Americans

Native Web: <http://www.nativeweb.org>

Oxford Companion to African American Literature

WWW Virtual Library: Migration and Ethnic Relations: <http://www .ercomer.org/wwwvl>

GEOGRAPHY

Companion Encyclopedia of Geography

Geographical Abstracts (online)

Geography Web Ring: <http://www.zephryus.demon.co.uk/education/ webring>

U.S. Census Bureau: U.S. Gazetteer: <http://www.census.gov/cgi-bin/ gazetteer>

GEOLOGY

AGI (American Geological Institute): <http://www.agiweb.org>

GeoRef (electronic index produced by American Geological Institute): <http://www.agiweb.org/georef>

Glossary of Geology and Earth Sciences

Macmillan Encyclopedia of Earth Sciences

New Penguin Dictionary of Geology

USGS (United States Geological Survey): <http://www.usgs.gov>

USGS Library: <http://www.usgs.gov/library>

HISTORY

Dictionary of Medieval History (Scribner)

Don Mabry's Historical Text Archive: <http://historicaltextarchive.com/>

Great Events from History series

Historical Abstracts and America: History and Life from ABC-CLIO (print and online): <http://www.abc-clio.com>

WWW Virtual Library: History Central Catalogue: <http://www.ukans .edu/history/VL>

LINGUISTICS

Cambridge Encyclopedia of the English Language (ed. David Crystal)
Center for Applied Linguistics: <http://www.cal.org>
Linguistics: A Guide to the Reference Literature (ed. Anna L. DeMiller)
Oxford Companion to the English Language (ed. Tom McArthur)
WWW Virtual Library: Applied Linguistics: <http://alt.venus.co.uk/VL/AppLingBBK/welcome.html>

LITERATURE

Complete Works of Shakespeare: <http://the-tech.mit.edu/Shakespeare>
Dictionary of Literary Biography
MLA International Bibliography of Books and Articles on the Modern Languages and Literature (online)
New Cambridge Bibliography of English Literature
Oxford Companion to Contemporary Authors
Project Bartleby (complete texts of books no longer in copyright): <http://www.bartleby.com>
Victorian Women Writers Project: <http://www.indiana.edu/~letrs/vwwp>
Voice of the Shuttle: <http://vos.ucsb.edu>

MATHEMATICS AND STATISTICS

American Mathematical Society MathSciNet (index and abstracts of articles): <http://www.ams.org/mathscinet>
HarperCollins Dictionary of Mathematics
Mathematical Reviews (print and online)
Statistical Abstract of the United States (Government Printing Office: print and online): <http://www.census.gov/statab/www>
University of Tennessee Math Archives: <http://archives.math.utk.edu>
WWW Virtual Library: Statistics: <http://www.stat.ufl.edu/vlib/statistics.html>

MUSIC

Baker's Biographical Dictionary of Musicians
Classical USA: <http://classicalusa.com>
Indiana University Worldwide Internet Music Resources: <http://www.music.indiana.edu/music_resources>
International Index to Music Periodicals
New Grove Dictionary of Music and Musicians
New Harvard Dictionary of Music
New Oxford History of Music

RILM Abstracts of Musical Literature (online)

Thematic Catalogues in Music: An Annotated Bibliography Including Printed, Manuscript, and In-Preparation Catalogues

The Music Index

WWW Virtual Library: Classical Music: <http://www.gprep.org/classical/>

WWW Virtual Library: Music: <http://www.vl-music.com>

NURSING

Allnurses.com: <http://allnurses.com>

American Nurses Association Nursing World: <http://www.nursingworld.org>

Cambridge World History of Human Disease

Culture and Nursing Care

Dorland's Illustrated Medical Dictionary

Gray's Anatomy

Health Web: <http://healthweb.org/>

National Institute of Nursing Research: <http://www.nih.gov/ninr>

Nursing Net: <http://www.nursingnet.org>

PHILOSOPHY

American Philosophical Association: <http://www.apa.udel.edu/apa/index.html>

Cambridge Dictionary of Philosophy

Guide to Philosophy on the Internet: <http://www.earlham.edu/~peters/philinks.htm>

Handbook of Western Philosophy

Internet Encyclopedia of Philosophy: <http://www.utm.edu/research/iep>

Oxford Companion to Philosophy

Philosopher's Index

Philosophy in Cyberspace: <http://www-personal.monash.edu.au/~dey/phil>

Routledge History of Philosophy

PHYSICS

American Institute of Physics: <http://www.aip.org>

American Physical Society: <http://www.aps.org>

Physics Abstracts (online)

Physics Today: <http://www.physicstoday.org>

WWW Virtual Library: Physics: <http://vlib.org/Physics.html>

POLITICAL SCIENCE

American Statistics Index

Congressional Quarterly Weekly Reports

International Political Science Abstracts

PAIS (Public Affairs Information Service) database (online and CD-ROM)

Political Handbook of the World (Annual)

Political Science Links: <http://www.loyola.edu/dept/politics/polilink.html>

Political Science Resources on the Web: <http://www.lib.umich.edu/govdocs/polisci.html>

The White House: <http://www.whitehouse.gov>

THOMAS: Legislative Information on the Internet: <http://thomas.loc.gov>

United Nations: <http://www.un.org>

U.S. Census Bureau: The Official Statistics: <http://www.census.gov>

PSYCHOLOGY

American Psychological Association: <http://www.apa.org>

CyberPsychLink: <http://cctr.umkc.edu/user/dmartin/psych2.html>

Handbook of Practical Psychology

Psychological Abstracts

PsycINFO (database of online abstracts)

The Social Psychology Network, Wesleyan University: <http://www.socialpsychology.org>

WWW Virtual Library: Psychology: <http://www.clas.ufl.edu/users/gthursby/psi/>

RELIGION

Academic Info: Religious Studies: <http://www.academicinfo.net/Religion.html>

Anchor Bible Dictionary

ATLA Religion Database

Encyclopedia of the American Religious Experience

Encyclopedia of World Religions

New Interpreter's Bible

Religion Index

Wabash Center Guide to Internet Resources for Teaching and Learning in Theology and Religion: <http://www.wabashcenter.wabash.edu/Internet/front.htm>

SOCIOLOGY

CIA Factbook: <http://www.odci.gov/cia/publications/factbook/index.html>

Data on the Net: <http://odwin.ucsd.edu/idata>

Firstgov (U.S. Government site): <http://firstgov.gov>

Handbook of Sociology (ed. Neil Smelser)

International Encyclopedia of the Social and Behavioral Sciences (print and online)

Public Agenda (public opinion data): <http://www.publicagenda.org/>

Social Sciences Abstracts (print and online)

Sociological Abstracts (print and online)

Sociological Tour through Cyberspace: <http://www.trinity.edu/~mkearl/index.html>

Statistical Abstract of the United States: <http://www.census.gov/statab/www/>

Statistical Resources on the Web: <http://www.lib.umich.edu/govdocs/stats.html>

U.S. Census Bureau: <http://quickfacts.census.gov/qfd>

WWW Virtual Library: Sociology: <http://vlib.org/SocialSciences.html>

WOMEN'S STUDIES

ABC-CLIO Guide to Women's Progress in America

Encyclopedia of Feminism

Feminism and Women's Studies: <http://eserver.org/feminism/index.html>

Gender Studies Page: <http://vos.ucsb.edu/browse.asp?id=2711>

Handbook of American Women's History

Notable American Women

Women in the World

WWW Virtual Library: Women's History: <http://www.iisg.nl/~womhist/vivalink.html>

8 Evaluating Sources

Finding sources is only half the battle. The other half is finding good, relevant sources. How can you tell which sources to use and which to reject? Use the following guidelines.

8a Reading critically

Reading what others write always provides ideas, but not just the ideas you absorb from the page or screen. If you read critically, you will generate ideas of your own as you read. Reading critically does not mean criticizing a writer's views, though it may sometimes include that. Rather, it means reading with an open, questioning mind, examining the writer's assumptions and biases, and scrutinizing the evidence the writer provides.

KEY POINTS

Guidelines for Critical Reading

- Ask questions about the credentials and reputation of the author and the place of publication. What do you learn about the writer's purpose and the audience whom the author is addressing? Make sure you subject any material you find on Web pages to especially careful scrutiny (**8d**).

- Ask questions about the ideas you read. An easy way to do this is to write your annotations in the margin. If you find yourself thinking "But . . ." as you read, go with that sense of doubt, and make a note of what troubles you.

- Be on the lookout for assumptions that may be faulty. If you are reading an article on home-schooling and the writer favors home-schooling because it avoids subjecting students to violence in schools, the unstated assumption is that all schools are violent places. For more on the logic of argument, see **4h** and **4i**.

- Make sure the writer's evidence is adequate and accurate. For example, if the writer is making a generalization about all Chinese students based on a study of only three, you have cause to challenge the generalization as resting on inadequate evidence.

- Note how the writer uses language. Which terms does the writer use with positive—or negative—connotations, signaling the values the writer holds? Does the writer flamboyantly denigrate the views of others with such phrases as "a ridiculous notion" or "laughably inept policies"?

- Be alert for sweeping generalizations, bias, and prejudice: "Women want to stay home and have children." "Men love to spend Sundays watching sports."

Do your reading when you can write—not on the treadmill or while watching TV. Note any questions, objections, or challenges on the page, on self-stick notes, on index cards, in a response file on your computer, or in a double-entry journal (see p. 7). Your critical responses to your reading will provide you with your own ideas for writing.

8b   Recognizing a scholarly article

Learn to distinguish scholarly from nonscholarly articles. A scholarly article is not something you are likely to find in a magazine in a dentist's office. A scholarly article does the following—the first point being the most important:

- refers to the work of other scholars (look for in-text citations and a bibliographical list of works cited, footnotes, or endnotes)
- names the author and usually describes the author's credentials
- includes notes, references, or a bibliography
- deals with a serious issue in depth
- uses academic or technical language for informed readers
- appears in journals that do not include colorful advertisements or eye-catching pictures (a picture of two stunning models is an indication that you are not looking at a scholarly article)

While reading scholarly articles, scan any section headings, read the abstract and any section headed "Summary" or "Conclusions," and skim for the author's main idea to find out whether the article addresses your topic. If you are working on a topic related to current events, you will probably need to consult newspapers, magazines, and online sources as well as or in place of scholarly journals. See **8c** for more on the various types of periodicals. See the following Web site for more on distinguishing types of periodicals: <http://www .library.cornell.edu/okuref/research/skill20.html>.

8c   Evaluating works originating in print

Before you make detailed notes on a book or an article that began its life in print, be sure it will provide suitable information to help answer your research question.

Print books   Check the date of publication, notes about the author, table of contents, and index. Skim the preface, introduction, chapter headings, and summaries to give yourself an idea of the information in the book and the book's theoretical basis and perspective. Do not waste time making detailed notes on a book that deals only tangentially with your topic or on an out-of-date book (unless your purpose is to discuss and critique its perspective or examine a topic historically). Ask a librarian or your instructor for help in evaluating the appropriateness of sources you discover. If your topic concerns a serious academic issue, readers will expect you to consult books and not limit your references to popular magazines, newspapers, and Internet sources.

Periodical articles in print   Take into account the type of periodical, any organization with which it is affiliated, and the intended audience. Differentiate among the following types of articles (listed in descending order of reliability, with the most reliable first):

- scholarly articles (see **8b**)
- articles, often long, in periodicals for nonspecialist but serious, well-educated readers, such as *New York Review of Books, Atlantic Monthly, Economist, Scientific American,* and *Nation*
- shorter articles, with sources not identified, in popular magazines for a general audience, such as *Ebony, Time, Newsweek, Parents, Psychology Today,* and *Vogue*
- articles with dubious sources, written for sensational tabloid magazines, such as *National Enquirer, Globe,* and *Star*

KEY POINTS

Questions to Evaluate a Print Source

1. *What does the work cover?* It should be long enough and detailed enough to provide adequate information.
2. *How objective is the information?* The author, publisher, or periodical should not be affiliated with an organization that has an ax to grind—unless, of course, your topic entails reading critically and making comparisons with other points of view.
3. *How current are the views?* Check the date of publication. The work should be up-to-date if you need a current perspective.
4. *How reputable are the publisher and author?* The work should be published by a reputable publisher in a source that is academically reliable, not one devoted to gossip, advertising, propaganda, or sensationalism. Check *Books in Print* or *Literary Market Place* for details on publishers. The author should be an authority on the subject. Find out what else the author has written (in Google, in *Books in Print,* or at <http://www.amazon.com>) and what his or her qualifications are as an authority.

Newspaper articles The *New York Times, Washington Post,* and *Los Angeles Times,* for example, provide mostly reliable accounts of current events, daily editorial comments, and reviews of books, film, and art. Be aware that most newspapers have political leanings, so reports of and comments on the same event may differ.

8d Evaluating Internet sources

What makes the Internet so fascinating is that it is wide open, free, and democratic. Anyone can "publish" anything, and thousands or millions can read it. For scholars looking for information and well-presented, informed opinion, however, the Internet can pose a challenge.

If you find an article in a CD-ROM or subscription database (*InfoTrac* or *LexisNexis,* for example), you will know that the article has been published in print, so you can use the criteria for print works (**8c**) to evaluate it. If the article has been published in a reputable periodical or in an online journal sponsored by a professional organization or a university, you can assume that it is a valid source for a research paper.

For works devised specifically for the Internet, use the strategies in the Key Points box to separate the information from the junk.

KEY POINTS

Developing Your Junk Antennae

1. *Scrutinize the domain name of the URL.* Informational Web pages tend to come from .gov and .edu addresses, which will have used a review process. Nonprofit organizations (.org) provide interesting mission statements. With .com ("dot com") sources, always assess whether the source is informational or is basically an advertisement or self-promotion.

2. *Check the home page.* Always take the link from a Web site to its home page, if you are not already there. The home page often provides more information about the author, the sponsor, the purpose, and the date of posting.

3. *Assess the originator of an .edu source.* Is the educational institution or a branch of it sponsoring the site? A tilde (~) followed by a name in the URL indicates an individual posting from an academic source. Try to ascertain whether the individual is a faculty member or a student. Increasingly, though, individuals are setting up Web sites under their own domain name.

(Continued)

(Continued)

4. *Discover what you can about the author.* Look for a list of credentials, a home page, a résumé, or Web publications. In Google, use the author's name as a search term to see what the author has published on the Internet or who has cited the author.

5. *Investigate the purposes of a Web page author or sponsor.* Objectivity and rationality are not necessarily features of all Web pages. You may come across propaganda, hate sites, individuals purporting to have psychic powers, religious enthusiasts, and extreme political groups. The sponsor of a site may want to persuade, convert, or sell. Go to the home page and to linked sites, and in addition, note any postal or e-mail address or phone number you can use to get more information about the page and the sponsor. Even if the message is not pointedly biased and extreme, be aware that most authors write from some sense of conviction or purpose. (Note, though, that a Web site can be oriented toward a specific view without necessarily being irresponsible.)

6. *Evaluate the quality of the writing.* A Web page filled with spelling and grammatical errors should not inspire confidence. If the language has not been checked, the ideas probably haven't been given much time and thought, either. Don't use such a site as a source. Exceptions are discussion lists and Usenet postings. They are written and posted quickly, so even if they contain errors, they can also contain useful ideas to stimulate thinking on your topic.

7. *Follow the links.* See whether the links in a site take you to authoritative sources. If the links no longer work (you'll get a 404 message: "Site Not Found"), the home page with the links has not been updated in a while—not a good sign.

8. *Check for dates, updates, ways to respond, and ease of navigation.* A recent date of posting or recent updating; information about the author; ways to reach the author by e-mail, regular mail, or phone; a clearly organized site; easy navigation; and up-to-date links to responsible sites are all indications that the site is well managed and current.

Useful information on evaluating sources is available at a Widener University (Chester, PA) site at <http://www2.widener.edu/ Wolfgram-Memorial-Library/webevaluation/webeval.htm> and at a site called *Thinking Critically about World Wide Web Resources* at <http:// www.library.ucla.edu/libraries/college/help/critical/index.htm>.

9   Avoiding Plagiarism

Once you have found useful sources for your paper, you then need to know how to record the information and use your sources to support your points. It is especially important to know how to cite any source that you refer to, summarize, paraphrase from, or quote from, so that you avoid plagiarizing. First, though, understand what plagiarism is and how careful documentation can steer you clear of it.

9a   What is plagiarism?

The word *plagiarize* is derived from a Latin verb meaning "to kidnap," and kidnapping or stealing someone else's ideas and presenting them as your own is regarded as a serious offense in Western academic culture and public life. Any of the following are regarded as plagiarizing:

- presenting the work of others as your own work
- downloading material from the Internet without acknowledgment
- using the ideas or words you find in a print or Web source without acknowledging where those ideas or words come from
- forgetting to add a citation to ideas that are not your own

In short, plagiarizing is seen as stealing somebody else's words and ideas. It can be done intentionally; it can also occur unintentionally (as some writers have claimed), as a result of sloppy research and acknowledgment. Either way, intentional or not, plagiarizing is a serious offense. Avoid it by always using your own work and always documenting a source.

 TechNote   A Web Site on Plagiarism

For more on the topic of plagiarism, see the Georgetown University Web site *What Is Plagiarism?* at <http://www.georgetown.edu/honor/plagiarism.html>. ■

9b   How to avoid even the suspicion of plagiarism

Research and clear documentation open a channel of communication between you and your readers. They learn what your views are and what has influenced those views. They will assume that anything not documented is your original idea and your wording. So if you even accidentally present someone else's words or ideas as if they were your own, readers may suspect you of plagiarizing. Avoiding plagiarism begins early, with accurate recording and careful management of source material so that you do not end up confused about which parts of your notes contain your ideas and which are derived from the works of others.

KEY POINTS

How to Avoid Plagiarizing

1. Make a record of each source, so that you have all the information you need for appropriate documentation.

2. Set up a working annotated bibliography.

3. Take notes from the sources, with a systematic method of indicating quotation, paraphrase, and your own comments. For example, use quotation marks around quoted words, phrases, sentences, and passages; introduce a paraphrase with a tag, such as "Laird makes the point that . . ."; in your notes about a source, write your own comments in a different color. Then, later, you will see immediately which ideas are yours and which come from your source.

4. Never include in your own essay a passage, an identifiable phrase, or an idea that you have copied from someone else's work without acknowledging and documenting the source.

5. Never use exactly the same sequence of ideas and organization of argument as your source.

6. When you use a single key word from your source or three or more words in sequence from your source, use the appropriate format for quoting and documenting.

7. Always cite the source of any summary or paraphrase. Not only exact words but also ideas need to be credited.

8. Never simply substitute synonyms for a few words in the source or move a few words around.

9. Never use in your paper passages that have been written or rewritten by a friend or a tutor.

10. Never buy, find, download from the Internet, or "borrow" a paper or a section of a paper that you turn in as your own work.

Ownership Rights across Cultures

The Western view takes seriously the ownership of words and text. It respects both the individual as author (and authority) and the originality of the individual's ideas. Copyright laws define and protect the boundaries of intellectual property. However, even the Western world acknowledges that authors imitate and borrow from others' work, as Harold Bloom notes in *The Anxiety of Influence*. In some cultures, memorization and the use of classic texts are common in all walks of life. And worldwide, the ownership of language, texts, and ideas is being called into question by the democratic, interactive nature of the Internet. In short, therefore, plagiarism is not something universal and easy to define. In Western academic culture, basic ground rules exist for the "fair use" of another writer's work without payment, but acknowledging the source of borrowed material is always necessary.

9c   Keeping track of sources

The first step toward avoiding plagiarism is keeping track of what your sources are and which ideas come from your sources and which from you. You will find that one of the frustrating moments for you as a researcher occurs when you find some notes about an interesting point you read—but cannot remember where you found the passage or who wrote it or whether your notes represent an author's exact words. You can spend hours in tedious retracing of your steps. Avoid this frustration by keeping track as you go along.

Use the Bookmarks or Favorites feature.   Many browsers have a Bookmarks or Favorites feature that allows you to compile and save a list of useful sites you have visited. You can then easily revisit these sites by simply clicking on the bookmark. Bookmarks can be deleted later when you no longer need them. If you work on a networked computer in a lab where you cannot save your work on the hard drive, save your bookmarks to your own bookmark file on a diskette or CD.

Record URL and date of access.   Note that bookmarking will not always last with a long URL, such as URLs of online subscription services. To be safe, also use the Copy and Paste features to copy the URL on your hard drive, diskette, or CD, along with the date on which you access the source. As a last resort, copy the URL by hand, but take care to get it exactly right: every letter, symbol, and punctuation mark is important.

 TechNote   Keeping a Bookmark or Favorites File on the Internet

If you do most of your writing in a college computer lab, you may not be able to use the Bookmark or Favorites feature of the browser. In that case, try the free bookmark service on the Internet at <http://www.blink.com>. ■

Highlight, copy, and paste.   As you read material on the Web, most reasonably powerful computers allow you to highlight a passage you find, copy it, and then paste it into a file on your own disk. Make sure that you indicate clearly in your new document that you have included a direct quotation: use quotation marks or a bigger or colored font along with an author/page citation. Save as much information as you can about the original document in your working bibliography (**9d**).

Make photocopies of sources.   Photocopying print articles and printing or downloading online articles allow you to devote research time to locating relevant sources and taking notes from reference works and books; you can take the copies of articles with you and use them when you are unable to be in the library. A quick way to make a copy of an Internet source or material in an online database is to e-mail it to yourself (File/Send).

9d   Setting up a working bibliography

From the first steps of your research, keep accurate records of each source in a working bibliography. Record enough information so that you will be able to make up a list of references in whichever style of documentation you choose, though not all the points of information you record will be necessary for every style of documentation. Use the following templates as guides for what to record, but be aware that with online sources, especially, much of the information may not be available. Essential information for an online source is always the URL and the date on which you access the material. Always make a note of that information. The templates are available for printing and filling out at <http://college.hmco.com/keys.html> (click on Downloadable Forms).

PRINT BOOK

1. Author(s), editor(s), translator(s): last name, first name
2. Title and subtitle
3. Publication information

   place of publication

   name of publishing company

   year of publication
4. If available, volume number or edition number
5. Call number (not needed for list of works cited)

Hint: Photocopy the title page and the copyright page, where the first four items of information are available.

PRINT ARTICLE

1. Author(s), editor(s) translator(s): last name, first name
2. Title and subtitle
3. Name of periodical
4. Publication information

   a. For a periodical

      volume number (scholarly article)

      issue number (scholarly article paged by issue)

      date of publication

      inclusive page numbers of article

   b. For an article in a book

      title of book, name of editor

      publisher, place, and year of publication

      inclusive page numbers of article

Hint: Photocopy the table of contents of the periodical or anthology.

ELECTRONIC OR ONLINE SOURCE

1. Author(s), editor(s), translator(s): last name, first name
2. Title and subtitle of work
3. Any print publication information (as for a book or an article)
4. Name of site (for example, title of online periodical or Web site, database, name of discussion list or forum, home page, subject line of e-mail message)

5. Electronic publication information, as available, for

a document in a database: name of database and service

an article in an online journal: volume, issue number, and date of publication

a Web site: date of online publication or latest update

electronic or online material: number of paragraphs, but only if paragraph numbers actually appear on the screen

a CD-ROM: version number

6. Compiler or sponsor of Web site or distributor of CD-ROM

7. For an e-mail message or discussion list posting: name of sender, subject line, date of posting, name of discussion list, your date of access

8. MOST IMPORTANT! For any Web source, the date when you access the source and the complete URL—or home page URL of a subscription service.

Hint: Save to disk, e-mail yourself a copy, or print out an online source. For a printout of a Web document, you can set your computer so that the URL appears on the printout, along with the date on which you print the document (the date of access). If you are saving information in a computer program, use the Copy and Paste functions to copy the URL accurately into your own document.

Keep your list of sources in a form that you can work with to organize them alphabetically, add and reject sources, and add summaries and notes. Note cards and computer files have the advantage over sheets of paper or a research journal. They don't tie you to page order.

Here is a sample index card for an article accessed in an online subscription database.

Laird, Ellen. "Internet Plagiarism: We All Pay the Price." *Chronicle of Higher Education* 13 July 2001: 5. *Academic Universe: News.* Lexis Nexis. City U of New York Lib. 5 May 2003 < http://web.lexis-nexis.com>.

9e Annotating and taking notes

Printing and saving from online sources make a source text available for you to annotate. You can interact with the author's ideas, asking questions, writing comments, and jotting down your own ideas. Here is a passage from the article by Ellen Laird on plagiarism (see the bibliography card on p. 121). As Laird, a college professor, discusses the case of Chip, a student who has plagiarized, she is considering her own role and her student's explanation. The passage shows student Juana Mere's annotations as she gave the article a critical reading.

But what if her instructions weren't as clear as she thought?
To save face with myself, I must assume that Chip understood that downloading an essay and submitting it as his own was an *Look up* egregious act. Why, then, did he do it? *Can she ever really know?*

But it's   Chip explained he had been "mentally perturbed" the weekend *Sounds*
specula- before the paper was due and that the essay he had written failed *like a*
tion on to meet his high standards. But I <u>sensed</u> that Chip felt he had made *very*
her part a choice akin to having a pizza delivered. He had procrastinated *genera*
     on an assignment due the next day, had no time left in which to *excuse*
     prepare his work from scratch, and had to get on to those <u>pressing</u>
Is this <u>matters that shape the world of an 18-year-old.</u> He dialed his
conde- Internet service provider, ordered takeout, and had it delivered.
scending? *Nice analogy* *Good quotation*

Annotating is useful for comments, observations, and questions. You also will need to make notes when you do not have a copy that you can write on or when you want to summarize, paraphrase, and make detailed connections to other ideas and other sources. Write notes on the computer, on legal pads, in notebooks, or on index cards—whatever works best for you. Index cards—each card with a heading and only one note—offer the advantage of flexibility: you can shuffle and reorder them to fit the organization of your paper. In your notes, always include the author's name, a short version of the title of the work, and any relevant page number(s) whenever you summarize, paraphrase, or quote. Include full bibliographical information in your working bibliography (9d). Then when you start to write your paper, you will have at your fingertips all the information necessary for a citation.

9f Summarizing and paraphrasing

Summary   Summaries are useful for giving readers basic information about the work you are discussing. To summarize a source or a passage in a source, select only the main points as the author presents them, without your own commentary or interpretation. Be brief, and use your own words at all times. To ensure that you use your own words, do not have the original source in front of you as you write. Read, understand, and then put the passage away before writing your summary. If you find that you must include some particularly apt words from the original source, put them in quotation marks.

Use summaries in your research paper to let readers know the gist of the most important sources you find. When you include a summary in a paper, introduce the author or the work to indicate where your summary begins. At the end of the summary, give the page numbers you are summarizing. Do not include page numbers if you are summarizing the complete work or summarizing an online source; instead, indicate where your summary ends and your own ideas return (see **9h**). When you write your paper, provide full documentation of the source in the list of works cited at the end.

After reading the article by Laird on plagiarism, Mere decided to write a research paper on Internet plagiarism. She wrote this 65-word summary of an article of 1,635 words in a computer file headed "College plagiarism." (She could also have used an index card.) The heading of the summary refers directly to the first word on the bibliography card on page 121.

Laird   Summary

"Internet plagiarism"

College professor Ellen Laird explores the possible reasons why a student might have plagiarized a whole essay. She concludes that Chip, otherwise a good student, knew what he was doing, but taking material from the Internet while at home might not have seemed unethical. Laird connects his behavior to our contemporary culture and laments that teaching will have to change to counteract opportunities for plagiarism.

Paraphrase   When you need more details than a summary provides, paraphrasing offers a tool. Use paraphrase more often than you use quotation. A paraphrase uses your words and your interpretations of and comments on the ideas you find in your sources. Many instructors feel that if you cannot paraphrase information, then you probably do not understand it. So paraphrase serves the purpose of showing that you have absorbed your source material.

A paraphrase is similar in length to the original material— maybe somewhat longer. In a paraphrase, present the author's argument and logic, but be very careful not to use the author's exact words or sentence structure.

KEY POINTS

How to Paraphrase

1. Keep the source out of sight as you write a paraphrase, so you will not be tempted to copy the sentence patterns or phrases of the original.

2. Do not substitute synonyms for some or most of the words in an author's passage.

3. Use your own sentence structure as well as your own words. Your writing will still be regarded as plagiarized if it resembles the original in sentence structure as well as in wording.

4. Do not comment or interpret: just tell readers the ideas that the author of your source presents.

5. Check your text against the original source to avoid inadvertent plagiarism.

6. Cite the author (and page number if a print source) as the source of the ideas, introduce and integrate the paraphrase, and provide full documentation. If the source does not name an author, cite the title.

When Mere was making notes for her paper on Internet plagiarism, she decided to paraphrase one of the key paragraphs from Laird's article, one that she had previously annotated (**9e**).

ORIGINAL SOURCE

Chip explained that he had been "mentally perturbed" the weekend before the paper was due and that the essay he had written failed to meet his high standards. But I sensed that Chip felt that he had made a choice akin to having a pizza delivered. He had procrastinated on an assignment due the next day, had no time left in which to prepare his work from scratch, and had to get on to those pressing matters that shape the world of an 18-year-old. He dialed his Internet service provider, ordered takeout, and had it delivered.

—Ellen Laird, "Internet Plagiarism: We All Pay the Price"

You can use common words and expressions such as "made a choice" or "due the next day." But if you use more unusual expressions from the source ("a choice akin to having pizza delivered"; "pressing matters"; "dialed his Internet service provider"), you need to enclose them in quotation marks. In Mere's first attempt at paraphrase on a 6″ × 4″ note card, she does not quote, but her words and structure resemble the original too closely.

PARAPHRASE TOO SIMILAR TO THE ORIGINAL

Laird   Paraphrase, p. 5, ninth paragraph

Laird knew that Chip was mentally perturbed before he wrote his paper and his high standards prevented him from writing his own essay. But she felt that what he did was like having a pizza takeout. He had procrastinated so long that he could not write an essay from scratch and wanted to enjoy his life. So he ordered a takeout essay from his ISP (5).

Mere gives the name of the author and the page number of the source material (given in the online version) using the MLA style of documentation. Documentation, however, is not a guarantee against plagiarism. Mere's wording and sentence structure follow the original too closely. When classmates and her instructor pointed this out, she revised the paraphrase by keeping the ideas of the original, using different wording and sentence structure, and quoting what she regarded as a unique phrase.

REVISED PARAPHRASE

Laird   Paraphrase, p. 5, ninth paragraph

Laird's student Chip might have felt psychologically stressed and that might have affected his attitude to the paper he wrote, forcing him to reject it as not good enough to hand in for a grade. Laird, however, sees his transgression not so much as one of high moral principles as of expediency. He chose the easiest way out. He had left the assignment until the last minute. He had no time to do the work. He wanted to go out and have fun. So what did he do? He went on the Web, found an essay, and "ordered takeout" (5).

9g What to cite

When you refer to a source in your work, carefully cite and document it. Systematically provide information about the author, title, publication data, page numbers, Internet address, dates—whatever is available (see **9d** for the information you need to collect). You provide such documentation so that your readers can locate the sources and read them for further information. (See Part 3 and Part 4 for guides to specific systems of documentation.) You also document sources so that there will be no question about which words and ideas are yours and which belong to other people.

KEY POINTS

What to Cite

1. Cite all facts, statistics, and pieces of information unless they are common knowledge and are accessible in many sources.

2. Cite exact words from your source, enclosed in quotation marks.

3. Cite somebody else's ideas and opinions, even if you restate them in your own words in a summary or paraphrase.

4. Cite each sentence in a long paraphrase (if it is not clear that all the sentences paraphrase the same original source).

Note how James Stalker, in his article "Official English or English Only," does not quote directly but still cites Anderson as the source of the specialized facts mentioned in the following passage:

> By 1745 there were approximately 45,000 German speakers in the colonies, and by 1790 there were some 200,000, nine per cent of the population (Anderson 80).

Citation is not necessary for facts regarded as common knowledge, such as the dates of the Civil War; facts available in many sources, such as authors' birth and death dates and chronological events; or allusions to folktales that have been handed down through the ages. When you are in doubt about whether a fact is common knowledge, play it safe, and cite your source.

9h Indicating the boundaries of a citation

Naming an author or title in your text tells readers that you are citing ideas from a source, and citing a page number at the end of a summary or paraphrase lets them know where your citation ends.

However, for one-page print articles and for Internet sources, a page citation is not necessary, so indicating where your comments about a source end is harder to do. You always need to indicate clearly where your summary or paraphrase ends and where your own comments take over. Convey the shift to readers by commenting on the source in a way that clearly announces a statement of your own views. Use expressions such as *it follows that, X's explanation shows that, as a result, evidently, obviously,* or *clearly* to signal the shift.

UNCLEAR CITATION BOUNDARY

According to a Sony Web site, Mozart Makes You Smarter, the company has decided to release a cassette on the strength of research indicating that listening to Mozart improves IQ. The products show the ingenuity of commercial enterprise while taking the researchers' conclusions in new directions.

[Does only the first sentence refer to material on the Web page, or do both sentences?]

REVISED CITATION, WITH SOURCE BOUNDARY INDICATED

According to a Sony Web site, Mozart Makes You Smarter, the company has decided to release a cassette on the strength of research indicating that listening to Mozart improves IQ. Clearly, Sony's plan demonstrates the ingenuity of commercial enterprise, but it cannot reflect what the researchers intended when they published their conclusions.

Another way to indicate the end of your citation is to include the author's or authors' name(s) at the end of the citation instead of (or even in addition to) introducing the citation with the name.

UNCLEAR CITATION BOUNDARY

For people who hate shopping, Web shopping may be the perfect solution. Jerome and Taylor's exploration of "holiday hell" reminds us that we get more choice from online vendors than we do when we browse at our local mall because the online sellers, unlike mall owners, do not have to rent space to display their goods. In addition, one can buy almost anything online, from CDs, cassettes, and books to cars and real estate.

REVISED CITATION, WITH SOURCE BOUNDARY INDICATED

For people who hate shopping, Web shopping may be the perfect solution. An article exploring the "holiday hell" of shopping reminds us that we get more choice from online vendors than we do when we browse at our local mall because the online sellers, unlike mall owners, do not have to rent space to display their goods (Jerome and Taylor). In addition, one can buy almost anything online, from CDs, cell phones, and books to cars and real estate.

10 Writing the Research Paper

10a Guidelines for writing research paper drafts

WHAT NOT TO DO

1. Do not expect to complete a polished draft at one sitting.
2. Do not write the title and the first sentence and then panic because you feel you have nothing left to say.
3. Do not constantly imagine your instructor's response to what you write.
4. Do not worry about coherence—a draft by its nature is something that you work on repeatedly and revise for readers' eyes.
5. Do not necessarily begin at the beginning; do not think you must first write a dynamite introduction.

WHAT TO DO

1. Wait until you have a block of time available before you begin writing a draft of your paper.
2. Turn off the phone, close the door, and tell yourself you will not emerge from the room until you have written about six pages.
3. Promise yourself a reward when you meet your target—a refrigerator break or a trip to a nearby ice cream store, for instance.
4. Assemble your copy of the assignment, your thesis statement, all your copies of sources, your research notebook and any other notes, your working bibliography, and your proposal or outline.
5. Write the parts you know most about first.
6. Write as much as you can as fast as you can. If you only vaguely remember a reference in your sources, just write what you can remember—but keep writing, and don't worry about gaps:

   As so and so (who was it? Jackson?) has observed, malls are taking the place of city centers (check page reference).

7. Write the beginning—the introduction—only after you have some ideas on paper that you feel you can introduce.

8. Write at least something on each one of the points in your outline. Start off by asking yourself: What do I know about this point, and how does it support my thesis? Write your answer to that in your own words without worrying about who said what in which source. You can check your notes and fill in the gaps later.

9. Write until you feel you have put down on the page or screen your main points and you have made reference to most of your source material.

Now here is the hard part. Do not go back over your draft and start tinkering and changing—at least not yet. Congratulate yourself on having made a start and take a break, a long one. Put your draft in a drawer and do not look at it for at least a few days. In the meantime, you can follow up on research leads, find new sources, and continue writing ideas in your research notebook.

10b Getting mileage out of your sources

You have done hours, days, maybe weeks of research. You have found useful sources. You have a working bibliography and masses of photocopies, printouts, and notes. You have made a scratch outline. Now comes the time to write your draft.

Let readers know about the sources that support your point effectively. Don't mention an author of an influential book or long, important article just once and in parentheses. Let readers know why this source adds so much weight to your case. Tell about the expert's credentials, affiliations, and experience. Tell readers what the author does in the work you are citing. A summary of the work along with a paraphrase of important points may also be useful to provide context for the author's remarks and opinions. Show readers that they should be impressed by the heavyweight opinions and facts you present.

10c Putting yourself in your paper and synthesizing

Never get so involved in your mountains of notes and copies of sources that you include everything you have read and string it all together. Large amounts of information are no substitute for a thesis with relevant support. Your paper should *synthesize* your sources, not just tell about them, one after the other. When you synthesize, you connect the ideas in individual sources to create a larger picture, to inform yourself about the topic, and to establish your own ideas on the topic. So leave plenty of time to read through your notes, think about what you have read, connect with the material, form responses to it, take into account new ideas and opposing arguments, and find connections among the facts and the ideas your sources offer. Avoid sitting down to write a paper at the last minute, surrounded by library books or stacks of photocopies. In this scenario, you might be tempted to lift material, and you will produce a lifeless paper. Remember that the paper is ultimately your work, not a collection of other people's words, and that your identity and opinions as the writer should be evident.

10d Driving the organization with ideas, not sources

Let your ideas, not your sources, drive your paper. Resist the temptation to organize your paper in the following way:

1. What points Smith makes
2. What points Jones makes
3. What points Fuentes makes
4. What points Jackson and Hayes make in opposition
5. What I think

That organization is driven by your sources, with the bulk of the paper dealing with the views of Smith, Jones, and the rest. Instead, let your thesis and its points of supporting evidence determine the organization:

1. First point of support: what ideas I have to support my thesis and what evidence Fuentes and Jones provide
2. Second point of support: what ideas I have to support my thesis and what evidence Smith and Fuentes provide
3. Third point of support: what ideas I have to support my thesis and what evidence Jones provides
4. Opposing viewpoints of Jackson and Hayes
5. Common ground and refutation of those viewpoints
6. Synthesis

To avoid producing an essay that reads like a serial listing of summaries or references ("Crabbe says this," "Tyger says that,"

"Tyger also says this"), spend time reviewing your notes and synthesizing what you find into a coherent and convincing statement of what you know and believe.

- Make lists of good ideas your sources raise about your topic.
- Look for the connections among those ideas: comparisons and contrasts.
- Find links in content, examples, and statistics.
- Note connections between the information in your sources and what you know from your own experience.

If you do this, you will take control of your material instead of letting it take control of you.

10e Introducing and integrating source material

When you provide a summary, paraphrase, or quotation to support one of the points in your paper, set up the context. Don't drop in the material as if it came from nowhere. Think about how to introduce and integrate the material into the structure of your paper.

If you quote a complete sentence, or if you paraphrase or summarize a section of another work, prepare readers for your summary, paraphrase, or quotation by mentioning the author's name in an introductory phrase. In your first reference to the work, give the author's full name. To further orient readers, you can also provide the title of the work or a brief statement of the author's expertise or credentials and thesis. Here are some useful ways to introduce source material:

X has pointed out that	According to X,
X has made it clear that	As X insists,
X explains that	In 2003, X, the vice president
X suggests that	of the corporation, declared

The introductory verbs *say* and *write* are clear and direct. For occasional variety, though, use verbs that offer shades of meaning, such as *acknowledge, agree, argue, ask, assert, believe, claim, comment, contend, declare, deny, emphasize, insist, note, observe, point out, propose, speculate.*

10f Quoting

Readers should immediately realize why you quote a particular passage and what the quotation contributes to the ideas you want to convey. They should also learn who said the words you are quoting and, if the source is a print source, on which page of the original work the quotation appears. Then they can look up the author's name in the list of works cited at the end of your paper and find out exactly where you found the quotation.

The Modern Language Association (MLA) format for citing a quotation from an article by one author is illustrated in this section and in Part 3. See Part 4 for examples of citations of other types of sources in APA and other styles of documentation. For punctuation with quotation marks, see **49**.

Deciding what and when to quote Quote when you use the words of a well-known authority or when the words are particularly striking. Quote only when the original words express the exact point you want to make and express it succinctly and well. Otherwise, paraphrase. When you consider quoting, ask yourself: Which point of mine does the quotation illustrate? Why am I considering quoting this particular passage? Why should this particular passage be quoted rather than paraphrased? What do I need to tell my readers about the author of the quotation?

Quoting the exact words of the original To understand how to deal with quotations in your paper, consider the following article a student used as he was working on a paper on students' rights to free speech.

> Late last month, Charles Carithers got an English assignment: Write "a vivid horror story" about a mysterious person in the community who had a "shocking" secret in his past. So the 11th-grader at Boston Latin Academy, a competitive-admissions public school, wrote about a student athlete (which he is) who went after his English teacher with a chain saw.
>
> The teacher saw details that hit too close to home. Charles got a three-day suspension. The school is defending the action, and Charles's mother is appealing it.
>
> In the current climate of jitters in schools across the United States, chainsaw murders might not be the best topic for an essay. But assignments that open the door to writing about chainsaw murders might not be all that inspired, either. Adults can say that they weren't as prone to writing about such gore in their day, or that horror is more effective when less crudely rendered. But high-schoolers don't think like adults—and they are routinely doused with ridiculously crude and gory films like *Scream* (1, 2, and 3) and *I Know What You Did Last Summer*, all of which Charles said he pondered as he created

his opus. (As did perhaps a peer—not suspended—whose protagonist murdered children and cut them up for fertilizer.)

It seems like a "teachable moment" that engendered a hard-line response. And such debacles happen across the U.S. Why no open discussion of what's acceptable? Or specifics: a horror story, children, but no guns or chain saws allowed. Or, show me the difference between horror and tension.

Assignments can't be created in a cultural vacuum—and no one should expect the results to be, either.

—Amelia Newcomb, "Suspense and Suspension," *Christian Science Monitor,*
2 May 2000: 13

Any words you use from a source must be included in quotation marks (unless they are long quotations) and quoted exactly as they appear in the original, with the same punctuation marks and capital letters. Do not change pronouns or tenses to fit your own purpose, unless you enclose changes in square brackets (see the examples on p. 134).

NOT EXACT QUOTATION
Newcomb reports that Charles Carithers wrote an essay about "someone in his community with a secret in his past."

EXACT QUOTATION, WITHOUT CITATION
Newcomb reports that Charles Carithers wrote an essay "about a mysterious person in the community who had a 'shocking' secret in his past."

EXACT QUOTATION, WITH CITATION
Newcomb reports that Charles Carithers wrote an essay "about a mysterious person in the community who had a 'shocking' secret in his past" (13).

Note that if your quotation includes a question mark or exclamation point, you must include it within the quotation. Your sentence period then comes after your citation.

Newcomb wonders, "Why no open discussion of what's acceptable?" (13).

Quoting part of a sentence You can make sure that quotations make a point and are not just dropped into your paper if you integrate parts of quoted sentences into your own sentences. When it is obvious that parts of the quoted sentence have been omitted, you do not need to use ellipsis dots.

Reporter Amelia Newcomb wonders about the influence of "ridiculously crude and gory films."

Omitting words in the middle of a quotation If you omit as irrelevant to your purpose any words from the middle of a quotation, signal the omission with an ellipsis mark, three dots separated by spaces. See **51g**.

> According to Newcomb, a high school teacher asked students to write about a "mysterious person . . . who had a 'shocking' secret in his past."

In MLA style, if your source passage uses other ellipses, place the dots within square brackets to indicate that your ellipsis mark is not part of the original text: [. . .].

Omitting words at the end of a quotation If you omit the end of the source's sentence at the end of your own sentence, and your sentence is not followed by a page citation, signal the omission with three ellipsis dots following the sentence period—four dots in all—and then the closing quotation marks.

> With resignation, Newcomb concedes that "such debacles happen. . . ."

When you include a page citation for a print source, place it after the ellipsis dots and the closing quotation marks and before the final sentence period.

> With resignation, Newcomb concedes that "such debacles happen . . ." (13).

Also use three dots after the period if you omit a complete sentence (or more). Use a line of dots for an omitted line of poetry (**51g**).

Adding or changing words If you add any comments or explanations in your own words, or if you change a word in the quotation to fit it grammatically into your sentence, enclose the added or changed material in square brackets (**51e**). Generally, however, it is preferable to rephrase your sentence, because bracketed words and phrases make sentences difficult to read.

AWKWARD Newcomb wonders whether we as adults were not "as prone to writing about such gore [in a high school essay assignment] in [our] day."

REVISED Newcomb wonders whether we as adults were not "as prone to writing about such gore" in our high school essays.

Quoting longer passages If you quote more than three lines of poetry or four typed lines of prose, do not use quotation marks. Instead, begin the quotation on a new line and indent the quotation one inch or ten spaces from the left margin in MLA style, or indent it five spaces from the left margin if you are using APA style. Double-space throughout. Do not indent from the right margin. You can establish the context for a long quotation and integrate it effectively into your text if you state the point that you want to make and name the author of the quotation in your introductory statement.

Author mentioned in introductory statement
> Newcomb lays some blame on the teacher and uses sentence fragments to make a strong point about the way the teacher neglected to discuss the specifics of the assignment:

No quotation marks around indented quotation

Quotation indented one inch or 10 spaces (MLA)

> It seems like a "teachable moment" that engendered a hardline response. And such debacles happen across the U.S. Why no open discussion of what's acceptable? Or specifics: a horror story, children, but no guns or chain saws allowed. Or, show me the difference between horror and tension. (13)

Page citation (only for a print source) after period

Note: After a long indented quotation, put the period before the parenthetical citation.

Avoiding a string of quotations Use quotations, especially long ones, sparingly, and only when they bolster your argument. Readers do not want to read snippets from the works of other writers. They want your analysis of your sources, and they are interested in the conclusions you draw from your research.

Fitting a quotation into your sentence When you quote, use the exact words of the original, and make sure that those exact words do not disrupt the flow of your sentence and send it in another direction.

A BAD FIT   Newcomb says that a teacher suspending a student for writing a gory essay, "such debacles happen across the U.S."

A BETTER FIT   Newcomb says that the teacher who suspended a student was influenced by the contemporary climate since "such debacles happen across the U.S."

A BAD FIT   I wonder if Newcomb is biased when she claims that some "assignments that open the door to writing about chainsaw murders."

A BETTER FIT   I wonder if Newcomb is biased when she claims that some "assignments . . . open the door to writing about chainsaw murders."

 KEY POINTS

Using Quotations: A Checklist

Examine a draft of your paper, and ask questions about each quotation you have included.

1. Why do you want to include this quotation? How does it support a point you have made?

2. What is particularly remarkable about this quotation? Would a paraphrase be better?

3. Does what you have enclosed in quotation marks exactly match the words and punctuation of the original?

4. Have you told your readers the name of the author of the quotation?

5. Have you included the page number of the quotation from a print source?

6. How have you integrated the quotation into your own passage? Will readers know whom you are quoting and why?

7. What verb have you used to introduce the quotation?

8. Are there any places where you string quotations together, one after another? If so, revise. Look for quotation marks closing and then immediately opening again. Also look for phrases such as "X goes on to say . . ."; "X also says . . ."; "X then says . . . ."

9. Have you indented quotations longer than four lines of type and omitted quotation marks?

10. Have you used long quotations sparingly?

10g Researching across the curriculum

Writing research papers in the humanities and arts

- Consult primary sources, such as original works of literature, or attend original performances, such as plays, films, poetry readings, and concerts.
- Form your own interpretations of works.
- Use secondary sources (works of criticism) only after you have formed your own interpretations and established a basis for evaluating the opinions expressed by others.

- Look for patterns and interpretations supported by evidence, not for one right answer to a problem.

- Use the present tense to refer to what writers have said (*Emerson points out that* . . .).

- Use MLA guidelines (see **11–13**) or *Chicago Manual of Style* (see **18**) for documentation style. Consult with your instructor about whether to use the style for online sources described in *The Columbia Guide to Online Style* (CGOS; see **19**).

Writing in the social sciences

- Examine research studies in the field, evaluate their methodology, compare and contrast results with those of other studies, and draw conclusions based on the empirical evidence uncovered. Devote a section of the paper to a review of the literature. (If your field is public policy, international relations, or ethnography, however, your writing will examine trends and draw conclusions, an approach closer to the humanities than to the natural sciences.)

- Look for accurate, up-to-date information, and evaluate it systematically against stated criteria.

- Use the first person (*I* and *we*) less frequently than in the humanities.

- Use the present perfect tense to refer to what researchers and writers have reported (*Smith's study has shown that* . . .).

- Use the passive voice as appropriate when reporting on scientific and experimental procedures (*The stimulus was repeated* in place of *I repeated the stimulus*).

- Where possible and appropriate, present graphs, charts, and tables in support of your conclusions.

- Use APA (**14–16**) or *Chicago* documentation style (**18**). Consult with your instructor about whether to use *The Columbia Guide to Online Style* (CGOS; see **19**) for citing online sources.

Writing in the natural sciences and mathematics

- Use primary sources more frequently than secondary sources.
- Avoid personal anecdotes.
- Report firsthand original experiments and calculations.
- Refer to secondary sources in the introductory section of your paper, a section sometimes called "Review of the Literature."

- Use the present perfect tense to introduce a survey of the literature (*Several studies have shown that . . .*).
- Use the past tense for details of specific studies (*Cocchi et al. isolated the protein fraction . . .*).
- Use the passive voice more frequently than in other types of writing (*The muscle was stimulated . . .*) (**42a**).
- Be prepared to write according to a set format, using sections with headings (see Writing laboratory reports, **5d**).
- Use APA (**14–16**) or CBE/CSE (**17**) documentation style, or follow specific style manuals in scientific areas. Ask your instructor whether you should use *The Columbia Guide to Online Style* (CGOS; see **19**) for citing online sources.

See **7g** for sources to get you started in twenty-seven subject areas.

MLA Documentation

PART 3   MLA Documentation

AT A GLANCE: INDEX OF MLA STYLE FEATURES

SAMPLES OF MLA IN-TEXT CITATIONS (11c)

SAMPLES OF ENTRIES IN MLA LIST OF WORKS CITED

Print Books and Parts of Books (12c)

Print Articles in Periodicals (12d)

Internet and Other Electronic Sources (12e)

Miscellaneous Sources (12f)

You need to document the sources of your information, not only in research papers but also in shorter essays in which you mention only a few books, articles, or other sources to illustrate a point or support your case. Sections **11–13** provide information on the system commonly used to document sources in the humanities, the Modern Language Association (MLA) system, as recommended in Joseph Gibaldi, *MLA Handbook for Writers of Research Papers*, 6th ed. (New York: MLA, 2003), in Joseph Gibaldi, *MLA Style Manual*, 2nd ed. (New York: MLA, 1998), and on the MLA Web site (http://www.mla.org).

11   Citing Sources, MLA Style

11a   Two basic features of MLA style

KEY POINTS

Two Basic Features of MLA Style

1. *In the text of your paper,* include an author/page citation for each source: the **last name(s)** of the author (or authors) and **page number(s)** where the information is located, unless the source is online or only one page long. See **11c** for examples.

2. *At the end of your paper,* include a list of all the sources you refer to in the paper, alphabetized by author's last name or by title if the author is not known. Begin the list on a new page, and title it "Works Cited." See **12**.

Illustrations of the two basic features

1. Reference in the text of your paper:

> Historian and biographer Robert Caro calls Lyndon Johnson "not only the youngest but the greatest Senate Leader in America's history" (xxii).

2. Entry in the works-cited list:

> Caro, Robert A. Master of the Senate. New York: Knopf, 2002.

When readers see *Caro* in your text, they can find the name easily in the alphabetical listing of works cited. There they find all the details of the source, so they can retrieve it from a library if they want to. The page citation in your text (*xxii*) pinpoints for them the exact place you refer to.

11b FAQs about MLA in-text citations

FREQUENTLY ASKED QUESTIONS	SHORT ANSWER	MORE INFORMATION AND EXAMPLES
What information do I put into the body of my essay?	Give only the name of the author(s) (if available) and the page number (for a print source of more than one page).	**11c**, G, H, I, J
Where do I supply that information?	Either name the author as you introduce the information, or put both author and page number in parentheses at the end of the sentence containing the citation.	**11c**, A, B
How do I refer to an author?	In your text, use both names (and maybe a brief identification of position or credentials) for the first mention. Use only the last name for subsequent references and within parentheses.	**11c**, A, B
What if no author is named?	Give the title of the work or, in a parenthetical citation, an abbreviation containing the word of the title alphabetized in the works-cited list.	**11c**, I, J

(Continues)

FREQUENTLY ASKED QUESTIONS	SHORT ANSWER	MORE INFORMATION OR EXAMPLES
How do I give page numbers?	Do not use "p." or "pp." Give inclusive page numbers for information that spans pages: 35–36; 257–58; 305–06; 299–300.	**11c**, C
When can I omit a page number?	Do so for a reference to a whole work, to a work only one page long, or to an online work with no visible page numbers.	**11c**, G, H, J

See the samples in **11c** to answer other questions.

11c MLA sample author/page citations in text

A. One author, named in your introductory phrase Naming the author in an introductory phrase allows you to supply information about the author's credentials as an expert and so increases the credibility of your source for readers. Another advantage of naming your source in your text is that readers then know that everything between the mention of the author and the cited page number is a reference to your source material. See **12c**, item 1, to observe how the source used below appears in a works-cited list.

┌────── author and credentials ──────┐
Renowned historian David McCullough paints a vivid picture of

┌────────── quotation ──────────┐
the army's retreat from Boston: "The British had been outwitted,

humiliated. The greatest military power on earth had been forced

to retreat by an army of amateurs; it was a heady realization" (76).
                                              page number period

When a quotation ends the sentence, as above, close the quotation marks before the parentheses, and place the sentence period after the parentheses. (Note that this rule differs from the one for undocumented writing, which calls for a period *before* the closing quotation marks.)

When a quotation includes a question mark or an exclamation point, also include a period after the citation:

question mark   period
Mrs. Bridge wonders, "Is my daughter mine?" (Connell 135).

B. Author not named in your introductory text If you have referred to an author previously or if you are citing statistics, you do not need to mention the author while introducing the reference. In that case, include the author's last name in the parentheses before the page number, with no comma between them.

> The army retreated from Boston in disarray, making the victors realize
>
> that they had defeated the "greatest military power on earth"
>
> author and page
> ┌── number──┐
> (McCullough 76).

C. Two or more authors For a work with two or three authors, include all the names, either in your text sentence or in parentheses.

> (Lakoff and Johnson 42)
>
> (Hare, Moran, and Koepke 226–28)

For a work with four or more authors, use only the first author's last name followed by "et al." (*Et alii* means "and others.") See **12c**, item 2.

> Some researchers have established a close link between success at work and the pleasure derived from community service (Bellah et al. 196–99).

D. Author with more than one work cited You can include the author and title of the work in your text sentence.

> Alice Walker, in her book In Search of Our Mothers' Gardens, describes revisiting her past to discover more about Flannery O'Connor (43-59).

If you do not mention the author in your text, include in your parenthetical reference the author's last name, followed by a comma, an abbreviated form of the title, and the page number.

comma
> O'Connor's house still stands and is looked after by a caretaker (Walker,
>
> abbreviated title ┌─page number
> In Search 57).

E. Work in an anthology Cite the author of the included or reprinted work (not the editor of the anthology) and the page number in the anthology. The entry in the works-cited list will include the title of the article, its inclusive page numbers, and full bibliographical details for the anthology: title, editor(s), place of publication, publisher, and date. See **12c**, items 5 and 6, for examples.

> Des Pres asserts that "heroism is not necessarily a romantic notion" (20).

F. Work quoted in another source Use "qtd. in" (for "quoted in") in your parenthetical citation, followed by the last name of the author of the source in which you find the reference (the indirect source) and the page number where the reference appears. List the indirect source in your list of works cited. In the following example, the indirect source Smith would be included in the list of works cited, not Britton.

> We generate words unconsciously, without thinking about them; they appear, as James Britton says, "at the point of utterance" (qtd. in Smith 108).

G. Reference to an entire work and not to one specific page If you are referring not to a quotation or idea on one specific page, but rather to an idea that is central to the work as a whole, use the author's name alone. Include the work in your works-cited list.

> We can learn from diaries about people's everyday lives and the worlds they create (Mallon).

H. One-page work If an article is only one page long, cite the author's name alone; include the page number in your works-cited list (**12d**, item 22).

I. No author or editor named In your text sentence, give the complete title to refer to the work. In parentheses, use a short title to refer to the work. See **12c**, item 8, for the works-cited list entries.

> According to Weather, one way to estimate the Fahrenheit temperature is to count the number of times a cricket chirps in 14 seconds and add 40 (18).

> Increasing evidence shows that glucosamine relieves the symptoms of arthritis (PDR Family Guide 242).

J. Electronic and Internet sources Electronic database material and Internet sources, which appear on a screen, have no stable page numbers that apply across systems or when printed, unless they are in PDF files. If your source as it appears on the screen includes no numbered pages or numbered paragraphs, provide only the author's name. In the first mention, establish the authority of your source. If no author's name is given, refer to the title.

> Science writer Stephen Hart describes how researchers Edward Taub and Thomas Ebert conclude that for musicians, practicing "remaps the brain."
> Online source has no numbered pages or paragraphs.

With no page number to indicate the end of a citation, be careful to define where your citation ends and your own commentary takes over. See **9h** for more on defining the boundaries of a citation.

If possible, locate online material by the internal headings of the source (for example, *introduction, chapter, section*). Give paragraph numbers only if they are supplied in the source and you see the numbers on the screen (use the abbreviation "par." or "pars."). And then include the total number of numbered paragraphs in your works-cited list (see **12e**, item 35).

> Hatchuel discusses how film editing "can change points of view and turn objectivity into subjectivity" (par. 6).

> Film editing provides us with different perceptions of reality (Hatchuel, par. 6).

To cite an online source with no author, give the title of the Web page or the posting, either in full or abbreviated to begin with the first word you alphabetize (see **12e**, item 40).

> A list of frequently asked questions about documentation and up-to-date instructions on how to cite online sources in MLA style can be found on the association's Web site (MLA).

K. Other nonprint sources For radio or TV programs, interviews, live performances, films, computer software, recordings, and other nonprint sources, include only the title or author (or, in some cases, the interviewer, interviewee, director, performer, or producer, and so on, corresponding to the first element of the information you provide in the entry in your list of works cited). See **12f**, item 59.

> Some playwrights might take a lesson from seeing how Talking Heads holds an audience in thrall with one actor and minimal sets.

> It takes an extraordinary actor to keep an audience enthralled by the topic of visits to a chiropodist (Redgrave).

L. Work by a corporation, government agency, or some other organization Give the complete name of the organization or agency in the introductory passage, or give a shortened form in parentheses. (See **12c**, item 9.)

```
                  ┌──────── full name ────────┐
```
A recent survey by the College Entrance Examination Board (CEEB) has shown that 43% of total enrollment in higher education is in two-year public institutions (14).

A recent survey shows that 43% of total enrollment in higher education is in two-year public institutions (College Board 14).
```
                                              └──────┬──────┘
                                               shortened name
```

M. Two authors with the same last name Include each author's first initial, or the whole first name if the authors' initials are the same.

A writer can be seen as both "author" and "secretary" and the two roles can be seen as competitive (F. Smith 19).

N. Multivolume work Indicate the volume number, followed by a colon, a space, and the page number. List the number of volumes in your works-cited list. (See **12c**, item 11.)

Barr and Feigenbaum note that "the concept of translation from one language to another by machine is older than the computer itself" (1: 233).

O. More than one work in a citation Separate two or more works with semicolons. Avoid making a parenthetical citation so long that it disrupts the flow of your text.

The links between a name and ancestry have occupied many writers and researchers (Waters 65; Antin 188).

P. Lecture, speech, or personal communication such as a letter, an interview, an e-mail, or a conversation In your text, give the name of the lecturer or person you communicated with. In your works-cited list, list the type of communication after the author or title. (See **12e**, item 49, and **12f**, item 53.)

According to George Kane, a vice president at Learning Network, Inc., online courses are more convenient, and often less expensive, than courses in actual classrooms.

Q. Literary works: fiction, poetry, and drama For well-known works published in several different editions, include information so readers may locate material in whatever edition they are using.

FOR A NOVEL Give the chapter or section number in addition to the page number in the edition you used: (104; ch. 3).

FOR A POEM Give line numbers, not page numbers: (lines 62–73). Subsequent line references can omit the word *lines*. Include up to three lines of poetry sequentially in your text, separated by a slash with a space on each side (/) (see **51f**). For four or more lines of poetry, begin on a new line, indent the whole passage one inch from the left, double-space throughout, and omit quotation marks from the beginning and end of the passage (see **10f**).

FOR CLASSIC POEMS, SUCH AS THE *ILIAD* Give the book or part number, followed by the line numbers, not page numbers: (8.21–25).

FOR A PLAY For dialogue, set the quotation off from your text, indented one inch with no quotation marks, and write the name of the character speaking in all capital letters, followed by a period. Indent subsequent lines of the same speech another quarter inch (three spaces). For a classic play, one published in several different editions (such as plays by William Shakespeare or Oscar Wilde), omit page numbers and cite in parentheses the act, scene, and line numbers of the quotation, in Arabic numerals. In your works-cited list, list the bibliographical details of the edition you used.

> Shakespeare's lovers in A Midsummer Night's Dream appeal to
> contemporary audiences accustomed to the sense of loss in love songs:
>> LYSANDER. How now, my love! Why is your cheek so pale?
>> How chance the roses there do fade so fast?
>> HERMIA. Belike for want of rain, which I could well
>> Beteem them from the tempest of mine eyes.
>> (1.1.133-36)

For a new play available in only one published edition, cite author and page numbers as you do for other MLA citations.

FOR SHAKESPEARE, CHAUCER, AND OTHER LITERARY WORKS Abbreviate titles cited in parentheses, such as the following: *Tmp.* for *The Tempest; 2H4* for *Henry IV, Part 2; MND* for *A Midsummer Night's Dream; GP* for the *General Prologue; PrT* for *The Prioress's Tale; Aen.* for *Aeneid; Beo.* for *Beowulf; Prel.* for Wordsworth's *Prelude.*

R. The Bible and other sacred texts Give book, chapter, and verse(s) in your text—Genesis 27.29 (with no underlining; see **52a**)—or abbreviate the book in a parenthetical citation (Gen. 27.29). Include an entry in your works-cited list only if you do not use the King James Version as your source. For other versions—and for other sacred texts—give the appropriate information in your works-cited list. See **12c**, item 18.

S. Two or more sequential references to the same work If you rely on several quotations from the same page within one of your paragraphs, one parenthetical reference after the last quotation is enough, but make sure that no quotations from other works intervene. If you are paraphrasing from and referring to one work several times in a paragraph, mention the author in your introductory phrase; cite the page number at the end of a paraphrase and again if you paraphrase from a different page. Make it clear to a reader where the paraphrase ends and your own comments take over (**9h**).

T. A long quotation Indent a quotation of four or more lines one inch or ten spaces, without enclosing the quotation in quotation marks. See page 135 for an example.

11d MLA explanatory footnotes and endnotes

With the MLA parenthetical style of documentation, use a footnote (at the bottom of the page) or an endnote (on a separate numbered page at the end of the paper before the works-cited list) only for notes giving supplementary information that clarifies or expands a point. You might use a note to refer to several supplementary bibliographical sources or to provide a comment that is interesting but not essential to your argument. Indicate a note with a raised number (superscript) in your text, after the word or sentence your note refers to. Begin the first line of each note one-half inch (or five spaces) from the left margin. Do not indent subsequent lines of the same note. Double-space endnotes. Single-space within each footnote, but double-space between notes.

NOTE NUMBER IN TEXT

Ethics have become an important part of many writing classes.[1]

CONTENT ENDNOTE

five spaces ———— raised number followed by space

←—↗[1] For additional discussion of ethics in the classroom, see Stotsky 799–806; Knoblauch 15–21; Bizzell 663–67; Friend 560–66.

The *MLA Handbook* also describes a system of footnotes or endnotes as an alternative to parenthetical documentation of references. This style is similar to the footnote and endnote style described in *The Chicago Manual of Style* (see **18**).

12 The MLA List of Works Cited

The references you make in your text to sources are brief—usually only the author's last name and a page number—so they allow readers to continue reading without interruption. For complete information about the source, readers can use your brief in-text citation as a guide to the full bibliographical reference in the list of works cited at the end of your paper.

12a Format and organization of the MLA list of works cited

Here are the basics for formatting and organizing your list.

KEY POINTS

Setting Up the MLA List of Works Cited

1. *What to list* List only works you actually cited in the text of your paper, not works you read but did not mention, unless your instructor requires you to include all the works you consulted as well as those mentioned in your text.

2. *Format of the list* Begin the list on a new numbered page after the last page of the paper or any endnotes. Center the heading (Works Cited) without quotation marks, underlining, or a period. Double-space throughout the list.

3. *Organization* Do not number the entries. List works alphabetically by author's last name (**12b**). List works with no stated author by the first main word of the title (**12c**, item 8, and **12d**, item 26).

4. *Indentation* To help readers find an author's name and to clearly differentiate one entry from another, indent all lines of each entry, except the first, one-half inch (or five spaces). A word processor can provide these "hanging indents" (**20a**, item 4).

(Continued)

(Continued)

 **TechNote**   Indentation Online

If you intend to publish on the Internet, it is often preferable to use no indentation at all (HTML does not support hanging indents well). Instead, follow each bibliographical entry with a line space. ■

5. *Periods*   Separate the main parts of each entry—author, title, publishing information—with a period, followed by one space.

6. *Capitals*   Capitalize the first letter of all words in titles of books and articles except *a, an, the,* coordinating conjunctions, *to* in an infinitive, and prepositions (such as *in, to, for, with, without, against*) unless they begin or end the title or subtitle.

7. *Underlining or italics*   Underline the titles of books and the names of journals and magazines as in the examples in this section. You may use italics instead if your instructor approves and if your printer makes a clear distinction from regular type.

 TechNote   Underlining versus Italics

If you write for publication on a World Wide Web site, avoid underlining titles of books and journals, because underlining is a signal for a hypertext link. Use italics, or consult your instructor or editor. ■

8. *Page numbers*   Give inclusive page numbers for print articles and sections of books. Do not use "p." ("pp.") or the word *page* (or *pages*) before page numbers in any reference. For page citations over 100 and sharing the same first number, use only the last two digits for the second number (for instance, 683–89, but 798–805). For an unpaginated work, write "n. pag."

12b   Guidelines for listing authors in the MLA list of works cited

Name of author(s)   Put the last name first for a single author or the first author: *Caro, Robert.* For two or more authors, reverse the names of only the first author: *Engleberg, Isa, and Ann Raimes.*

Alphabetical order   Alphabetize entries in the list by authors' last names. Note the following:

- Alphabetize by the exact letters in the spelling: *MacKay* precedes *McHam.*

- Let a shorter name precede a longer name beginning with the same letters: *Linden, Ronald* precedes *Lindenmayer, Arnold.*

- With last names using a prefix such as *le, du, di, del,* and *des,* alphabetize by the prefix: *Le Beau, Bryan F.*

- When *de* occurs with French names of one syllable, alphabetize under *d: De Jean, Denise.* Otherwise, alphabetize by last name: *Maupassant, Guy de.*

- Alphabetize by the first element of a hyphenated name: *Sackville-West, Victoria.*

- Alphabetize by the last name when the author uses two names without a hyphen: *Thomas, Elizabeth Marshall.*

Author not known For a work with no author named, alphabetize by the first word in the title other than *A, An,* or *The* (see **12c**, item 8, and **12d**, item 26).

Several works by the same author(s) For all entries after the first, replace the name(s) of the author(s) with three hyphens followed by a period, and alphabetize according to the first significant word in the title. If an author serves as an editor or translator, put a comma after the three hyphens, followed by the appropriate abbreviation ("ed." or "trans."). If, however, the author has coauthors, repeat all authors' names in full and put the coauthored entry after all the single-name entries for the author.

Goleman, Daniel. Destructive Emotions: A Scientific Dialogue with the
     Dalai Lama. New York: Bantam-Dell, 2003.

---. Working with Emotional Intelligence. New York: Bantam, 2000.

Goleman, Daniel, Paul Kaufman, and Michael L. Ray. "The Art of Creativity."
     Psychology Today Mar.–Apr. 1992: 40–47.

Authors with the same last name Alphabetize by first names: *Smith, Adam* precedes *Smith, Frank.*

12c Sample MLA entries: Print books and parts of books

On the title page of a book and on the copyright page (usually on the back of the title page), you will find the information you need for an entry.

- For place of publication when more than one city is mentioned, list only the first city mentioned.
- Use a shortened form of the publisher's name; usually one word is sufficient: *Houghton* (not *Houghton Mifflin*); *Basic* (not *Basic Books*). For university presses, use the abbreviations "U" and "P" (no periods): *Columbia UP; U of Chicago P.*
- Use the most recent year of copyright.

1. Basic form for a book with one author

first name
comma — period
last name
Sidel, Ruth. On Her Own: Growing Up in the Shadow of the American ——— title: underlined and initial letters capitalized ———

← Dream. New York: Viking, 1990. —period
indented 5 spaces   period | colon \ comma \ year
city of publication   publisher year

McCullough, David. John Adams. New York: Simon, 2001.

2. Book with two or more authors
Use authors' names in the order in which they appear in the book. Separate the names with commas. Reverse the order of only the first author's name.

second author's name
comma   not reversed
Lakoff, George, and Mark Johnson. Metaphors We Live By. Chicago:
U of Chicago P, 1980.

For a work with four or more authors, either list all the names or use only the first author's name followed by "et al." (Latin for "and others").

Bellah, Robert N., et al. Habits of the Heart: Individualism and
Commitment in American Life. Berkeley: U of California P, 1985.

3. Edited book
Use the abbreviation "ed." or "eds.," preceded by a comma, after the name(s) of the editor or editors.

Gates, Henry Louis, Jr., ed. Classic Slave Narratives. New York: NAL, 1987.

For a work with four or more editors, use only the name of the first, followed by a comma and "et al."

4. Author and editor
When an editor has prepared an author's work for publication, list the book under the author's name if you cite the author's work. Then, in your listing, include the name(s) of

the editor or editors after the title, introduced by "Ed." for one or more editors. "Ed." here stands for "edited by."

┌ author of letters ┐   name
                                                      ┌─ of editor ─┐
Bishop, Elizabeth. <u>One Art: Letters</u>. Ed. Robert Giroux.
    New York: Farrar, 1994.

If you cite a section written by the editor, such as a chapter introduction or a note, list the source under the name of the editor.

        name
┌── of editor ──┐ editor   ┌ author of letters ┐
Giroux, Robert, ed. <u>One Art: Letters</u>. By Elizabeth Bishop.
    New York: Farrar, 1994.

5. One work in an anthology (original or reprinted)   For a work included in an anthology, first list the author and title of the included work. Follow this with the title of the anthology, the name of the editor(s), publication information (place, publisher, date) for the anthology, and then, after the period, the pages in the anthology covered by the work you refer to.

  author of article
┌── or chapter ──┐
Des Pres, Terrence. "Poetry and Politics." <u>The Writer in Our World</u>.
means   name of editor
"edited by" ┌─ of anthology ─┐
    Ed. Reginald Gibbons. Boston: Atlantic Monthly, 1986. 17–29.
                          inclusive page numbers of article or chapter

Nye, Naomi Shihab. "My Brother's House." <u>The Riverside Reader</u>. 7th ed.
    Ed. Joseph Trimmer and Maxine Hairston. Boston: Houghton, 2002.
    171–81.

If the work in the anthology is a reprint of a previously published scholarly article, supply the complete information for both the original publication and the reprint in the anthology.

Gates, Henry Louis, Jr. "The Fire Last Time." <u>New Republic</u> 1 June 1992:
    37–43. Rpt. in <u>Contemporary Literary Criticism</u>. Ed. Jeffrey W. Hunter.
    Vol. 127. Detroit: Gale, 2000. 113–19.

6. More than one work in an anthology, cross-referenced   If you refer to more than one work from the same anthology, list the anthology separately, and list each essay with a cross-reference to the anthology. Alphabetize in the usual way, as in the following examples.

title of
┌─ author of article ─┐ ┌─ article in anthology ┐ editor of anthology
Des Pres, Terrence. "Poetry and Politics." Gibbons 17–29.
page numbers of article

editor of
┌─── anthology ───┐ ┌─── title of anthology ───┐
Gibbons, Reginald, ed. The Writer in Our World. Boston: Atlantic
Monthly, 1986.

author
┌─ of article ─┐ ┌─── title of article in anthology ───┐ editor of anthology
Walcott, Derek. "A Colonial's-Eye View of America." Gibbons 73–77.
page numbers of article

7. Entry in a reference book For a well-known reference book, give only the edition number and the year of publication. When entries are arranged alphabetically, omit volume and page numbers.

"Multiculturalism." The Columbia Encyclopedia. 6th ed. 2000.

8. Book with no author named Put the title first. Do not consider the words *A, An,* and *The* when alphabetizing the entries. The following entries would be alphabetized under *P* and *W.*

The PDR Family Guide to Natural Medicines and Healing Therapies.
New York: Three Rivers-Random, 1999.

Weather. New York: Discovery-Random, 1999.

9. Book by a corporation or government organization Alphabetize by the name of the corporate author. If the publisher is the same as the author, include the name again as publisher.

College Board. Trends in College Pricing: Annual Survey of Colleges.
New York: College Entrance Examination Board, 2002.

If no author is named for a government publication, begin the entry with the name of the federal, state, or local government, followed by the agency.

United States. Department of Labor. Occupational Outlook Handbook
2002–2003. Indianapolis: JIST, 2002.

10. Translated book After the title, include "Trans." followed by the name of the translator, first name first.

Grass, Günter. <u>Novemberland: Selected Poems, 1956–1993</u>. Trans.
Michael Hamburger. San Diego: Harcourt, 1996.

11. Multivolume work If you refer to more than one volume of a multivolume work, indicate the number of volumes (abbreviated "vols.") after the title.

Barr, Avon, and Edward A. Feigenbaum, eds. <u>The Handbook of Artificial
Intelligence</u>. 4 vols. Reading: Addison, 1981–86.

If you refer to only one volume of a work, limit the information in the entry to that one volume.

Feigenbaum, Edward A., and Paul R. Cohen, eds. <u>The Handbook of Artificial
Intelligence</u>. Vol. 3. Reading: Addison, 1985.

12. Book in a series Give the name of the series after the book title.

Connor, Ulla. <u>Contrastive Rhetoric: Cross-Cultural Aspects of Second Language
Writing</u>. Cambridge Applied Linguistics Ser. New York: Cambridge UP, 1996.

13. Book published under publisher's imprint State the names of both the imprint (the publisher within a larger publishing enterprise) and the larger publishing house, separated by a hyphen.

Richards, Thomas. <u>The Meaning of Star Trek</u>. New York: Anchor-Doubleday,
1999.

14. Foreword, preface, introduction, or afterword List the name of the author of the book element cited, followed by the name of the element, with no quotation marks. Give the title of the work; then use "By" to introduce the name of the author of the book (first name first). After the publication information, give inclusive page numbers for the book element cited.

Hemenway, Robert. Introduction. <u>Dust Tracks on a Road: An Autobiography</u>.
By Zora Neale Hurston. Urbana: U of Illinois P, 1984. ix–xxxix.

15. Republished book For a paperback edition of a hardcover book, give the original date of publication. Then cite information about the current publication.

Walker, Alice. <u>The Color Purple</u>. 1982. New York: Pocket, 1985.

16. Edition after the first After the title, give the edition number, using the abbreviation "ed."

Raimes, Ann. Keys for Writers. 4th ed. Boston: Houghton, 2005.

17. Book title including a title Do not underline a book title that is part of the source title. (However, if the title of a short work, such as a poem or short story, is part of the source title, enclose it in quotation marks.)

Hays, Kevin J., ed. The Critical Response to Herman Melville's

book title not underlined
Moby Dick. Westport: Greenwood, 1994.

18. The Bible or other sacred text For the King James Version of the Bible, no entry is necessary in the works-cited list (see **11c**, item R for the information to include in your in-text citation). For other versions and other religious texts, give the usual bibliographical details for a book.

Koran. Trans. George Sales. London: Warne, n.d.

(*n.d.* means no date is given.)

The New Testament in Modern English. Trans. J. B. Phillips. New York:
    Macmillan, 1972.

19. Dissertation For an unpublished dissertation, follow the title (in quotation marks) with "Diss." and the university and date.

Hidalgo, Stephen Paul. "Vietnam War Poetry: A Genre of Witness." Diss.
    U of Notre Dame, 1995.

Cite a published dissertation as you would a book, with place of publication, publisher, and date, but also include dissertation information after the title (for example, "Diss. U of California, 1998.").

If the dissertation is published by University Microfilms International (UMI), underline the title and include "Ann Arbor: UMI," the date, and the order number at the end of the entry.

Diaz-Greenberg, Rosario. The Emergence of Voice in Latino High School
    Students. Diss. U of San Francisco, 1996. Ann Arbor: UMI, 1996. 9611612.

If you cite an abstract published in *Dissertation Abstracts International,* give the relevant volume number and page number.

Hidalgo, Stephen Paul. "Vietnam War Poetry: A Genre of Witness." Diss.
    U of Notre Dame, 1995. DAI 56 (1995): 0931A.

12d Sample MLA entries: Print articles in periodicals

The conventions for listing print articles depend on whether the articles appear in newspapers, popular magazines, or scholarly journals. For distinguishing scholarly journals from other periodicals, see **8b**.

- For all types of periodicals, omit from your citation any introductory *A, An,* or *The* in the name of a newspaper, magazine, or scholarly journal.

- When giving dates of articles in journals, newspapers, and magazines, abbreviate all months except May, June, and July.

- If an article is only one page long, give that page number. For a longer article, give the range of page numbers (such as 24–27; 365–72). Your in-text citation will give the exact page on which you found the information.

- Do not use "p." or "pp." before page numbers.

20. Article in a scholarly journal: pages numbered consecutively through each volume   For journals with consecutive pagination through a volume (for example, the first issue of volume 1 ends with page 174, and the second issue of volume 1 begins with page 175), give the volume number, the year in parentheses, and page numbers.

Hesse, Douglas. "The Place of Creative Nonfiction." College English 65
     (2003): 237–41.

21. Article in a scholarly journal: each issue paged separately   For journals in which each issue begins with page 1, include the issue number after the volume number, separated from the volume number by a period, or include the issue number alone if no volume number is given.

Ginat, Rami. "The Soviet Union and the Syrian Ba'th Regime: From Hesitation
     to *Rapprochement.*" Middle Eastern Studies 36.2 (2000): 150–71.

22. Article in a magazine   For a magazine published every week or biweekly, give the complete date (day, month, and year, in that order, with no commas between them). For a monthly or bimonthly magazine, give only the month and year (see item 27). In either case, do not include volume and issue numbers. If the article is on only one page, give that page number. If the article covers two or more consecutive pages, list inclusive page numbers.

McGuigan, Cathleen. "Down from the Clouds." Newsweek 17 Mar. 2003: 64.

Scahill, Jeremy. "Inside Baghdad." Nation 7 Apr. 2003: 11–13.

MLA (Modern Language Association)

23. Article in a newspaper Omit an initial *The* in a newspaper title. Include the date after the newspaper title and the edition. For a newspaper that uses letters to designate sections, give the letter before the page number: "A23." For a numbered section, write, for example, "sec. 2: 23." See **12e**, item 37, for the online version of the article below.

Smith, Dinitia. "Critic at the Mercy of His Own Kind." New York Times
    24 May 2003, natl. ed: B9.

24. Article that skips pages When an article does not appear on consecutive pages (the one by Kilgannon begins on p. B1 and skips to p. B6), give only the first page number followed by a plus sign.

Kilgannon, Corey. "Get That Oak an Accountant." New York Times
    12 May 2003: B1+.

25. Review Begin with the name of the reviewer and the title of the review article, if these are available. After "Rev. of," provide the title and author of the work reviewed, followed by publication information for the periodical in which the review appears.

Hollander, Anne. "Men in Tights." Rev. of Why We Are What We Wear, by
    Paul Fussell. New Republic 10 Feb. 2003: 33–36.

26. Unsigned editorial or article Begin with the title. For an editorial, include the label "Editorial" after the title. In alphabetizing, ignore an initial *A, An,* or *The*.

"Santorum and Tolerance." Editorial. Wall Street Journal 25 Apr. 2003: A8.

27. Letter to the editor Write "Letter" or "Reply to letter of . . . " after the name of the author.

Ronk, Chris. Letter. Harper's May 2003: 5–6.

28. Abstract in an abstracts journal For abstracts of articles, provide exact information for the original work and add information about your source for the abstract: the title of the abstract journal, volume number, year, and item number or page number. (For dissertation abstracts, see **12c**, item 19.)

Van Dyke, Jan. "Gender and Success in the American Dance World."
    Women's Studies International Forum 19 (1996): 535–43.
    Studies on Women Abstracts 15 (1997): item 97W/081.

29. Article on microform (microfilm and microfiche) To cite sources that are neither in hard copy nor in electronic form, provide as much print publication information as is available along with the name of the microfilm or microfiche and any identifying features. Many newspaper and magazine articles published before 1980 are available only in microfiche or microfilm, so you will need to use this medium for historical research. However, be aware that such collections may be incomplete and difficult to read and duplicate clearly.

"War with Japan." Editorial. New York Times 8 Dec. 1941: 22.
    UMI University Microfilm.

Savage, David. "Indecency on Internet Faces High Court Test." Los Angeles
    Times 16 Mar. 1997. Newsbank: Law (1997): fiche 34, grid A6.

12e Sample MLA entries: Internet and other electronic sources

30. Internet and other electronic sources: information to include With the fast pace of change in the electronic world, standards are continually evolving for citing sources. For more information on citing Internet sources, refer to the MLA Web site at <http://www .mla.org>.

With whatever system of documentation you use, the basic question you need to ask is "What information does my reader need in order to access the same site and find the same information I found?" Internet sites vary in the amount of information they provide, and with some you need to go to the home page or search the site to find information. Scroll to the end of a page—the author's name and the date of posting often lurk there. *Note:* For all Web sources, you *must* provide the date when you found the material (your date of access) and the URL.

KEY POINTS

Documenting Internet Sources

1. *Information to include* As a general rule, follow this pattern, including as much of the information as is available:
    - author(s)
    - title of work
    - print publication information

(Continued)

(Continued)

- title of online site, project, journal, or database, underlined
- online publication information: date of latest update, volume and issue number of online journal, name of online service, sponsor of site, or name of discussion list
- date when you accessed the site
- electronic address (URL) enclosed in angle brackets and followed by a period

For specific examples, see **12e**, items 31–50.

2. *Dates* The last date in your source reference, immediately before the URL or keywords, should be the date when you accessed the material. Two dates might appear next to each other in a source reference, as in **12e**, items 36 and 37, but both are necessary: the first, the date when the work was posted or updated electronically; the second, the date when you found the material.

3. *URL* Break a URL for a new line only after a slash. Never insert a hyphen into a Web address (a URL), and never split a protocol (for example, http://) across lines.

4. *Page numbers only for print version* Include in your citation the page numbers for any print version of the source. For the electronic versions, include page or paragraph numbers of the on-screen version *only* if they are indicated on the screen. Page numbers are shown in PDF files, but otherwise they usually are not, so the page numbers on your printout of a source would not necessarily correspond to the page numbers on other printouts. When no page or paragraph information for the online version appears on the screen, include no page numbers in your list of references. For how to cite unpaged online material in your text, see **11c**, item J. See also **9h** on how to indicate where your citation ends.

5. *Permissions* Request permission to use any graphics or e-mail postings you include in your paper, especially if you intend to post your paper on a Web site. Make this request via e-mail.

---

31. Work in an online database or subscription service Libraries subscribe to large information services (such as *InfoTrac, FirstSearch, EBSCO, SilverPlatter, Dialog, SIRS,* and *LexisNexis*) to gain access to extensive databases of online articles, as well as to specialized databases (such as *ERIC, Contemporary Literary Criticism, and PsycINFO*). You can use these databases to locate abstracts and full texts of thousands of articles.

The URLs used to access databases are useful only to those accessing them through a subscribing organization such as a college library or a public library. In addition, database URLs tend not to remain stable, changing day by day, so providing a URL at the end of your citation will not be helpful to your readers unless you know it will be persistent. Cite articles in library databases by providing the following information:

- last and first name of author(s)
- title of article, in quotation marks
- print information for the article (name of journal, underlined; date and pages, if the full range of pages is given online), or the starting page followed by a hyphen, space, and period (for example, 26- .)
- name of the database (underlined)
- name of the service providing the database (for example, *Lexis-Nexis, EBSCO, InfoTrac*)
- name of library system (add city and state if necessary)
- your date of access
- the URL of the document only if it is persistent and not impossibly long, otherwise the URL of the search page or home page—or no URL at all
- a period at the end

The examples that follow show citations of a magazine article, a scholarly article, an article in an academic journal, and a newspaper article, all accessed from different databases.

print publication
information   starting page of article

Gray, Katti. "The Whistle Blower." Essence Feb. 2001: 148- . Academic

date
of access

database   service   library

Search Premier. EBSCO. City U of New York Lib. 12 May 2003

EBSCO database provides a persistent URL

<http://search.epnet.com/direct.asp?an=4011390&db=aph>.

The screenshots on page 165 show the information you need to include.

Lowe, Michelle S. "Britain's Regional Shopping Centres: New Urban
    volume and issue number for print version of scholarly article
    Forms?" Urban Studies 37.2 (2000): 261– . Academic Search Elite.

    EBSCO. Brooklyn Public Lib., Brooklyn, NY. 3 May 2003

    <http://search.epnet.com/direct.asp?an=2832704&db=afh>.

Toplin, Robert Brent. "Cinematic History: A Defense of Hollywood."
    National Forum Spring 2000: 10– . Expanded Academic ASAP.
    InfoTrac. City U of New York Lib. 13 May 2003
          URL of home page
         — of service —
    <http://www.galegroup.com>.

Weeks, Linton. "History Repeating Itself; Instead of Describing Our
    Country's Past, Two Famous Scholars Find Themselves Examining
    Their Own." Washington Post 24 Mar. 2002: F01– . Academic
    Universe: News. LexisNexis. City U of New York Lib. 8 Sept. 2003
        — URL of home page —
    <http://web.lexis-nexis.com/>.

If the service provider provides a direct link to a licensed database
without displaying the URL of the accessed database, give the name
of the database, the name of the subscription service or library, and
your date of access. Specify any path or keywords that you used to
access the source.

"Parthenon." The Columbia Encyclopedia. 6th ed. 2000. America Online.
    12 Apr. 2003. Keywords: Reference; Encyclopedias; Encyclopedia.com;
    Bartleby.com; Columbia Encyclopedia 6th ed.

Verdon, Mary E., and Leonard H. Sigel. "Recognition and Management of
    Lyme Disease." American Family Physician 56.2 (1997). NOAH
    (New York Online Access to Health). Brooklyn Public Lib., Brooklyn, NY.
    2 Apr. 2002. Path: Health Topics; Lyme Disease; Diagnosis and Symptoms.

32. Online book or text   Give whatever is available of the following: author, title, editor or translator (if applicable), print publication
information, electronic publication information and date, date of
access, and complete electronic address (URL).

```
     ┌── author ──┐  ┌──── title of work ────┐
```
               print publication
               ┌──── information ────┐
Darwin, Charles. The Voyage of the Beagle. London: John Murray, 1859.

```
                    date of electronic
┌─ title of database ─┐  ┌─ publication ─┐  ┌─name of sponsor of site ─┐
```
               Oxford Text Archive. 28 Mar. 2000. Arts and Humanities Data

```
                                          date of
                                        ┌─ access ─┐
```
Service, Oxford Computing Services. 11 May 2003

```
electronic address enclosed
┌─ in angle brackets ─┐
```
<http://ota.ahds.ac.uk>.

FULL TEXT OF ARTICLE

URL is not persistent and is too long for a citation.

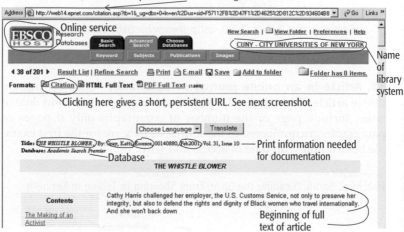

INFORMATION IN "CITATION" LINK

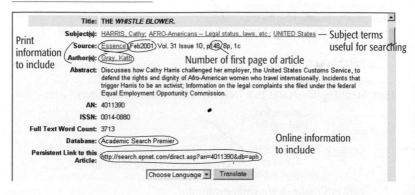

33. Online poem

print   print publication

┌── author ──┐ ┌ title of poem ┐ ┌── source ──┐ ┌────── information ──────┐
Levine, Philip. "What Work Is." <u>What Work Is</u>. New York: Knopf, 1991.

date of electronic   sponsor
┌────── title of database ──────┐ ┌ updating ┐ ┌────── of site ──────┐
<u>Internet Poetry Archive</u>. 4 Apr. 2000. U of North Carolina P.

date of   electronic address (URL)
┌── access ──┐ ┌────── enclosed in angle brackets ──────┐
12 May 2003 <http://www.ibiblio.org/ipa/levine/work.html>.

34. Article in a reference database

date of electronic
┌── title of article ──┐ ┌────── title of database ──────┐ ┌ update ┐
"Bloomsbury Group." <u>Columbia Encyclopedia</u> 6th ed. 7 July 2000.

date of
┌── sponsor ──┐ ┌── access ──┐
Bartleby.com. 7 Sept. 2003 <http://www.bartleby.com/65/

bl/Bloomsbury.html>.

35. Article in an online journal or newsletter

Give the author, title of article, title of journal, volume and issue numbers, and date of issue. Include page or the number of paragraphs only if pages or paragraphs are numbered in the source, as they are for the first example below. End with date of access and URL.

┌── author ──┐ ┌────────── title of article ──────────┐
Hatchuel, Sarah. "Leading the Gaze: From Showing to Telling in Kenneth

name of   volume and
┌────── online journal ──────┐ issue number
Branagh's <u>Henry V</u> and <u>Hamlet</u>." <u>Early Modern Literary Studies</u> 6.1

date of online number of paragraphs date of
publication (numbered in the text) access
(2000): 22 pars. 10 May 2003 <http://www.shu.ac.uk/emls/06-1/

hatchbra.htm>.

┌── author ──┐ ┌────── title of article ──────┐
Hart, Stephen. "Overtures to a New Discipline: Neuromusicology." <u>21st</u>

volume and
issue numbers date of
title of online journal ┌── access ──┐
<u>Century</u> 1.4 (July 1996). 8 Sept. 2003 <http://www.columbia.edu/
└ date of ┘ └── no numbered pages or paragraphs ──┘
electronic publication

cu/21stC/issue-1.4/mbmmusic.html>.

36. Article in an online magazine

Charoenying, Timothy. "Jazz at the Crossroads." Atlantic Online 26 Feb. 2003.
10 Sept. 2003 <http://www.theatlantic.com/unbound/flashbks/jazz.htm>.

37. Article in an online newspaper

Smith, Dinitia. "Critic at the Mercy of His Own Kind." New York Times
on the Web 24 May 2003. 25 May 2003 <http://www.nytimes.com/
2003/05/24/books/24WOOD.html>.

Daley, Beth. "U.S. Is Seeking New Riches with Claims to Ocean Floor."
Boston Globe Online 11 May 2003. 12 May 2003 <http://boston.com/
dailyglobe2/131/nation/US_is_seeking_new_riches_with_claims_to
_ocean_floor+.shtml>.

38. Review, editorial, abstract, or letter in an online publication

After author and title, identify the type of text: "Letter," "Editorial,"
"Abstract," or "Rev. of . . . by . . ." (see **12d**, items 25–28). Continue
with details of the electronic source.

39. Scholarly project online

   title of scholarly   date of electronic   sponsor
 ┌────── project ──────┐   ┌──── editor ────┐ ┌─ publication ─┐ ┌────┐
Perseus Digital Library. Ed. Gregory Crane. Updated daily. Tufts U.

      date of
  ┌─ access ─┐
  9 Sept. 2003 <http://www.perseus.tufts.edu>.

40. Professional site online

                            date of
 ┌────── title of professional site ──────┐ ┌─ update ─┐ ┌─── sponsor ───
MLA: Modern Language Association. 9 May 2003. Mod. Lang. Assn.

        date of
      ┌─ access ─┐
 ────┐ ┌──────┐
of Amer. 8 Sept. 2003 <http://www.mla.org>.

41. Government publication online

Begin with the government
and agency, title of the work, and place and date of print publication.
Follow this with the date of electronic posting or update, the date of
access, and the URL.

United States. Dept. of Educ. Office of Educ. Research and Improvement.
Natl. Center for Educ. Statistics. Digest of Education Statistics, 2000.
Washington: GPO, 2001. Jan. 2001. 5 Feb. 2002 <http://nces.ed.gov/
pubs2001/digest>.

42. Personal Web page   If a personal Web page has a title, supply it, underlined. Otherwise, use the designation "Home page."

personal site with   date of
  ┌─ no title ─┐ ┌─ update ─┐
Heiss, Jon. Home page. 3 Dec. 2002. 14 May 2003
    <http://www.unity.edu/WebDesign/jheiss.html>.

43. Course page   For a course home page, give name of instructor and course, the words *course home page,* the dates of the course, the department and institution, and then your access date and the URL.

Raimes, Ann. Expository Writing. Course home page. Sept. 2002–Dec. 2002.
    Dept. of English, Hunter Coll. 12 Dec. 2002 <http://bb.hunter.cuny.edu>.

44. Online posting in a discussion list, Web forum, bulletin board service or Usenet   Give the author's name, title of document (as written in the subject line), the label "Online posting," and the date of posting. Follow this with the name of the forum, date of access, and URL or address of discussion list. For a Usenet newsgroup, give the name and address of the group, beginning with the prefix "news:".

Desai, Satish. "Foreign Expense Deductions." Online posting. 11 May 2003.
    Explainer Forum in "The Fray" in Slate. 12 May 2003 <http://
    bbs.slate.msn.com/?id=3936&m=6843070>.

Cromm, Oliver. "Crossers of the Atlantic." Online posting. 6 May 2003.
    9 May 2003 <news:alt.usage.english>.

Howard, Rebecca Moore. "Institutional Pressures." Online posting.
    16 Apr. 2003. WPA-L. 18 Apr. 2003 <WPA-L@asu.edu>.

To make it easy for readers to find a posting, refer whenever possible to one stored in Web archives.

Howard, Rebecca Moore. "Institutional Pressures." Online posting. 16 Apr.
    2003. WPA-L Archives. 10 May 2003 <http://lists.asu.edu/cgi-bin/
    wa?A1=ind0304&L=wpa-l>.

To cite a forwarded document in an online posting, include author, title, and date, followed by "Fwd. by" and the name of the person forwarding the document. End with "Online posting," the date of the forwarding, the name of the discussion group, date of access, and address of the discussion list.

Assembly Internet Information Service. "Focus on the Legislative Budget
    Accord." 2 May 2003. Fwd. by Ken Sherrill. Online posting. 2 May
    2003. Hunter–l. 4 May 2003 <http://hunter.listserv.cuny.edu>.

45. Synchronous communication When citing a source from a chat room, a MUD (multiuser domain), or a MOO (multiuser domain, object-oriented), give the name of the person speaking or posting information, the type of event, title, date, forum, date of access, and electronic address. Refer to archived material whenever possible.

Day, Michael. Discussion of e-mail and argument. C-Fest 12. 19 June 1996. LinguaMOO. 9 May 2003 <http://lingua.utdallas.edu:7000/2007/>.

46. Work of art online

Duchamp, Marcel. Bicycle Wheel. 1951. Museum of Mod. Art, New York. 9 May 2003 <http://www.moma.org/exhibitions/1999/index.html>.

47. Television and radio programs online

Montagne, Renee. "Ed Ricketts and the 'Dream' of Cannery Row." Morning Edition. Natl. Public Radio. 7 May 2003. NPR Audio Online 8 May 2003 <http://www.npr.org/display-pages/features/feature_1252560.html>.

48. Film or film clip online

Hough, Paul, dir. End of the Line. 2001. 5 May 2003 <http://www.ifilm.com/filmdetail?ifilmid=2398940&cch=20>.

49. Personal e-mail message Treat this like a letter (**12f**, item 53).

Kane, George. "New Developments." E-mail to the author. 8 May 2003.

50. Other Internet sources Identify online interviews, maps, charts, sound recordings, cartoons, and advertisements as you would sources that are not online (see **12f**), with the addition of electronic publication information, date of access, and the URL.

51. Electronic source medium not known When you use a computer network to access information, you may not know whether the material is on the library's hard drive or on CD-ROM. In such a case, use the word *Electronic* for the medium, and give the name and sponsor of the network, followed by your date of access.

"Renaissance." 1996. Concise Columbia Electronic Encyclopedia. Electronic. ColumbiaNet. Columbia U Lib. 18 July 2000.

52. CD-ROM Cite material from a CD-ROM published as a single edition (that is, with no regular updating) in the same way you cite a book, but after the title add the medium of publication and any version or release number.

Keats, John. "To Autumn." Columbia Granger's World of Poetry. CD-ROM. Rel. 3. New York: Columbia UP, 1999.

To cite an updated database on CD-ROM, include any print publication information, the name of the database, the label "CD-ROM," the name of the producer or distributor, and the electronic publication date.

Dowd, Maureen. "Spite or Art?" New York Times 23 Apr. 2000: 11. New York Times Ondisc. CD-ROM. UMI-ProQuest. 2000.

12f Sample MLA entries: Miscellaneous sources

53. Lecture, speech, letter, personal communication, or interview For a lecture or speech, give the author and title, if known. For a presentation with no title, include a label such as "Lecture" or "Address" after the name of the speaker. Also give the name of any organizing sponsor, the venue, and the date.

Parry, Kate. Lecture. Hunter College, New York. 16 Apr. 2003.

For a letter that you received, include the phrase "Letter to the author" after the name of the letter writer. For an interview that you conducted, indicate the type of interview ("Personal interview," "Telephone interview").

Rogan, Helen. Letter to the author. 3 Feb. 2003.

Gingold, Toby. Telephone interview. 5 May 2003.

Cite a published letter as you would cite a work in an anthology. After the name of the author, include any title the editor gives the letter and the date. Add the page numbers for the letter at the end of the citation.

Bishop, Elizabeth. "To Robert Lowell." 26 Nov. 1951. One Art: Letters. Ed. Robert Giroux. New York: Farrar, 1994. 224–26.

54. Published or broadcast interview For print, radio, or TV interviews that have no title, include the label "Interview" after the name of the person interviewed, followed by the bibliographical information for the source.

Guest, Christopher. Interview. Charlie Rose. PBS. WNET, New York. 13 May 2003.

55. Map or chart Underline the title of the map or chart, and include the designation after that title.

Auvergne/Limousin. Map. Paris: Michelin, 1996.

56. Film or video   List the title, director, performers, and any other pertinent information. End with the name of the distributor and the year of distribution.

Sunshine. Dir. Istvan Szabo. Perf. Ralph Fiennes. Paramount, 2000.

When you cite a videocassette or DVD, include the date of the original film, the medium, the name of the distributor of the DVD or cassette, and the year of the new release.

Casablanca. Dir. Michael Curtiz. Perf. Humphrey Bogart and Ingrid Bergman.
　　　1943. DVD. MGM, 1998.

57. Television or radio program   Give the title of the program episode; the title of the program; any pertinent information about performers, writer, narrator, or director; the network; and the local station and date of broadcast.

"The Difference between Us." Race: The Power of an Illusion. Narr. C. C. H.
　　　Pounder. Dir. Christine Herbes-Sommers. PBS. WLIW, New York.
　　　18 May 2003.

58. Sound recording   List the composer or author, the title of the work, the names of artists, the production company, and the date. If the medium is not a compact disc, indicate the medium, such as "Audiocassette," before the name of the production company.

Scarlatti, Domenico. Keyboard Sonatas. Andras Schiff, piano. London, 1989.

Walker, Alice. Interview with Kay Bonetti. Audiocassette. Columbia:
　　　American Audio Prose Library, 1981.

59. Live performance   Give the title of the play, the author, pertinent information about the director and performers, the theater, the location, and the date of performance. If you are citing an individual's role in the work, begin your citation with the person's name.

Talking Heads. By Alan Bennett. Perf. Lynn Redgrave. Minetta Lane Theater,
　　　New York. 2 Apr. 2003.

Redgrave, Lynn, perf. Talking Heads. By Alan Bennett. Minetta Lane Theater,
　　　New York. 2 Apr. 2003.

60. Work of art, slide, or photograph   List the name of the artist, the title of the work (underlined), the name of the museum, gallery, or owner, and the city.

Johns, Jasper. Racing Thoughts. Whitney Museum of Amer. Art, New York.

For a photograph in a book, give complete publication information, including the page number on which the photograph appears.

Johns, Jasper. Racing Thoughts. Whitney Museum of Amer. Art, New York.
    The American Century: Art and Culture 1950–2000. By Lisa Phillips.
    New York: Norton, 1999. 311.

For a slide in a collection, include the slide number (Slide 17).

61. Cartoon   After the cartoonist's name and the title (if any) of the cartoon, add the label "Cartoon." Follow this with the usual information about the source, and give the page number.

Chast, Roz. "Cloud Chart." Cartoon. New Yorker 14 Apr. 2003: 59.

62. Advertisement   Give the name of the product or company, followed by the label "Advertisement" and publication information. If a page is not numbered, write "n. pag."

Scholastic. Advertisement. Ebony Feb. 2003: n. pag.

63. Legal or historical source   For a legal case, give the name of the case with no underlining or quotation marks; the number of the case; the name of the court deciding the case; and the date of the decision.

Roe v. Wade. No. 70–18. Supreme Ct. of the US. 22 Jan. 1973.

If you mention the case in your text, underline it.

Chief Justice Burger, in Roe v. Wade (209), noted that . . .

For an act, give the name of the act, its Public Law number, its date, and its Statutes at Large cataloging number.

USA Patriot Act. Pub. L. 107–56. 26 Oct. 2001. Stat. 115.272.

Cite the section of a familiar historical document, such as the Constitution, in parentheses in your text (US Const., art. 2, sec. 4), with no entry in your works-cited list.

13   Sample Documented Paper, MLA Style

Section **7f** shows how Lindsay Camp did research for a paper required in her first-year composition course. Here is her complete, revised paper, with citations for the sources she used and a corresponding works-cited list. If your instructor requires a separate title page, see **3f** or ask for guidelines.

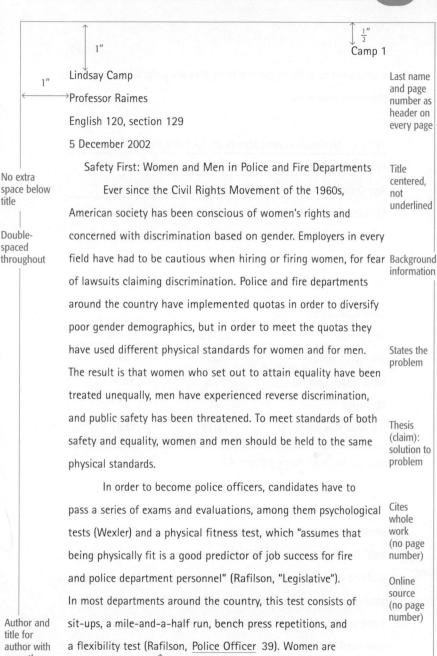

1"

1/2"

Camp 1

Last name and page number as header on every page

Lindsay Camp

1"

Professor Raimes

English 120, section 129

5 December 2002

Safety First: Women and Men in Police and Fire Departments

Title centered, not underlined

No extra space below title

Double-spaced throughout

Ever since the Civil Rights Movement of the 1960s, American society has been conscious of women's rights and concerned with discrimination based on gender. Employers in every field have had to be cautious when hiring or firing women, for fear of lawsuits claiming discrimination. Police and fire departments around the country have implemented quotas in order to diversify poor gender demographics, but in order to meet the quotas they have used different physical standards for women and for men. The result is that women who set out to attain equality have been treated unequally, men have experienced reverse discrimination, and public safety has been threatened. To meet standards of both safety and equality, women and men should be held to the same physical standards.

Background information

States the problem

Thesis (claim): solution to problem

In order to become police officers, candidates have to pass a series of exams and evaluations, among them psychological tests (Wexler) and a physical fitness test, which "assumes that being physically fit is a good predictor of job success for fire and police department personnel" (Rafilson, "Legislative"). In most departments around the country, this test consists of sit-ups, a mile-and-a-half run, bench press repetitions, and a flexibility test (Rafilson, <u>Police Officer</u> 39). Women are

Cites whole work (no page number)

Online source (no page number)

Author and title for author with more than one work cited

1"

Camp 2

encouraged to apply, but in the tests they are judged by lower

standards than men.

Table 1   Minimum Fitness Standards for Entry to the Academy

Female Candidates		
Age Group	20–29	30–39
Sit-ups (1 minute)	35	27
Sit & Reach (inches)	20	19
Push-ups	18	14
1.5-Mile Run (minutes)	14:55	15:26
Male Candidates	~	
Age Group	20–29	30–39
Sit-ups (1 minute)	40	36
Sit & Reach (inches)	17.5	16.5
Push-ups	33	27
1.5-Mile Run (minutes)	12:18	12:51

Source: Rafilson, Police Officer 47.

Comments on table and explains data

Table 1 shows that women are given from 2 minutes and 37

seconds to 3 minutes and 15 seconds extra to run a mile-and-a-

half. That could mean the difference between catching a suspect

and not catching a suspect. Men have to complete 13 to 15 more

push-ups than women because women generally do not have the

same amount of upper body strength as men. But police officers

may need to climb fences, lift heavy items, or carry injured people;

Camp 3

certainly firefighters may need to carry injured people and heavy hoses.

Recognizing that the physical fitness tests are flawed, police and fire departments have been turning to a different test, called a physical agility exam, in which the candidate must complete an obstacle course. For the New York Police Department's agility exam, candidates are required to wear a 10.5 lb utility belt as they run out of a patrol car, climb a six-foot wall, run up four flights of stairs, drag a 160 lb dummy 30 feet, run back down four flights of stairs, climb a four-foot wall, and run back to the patrol car (Rafilson, Police Officer 40-42). Such tasks are seen as relevant to what a police officer actually encounters while on duty. All candidates must complete every part of the obstacle course in the same amount of time in order to pass the exam, regardless of sex, age, or weight. The obstacles in the course and the time allotted may vary between departments, but there is no partiality given based on ethnicity, gender, or age. Women may need to be provided with preparation and training for the test, as an article in The Police Chief points out (Polisar and Milgram), but they should still be required to take and pass it.

More and more police and fire departments are now using the physical agility test instead of the fitness test. According to Dr. Fred M. Rafilson, the fitness model was popular because it "allows fire departments to hire more women because passing standards are adjusted based on a person's age, sex, and weight," but, as he says, a "woman can pass a fitness model test for the

Gives page numbers for print source

Online source

Gives author's credentials

Camp 4

fire service and still not be able to perform essential job functions that require a great deal of upper body and leg strength" ("Legislative"). Some programs have been established to help prepare women for the new tests. The program at the University of Victoria in British Columbia, Canada, culminates in having women carry "65-pound pumps and heavy fire hoses across the infield of the warm-up track" (Liscomb). Figure 1 shows a participant in action.

Fig. 1. From Robie Liscomb, "Preparing Women for Firefighting in B.C."

Many see upper body strength as crucial. Firefighters are very much like a family, trust each other like brothers, and in a fire emergency may have to make life and death decisions. They need to know that the person next to them can handle all of the duties of the job. Thomas P. Butler, a spokesman for the Uniformed Firefighters Association, the firefighters' union, points out that "this is a job

Camp 5

where one firefighter's life and safety depends on another. It is
important that we attract the best and the brightest" (qtd. in
Baker). Any person who cannot perform the tasks of a firefighter
poses "a direct threat to human life and safety" (Rafilson,
"Legislative") and does not belong on the job.

Work is one page long--no page number necessary in citation

Frances Heidensohn's thorough study of women in law
enforcement in the U.S.A. and in Britain does, however, point out that
many women have "questioned the relevance and purpose of the
physical standards as . . . irrelevant to policing" (170). Women in the
police force testified that while they had been tested on doing a
"body drag," they never had seen it done or had to do this on the job.
And, of course, we all can recognize that having different (and lower)
standards for women does allow more women to be hired as career
officers and helps departments with affirmative action requirements.

Considers opposing views

Establishes common ground ("we all")

Those on the job, however, still question the wisdom of
different testing criteria. Douglass Mignone, a first lieutenant of the
Purchase Fire Department and a New York City Fire Department
applicant, for example, sees the situation as one of safety rather
than equality of opportunity. When asked in a telephone interview
for his view on women in the Fire Department, he replied:

Uses evidence from interview to refute the opposing views

> If you were in a burning building and had the choice
> between my girlfriend Sinead, a five-foot-five, 130 lb
> woman, or myself, a six-foot-two, 200 lb man, to get you
> out alive, who would you choose? I have no problem with
> women being firefighters as long as they meet the same
> requirements and undergo the same training as myself.

Indents a long quotation

Camp 6

This view is the consensus among male police officers and male firefighters, but not that of the general public. The general idea of safety seems to be slipping past the newspapers and television. There are no activists standing outside City Hall crying, "What about our safety?" "Make physical requirements equal" (Rafilson, "Legislative"). There will be no activists, no protests, and no media until someone dies or until there is a tragedy.

Added to the issue of safety is the issue of equality. In 1964, Congress prohibited discrimination based on race, color, sex, national origin, or religion under the Civil Rights Act of 1964

Broadens the picture to legislation

(Brooks 26). In 1991, Congress passed the 1991 Civil Rights Act, which made it illegal to use different standards for hiring men and women. The 1991 Civil Rights Act says it like this:

> It shall be an unlawful employment practice for a respondent in connection with the selection or referral of applicants to adjust the scores of, use different cut-off scores for, or otherwise alter the results of employment related tests on the basis of race, color,

Cites work in which quotation appears

> religion, sex, or national origin. (qtd. in Rafilson, "Legislative")

Title VII under this Act claims the employer accused of "disparate impact" would have to prove business necessity. This has left police and fire departments all over the country confused and asking themselves what to do and whom to hire next.

Camp 7

Are police and fire departments going to claim that the
physiological differences between men and women make different
physical standards a business necessity? According to Special Agent
Michael E. Brooks:

> The challenge comes when a male cannot meet the
> male standard but can meet the female standard. Such
> an action amounts to express disparate treatment of the
> male. Disparate treatment, like disparate impact, is only
> permissible under the business necessity justification.
> The administrator who uses different physical selection
> standards for female applicants would, therefore, have
> to show what business necessity justifies such a
> practice. (31)

Controversy and confusion abound, and male applicants are
filing lawsuits claiming reverse discrimination. The Edmonton Fire
Department has a "diversity" policy in which the 12 positions that
were available did not go to the top 12 applicants but to women
and minorities (Champion). Two groups of rejected applicants filed
complaints with the Alberta Human Rights Commission claiming
that "the City of Edmonton exercised race and gender bias in
denying them employment" (Champion).

The process of applying to be hired in a police or fire
department must be clear to all and equitable to all. Only those
with the highest scores on the written exam should be eligible to
take the physical agility test. Then only the candidates who pass

Question draws readers into issue

Summation

the physical should qualify for further testing and employment. Men who fail any of the tests should not be hired--nor should women. If police and fire departments lower standards for anyone, they are putting the general public's safety on the line as well as their fellow officers'. Peter Horne, an assistant professor at Meramec Community College, says it succinctly: "Females and males should take the same physical agility test. Then it would not matter whether a recruit is 5'8" or 5'4", or a male or female, but only whether he/she possesses the physical capability to do the job" (33-34). The cost to safety is much too great for women to be held to lower requirements than men.

Reiteration of thesis

Camp 9

Works Cited

Baker, Al. "Fire Department Looks to Diversify the Ranks." New York
Times 3 Apr. 2002: B3. Academic Universe: News. LexisNexis.
City U of New York Lib. 25 Oct. 2002
<http://web.lexis-nexis.com/>.

Brooks, Michael E. "Law Enforcement Physical Fitness Standard and
Title VII." FBI Law Enforcement Bulletin May 2001: 26–33.

Champion, Chris. "Male Honkies Need Not Apply." Western Report
7 Aug. 1996: 24– . Academic Search Premier. EBSCO. City U
of New York Lib. 27 Oct. 2002 <http://search.epnet.com/
direct.asp?an=9607267865&db=aph>.

Heidensohn, Frances. Women in Control? The Role of Women in
Law Enforcement. New York: Oxford UP, 1992.

Horne, Peter. Women in Law Enforcement. 2nd ed. Springfield:
Thomas, 1980.

Liscomb, Robie. "Preparing Women for Firefighting in B.C."
The Ring 6 Feb. 1998. University of Victoria Sport and
Fitness Centre. 28 Oct. 2002 <http://
communications.uvic.ca/ring/98feb06/firefighting.html>.

Mignone, Douglass. Telephone interview. 19 Oct. 2002.

Polisar, Joseph, and Donna Milgram. "Recruiting, Integrating
and Retaining Women Police Officers: Strategies That
Work." The Police Chief Oct. 1998. IWITTS in the News.
Institute for Women in Trades, Technology, and Science.
27 Oct. 2002 <http://www.iwitts.com/html/
the_police_chief.htm>.

Entries
organized
alphabetically

Article from a
subscription
database
with URL of
home page

Database
gives first
page
number
only

Title
centered,
not
underlined

Article
spans
consecutive
pages

EBSCO
provides
persistent
URL

½″

Published
work on
Web site

Camp 10

Rafilson, Fred M. "Legislative Impact on Fire Service Physical

Fitness Testing." Fire Engineering Apr. 1995: 83- .

Academic Search Premier. EBSCO. City U of New York Lib.

23 Oct. 2002 <http://search.epnet.com/

direct.asp?an=9505024136&db=aph>.

Second entry for author ———. Police Officer. 15th ed. United States: Arco, 2000.

Wexler, Ann Kathryn. Gender and Ethnicity as Predictors of

Psychological Qualification for Police Officer Candidates.

Diss. California School of Professional Psychology, 1996.

Ann Arbor: UMI, 1996. 9625522.

List includes only sources actually cited in the paper

APA, CBE, *Chicago*, and CGOS Documentation

PART 4   APA, CBE, *Chicago*, and CGOS Documentation

AT A GLANCE: INDEX OF APA STYLE FEATURES

SAMPLES OF APA IN-TEXT CITATIONS (14b)

SAMPLES OF ENTRIES IN APA LIST OF REFERENCES
Print Books and Parts of Books (15c)

Print Articles in Periodicals (15d)

Internet and Other Electronic Sources (15e)

Miscellaneous Sources (15f)

APA (American Psychological Association)

In Part 4 you will find descriptions of documentation systems other than the MLA system. Sections **14**, **15**, and **16** focus on the style recommended for the social sciences by the *Publication Manual of the American Psychological Association*, 5th ed. (Washington, DC: Amer. Psychological Assn., 2001), and on the APA Web site at <http://www.apastyle.org>. A student's paper written in APA style is presented in section **16**. Section **17** describes the citation-sequence style recommended by the Council of Biology Editors, now renamed the Council of Science Editors (CBE/CSE). Section **18** describes the endnote and footnote style recommended in *The Chicago Manual of Style*, 15th ed. (Chicago: U of Chicago P, 2003), for writing in the humanities; it is sometimes used as an alternative to MLA style. Section **19** outlines the system recommended in *The Columbia Guide to Online Style* (New York: Columbia UP, 1998) and at <http://www.columbia.edu/cu/cup/cgos> for citing online sources in the humanities and sciences.

14 Citing Sources, APA Style

14a Two basic features of APA style

KEY POINTS

Two Basic Features of APA Style

1. *In the text of your paper*, include at least two pieces of information each time you cite a source:

    the last name(s) of the author (or authors);

    the year of publication.

2. *At the end of your paper*, include on a new numbered page a list entitled "References," double-spaced and arranged alphabetically by authors' last names, followed by initials of first and other names, the date in parentheses, and other bibliographical information. See **15** for the information to include in an APA-style reference list.

14b APA author/year style for in-text citations

A. One author If you mention the author's last name in your own sentence, include the year in parentheses directly after the author's name.

author   year
Wilson (1994) has described in detail his fascination with insects.

(See **15c**, item 1, to see how this work appears in a reference list.)

If you do not name the author in your sentence, include both the name and the year, separated by a comma, in parentheses.

The army retreated from Boston in disarray, making the rebels realize that they had achieved a great victory (McCullough, 2001).
                                 author   comma year

If you use a direct quotation, include in parentheses the abbreviation "p." or "pp." followed by a space and the page number(s). Separate items within parentheses with commas.

Memories are built "around a small collection of dominating images" (Wilson, 1994, p. 5).
comma comma   page number
                  with a quotation

B. More than one author For a work by two authors, name both in the order in which their names appear on the work. Within parentheses, use an ampersand (&) between the names, in place of *and.*

Kanazawa and Still (2000) in their analysis of a large set of data show that the statistical likelihood of being divorced increases if one is male and a secondary school teacher or college professor.

Analysis of a large set of data shows that the statistical likelihood of being divorced increases if one is male and a secondary school teacher or college professor (Kanazawa & Still, 2000).
                     ampersand in parentheses

(See **15d**, item 13, to see how this work appears in a reference list.)

For a work with three to five authors or editors, identify all of them the first time you mention the work. In later references, use only the first author's name followed by "et al." (for "and others") in place of the other names.

Jordan, Kaplan, Miller, Stiver, and Surrey (1991) have examined the idea of *self*.

Increasingly, the self is viewed as connected to other human beings (Jordan et al., 1991).

(**15c**, item 2, shows how this work appears in a reference list.)

For six or more authors, use the name of the first author followed by "et al." both for the first mention and in a parenthetical citation.

C. Author with more than one work published in one year Identify each work with a lowercase letter after the date: (Zamel, 1997a, 1997b). Separate the dates with a comma. The reference list will contain the corresponding letters after the dates of each work. (See **15b** for how to order the entries in the list of references.)

D. Work in an anthology In your text, refer to the author of the work, not to the editor of the anthology. In the reference list, give the author's name, title of the work, and bibliographical details about the anthology, such as the editor, title, publisher, and date (**15c**, item 4).

> Seegmiller (1993) has provided an incisive analysis of the relationship between pregnancy and culture.

E. Work cited in another source Give the author or title of the work in which you find the reference, preceded by "as cited in" to indicate that you are referring to a citation in that work. List that secondary source in your list of references. In the following example, *Smith* will appear in the list of references; *Britton* will not.

> The words we use simply appear, as Britton says, "at the point of utterance" (as cited in Smith, 1982, p. 108).

F. An entire work or an idea in a work Use only an author and a year to refer to a complete work; for a paraphrase or a comment on a specific idea, a page number is not required but is recommended.

G. No author named In your text, use the complete title if it is short (capitalizing major words) or a few words for the title in parentheses, along with the year of publication.

> According to *Weather* (1999), one way to estimate the Fahrenheit temperature is to count the number of times a cricket chirps in 14 seconds and add 40.

> Increasing evidence shows that glucosamine relieves the symptoms of arthritis (*The PDR Family Guide*, 1999).

(See **15c**, item 5, for how to list the latter work.)

H. Electronic or other Internet source Give author, if available, or title, followed by the year of electronic publication or of the most recent update. Also provide the date on which you access the material. To locate a quotation in a source with no page or paragraph numbers visible on the screen, give the section heading, and indicate the paragraph within the section (such as "Conclusion section, para. 2").

Be wary of citing e-mail messages (personal, bulletin board, discussion list, or Usenet group) as these are not peer reviewed or easily retrievable. If you need to cite an e-mail message, cite from an archived list whenever possible (see examples in **15e**, item 30); otherwise, cite the message in your text as a personal communication (**14b**, item O), but do not include it in your list of references.

I. Entire Web site   Give the complete URL in the text of your paper. Do not list the site in your list of references.

> Research on the "Mozart effect" has generated an institute with a Web site providing links to research studies (http://www.mindinst.org).

J. Nonprint source   For a film, television or radio broadcast, recording, or other nonprint source, include in your citation the name of the originator or main contributor (such as the writer, interviewer, director, performer, or producer) or an abbreviated title if the originator is not identified, along with the year of publication—for example, "(Morris, 1993)." (See **15f**, item 32, for how to list this work.)

K. Work by a corporation or government organization   In the initial citation, use the organization's full name; in subsequent references, use an abbreviation if one exists.

> ┌──── first mention: full name ────┐
> A recent survey by the College Entrance Examination Board (CEEB) has shown that 43% of total enrollment in higher education is in two-year public institutions. Full-time enrollment is different, with only 24% enrolled in two-year public schools (CEEB, 2002).
>   abbreviation in citation

(**15c**, item 6, shows how to list this work.)

L. Two authors with the same last name   Include the authors' initials, even if the publication dates of their works differ.

> F. Smith (1982) has often described a writer as having two competitive roles: author and secretary.

(For the order of entries in the list of references, see **15b**.)

M. Multivolume work   In your citation, give the publication date of the volume you are citing: (Barr & Feigenbaum, 1982). If you refer to more than one volume, give inclusive dates for all the volumes you cite: (Barr & Feigenbaum, 1981–1986). (See **15c**, item 8, for how to list this work.)

N. More than one work in a citation List the sources in alphabetical order, separated by semicolons. List works by the same author chronologically (earliest source first) or by the letters *a, b,* and so on, if the works were published in the same year.

> Criticisms of large-scale educational testing abound (Crouse & Trusheim, 1988; Nairn, 1978, 1980; Raimes, 1990a,1990b; Sacks 2003).

O. Personal communication, such as a conversation, a letter, an e-mail, an unarchived electronic discussion group, or an interview Mention these only in your paper; do not include them in your list of references. Give the last name and initial(s) of the author of the communication and the exact date of posting.

> According to Dr. C. S. Apstein, Boston University School of Medicine, research in heart disease is critical to the well-being of society today (personal communication, January 7, 2004).

P. A classical work If the date of publication of a classical work is not known, use in your citation "n.d." for "no date." If you use a translation, give the year of the translation, preceded by "trans." You do not need a reference list entry for the Bible or ancient classical works. Just give information about book and line numbers in your text.

Q. Long quotation If you quote more than forty words of prose, do not enclose the quotation in quotation marks. Start the quotation on a new line, and indent the whole quotation half an inch or five spaces from the left margin. Double-space the quotation.

14c Notes, tables, and figures

Notes In APA style, you can use content notes to amplify information in your text. Number notes consecutively with superscript numerals. After the list of references, attach a separate page containing your numbered notes and headed "Footnotes." Use notes sparingly; include all important information in your text, not in footnotes.

Tables Place all tables at the end of your paper, after the references and any notes. Number each table and provide an italicized caption.

Figures After the references and any notes or tables, provide a separate page listing the figure captions, and place this page before the figures (see pages 208–209 for an example).

APA (American Psychological Association)

15   The APA List of References

15a   List format and organization

The APA *Publication Manual* and Web site provide guidelines for submitting professional papers for publication, and many instructors ask students to follow those guidelines to prepare them for advanced work. This section follows APA guidelines. Check with your instructor, however, as to specific course requirements for the reference list.

 KEY POINTS

Setting Up the APA List of References

1. *What to list* List only the works you cited (quoted, summarized, paraphrased, or commented on) in the text of your paper, not every source you found.

2. *Format* Start the list on a new numbered page after the last page of text or notes. Center the heading "References," without quotation marks, not underlined or italicized, and with no period following it. Double-space throughout the list.

3. *Organization* List the works alphabetically, by last names of primary authors. Do not number the entries. Begin each entry with the author's name, last name first, followed by an initial or initials. Give any authors' names after the first in the same inverted form, separated by commas. Do not use "et al." List works with no author by title, alphabetized by the first main word.

4. *Date* Put the year in parentheses after the authors' names. For journals, magazines, and newspapers, include also month and day, but do not abbreviate the names of the months.

5. *Periods* Use a period and one space to separate the main parts of each entry.

6. *Indentation* Use hanging indents. (Begin the first line of each entry at the left margin; indent subsequent lines one-half inch.)

7. *Capitals* In titles of books and articles, capitalize only the first word of the title or subtitle and any proper nouns or adjectives.

(Continued)

APA

(American Psychological Association)

(Continued)

8. *Italics* Italicize the titles of books, but do not italicize or use quotation marks around the titles of articles. For magazines and journals, italicize the publication name, the volume number, and the comma. Italicize the names of newspapers.

9. *Page numbers* Give inclusive page numbers for articles and sections of books, using complete page spans ("251–259"). Use the abbreviation "p." or "pp." only for newspaper articles and sections of books (such as chapters or anthologized articles).

15b Guidelines for listing authors in the APA reference list

Name of author(s) Put the last name first, followed by a comma and then the initials.

> Gould, S. J.

Reverse the names of all authors listed, except the editors of an anthology or a reference work (**15c**, item 4).

Alphabetical order Alphabetize letter by letter. Treat Mac and Mc literally, by letter.

> MacKay, M. D'Agostino, S.
> McCarthy, T. De Cesare, P.
> McKay, K. DeCurtis, A.

A shorter name precedes a longer name beginning with the same letters, whatever the first initial: *Black, T.* precedes *Blackman, R.*

For a work with no known author, list by the first word in the title other than *A, An,* or *The.*

Alphabetize numerals according to their spelling: 5 ("five") will precede 2 ("two").

Individual author(s) not known If the author is a group, such as a corporation, agency, or institution, give its name, alphabetized by the first important word (**15c**, item 6). Use full names, not abbreviations. If no author or group is named, alphabetize by the first main word of the title (**15c**, item 5).

Several works by the same author List the author's name in each entry. Arrange entries chronologically from past to present. Entries published in the same year should be arranged alphabetically by title and distinguished with lowercase letters after the date (*a, b,* and so on). Note that entries for one author precede entries by that author but written with coauthors.

Goleman, D. (1996a, July 16). Forget money; nothing can buy happiness, some researchers say. *The New York Times*, p. C1.

Goleman, D. (1996b). *Vital lies, simple truths*. New York: Simon & Schuster.

Goleman, D. (2000). *Working with emotional intelligence*. New York: Bantam.

Goleman, D., Kaufman, P., & Ray, M. L. (1992, March-April). The art of creativity. *Psychology Today, 25*, 40–47.

Authors with the same last name List alphabetically by first initial: Smith, *A.* precedes Smith, *F.*

15c Sample APA entries: Print books and parts of books

On the title page and the copyright page of the book, you will find the information you need for an entry.

- For the place of publication, give the state (abbreviated) as well as the city (but omit the state when a major city is cited or when the state is included in the name of a unversity press publisher, as in *University of Illinois Press*).

- Give the publisher's name in a short but intelligible form, spelling out *University* and *Press* but omitting *Co.* and *Inc.*

- Use the most recent copyright date.

1. Book with one author Give the last name first, followed by the initials.

periods

last name   initials   year in parentheses

comma   period   title and period italicized

Wilson, E. O. (1994). *Naturalist.* Washington: Island Press.

place of publication   colon   publisher   final period

2. Book with two or more authors List all authors' names in the order in which they appear on the book's title page. Reverse the order of each name: last name first, followed by initials. Do not use "et al." Separate all names with commas, and insert an ampersand (&) before the last name.

all names reversed ⸻ ampersand

Jordan, J. V., Kaplan, A. G., Miller, J. B., Stiver, I. P., & Surrey, J. L. (1991).

indented
5 spaces

↳*Women's growth in connection: Writings from the Stone Center.*

New York: Guilford Press.

3. Edited book Use "Ed." or "Eds." for one or more editors, in parentheses.

Denmark, F., & Paludi, M. (Eds.). (1993). *Psychology of women: A handbook of issues and theories.* Westport, CT: Greenwood Press.

4. Work in an anthology or reference book List the author, date of publication of the edited book, and title of the work. Follow this with "In" and the names of the editors (not inverted), the title of the book, and the inclusive page numbers (preceded by "pp.") of the work in parentheses. End with the place of publication and the publisher. If you cite more than one article in an edited work, include full bibliographical details in each entry.

names of editors
⸻ not reversed ⸻

Seegmiller, B. (1993). Pregnancy. In F. Denmark & M. Paludi (Eds.), *Psychology of women: A handbook of issues and theories* (pp. 437– 474). Westport, CT: Greenwood Press.

For a well-known reference book with unsigned alphabetical entries, begin with the title of the entry and include the page number(s).

Multiculturalism. (1993). In *The Columbia encyclopedia* (5th ed., p. 1855). New York: Columbia University Press.

5. Book with no author named Put the title first. Ignore *A, An,* and *The* when alphabetizing. Alphabetize the following under *P.*

The PDR family guide to natural medicines and healing therapies. (1999). New York: Three Rivers–Random House.

6. Book by a corporation or government or other organization
Give the name of the corporate author first. If the publisher is the same as the author, write "Author" for the name of the publisher.

College Entrance Examination Board. (2002). *Trends in college pricing: Annual survey of colleges.* New York: Author.

If no author is named for a government publication, begin with the name of the federal, state, or local government, followed by the agency.

United States. Department of Labor. (2002). *Occupational outlook handbook 2002–2003.* Indianapolis: JIST.

7. Translated book In parentheses after the title of the work, give the initials and last name of the translator, followed by a comma and "Trans."

name of translator not reversed

Jung, C. G. (1960). *On the nature of the psyche* (R. F. C. Hull, Trans.). Princeton, NJ: Princeton University Press.

8. Multivolume work When you refer to several volumes in a work of more than one volume, give the number of volumes after the title, in parentheses. The date should indicate the range of years of publication, when appropriate.

Barr, A., & Feigenbaum, E. A. (1981–1986). *The handbook of artificial intelligence* (Vols. 1–4). Reading, MA: Addison-Wesley.

9. Foreword, preface, introduction, or afterword List the name of the author of the book element cited. Follow the date with the name of the element, the title of the book, and, in parentheses, the page number or numbers on which the element appears, preceded by *p.* or *pp.*

Weiss, B. (Ed.). (1982). Introduction. *American education and the European immigrant, 1840–1940* (pp. xi–xxviii). Urbana: University of Illinois Press.

10. Republished book After the author's name, give the most recent date of publication. At the end, in parentheses add "Original work published" and the date. In your text citation, give both dates: (Smith, 1793/1976).

Smith, A. (1976). *An inquiry into the nature and causes of the wealth of nations.* Chicago: University of Chicago Press. (Original work published 1793)

11. Technical report If the report has a number, state it in parentheses after the title.

Breland, H. M., & Jones, R. J. (1982). *Perceptions of writing skill* (Rep. No. 82–4). New York: College Entrance Examination Board.

12. Dissertation or abstract For a manuscript source, give the university and year of the dissertation and the volume and page numbers of *DAI*.

Salzberg, A. (1992). Behavioral phenomena of homeless women in San Diego County (Doctoral dissertation, United States International University, 1992). *Dissertation Abstracts International, 52*, 4482.

For a microfilm source, also include in parentheses at the end of the entry the university microfilm number. For a CD-ROM source, include "CD-ROM" after the title. Then name the electronic source of the information and the *DAI* number.

15d Sample APA entries: Print articles in periodicals

When listing any periodical print article, do the following:

- Do not use quotation marks with the title of an article.
- Use a capital letter only for the first word of the title and subtitle (if any) and for proper nouns.
- Italicize the name of a journal, magazine, or newspaper.
- Do not use *p.* or *pp.* with page numbers of articles, except for the pages of newspaper articles (see **15d**, item 16).
- Use all the digits of page numbers in a range: 167–168; 256–289.
- Do not abbreviate months in magazine and newspaper dates.

13. Article in a scholarly journal: pages numbered consecutively through each volume Give only the volume number and year for journals with consecutive pagination through a volume (for example, the first issue of volume 1 ends on page 174, and the second issue of volume 1 begins on page 175). Italicize the volume number and the following comma as well as the title of the journal. See **8b** on recognizing a scholarly journal.

no quotation marks around
—————— article title ——————

Kanazawa, S., & Still, M. C. (2000). Teaching may be hazardous to your

journal title, volume number,
┌——————— and commas italicized ———————┐
marriage. *Evolution and Human Behavior, 21,* 185–190.

no "p." or "pp." before page numbers

14. Article in a scholarly journal: each issue paged separately
For journals in which each issue begins with page 1, include the issue number—in parentheses but not in italics—immediately after the volume number.

Ginat, R. (2000). The Soviet Union and the Syrian Ba'th regime: From

hesitation to *rapprochement. Middle Eastern Studies, 36*(2),

150–171.   issue number not in italics

15. Article in a magazine Include the year and month or month and day of publication in parentheses. Italicize the magazine title, the volume number, and the comma that follows; then give the page number or numbers.

Levy, S. (2003, April 21). The killer browser. *Newsweek, 141,* 6–12.

16. Article in a newspaper In parentheses, include the month and day of the newspaper after the year. Give the section letter or number before the page, where applicable. Use "p." and "pp." with page numbers. Do not omit *The* from the title of a newspaper or a magazine.

Revkin, A. C. (2003, April 28). At the bustling North Pole, here today, gone

tomorrow. *The New York Times,* pp. A1, A6.

17. Article that skips pages When an article appears on discontinuous pages, give all the page numbers, separated by commas, as in item 16 above.

18. Review After the title of the review article, add in brackets a description of the work reviewed and identify the medium: book, film, or video, for example.

Himmelfarb, G. (2003, March). The Victorian achievement [review of the

book *The Victorians*]. *The Atlantic, 291,* 113–120.

19. Unsigned editorial or article For a work with no author named, begin the listing with the title; for an editorial, add the label "Editorial" in brackets.

No nuke blackmail [Editorial]. (2003, April 26). *New York Post*, p. 14.

20. Letter to the editor Put the label "Letter to the editor" in brackets after the date or the title of the letter, if it has one.

Chapman, R. C. (2003, March). [Letter to the editor]. *Natural History, 112*, 13.

15e Sample APA entries: Internet and other electronic sources

The American Psychological Association supplements the fifth edition of its *Publication Manual* with a style Web site (http://www.apastyle .org) offering examples, periodic updates, and tips. Provide as many of the following elements as you can when citing Internet and electronic sources.

- name of author(s), if available
- date of work ("n.d." if no date is available)
- title of work (article, report, Web document or site, abstract, subject line of discussion list message), with additional necessary information added in brackets: [*letter to the editor, data file*, etc.]
- any print publication information, such as name of journal, volume number, and page numbers, if available (they will be available in PDF format, not HTML)
- chapter or section identification, if available, when no page numbers are given
- a retrieval statement containing the date you retrieved the information (month, day, year, with comma after day and after year) and the name of the database or the Internet address (URL) of the specific document you refer to, not just the home page
- a period at the end of the entry—except when the entry ends with a URL

The URL must be exact. Use the Copy function to copy it from the address window in your browser (making sure you have turned off automatic hyphenation: Tools/Language/Hyphenation), and then use the Paste function to paste the URL into your document.

21. Work in an electronic database Many universities, libraries, and organizational Web sites subscribe to large searchable databases, such as *InfoTrac, EBSCO, LexisNexis, OCLC, SilverPlatter, WilsonWeb, Dialog,* and *SIRS.* These databases provide access to large numbers of published, scholarly abstracts and full-text articles. In addition, available both online and on CD-ROM are specialized databases such as *ERIC, PsycINFO,* and *PAIS* (Public Affairs Information Service). However or wherever you access a source from an electronic database, cite it as follows:

Goldstein, B. S. C., & Harris, K. C. (2000). Consultant practices in two
heterogeneous Latino schools. *The School Psychology Review, 29,*
368–377. Retrieved June 4, 2003, from WilsonWeb Education Full
Text database.

22. Newspaper article retrieved from database or Web site Newspaper articles, as well as journal articles, are often available from several sources, in several databases and in a variety of formats, such as in a university online subscription database.

Wade, N. (2000, May 9). Scientists decode Down syndrome chromosome. *The*
New York Times, p. F4. Retrieved June 2, 2003, from LexisNexis
Academic Universe database.

Liptak, A. (2003, June 2). Internet battle raises questions about the First
Amendment. *The New York Times.* Retrieved June 4, 2003, from
http://www.nytimes.com/2003/06/02/national/02INTE.html

23. Online abstract For an abstract retrieved from a database or from a Web site, begin the retrieval statement with the words "Abstract retrieved" followed by the date and the name of the database or the URL of the Web site.

Zadra, A., & Donderi, D. C. (2000, May). Nightmares and bad dreams: Their
prevalence and relationship to well-being. *Journal of Abnormal*
Psychology, 109, 273–281. Abstract retrieved May 21, 2002, from
http://www.apa.org/journals/abn/500ab.html#11

24. Online article, based on a print source If you read a print article in electronic form, unchanged from the original and with no additional commentary (as in a PDF file), cite the article as you would a print article, with the addition of [Electronic version] after the title of the article. If information such as page numbers or figures is missing or if the document may have additions or alterations, give full retrieval information:

Jones, C. C., & Meredith, W. (2000, June). Developmental paths of psychological health from early adolescence to later adulthood. *Psychology and Aging, 15,* 351–360. Retrieved June 2, 2003, from http://www.apa.org/journals/pag/pag152351.html

25. Article in an online journal, no print source

Holtzworth-Munroe, A. (2000, June). Domestic violence: Combining scientific inquiry and advocacy. *Prevention & Treatment, 3.* Retrieved June 4, 2003, from http://journals.apa.org/prevention/volume3/pre0030022c.html

26. Article in an online site, no author identified

Division spotlight. (2003, February). *APA Monitor, 34*(2). Retrieved June 3, 2003, from http://www.apa.org/monitor/feb03/ds.html

27. Entire Web site Give the complete URL in the text of your paper, not in your list of references. For an example see **14b**, item I.

28. Document on a Web site, no author identified Italicize the title of the document (the Web page). Alphabetize by the first major word of the title.

APAStyle.org: Electronic references. (2003). Retrieved June 4, 2003, from http://www.apastyle.org/elecgeneral.html

29. Document on a university or government agency site Italicize the title of the document. In the retrieval statement, give the name of the university or government agency (and the department or division if it is named). Follow this with a colon and the URL.

McClintock, R. (2000, September 20). *Cities, youth, and technology: Toward a pedagogy of autonomy.* Retrieved May 30, 2003, from Columbia University, Institute for Learning Technologies Web site: http://www.ilt.columbia.edu/publications/cities/cyt.html

30. E-mail and contributions to electronic mailing lists Make sure that you cite only scholarly e-mail messages. Cite a personal e-mail message in the body of your text as "personal communication," and do not include it in your list of references (see **14b**, item O).

Gracey, D. (2001, April 6). Monetary systems and a sound economy [Msg 54]. Message posted to http://groups.yahoo.com/group/ermail/message/54

Cromm, O. (2003, May 6). Crossers of the Atlantic. Message posted to news:alt.usage.english

Whenever possible, cite an archived version of a message:

Howard, R. M. (2003, April 16). Institutional pressures. Message posted to WPA–L electronic mailing list, archived at http://lists.asu.edu

15f Sample APA entries: Miscellaneous sources

31. Personal communication (letter, telephone conversation, or interview)   Cite a personal communication only in your text. (See **14b**, item O.) Do not include it in your list of references.

32. Film, recording, or video   Identify the medium in brackets after the title.

Morris, E. (Director). (1993). *A brief history of time* [Video]. Hollywood: Paramount.

33. Television or radio program

Keach, S. (Narrator). (2000, July 9). *Storms of the century* [Television broadcast]. New York: WNET.

34. Computer software

Movie Magic Screenwriter (Version 4.5) [Computer software]. (2000). Burbank, CA: Storymind.

16 Sample Documented Paper, APA Style

The paper that follows was written for a college course in experimental psychology. Check with your instructor to see whether your title page should strictly follow APA guidelines, as this one does, or whether it should be modified to include the course name, instructor's name, and date.

APA
(American Psychological Association)

TITLE PAGE

Running head and page number on every page

Absolute Auditory Thresholds ⟷ 1
                                    5 spaces
                                         ⟷
                                      1" margin

Running head: ABSOLUTE AUDITORY THRESHOLDS

Absolute Auditory Thresholds in College Students

Todd Kray

Hunter College of the City University of New York

Centered title, writer's name, and writer's affiliation

APA ABSTRACT PAGE

Absolute Auditory Thresholds   2

Heading centered

Abstract

Seventeen college students participated in an auditory experiment, collecting data while working in pairs. In the experiment, absolute auditory thresholds were established and compared to "normal" thresholds. This study discusses details and plots results on two graphs for one pair of students: one 20-year-old female, and one 37-year-old male. While results paralleled the "norm" at many frequencies (125 Hz, 250 Hz, 500 Hz, 1000 Hz, 2 KHz, 4 KHz, and 8 KHz), strong evidence for high-frequency loss was discovered for the older of the two participants. Environmental conditions and subject fatigue were also seen to be influences on determining auditory thresholds.

Passive voice common in accounts of research

Results summarized

Absolute Auditory Thresholds   3

Absolute Auditory Thresholds in College Students

For decades, the branch of psychophysics known as psychoacoustics has concerned itself with the minimum amount of sound pressure level (SPL) required for detection by the human ear. An early landmark study by Sivian and White (1933) examined loudness thresholds by measuring minimum audible field (MAF) and minimal audible pressure (MAP) and found that the ear was not as sensitive as had been reported in earlier studies by Wien (as cited in Sivian & White, 1933). Parker and Schneider (1980) tested Fechner's and Weber's laws, both of which concern themselves with measuring changes in physical intensity and the psychological experiences of those changes (Jahnke & Nowaczyk, 1998; Noll, 2002) and determined that loudness is a power function of intensity, which was consistent with Fechner's assumption. In recent years, loudness thresholds have been measured under various experimental conditions, including quiet sedentary activity, exercise, and noise (Hooks-Horton, Geer, & Stuart, 2001).

An experiment was designed to utilize the method of limits, which establishes the absolute sensitivity (threshold) for a particular sound, to test auditory thresholds in college students and compare them to the "norm." Each threshold is determined by presenting the tone at a sound level well above threshold, then lessening it in discrete intervals until the tone is no longer perceived by the participant (Gelfand, 1981). The present study predicts that,

Annotations (margin notes):
- 1″ margin
- Brief review of the literature
- Title centered, not underlined
- Date after citation
- Ampersand within parentheses
- Author and year in parentheses
- Hypothesis
- 1″ margin

Absolute Auditory Thresholds   4

according to Gelfand's (1981) summary of the research on normal
hearing, college students' thresholds would be described as "normal."

Method

Participants

Seventeen college students in an introductory experimental
psychology course participated in the experiment. The median age
of the 5 males and 12 females was 24, with ages ranging from 20
to 37 years old. None of the participants claimed to be aware of
any significant hearing loss, and none claimed to have ever
participated in this or a similar experiment before. All appeared to
be in good overall physical and mental condition, though no formal
testing was done in these areas.

Apparatus

Pure tones were generated by a B&K waveform generator.
The intensity of the tones was controlled by a Hewlett-Packard
350D attenuator. Tones were gated on and off by a push-button-
controlled, light-dependent resistor. This provided for a gradual
"ramping" on and off of sound. The tones were presented to
the subject through a pair of Koss PRO/99 headphones. The
headphones were calibrated at all test frequencies on a Kemar
dummy head with a 6 cc coupler.

Procedure

Participants worked in pairs to run and participate in the
experiment. In each pair, one participant controlled the waveform

---

Margin annotations:

- Subheading italicized
- Specialized equipment described
- Main heading centered
- Details of participants
- Passive voice common in description of experiment

Absolute Auditory Thresholds   5

generator and attenuator while the other faced away from the tester toward the wall. Participants had been instructed to choose an order of frequencies prior to taking the test. They then administered the tests to each other, trading "roles" after one block of attenuated tones for each frequency was completed. On the first day of testing, the method of limits was utilized to determine a baseline threshold for each frequency. Seven frequencies were generated: 125 Hz, 250 Hz, 500 Hz, 1000 Hz, 2 KHz, 4 KHz, and 8 KHz.

The tests were administered in small cubicles that were quiet but not soundproof. Participants had been instructed to use their "good ear." Tones were heard monophonically, through one side of the headphones.

Details of procedure

Eight blocks were run for each frequency, 4 ascending and 4 descending, in a semirandomized order determined by the experimenter to help insure accurate responses rather than the participant being able to "guess it out." Participants were instructed to say "yes" after each audible tone for a descending block, until they could no longer hear the tone, at which point they would say "no" and that particular block would end. For an ascending block, participants were to say "no" for each ascending tone that they could not hear, until the first tone they heard, at which point they would say "yes" and that block would be complete. Each response was recorded on a sheet of paper by the experimenter, handwritten.

Absolute Auditory Thresholds   6

Results

Main
heading
centered

For this pair of participants, 2 audiograms were plotted to display dB SPL (decibel sound pressure level) thresholds for Subject A and Subject B. Threshold ranges for the subjects in one pair were quite different from each other. Subject A's ranged from 5.9 dB to

Reference to
figures at
end of paper

39.3 dB (Fig. 1); Subject B's ranged from 2.7 dB to 26.6 dB (Fig. 2), resulting in a more "normal" curve than the one for Subject A.

Discussion

Results
evaluated
with respect
to
hypothesis

Subject B's absolute threshold levels somewhat resemble those of "normal" hearing, as reported by Gelfand (1981) with a peculiar loss of sensitivity at 2 KHz and extreme sensitivity at 8 KHz. While loss of sensitivity is not uncommon for those who have had prolonged exposure to loud sounds, such as listening to a Walkman being played

Unusual
results
analyzed

at the maximum level or attending rock concerts frequently, it seems odd that Subject B, who claimed not to possess these conditions, would experience a loss of sensitivity at 2 KHz, particularly at age 20. In the light of that, it seems even stranger that Subject B would have sensitivity greater than the norm at both 4 KHz and 8 KHz. However,

Causes of
results
considered

the fact that both subjects had elevated thresholds at 2 KHz could lead to the suspicion of faulty apparatus.

Subject A seems to be a classic example of somebody who would be prone to loss of sensitivity at higher frequencies. He had

Details of
causes

constant exposure to loud sounds as a result of over 2 decades spent playing in rock bands, frequently attending rock concerts, wearing a Walkman often in his youth, working in extremely loud nightclubs, and

Absolute Auditory Thresholds   7

working in recording studios. In addition, he is currently 37 years old and may be experiencing the first symptoms of Presbyacusia--hearing loss at high frequencies due to aging. Subject A showed an extreme loss of sensitivity at 2 KHz (again, apparatus could be at fault here) and the loss at 4 KHz seems real when compared to Gelfand's (1981) norm.

Auditory testing over the years has provided us with no easy answers regarding absolute threshold. Many of the articles cited in this study provide more questions than conclusions. Sivian and White (1933) inquired as to whether ear sensitivity was determined by the actual physiological construction of the ear or if air as a transmitter was responsible. It would be helpful to test for this in the future.

The tests themselves are problematic as well. It is easy to wind up with a masked threshold if thresholds are not measured in absolute silence--not always an easy condition to create. Even under the best conditions that could be achieved in this experiment, demand characteristics and experimenter effects were unavoidable. The dial of the attenuator clicked loudly when turned, providing very definite clues that attenuation levels were being changed. In addition, the test, which took several hours to complete, caused subjects to feel fatigued and restless, making it difficult to concentrate at times.

Despite these hurdles, the experiment produced reasonable estimates for absolute auditory thresholds for college students and a reasonable estimate for a person experiencing symptoms of high-frequency loss due to abuse to the ear in the form of prolonged and excessive exposure to high volume.

Study related to prior research

Future research suggested

Problems with research procedures discussed

Results related to hypothesis

APA

(American Psychological Association)

Absolute Auditory Thresholds   8

References

Gelfand, S. A. (1981). *Hearing: An introduction to psychological and physiological acoustics.* New York: Marcel Dekker.

Hooks-Horton, S., Geer, S., & Stuart, A. (2001). Effects of exercise and noise on auditory thresholds and distortion-product otoacoustic emissions. *Journal of the American Academy of Audiology, 12,* 52–58. Retrieved April 28, 2003, from EBSCO database.

Jahnke, J. C., & Nowaczyk, R. H. (1998). *Cognition.* Englewood Cliffs, NJ: Prentice Hall.

Noll, T. (2002). *Tone apperception, relativity, and Weber-Fechner's law.* Paper presented at the 2002 2nd International Conference on Understanding and Creating Music. Retrieved June 2, 2003, from http://flp.cs.tu-berlin.de/~noll/ApperceptRelativity.pdf

Parker, S., & Schneider, B. (1980). Loudness and loudness discrimination. *Perception and Psychophysics, 28,* 398–406.

Sivian, L. J., & White, S. D. (1933). Minimum audible sound fields. *The Journal of the Acoustical Society of America, 4,* 288–321.

Organized alphabetically

Year in parentheses after author

Hanging indents

Italics extend through volume number and commas

Absolute Auditory Thresholds   9

Figure Captions

Figure 1. Comparison of thresholds for "normal" and Sub. A.

Figure 2. Comparison of thresholds for "normal" and Sub. B.

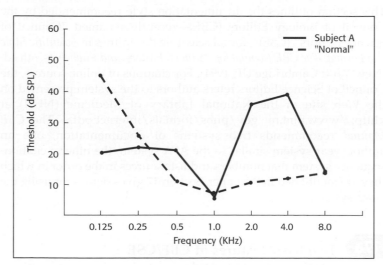

Figure 1

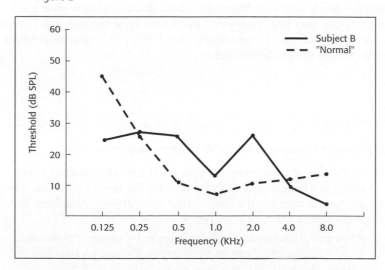

Figure 2

CBE/CSE

(Council of Science Editors)

17 The CBE/CSE Style of Documentation in the Sciences and Mathematics

This section outlines the documentation style recommended by the Council of Biology Editors (CBE)—recently renamed "Council of Science Editors" (CSE)—for all scientific disciplines in *Scientific Style and Format: The CBE Manual for Authors, Editors, and Publishers*, 6th ed. (New York: Cambridge UP, 1994). For citations of online sources, the Council of Science Editors refers authors to the system presented on the Web site of the National Library of Medicine (NLM) at <http://www.nlm.nih.gov/pubs/formats/internet.pdf>. The *CBE Manual* recommends two systems of documentation, one an author/year system similar to the APA system, the other a citation-sequence system that numbers and lists sources in the order in which they are mentioned in the paper. Section **17** gives details for using the latter system.

17a Two basic features of CBE/CSE citation-sequence style

Always check with your instructor about documentation style guidelines. Some may not specify one particular style but will ask you to select one and use it consistently. For CBE/CSE citation-sequence style, follow the guidelines below.

KEY POINTS

Two Basic Features of CBE/CSE Citation-Sequence Style

1. *In the text of your paper,* number each reference with a superscript in a smaller size than the type for the text, or place the reference number on the line within parentheses. Numbers run sequentially through your paper.

2. *At the end of your paper,* list the references by number, in the order in which you cite them in your paper. Do not alphabetize the entries. Begin the list on a new page, and title it "References."

CBE/CSE in-text citations

Use superscript numbers to refer readers to the list of references at the end of your paper.

superscript number
One summary of studies of the life span of the fruit fly[1] has shown . . .

Refer to more than one entry in the reference list as follows:

Two studies of the life span of the fruit fly[1,2] have shown that . . .

Several studies of the life span of the fruit fly[1-4] have shown that . . .

 Guidelines for listing CBE/CSE references

KEY POINTS

Setting Up the CBE/CSE List of References

1. After the last page of your paper, attach the list of references, headed "References" or "Cited References."

2. Number the works consecutively in the order in which you mention them in your paper. Invert all authors' names, and use the initials of first and middle names. Use no punctuation between last names and initials, and leave no space between initials.

3. Begin each entry with the note number followed by a period and a space. Do not indent the first line of each entry; indent subsequent lines to align beneath the first letter on the previous line.

4. Do not underline or use quotation marks for the titles of articles, books, or journals and other periodicals.

5. Capitalize only the first word of a book or article title, and capitalize any proper nouns.

6. Abbreviate titles of journals and organizations.

7. Use a period between major divisions of each entry.

(Continued)

(Continued)

8. Use a semicolon and a space between the name of the publisher and the publication date of a book. Use a semicolon with no space between the date and the volume number of a journal.

9. For books, give the total number of pages, followed by a space and "p." For journal articles, give inclusive page spans, using digits in the second number that are *not* included in the first: 135–6; 287–93; 500–1.

10. For online sources, provide author, title, print publication information, date and place of online publication, your date of access, and the URL.

17d Examples of entries in a CBE/CSE sequential list of references

Book with one author

title not underlined,
no punctuation ⎯⎯ only first word capitalized ⎯⎯⎯⎯⎯
2. Finch CE. Longevity, senescence and the genome. Chicago:
initials with abbreviated publishing
no periods
between ⎯ terms ⎯ semicolon number of pages in book
Univ Chicago Pr; 1990. 922 p.

Book with two or more authors

all authors'
⎯ names inverted ⎯
8. Ferrini AF, Ferrini RL. Health in the later years. 2nd ed. Dubuque (IA):
Brown & Benchmark; 1993. 470 p.
semicolon after publisher

Article in a scholarly journal

1. Kowald A, Kirkwood TB. Explaining fruit fly longevity. Science 1993;

no spaces in information about journal
260:1664–5.
volume number

In a journal paginated by issue, include the issue number in parentheses after the volume number.

Newspaper or magazine article

6. Altman LK. Study prompts call to halt a routine eye operation. NY Times 1995 Feb 22; Sect C:10.

Article with no author named   Begin with "[Anonymous]."

Editorial   After the title, insert "[editorial]."

Audiovisual materials   Begin the entry with the title, followed by the medium in brackets. Then include the author (if known), producer, place, publisher, and date. Include a description, such as number of cassettes, length, color or black and white, and accompanying material. End with a statement of availability, if necessary.

7. AIDS in Africa: living with a time bomb [videocassette]. Princeton: Films for the Humanities and Sciences; 1991. 33 min, sound, color, 1/2 in.

The following examples of Internet sources use the format suggested on the National Library of Medicine Web site, as recommended by CSE.

Electronic journal article with a print source   Cite as for a print journal article, and include the type of medium in brackets after the journal title. Include any document number, the accession date "[cited (year, month, date)]," and an availability statement with the URL.

12. Jones CC, Meredith W. Developmental paths of psychological health from early adolescence to later adulthood. Psych Aging [Internet] 2000 [cited 2002 May 3];15(2):351–60. Available from: http://www.apa.org/journals/pag/pag152351.html

Electronic journal article with no print source   If no print source is available, provide an estimate of the length of the document in pages, paragraphs, or screens. Place the information in square brackets, such as "[about 3 p.]," "[about 15 paragraphs]," or "[about 6 screens]."

9. Holtzworth-Munroe A. Domestic violence: Combining scientific inquiry and advocacy. Prev Treatment [serial on the Internet], 2000 June 2 [cited 2002 May 12];3 [about 6 pages]. Available from: http://journals .apa.org/prevention/volume3/pre0030022c.html

CBE/CSE *(Council of Science Editors)*

Article in an electronic database   After author, title, and print publication information, give the name of the database, the designation in square brackets "[database on the Internet]," any date of posting or modification, or the copyright date. Follow this with the date of access, the approximate length of the article, the URL, and any accession number.

15. Mayor S. New treatment improves symptoms of Parkinson's disease. Brit Med J 2002 324(7344):997. In: EBSCOhost Health Source: Nursing/Academic Edition [database on the Internet]; c2002 [cited 2002 May 14]. [about 1 screen]. Available from: http://ehostvgw17.epnet.com; Accession No.: 6609093.

Internet home page   Give author (if available) and title of page followed by "[Internet]." Follow this with any available information about place of home page publication and sponsor, and then include date of publication or copyright date, along with any update. End with your date of citation and the URL.

11. Anemia and iron therapy [Internet]. Hinsdale (IL): Medtext, Inc.; c1995–2002 [cited 2002 May 15]. Available from: http://www.hdcn.com/ch/rbc/

Posting to a discussion list   After the author's name and the subject line of the message, give information about the discussion list, including name of list; place and sponsor, if available; year, date, and time of posting; date of citation; and approximate length of the posting. End with an availability statement of the address of the discussion list or the archive.

10. Bishawi AH. Summary: hemangioendothelioma of the larynx. In: MEDLIB-L [discussion list on the Internet]. [Buffalo (NY): State Univ of NY]; 2002 May 6, 11:25am [cited 2002 May 15]. [about 4 screens]. Available from: MEDLIBL@LISTSERV.ACSU.BUFFALO.EDU

---

18 *Chicago Manual of Style:* **Endnotes, Footnotes, and Bibliography**

As an alternative to an author/year citation style similar to the APA system, *The Chicago Manual of Style,* 15th ed. (Chicago: University of Chicago Press, 2003), describes a system in which sources are documented in footnotes or endnotes. This system is used widely in the humanities, especially in history and art history. For a *Chicago*-style paper, include an unnumbered title page, and number the first page of your text as page "2."

18a Two basic features of *Chicago* endnotes and footnotes

KEY POINTS

Two Basic Features of *Chicago* Endnotes and Footnotes

1. Place a superscript numeral at the end of the quotation or the sentence in which you mention source material; place the number after all punctuation marks except a dash.

2. List all endnotes—single-spaced, but double-spaced between notes, unless your instructor prefers double-spaced throughout—on a separate numbered page at the end of the paper, and number the notes sequentially, as they appear in your paper. Your word processing program will automatically place footnotes at the bottom of each page (Insert/Footnote). See **20a**.

18b *Chicago* in-text citations, notes, and bibliography

In-text citation   Use the following format, and number your notes sequentially.

> George Eliot thought that Eliot was a "good, mouth-filling, easy to pro-nounce word."[1]

If you include at the end of your paper a bibliography listing all the sources cited in your notes (see **18h**), then the note citation can be concise. If no bibliography is attached to your paper, you need to give full information about a source the first time you include it in your notes.

First note for a source when a full bibliography is included   A bibliography includes full publication details, so in a short note, only the author's last name, a shortened form of the title, and the page number (if a specific reference is made) are necessary. Indent the first line of the note.

author's last name   short title   page number for a specific reference or a quotation
1. Crompton, *George Eliot*, 123.

Entry in bibliography

Crompton, Margaret. *George Eliot: The Woman.* London: Cox and Wyman, 1960.

Full first note for a source when no bibliography is included

         author's name   title underlined, all important
     ┌─ in normal order ─┐   ┌──── words capitalized ──┐
1. Margaret Crompton, <u>George Eliot: The Woman</u> (London: Cox

        comma   page number
and Wyman, 1960), 123.

Note referring to the immediately preceding source In a reference to the immediately preceding source, you may use "Ibid." (Latin *ibidem,* meaning "in the same place") instead of repeating the author's name and the title of the work. All the details except the page number must be the same as in the previous citation. If the page number is the same too, omit it following "Ibid."

    2. Ibid., 127.

However, avoid a series of "ibid." notes. These are likely to irritate your reader. Instead, place page references within your text: *As Crompton points out (127),* . . .

Any subsequent reference to a previously cited source For a reference to a source cited in a previous note, but not in the immediately preceding note, give only the author and page number. However, if you cite more than one work by the same author, include a short title to identify the source.

    6. Crompton, 124.

 18c Guidelines for *Chicago* endnotes and footnotes

 KEY POINTS

Setting Up *Chicago* Endnotes and Footnotes

1. In the list of endnotes, place each number on the line (not as a superscript), followed by a period and one space. For footnotes, word processing software will often automatically make the number a superscript number—just be consistent with whatever format you use.

(Continued)

(Continued)

2. Indent the first line of each entry three or five spaces. Single-space within a note and double-space between notes, unless your instructor prefers double-spacing throughout.

3. Use the author's full name, not inverted, followed by a comma and the title of the work. Put quotation marks around article titles, and italicize titles of books and periodicals.

4. Capitalize all words in the titles of books, periodicals, and articles except *a, an, the,* coordinating conjunctions, *to* in an infinitive, and prepositions. Capitalize any word that begins or ends a title or subtitle.

5. Follow a book title with publishing information in parentheses (city—and state if necessary: name of publisher, year) followed by a comma and the page number(s), with no "p." or "pp." Follow an article title with the name of the periodical and pertinent publication information (volume, issue, date, page numbers where appropriate). Do not abbreviate months.

6. Separate major parts of the citation with commas, not periods.

7. For online sources, provide the URL, and for time-sensitive material, end with the date on which you last accessed the source.

18d *Chicago* **print books and parts of books**

Note the indented first line, the full name of the author, the commas separating major sections of the note, and the publication details in parentheses (City: Publisher, year of publication). If you quote or refer to a specific page of the source, provide the page number following the publication details and a comma, as in item 1. For a general reference or a reference to the work as a whole, end the note after the closing parenthesis, as in item 2.

1. Book with one author

1. Robert A. Caro, *Master of the Senate: The Years of Lyndon Johnson* (New York: Knopf, 2002), 8.

2. Book with two or three authors

2. George Lakoff and Mark Johnson, *Metaphors We Live By* (Chicago: University of Chicago Press, 1980).

3. Book with four or more authors

For a book with four or more authors, use the name of only the first author followed by "et al." (for "and others").

> 3. Randolph Quirk and others, *A Comprehensive Grammar of the English Language* (London: Longman, 1985).

4. Book with no author identified

> 4. *Chicago Manual of Style*, 15th ed. (Chicago: University of Chicago Press, 2003).

5. Book with editor or translator

> 5. John Updike, ed., *The Best American Short Stories of the Century* (Boston: Houghton Mifflin, 1999).

For a translated work, give the author, title, and then the name of the translator after "trans."

6. Author's work quoted in another work

> 6. E. M. Forster, *Two Cheers for Democracy* (New York: Harcourt, Brace and World, 1942), 242, quoted in Phyllis Rose, *Woman of Letters, A Life of Virginia Woolf* (New York: Oxford University Press, 1978), 219.

Note, however, that *The Chicago Manual of Style* recommends that a reference be found in and cited from the original work.

7. Government document

> 7. U.S. Department of Education, Office of Educational Research and Improvement, *Digest of Education Statistics, 2000* (Washington, DC, 2002).

8. Scriptures, Greek and Latin works, classic works of literature

Provide the reference in the text or in a note. For the Bible, include the book (in abbreviated form, chapter, and verse, not a page number).

> 8. Gen. 27:29.

You do not need to include the Bible in your bibliography.

For Greek and Roman works and for classic plays in English, locate by the number of book, section, and line or by act, scene, and line. Cite a classic poem by book, canto, stanza, and line, whichever is appropriate. Specify the edition used only in the first reference in a note.

9. Article in an edited volume or anthology

9. Terrence Des Pres, "Poetry and Politics," in *The Writer in Our World*, ed. Reginald Gibbons (Boston: Atlantic Monthly Press, 1986), 17-29.

18e *Chicago* print articles in periodicals

10. Article in a scholarly journal, continuously paged through issues of a volume If journal volumes are paged continuously through issues (for example, if issue 1 ends on page 188 and issue 2 of the same volume begins with page 189) give only the volume number and year, not the issue number. If you refer to a specific page, put a colon after the year in parentheses and then add the page number or numbers. To cite an abstract, include the word *abstract* before the name of the journal. For more on scholarly journals, see **8b**.

10. Hesse, Douglas, "The Place of Creative Nonfiction," *College English* 65 (2003): 238.

11. Article in a scholarly journal, each issue paged separately When each issue of a journal is paged separately, with each issue beginning on page 1, include "no." for number after the volume number, and follow it with the issue number.

11. Rami Ginat, "The Soviet Union and the Syrian Ba'th Regime: From Hesitation to *Rapprochement*," *Middle Eastern Studies* 36, no. 2 (2000): 160.

12. Article in a magazine Include the month for monthly magazines and the complete date for weekly magazines (month, day, year). Cite only a specific page number in a note (after a comma), not the range of pages. Provide the range of pages of the whole article in a bibliographical citation.

12. Jeremy Scahill, "Inside Baghdad," *Nation*, April 7, 2003, 12.

13. Article in a newspaper Include the complete date, the edition, if relevant, and the section number. Do not include an initial *The* in the name of a newspaper. A page number is not necessary as a newspaper may appear in several editions. You may, however, give the edition and any section number.

13. Dinitia Smith, "Critic at the Mercy of His Own Kind," *New York Times*, sec. B, May 24, 2003.

If the city is not part of the newspaper title, include it in parentheses: *Times* (London).

14. Editorial, no author identified When no author is identified, begin the note with the title of the article.

> 14. "Santorum and Tolerance," *Wall Street Journal*, April 25, 2003.

15. Letter to the editor

> 15. Chris Ronk, letter to the editor, *Harper's*, May 2003, 5.

16. Review of book, play, or movie

> 16. Anne Hollander, "Men in Tights," review of *Why We Are What We Wear*, by Paul Fussell, *New Republic*, February 10, 2003, 34.

18f *Chicago* **Internet and electronic sources**

17. Online reference work Cite an online dictionary or an encyclopedia in a note, but do not include it in a bibliography. Because databases are frequently updated, you need to give the date on which you access the material. Precede the title of the article with the initials s.v. (Latin for *sub verbo*—"under the word").

> 17. *Columbia Encyclopedia*, 6th ed., s.v. "Bloomsbury group," http://www.bartleby.com/65/bl/Bloomsbury.html (accessed August 2, 2003).

18. Online book Include your date of access only for time-sensitive material or material that may be revised for different editions.

> 18. Mary Wollstonecraft Shelley, *Frankenstein, or, The Modern Prometheus* (London: Dent, 1912), http://ota.ahds.ac.uk.

19. Article obtained through an online database After any available print information, give the URL of the entry page of the service and other retrieval information, and (only if the material is time-sensitive or may exist in varying editions) the date you accessed the material.

> 19. Geoffrey Bent, "Vermeer's Hapless Peer," *North American Review* 282 (1997), http://www.infotrac.galegroup.com/.

20. Article in an online journal

> 20. Sarah Hatchuel, "Leading the Gaze: From Showing to Telling in Kenneth Branagh's *Henry V* and *Hamlet*," *Early Modern Literary Studies* 6 no. 1 (2000), http://www.shu.ac.uk.emls/06-1/hatchba.htm.

21. Article in an online magazine   Cite as for a print publication, but add the URL.

21. Timothy Charoenying, "Jazz at the Crossroads," *Atlantic*, February 26, 2003, http://www.theatlantic.com/unbound/flashbks/jazz.htm.

22. Article in an online newspaper   Cite as for a print publication, but add the URL. See item 13 above.

22. Dinitia Smith, "Critic at the Mercy of His Own Kind," *New York Times*, sec. B, May 24, 2003, http://www.nytimes.com/2003/05/24/books/24WOOD.html.

23. Government publication online

23. U.S. Department of Labor, "Labor Department Responds to Disaster Relief Effort," May 22, 2002, http://www.dol.gov/_sec/programs/responds.htm.

24. Web page or document from a Web site   Give the author of the content, if known, the title of the document, the owner or sponsor of the site, the URL, and your date of access if the material is frequently updated.

24. "MLA Style," Modern Language Association, http://www.mla.org (accessed August 3, 2003).

25. Personal home page   If a page does not have a title, use a descriptive phrase such as "home page."

25. Allison Marsh, "Business Portfolio," http://www.student.richmond.edu/2001/amarsh/public_html/profport/index.html.

26. E-mail communication

26. George Kane, e-mail message to the author, August 5, 2003.

27. Material posted on an electronic mailing list   Whenever possible, cite a URL for archived material. Otherwise, end the note after the date.

27. Rebecca Moore Howard, e-mail to WPA-L mailing list, April 16, 2003, http://lists.asu.edu/cgi-bin/wa?A1=ind0304&L=wpa-l.

28. CD-ROM, DVD, e-book Indicate the medium.

28. Ann Raimes, *Digital Keys 3.1* (Boston: Houghton Mifflin, 2004), CD-ROM.

18g Miscellaneous sources

29. Interview Treat a published interview like an article or a book chapter, including the phrase "interview with." For unpublished interviews, include the type of interview and the date.

29. Douglass Mignone, telephone interview with the author, October 19, 2002.

30. Lecture or speech Give location and date.

30. Trudy Smoke, "The History of Rhetoric" (lecture, Hunter College, New York, April 7, 2003).

31. Film, filmstrip, slides, videocassette, or audiocassette End the note with an indication of the type of medium, such as *film, filmstrip, slide, videocassette, audiocassette.* For online multimedia, include the type of medium, such as *MP3 audio file.*

31. *Citizen Kane*, produced, written, and directed by Orson Welles, 119 min., RKO, 1941, film.

18h *Chicago* bibliography guidelines and sample

Check whether your instructor wants you to include a bibliography of works cited (or a bibliography of works consulted) in addition to notes. If you do, you can use the short form for notes (**18b**).

- Begin a bibliography on a new, numbered page after the endnotes.
- List entries alphabetically, by authors' last names.
- Include authors' full names, the first author's inverted.
- Indent all lines three or five spaces except the first line of each entry.
- Single-space entries and double-space between entries, or double-space the whole list.
- Separate the major parts of each entry with a period and one space.

Here is the bibliography from a student's paper on the seventeenth-century Dutch painter Pieter de Hooch.

Quinones 16

Bibliography

Bent, Geoffrey. "Vermeer's Hapless Peer." *North American Review*
282 (1997). http://www.infotrac.galegroup.com/.

Botton, Alain de. "Domestic Bliss: Pieter de Hooch Exhibition."
New Statesman, October 9, 1998, 34–35.

Franits, Wayne E. "The Depiction of Servants in Some Paintings by
Pieter de Hooch." *Zeitschrift für Kunstgeschichte* 52 (1989):
559–66.

Sutton, Peter. *Pieter de Hooch: Complete Edition, with a Catalogue
Raisonné.* Ithaca, NY: Cornell University Press, 1980.

19   CGOS Style for Online Sources

Your instructor may refer you to Janice Walker and Todd Taylor's
book *The Columbia Guide to Online Style* (New York: Columbia UP,
1998) for formats to use when you are citing online sources in the
humanities or sciences, especially when a specific style manual is not
up-to-date with its recommendations on citing Internet sources.
CGOS provides full details, and updates are available at
<http://www.columbia.edu/cu/cup/cgos>.

CGOS recommends indenting all but the first line of each entry
in lists of works cited in the humanities and the sciences. However,
if you publish a paper online, such hanging indents may cause problems, and it may be preferable to use no indentation at all and
instead separate entries with a line of space. Check with your
instructor.

19a Two basic features of CGOS humanities style

The CGOS style for the humanities is based on the MLA style but differs in its recommendations for citing online material.

KEY POINTS

Two Basic Features of CGOS Humanities Style

1. Use MLA style to cite the author (or title) of the source in your text, giving page or paragraph numbers for online sources only if these are provided in the online site. They rarely are, however.

   ▶ **Science writer Stephen Hart claims that neuromusicology is being hailed as a "new discipline."**

   ▶ **Neuromusicology is being hailed as a "new discipline" (Hart).**

2. In your list of works cited, follow MLA style to include information about authors and titles and any basic print information, and then include information about the online source. Include whatever is available of the following items in the order indicated, each item ending with a period. Use italics (as shown below) in place of underlining if you post your paper online.

   Last name of author, first name. "Title of document." Print publication information for book or article in MLA style. *Title of complete work or Web site.* Any version number, volume, issue number, or access number. Date of online posting or update. URL (date of access).

   You can omit the URL if the database is licensed and access is limited to a specific library or institution.

19b Sample list entries in CGOS humanities style

In a works-cited list in print, titles would be underlined, not italicized. But in online documents, underlining is reserved for links, so italics for titles are preferable.

Article in an online database

Lowe, Michelle S. "Britain's Regional Shopping Centres: New Urban Forms?"
Urban Studies 37 (Feb. 2000). *InfoTrac: Expanded Academic ASAP.*
Article A61862666. (14 Apr. 2003).

Article in an online journal

Hart, Stephen. "Overtures to a New Discipline: Neuromusicology."
21st Century 1:4 (1996). http://www.columbia.edu/cu/
21stC/issue–1.4/mbmmusic.html (3 Jun. 2003).

Online posting to a discussion group

Howard, Rebecca Moore. "Institutional Pressures." 16 Apr. 2003. WPA-L.
http://lists.asu.edu (5 May 2003).

 19c Two basic features of CGOS scientific style

 KEY POINTS

Two Basic Features of CGOS Scientific Style

1. As with APA style, in your text give the author's name and year of online publication:

   ▶ **Analysis of a large set of data shows that the statistical likelihood of being divorced increases if one is male and a secondary school teacher or college professor (Kanazawa & Still, 2000).**

2. Follow APA style for the list of references. Include whatever is available of the following information in the order indicated, ending each part with a period.

   Author's last name, initial(s). (Date of online publication). Title of online work. Any print publication information. *Title of complete work, online service, or site* (with any version, volume, issue number(s)). URL (date of access).

   You can omit the URL if the database is a licensed database and access is limited to a specific library or institution.

19d Sample entries in CGOS scientific style

Article from an online database

Lowe, M. S. (2000, February). "Britain's regional shopping centres: New urban forms?" *Urban Studies 37*(2). *InfoTrac: Expanded Academic ASAP* (Article A61862666). (14 Jan. 2001).

Article in an online journal

Holtzworth-Munroe, A. (2000, June). Domestic violence: Combining scientific inquiry and advocacy. *Prevention & Treatment 3* (Article 22). http://journals .apa.org/prevention/volume3/pre0030022c.html (4 Jun. 2003).

Document Design/
Online and Workplace

Writing an essay, a research paper, a business report, a résumé, or a Web page involves not just writing but presenting. How can we make those documents we have labored over attractive and appealing to readers—and how can we make the design of those documents enhance the content and highlight our ideas? With all the technological tools at our disposal, the designing of documents is increasingly exciting and complex.

20 Design Tools, Design Features

20a Basic design functions in Word

The following functions are useful for college essays and for community and work-related documents.

1. Setting up the page and previewing it before printing Before you start your document, go to File/Page Setup to set page size, paper orientation, margins, and layout for headers and footers, and so on. When you have written your document, Print Preview shows what each page will look like, before you actually print. The screenshot shows Word XP; other versions of Word may vary, as will individual settings.

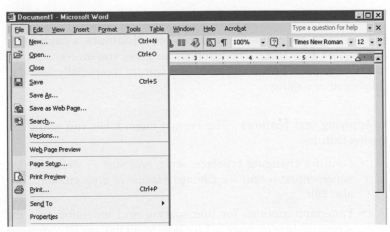

2. Adding a header or footer on every page When you open the View menu, you will see the header/footer option. The toolbar allows you to (a) include a page number along with any text, such as your name or a short running head; (b) include the date and time; (c) toggle between the choice of headers or footers. Headers and footers will adjust automatically to any changes in the pagination of your document. You type the information once only, and it appears in the place you specify on every page, however much material you add or delete.

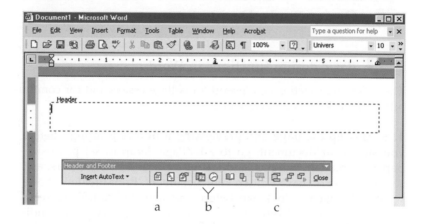

3. Inserting a page number, a comment, a footnote, a caption, or a hyperlink to a URL The Insert menu gives you access to all the functions above. The Insert/Comments feature is especially useful in collaborative writing.

4. Applying text features The Format menu takes you to the following features:

- Font: for changing typeface, style, and size as well as using superscripts; useful for *Chicago Manual of Style* citations; see also **20b**

- Paragraph: options for line spacing and indenting (see the screen capture on page 231 for how to set the special command for the hanging indents used in an MLA list of works cited)

- Bullets and Numbering for lists, Borders and Shading, Columns, Tabs, Dropped Capitals (just highlight the text to be formatted)

- Change Case: for changing your text from capital letters to lowercase or vice versa

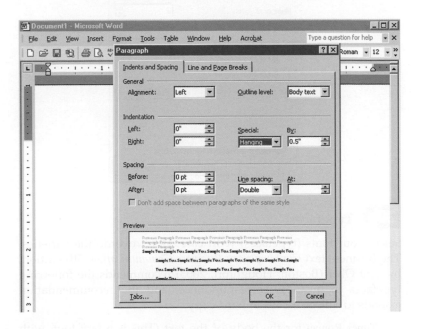

5. Getting a word count The Tools menu gives you access to a word count, to spelling and grammar checkers and a thesaurus, and to AutoCorrect and AutoFormat functions (such as turning off the automatic hyperlinks when you do not need them underlined for an MLA list of works cited). Note that you can set a grammar checker to look for specific features, such as "Punctuation with quotes" and "Passive sentences": from the Tools menu, go to Options/Spelling and Grammar/Check Grammar with Spelling/Settings. In the Tools menu you will also find the Track Changes feature, a useful tool for adding editing suggestions to your own or somebody else's text.

6. Inserting a table When you click on Table/Insert Table, you can then select the numbers of columns and rows you want.

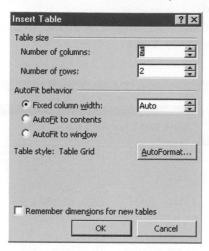

20b Typefaces

Select your fonts (typefaces) with care. Don't overdo the varieties. The business text *Contemporary Business Communication,* 5th edition, by Scot Ober (Boston: Houghton, 2003) recommends the following typefaces in business correspondence, and the recommendation extends to college essays in hard copy:

> Times Roman for the body of the text (This is a *serif* font, with little strokes—serifs—at the top and bottom of individual characters: Times Roman.)

> Arial or some other *sans serif* font for captions and headings (The word *sans* is French for "without"; a sans serif font does not have the little strokes at the top and bottom of the characters.)

> Courier, an alternative for the typewriter look, with all characters the same width. (Avoid ornamental fonts such as **Dom Casual** and *Brush Script.* They are distracting and hard to read.)

Note that if you are designing a Web page or an online communication, readers' settings of their browser configurations determine which fonts can be displayed. The simpler the font you choose, the more likely readers are to see the font of your choice.

For the body of your text in a college essay or a business communication, stick to 10- to 12-point type. Use larger type only for headings and subheadings in business, technical, or Web documents. Never increase or decrease font size in order to achieve a required page length. You will convey desperation, and you will certainly not fool your instructor.

Note: MLA and APA guidelines do not recommend typeface changes or bold type for titles and headings.

20c Color

Color printers and online publication have made the production of documents an exciting enterprise for both writers and readers. You can include graphs and illustrations in color, and you can highlight headings or parts of your text by using a different color typeface. However, simplicity and readability should prevail. Use color only when its use will enhance your message. Certainly, in the design of business reports, newsletters, brochures, and Web pages, color can play an important and eye-catching role (see **23** and **25**). But for college essays, the leading style manuals ignore and implicitly discourage the use of color.

20d Headings

Headings divide text into helpful chunks and give readers a sense of your document's structure. Main divisions are marked by first-level headings, subdivisions by second-level and third-level headings. In the heading structure of section **21**, for example, the main heading is "Visuals" and the subheadings are "Tables," "Graphs and Charts," and "Illustrations, clip art, Web downloads, and copyright issues."

For headings, bear in mind the following recommendations:

- If you use subheadings, use at least two—not just one.
- Whenever possible, use the Style feature from the Format menu to determine the level of heading you need: heading 1, 2, 3, and so on.
- Style manuals, such as the one for APA style, recommend specific formats for typeface and position on the page for levels of headings. Follow these recommended formats. See section **16** for an APA paper with headings.
- Keep headings clear, brief, and parallel in grammatical form (for instance, all commands: "Set Up Sales Strategies"; all beginning with -*ing* words: "Setting Up Sales Strategies"; or all noun-plus-modifier phrases: "Sales Strategies").

TECHNOTE Using Outline View

Note that if you are careful in applying the correct levels of headings, you can then switch to the Outline View of your document, which will collapse the body text for you and let you view only the headings above a certain level—only first-level and second-level headings, for example. This view omits all the text except for the headings you specify, so it lets you see how you have structured the organization of your document. It also helps you create an accurate table of contents for longer papers. ■

20e Lists

Lists are particularly useful in business reports, proposals, and memos. They direct readers' attention to the outlined points or steps. Decide whether to use numbers, dashes, or bullets to set off the items in a list (see **20a**, item 4). Introduce the list with a sentence ending in a colon (see **20d** for an example.) Items in the list should be parallel in grammatical form: all commands, all *-ing* phrases, or all noun phrases, for example (see **40j**). Listed items should not end with a period unless they are complete sentences.

20f Columns

Columns are useful for preparing newsletters and brochures. In Word, go to Format/Columns to choose the number of columns and the width. Your text will be automatically formatted. This feature is especially useful for creating brochures and newsletters.

21 Visuals

The technology of scanners, photocopiers, digital cameras, and downloaded Web images provides the means of making documents more functional and more attractive by allowing the inclusion of visual material. Frequently, when you are dealing with complicated data, the best way to get information across to readers is to display it visually. Consult the Key Points box on page 235.

Computer software and word processing programs make it easy for you to create your own tables and graphs to accompany your written text. For detailed information on using and creating visual material, a valuable resource is Edward Tufte, *The Visual Display of Quantitative Information,* 2nd ed. (Cheshire, CT: Graphics Press, 2001).

Tables

Tables are useful for presenting data in columns and rows. They can be created easily with word processing programs using figures from large sets of data, as the table below was (see **20a**, item 6).

TABLE 1   Internet Use by Educational Attainment: December 1998 and September 2001

Educational Attainment	Internet Use (as percentage of education group)		
	Dec 1998	Sep 2001	Difference
Less than high school	4.2	12.8	8.6
HS diploma/GED	19.2	39.8	20.6
Some college	38.6	62.4	23.8
Bachelors degree	58.4	80.8	22.4
Higher degree	66.4	83.7	17.3

Source: *A Nation Online: How Americans Are Expanding Their Use of the Internet,* February 2002: 28. National Telecommunications and Information Administration, data taken from Table 2-3 at <http://www.ntia.doc.gov/ntiahome/dn/anationonline2.pdf>. Data were collected by the U.S. Census as part of the CPS (Current Population Survey) in September 2001 from a representative sample of 137,000 adults in the United States.

KEY POINTS

On Using Visuals

1. Decide which type of visual presentation best fits your data, and determine where to place your visuals—within your text or in an appendix.

2. When you include a visual from the Web in your own online document, make sure the image file is not so large that it will take a long time for readers to download.

3. Whenever you place a visual in your text, introduce it and discuss it fully before readers come across it. Do not just make a perfunctory comment like "The results are significant, as seen in Figure 1." Rather, say something like "Figure 1 shows an increase in the number of accidents since 1997." In your discussion, indicate where the visual appears ("In the graph below" or "In the pie chart on page 8"), and carefully interpret or analyze

(Continued)

(Continued)

the visual for readers, using it as an aid that supports your points, not as something that can stand alone.

4. Give each visual a title, number each visual if you use more than one of the same type, and credit the source.

5. Do not include visuals simply to fill space or make your document look colorful. Every visual addition should enhance your content and provide an interesting and relevant illustration.

21b Graphs and charts

Graphs and charts (the terms are used interchangeably in many cases) are useful for presenting data and comparisons of data. Many software products allow you to produce graphs easily, and even standard word processing software gives you several ways to present your numbers in visual form. In Microsoft Office you can create graphs and charts in Word or Excel. In Word, for example, go to Insert/Picture/Chart and in the Chart screen go to Chart/Chart Type. You will be able to select a type of chart, such as a pie chart or a bar chart, and enter your own details, such as title, labels for the vertical and horizontal axes of a bar graph, numbers, and data labels.

Simple line graph Use a line graph to show changes over time. Figure 1 has a clear caption and is self-explanatory.

FIGURE 1 Danger on the Road

The fatality rate among motorcyclists declined for many years, partly as a result of better safety equipment and laws requiring that riders wear helmets. Now, many states have relaxed their helmet laws at the same time the median age of riders has risen, causing the fatality rate to rise again.

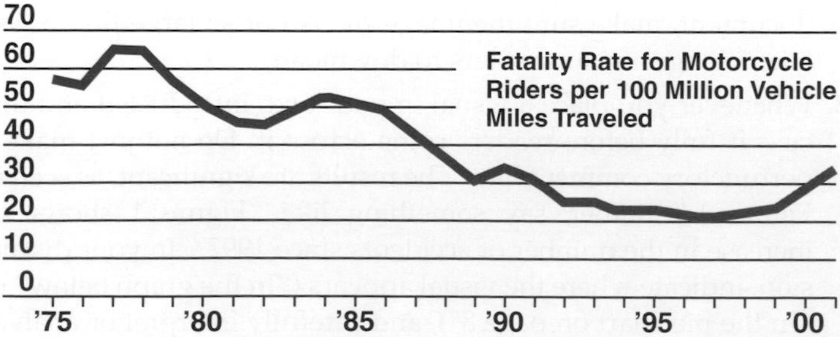

Fatality Rate for Motorcycle Riders per 100 Million Vehicle Miles Traveled

Source: Insurance Institute for Highway Safety, *New York Times,* 22 Apr. 2003: A16.

Comparative line graph   Line graphs such as Figure 2 are especially useful for comparing data over time.

FIGURE 2   **Average Tuition and Fee Charges (Enrollment-Weighted), in Constant (2002) Dollars, 1971–1972 to 2002–2003**

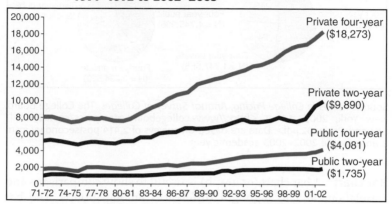

Source: *Trends in College Pricing, Annual Survey of Colleges,* The College Board, New York, 2002, 8 at <http://www.collegeboard.com/press/cost02/html/CBTrendsPricing02.pdf>. Data are based on surveys of 2,414 postsecondary institutions for the 2002–2003 academic year.

KEY POINTS

Using Graphs and Charts

- Use a graph or chart only to help make a point.
- Set up a graph or chart so that it is self-contained and self-explanatory.
- Make sure that the items on the time axis of a line graph are proportionately spaced.
- Always provide a clear caption.
- Use precise wording for labels.
- Always give details about the source of the data or information.

Pie chart   Use a pie chart (or pie graph) to show how fractions and percentages relate to one another and make up a whole. The two pie charts in Figure 3 show enrollment in four types of higher education institutions, both full-time enrollment and total enrollment.

FIGURE 3   Undergraduate Enrollment, 2002–2003

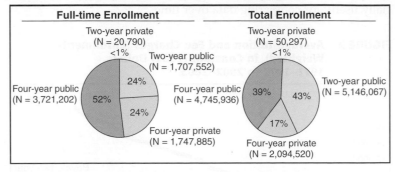

Source: *Trends in College Pricing, Annual Survey of Colleges,* The College Board, New York, 2002, 14 at <http://www.collegeboard.com/press/cost02/html/CBTrendsPricing02.pdf>. Data are based on surveys of 2,414 postsecondary institutions for the 2002–2003 academic year.

Bar chart   A bar chart (or graph) is useful to show comparisons and correlations and to highlight differences among groups. The bar chart in Figure 4 presents clear data for grade inflation over time at a variety of institutions.

FIGURE 4   Grade Inflation among Students Entering Different Types of Institutions (Percentage Earning A Averages)

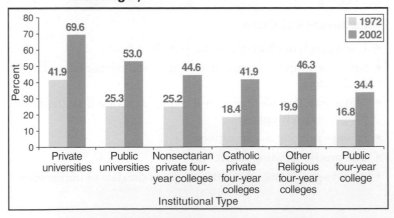

Source: L. J. Sax et al., *The American Freshman: National Norms for Fall 2002,* Los Angeles, Higher Education Research Institute, UCLA, 2003 at <http://www.gseis.ucla.edu/heri/norms.charts.pdf>. Data are from 282,549 students at 437 higher education institutions.

See also the bar charts that student Emily Luo included in her PowerPoint presentation on genetically modified crops (**28f**).

A bar chart can also be presented horizontally, which makes it easier to attach labels to the bars. Figure 5 below was produced in MS Office using the data from Table 1.

FIGURE 5   Internet Use by Educational Attainment: December 1998 and September 2001

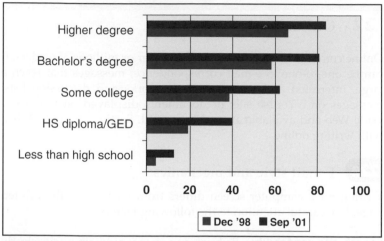

21c Illustrations, clip art, Web downloads, and copyright issues

Your computer software provides many standard images (clip art) and photographs that you can use free in your documents, without any copyright concerns. Web sites offer images to download, either free or at a small cost: try < http://www.freegraphics.com/>, <http://www.clipart.com/>,   <http://www.screamdesign.com>, <http://www.angelfire.com/wv/hmfic/free.html>, and <http://www.barrysclipart.com>. AltaVista at <http://www.altavista.com/image/default> and Google at <http://www.google.com/imghp> also let you search for specific images.

Note that if your document is to be posted on the Web, readers who have slow Internet connections may find it time-consuming or even impossible to download images with a large file size. Use a lower-quality setting for .jpg files or the .gif or .png format instead (resave if necessary).

Sophisticated and original graphics are usually copyrighted, so if you intend to use an image in a document that you post on the Web or make available in print, you need not only to download the image and cite the source, but also to write to the originator for permission to use the image. If you do not do this, you will violate copyright law.

For a college paper, you may want to include an illustration you find on the Web, such as a graph, a map, a photograph of an author or artist, a work of art, or an illustration from an online encyclopedia. You can do so without getting permission, but you must cite the source.

22   Online Communication

Online communication can reach one reader or millions of readers. It can be one-to-one in e-mail correspondence; messages that reach a large, interested audience through networks and discussion lists; messages on a course site; or documents displayed on the World Wide Web and available around the world. Sections **22** and **23** deal with writing online.

22a   E-mail style and mechanics

Writing for a computer screen differs from writing for the printed page. Pay careful attention to the following factors.

Length and readability   Be brief, and state your main points clearly at the start. One screen holds about 250 words, and online readers do not want to scroll repeatedly to find out what you are saying. Keep paragraphs short and manageable, so readers can take in the information at a glance. Use numbered or bulleted lists to present a sequence of points as brief items that can be readily seen and absorbed.

Font   Avoid using all capital letters in an e-mail message. To readers, it looks as if you are shouting.

URLs   Pay attention to accuracy of punctuation and capital letters. Both matter; one slip can invalidate an address and cause you great frustration. Whenever possible, to avoid having to write out a long URL, simply copy that URL from a document and paste it into your own document (Select/Copy/Paste). If you need to spread an address over two lines, break it after a slash (MLA style) or before a dot.

Accuracy   Use a spelling checker and edit your e-mail before sending if you are writing to people you do not know well and if you want them to take your ideas seriously—for example, your boss, business associates, classmates using a course Web page, or the unknown subscribers to a discussion list.

Subject heading Subscribers to a list and regular e-mail correspondents are likely to receive a great deal of mail every day. Be clear and concise when composing a subject heading, so readers will know at a glance what your message is about.

Flames Sometimes a writer fires off a message full of anger and name-calling. Such a message is called a *flame.* Avoid flaming. If someone flames you, do not get drawn into battle.

Signing off Always put your actual name (not just <cutiepie3@aol.com>) at the end of your online message. You can also construct a "signature file," which will appear automatically at the end of every message you send. Find out how to do this from the Help or Tools menu of your e-mail program.

The danger of attachments Attachments can harbor computer viruses, so always be cautious about opening any attachments to an e-mail message. Open attachments only from known senders, and keep your own antivirus software up-to-date so that you will not spread a virus.

22b E-mail discussion lists, bulletin boards, and discussion boards

Are you interested in Philip Glass, the St. Louis Cardinals, bonsai, beagle puppies, orchids, the Argentine tango, the Battle of Antietam? Both e-mail discussion lists and discussion/bulletin boards provide a forum for a virtual community of people sharing an interest in a topic. Thousands of these forums exist—some public, some private—providing opportunities for you to find information and to enter discussions with others and make your own contributions. Since many of the groups and forums may not be moderated or refereed in any way, you must always be careful about evaluating the reliability of a source of information. However, any discussion group can be valuable not only for the information it provides but also for the ideas that emerge as participants discuss an issue and tease out its complexities. As a general rule, e-mail lists to which it is necessary to first subscribe or register tend to be more substantive and professional than lists or boards with no access control.

Finding discussion lists Use the following directories to find the public lists that are available:

- CataList, the official catalog of LISTSERV® lists at <http://www.lsoft.com/catalist.html>. As of October 12, 2003, it contained 71,307 public lists out of a total of 303,670 LISTSERV lists.
- Topica/LISZT, a catalog of e-mail lists of all types at <http://www.topica.com>.

E-mail discussion lists The administrators of even a public list may screen potential subscribers carefully, even though generally there is no fee for subscribing. (To participate in an e-mail list, you need only an e-mail address and a mail program.) Private lists and professionally moderated lists, especially those with a technical focus, can be reliable sources of factual information and informed opinion. When you join an e-mail list (discussion group), all the messages posted are sent automatically to the e-mail accounts of all those who have registered as "subscribers." Subscribing simply means registering, not paying a fee. Lists are managed by specific software programs, such as Listserv, Listproc, and Majordomo, which have similar but not identical procedures.

Caution: Discussion lists often sell e-mail addresses, so you may get huge amounts of spam. Be careful about giving out your e-mail address. If there is a box you can check to prohibit giving out your address, be sure to check it.

KEY POINTS

Guidelines for Participating in Online Discussion Lists

1. If a Web interface is available for an e-mail discussion list, use it. Subscription management and posting, each with its own address, will be all in one place and therefore easier to manage.

2. If you do subscribe via e-mail, remember that a list has two addresses: the *posting* address (to send messages to all subscribers) and the *subscription* address (to send commands about managing your subscription). To differentiate between them, think of the difference between sending a letter to the editor of a printed newspaper for publication and sending a note to the circulation manager about a vacation suspension of your subscription. Use the subscription address (not the posting address) to subscribe to a list, suspend your subscription, unsubscribe from a list, or make other changes to your

(Continued)

(Continued)

subscription details. The wording you use must be exact. Follow the list's directions for the commands, and save a copy.

3. Lurk before you post! Spend time reading and browsing in the Web archives in order to learn the conventions and the types of topics before you start sending messages to everyone on the list.

4. Manage the volume of mail. A mailing list may generate thirty, one hundred, or more messages a day, so after a few days away, you may feel overwhelmed. Use the options the list provides to select—for example—Nomail, Digest, or Index. Nomail temporarily suspends the sending of messages to your mailbox; Digest allows you to get only one bundle of mail every day; Index simply lists the messages once a day, and you retrieve the ones you want to read. However, not all options are available for all lists. You can also use filters to put messages into a special folder, so that you can read them when you are ready.

5. Pay close attention to who the actual recipient is—the whole list or the person who posted the original message. Make sure you know who will actually receive your message. If you want to reply to only the individual sender of a message, do not send your message to the whole list; choose "Reply," not "Reply All." (Don't complain to Manuel about Al's views and then by mistake send your reply to the whole list, including Al!)

6. Do not quote the whole original message. Select only a short passage, the one you immediately refer or reply to.

7. Avoid sending a message like "I agree" to the many subscribers to the list. Make your postings substantive and considerate, so subscribers find them worth reading.

8. Do not forward a posting from one list to another unless you ask the sender for permission or unless the posting is a general informational announcement.

Bulletin boards and discussion boards   Now sharing many features with discussion lists, bulletin boards, and discussion boards are Web pages to which you can post messages directly. Sometimes you can do this spontaneously; in other instances, you have to register first. Discussion boards, such as those hosted by the *New York Times* on a variety of topics (at <http://www.nytimes.com/pages/readersopinions/index.html>), are included in many online magazine and media Web sites and in course Web sites, which provide a forum for students' discussions.

22c Newsgroups, blogs, and synchronous communication

Less reliable to researchers as sources of information are the following, though they can provide participants with a sense of current concerns on a topic.

Newsgroups   Tens of thousands of "Usenet newsgroups" cover every imaginable topic. Anyone can post anything on any subject. Messages are archived at <http://groups.google.com>, where you can use a search engine to find subjects and keywords that interest you, and you can read recent postings. As no control exists over the postings, they may contain material that some consider offensive, and they offer little that is useful for scholarly research.

Blogs   Web logs, known as *blogs*, are publicly posted personal diaries. Several providers offer free server space for blogs, such as Blogger at <http://www.blogger.com>. Groups as well as individuals can be given posting rights, so blogs are useful and affordable for student groups. Blogs have been called the soap boxes of the electronic age.

Synchronous communication   None of the discussions in the forums described so far in section **22** take place in real time. For all of them, you post a message, and then later, when someone else logs on and takes the time to write, you may get a response. Instant messaging, chat rooms, buddy lists, MUDs (multiuser domains), and MOOs (multiuser domains, object oriented), in contrast, operate in real time. You may want to use such instant messaging to connect with classmates or colleagues to discuss a group project.

Course management systems such as Blackboard and WebCT provide virtual classrooms, cyberspaces in which a whole class or a group of students can log on at the same time and communicate in real time. These virtual classrooms are used for serious instruction in distance learning. They can provide videoconferencing tools for group projects and give online students opportunities for discussions.

23 Web Site Design

The language commonly used for Web site design is HTML (see **24b**). For a HTML tutorial, try the following sites:

<http://webknowhow.net/dir/HTML/Tutorials/>

<http://www.htmlprimer.com>

23a Planning and organizing a Web site

Though the terms are often used rather loosely, a "Web page" can be viewed in a single window (though some scrolling may be necessary), whereas a "Web site" consists of a number of interrelated (linked) Web pages. Strictly speaking, Allison Marsh's Web site at <http://www.student.richmond.edu/2001/amarsh/public_html> (illustrated in **23d**) consists of one start page, three second-level pages (university and professional information, personal information, and e-mail), and many third-level pages. In addition, many pages are subdivided into frames, with a decorative "side frame" used on more than one page. You will generate one page at a time, but you should start by considering the following:

- What is your purpose? What content do you want to provide? What message do you want to get across?

- Who do you think will visit your site? What will your visitors expect?

- How do you want to structure the site? How will visitors navigate around the site?

- How much maintenance will the site need (updating links and content, for example)?

- How will you make your site accessible to those with disabilities?

Decide which you want to use, single pages or pages divided into frames. Keep in mind that the way Web pages are displayed on a visitor's screen depends much on the size and setup of the visitor's monitor and the type, version, and setup of the browser he or she uses. What may look terrific on your own station may look messy on the station of a visitor, or—worse yet—parts of your page may not display at all. Basic HTML gives you only limited control of how your pages display on other stations. Therefore, keep your start (home) page simple, think twice before using nonstandard features (Javascripts, Java applets, and so on), and make sure that all links to the other pages within your own site and to external sites are easily recognizable and indicate clearly what content they lead to.

Then draw a site map—that is, a flow chart that shows the logic of how the different parts of the site relate to each other. Allison Marsh's home page (p. 248) clearly links to three other pages within her site, which in turn link to other pages, internally and externally. Here is the site map for the first levels of her site.

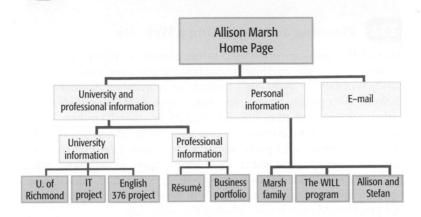

KEY POINTS

Web Site Design Guidelines

- Keep pages short—as a general rule, no more than 2–3 screens.
- Set your own monitor to a resolution not higher than 800×600, and make sure all the text is visible on your screen without horizontal scrolling.
- Keep sentences short and direct.
- Break text into short passages.
- Use headings, and provide internal links to the headings.
- Use visuals—such as pictures, diagrams, photographs, graphs, clip art, or animations—to enhance and illustrate ideas. Graphics should offer more than a distraction. Pay attention to the file size of such add-ons. It is often possible to reduce the file size significantly with only a minimal loss of image quality.
- Choose descriptive text or images as "anchors" for links. Check on their reliability and keep them up-to-date.
- Use color and background patterns judiciously. Blue type on a black swirling background may look interesting, but it can be difficult to read.
- Be sensitive to issues of accessibility for people with disabilities, such as using descriptive text as well as images and offering alternatives to visual and auditory material. Refer to the Bobby

(Continued)

(Continued)

site at the Center for Applied Special Technology for guidelines: <http://bobby.watchfire.com/bobby/html/en/index.jsp>.

- Keep the site uncluttered for ease of navigation.

- Include relevant navigational links from each page of your site to other pages, such as the home page. Consider the use of a "navigation bar" that appears on each page of your site. Update your site regularly to maintain the links to external URLs.

- Include your own e-mail address for comments and questions about your site. State the date of the last page update.

- Think about whether you really want to include personal information, such as your home address and telephone number.

If you download and use text and graphics in your own site, ask for permission and acknowledge the fact that you received permission to use the material. Be aware that you may have to pay a fee to use copyrighted material. Also, provide full documentation for your sources (see **21c**).

23c Useful resources for site design

A writing handbook cannot cover many of the intricate details of Web site preparation. For more complete coverage, consult the following:

- Johndan Johnson-Eilola, *Designing Effective Web Sites: A Concise Guide* (Boston: Houghton, 2002)

- Elizabeth Castro, *HTML 4 for the World Wide Web,* 5th ed. (Berkeley: Peachpit, 2002)

- Jakob Nielsen, *Designing Web Usability* (Indianapolis: New Riders, 2000); also the Web sites at <http://www.useit.com> and <http://www.useit.com/jakob/webusability>

- Jakob Nielsen and Marie Tahir, *Homepage Usability: Fifty Websites Deconstructed* (Indianapolis: New Riders, 2001)

- Jennifer Niederst, *Web Design in a Nutshell,* 2nd ed. (Cambridge: O'Reilly, 2001)

- *Builder.com* offering help for site builders and useful Web page design tips at <http://builder.com.com/>

- Library of Congress Guidelines for HTML 4.01 at <http://www.loc.gov/iug/html40>

23d Sample student Web site

Allison Marsh, now working for a consulting firm, graduated from the University of Richmond, Virginia. Here are two pages from her undergraduate Web site, available at <http://www.student.richmond.edu/2001/amarsh/public_html>.

Home Page

Link from "University of Richmond & Professional Information"

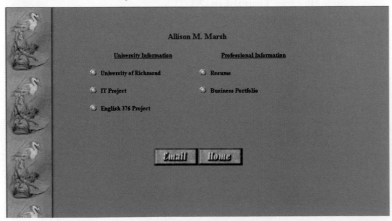

24 Academic Writing Online

A document written for presentation online has requirements very different from those for a document designed to be printed on paper.

24a Hypertext

When we read a printed document, we often read from beginning to end, though we may do some skimming and scanning and take an advance peek at the end of a murder mystery to see whether the butler actually did it. Other than reading technical texts with their many footnotes and endnotes, however, reading print is basically a linear process, as one word follows another, one idea follows another, one paragraph follows another. In contrast, when we read HTML-created documents in e-mail or on the Web, we can follow the links by opening an additional window. So when we write for online readers, we need to provide those associative links. It is not appropriate to write for the printed page and then simply slap the document up on a screen.

24b HTML

Text posted on the Web will usually be in HTML (hypertext markup language) format, which any browser can display (though other extensions—such as XML—and supplements—such as Javascript—are available for advanced Web pages). In HTML files, the visible text is supplemented by specific instructions, known as "tags," that are enclosed in angle brackets (< . . . >). However, if the sight of such tags and the often rather messy-looking source code makes you shudder, you can begin by using a program that creates the underlying HTML tags automatically (this is like driving a car without knowing or caring what the carburetor does).

Recent versions of word processing programs can automatically convert a document and save it as an HTML file. In Word, for example, you simply produce your document in the usual way but then, when you save it, go to "Save As" and change "Save as type" from "Word" to "Web page." The HTML commands are done for you, automatically. In addition, Netscape Composer provides an HTML editor that tends to be more efficient in display speed.

24c Guidelines for posting academic writing online

You may be required to submit an essay for a course online rather than in hard copy. Your instructor may ask you to e-mail him or her an attachment, or in a hybrid or a synchronous distance-learning course, you may be required to submit your essays in a dropbox or post them on a class bulletin board for the instructor and other students to read and comment on. In either case, keep in mind the following general guidelines, and ask your instructor for instructions specific to the course, format, and type of posting.

KEY POINTS

Posting an Essay or a Research Paper Online

1. *Structure* Set up a structure with sections and subsections (called "fragments"), all with headings, that allows each section to be accessed directly—for example, from your table of contents (see item 2 below) and from any other part of your paper as well. So instead of saying diffusely "see above" or "see below," you can provide a specific link allowing readers to jump directly to this part (see item 3).

2. *Links to sections from a table of contents* Provide a table of contents, with an internal link anchored to each fragment, marked with a "bookmark" or "target," and give each bookmark (MS IE) or target (Netscape) a name. Readers can then click on and go directly to any section they are interested in.

3. *Internal hyperlinks* Use internal hyperlinks (Insert/Hyperlink) to connect readers directly to relevant sections of your text, content notes, and visuals. Also provide a link from a source cited in the body of your paper to the entry in your list of works cited.

4. *External hyperlinks* Use external hyperlinks to connect to Web documents from references in the body of your paper and from your list of works cited. Useful for the works-cited list, Word has a function that will automatically convert any string starting with <http://> into a hyperlink (go to Tools/Auto Correct/ Auto Format, and then check Replace Internet and Network Paths with Hyperlinks).

(Continued)

(Continued)

5. *No paragraph indentation* Do not indent for a new paragraph. Instead, leave a line space between paragraphs.

6. *Attribution of sources* Make sure that the link you give to an online article in a database is a persistent link, not a link that works for only a few hours or days. It is often difficult to determine at first glance whether a link is persistent or not. Some databases are explicit; others are not. Double-check your links after a few days to see whether the links are still working. Some sites (such as Thomas at Library of Congress at <http://thomas.loc.gov) give instruction on how to turn non-persistent links into persistent ones).

7. *List of works cited or list of references.* Give a complete list, with visible hyperlinked URLs, even if you provide some external links to the sources from the body of your paper. If a reader prints your paper, the exact references will then still be available.

25 Flyers, Brochures, and Newsletters

25a Design principles for flyers, brochures, and newsletters

When you are producing material that will be printed or photocopied and then distributed to many people, you will want to take extra care to create a document that is attractive and effective. Attention to design increases the chance that your brochure, newsletter, or flyer will be read and have the effect that you intend. While there is never a single "right" way to arrange information and images on a page, some basic principles can help you design a successful print communication.

1. *Plan.* Consider the audience and the purpose of your document: Who will read the document? How and when will people see the document? What is the most important message you are communicating? Does the document need to relate to any other documents in a series from your school or organization?

2. *Experiment.* Leave time to try out variations in the document format: to experiment with type sizes and fonts, to add more or less white space at different places, to test various colors or arrangements—in short, to play with the design and get feedback from sample audience members. This way you can see what surprises and delights people and what puzzles or bores them.

3. *Value readability and clarity.* Consider the proportion of one element to another within your piece, so that important information is highlighted or given priority and nothing appears overly crowded or illegibly small.

4. *Keep consistency and coherence* from page to page in matters of margins, typefaces, headings, captions, borders, column widths, and so forth. While you do not want the document to be dull, you also do not want it to be a distracting, shifting jumble of formats and type styles. *Note:* If you are using a desktop publishing program, set up a grid or template to block out the consistent placement of headings, columns, margins, and boxed features for each document you are designing. The lines of a grid appear on your computer but will not appear when the document is printed; they become like an empty vessel into which you "pour" your content.

5. *Give careful consideration to the following design variables:*

   - *Type size and font* For the main text of your document, choose a readable type size, not one that is uncomfortably small or that has letters that are hard to decipher. Serif fonts (the ones with little strokes at the top and bottom of each letter) are more readable and thus the best choice for the main body of a print document. For headlines and headings, use a limited number of other larger type sizes. Headings should help organize material for the reader and establish a hierarchy of importance among different sections of the document.

   - *Use of white space* Cut and condense your text as necessary to allow for a generous amount of white space in your margins and borders and above and below headings.

   - *Leading (the amount of space between lines of type)* When lines of type are set too close together, one on top of the other, they are hard to read, so adequate line spacing is important. Extra line spacing can also be used to indicate paragraph breaks.

- *End-of-line alignment* Lines of type can be justified—spaced out uniformly to be all the same length—or set with a "ragged right" margin. Justified lines appear more formal, have a greater type density, and can create a lot of hyphenated words; lines that are ragged right create a less formal and more open look.

- *Column width and line length* In general, the wider the column or line of type, the easier it is for a reader to lose his or her place. Shorter columns and shorter lines of type are easier to read.

- *Rules (printed lines)* Horizontal and vertical rules of various thicknesses can be effective in setting off columns, headings, pull-out quotations, photos, and captions.

- *Boxes and sidebars* These elements separate smaller segments of material from the larger flow of text. Boxing a part of your document can give it extra emphasis or attention.

- *Reversed type* With this technique, type appears white against a black or other colored background. *Note:* Reversed type becomes hard to read when the type is very small.

- *Screened backgrounds or images* If your document is to be printed with black ink and you want a certain section of your document to have a gray background, printers can create that effect by "screening" the section at a certain percentage, which you specify. They apply the print at a graded density, from 100 percent (solid color) to 10 percent (very light gray). Ink of any color can be screened. Red ink will become pink if screened, blue ink will become light blue if screened, and so on.

- *Bleed images or bleed type* This effect makes an image or word appear to be running off the side of the page. It can be used to create drama, excitement, and a sense of an expanded design space.

In college and community life, much information is shared through brochures, newsletters, and flyers. The following sample demonstrates some principles of effective design for a brochure.

25b Sample community brochure

Community Brochure Offering Volunteer Opportunities (Front)

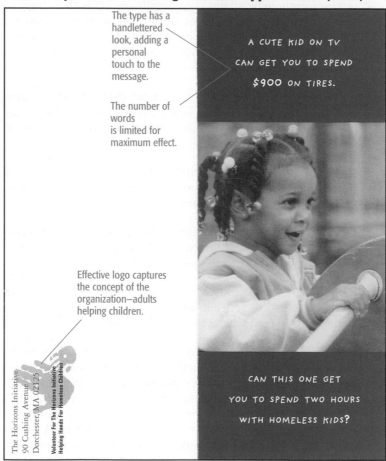

The type has a handlettered look, adding a personal touch to the message.

The number of words is limited for maximum effect.

A CUTE KID ON TV CAN GET YOU TO SPEND $900 ON TIRES.

Effective logo captures the concept of the organization—adults helping children.

The Horizons Initiative
90 Cushing Avenue
Dorchester, MA 02125

Volunteer For The Horizons Initiative
Helping Hands For Homeless Children

CAN THIS ONE GET YOU TO SPEND TWO HOURS WITH HOMELESS KIDS?

See the next page for the reverse side of this brochure.

Community Brochure Offering Volunteer Opportunities (Back)

Tan background sets off introduction.

EVERY CHILD DESERVES A CHILDHOOD.

Research shows that the first years in a child's life are critical for health, self-esteem and intellectual development. For homeless children, those needs are often overlooked.

There are more than 1.5 million homeless children in the U.S. In Boston, there are 500 homeless families and 1,500 homeless children each year. Over half of the homeless children in Massachusetts are under 5 years old.

WHAT IS OUR MISSION?

The Horizons Initiative is a non-profit organization in Boston that is exclusively dedicated to serving homeless children and their families.

Extra space between lines enhances readability of message.

Our mission is to provide homeless children in our community with the nurturing, stimulation and opportunities for educational play that all children need to learn and grow in healthy ways; and to improve these children's lives over the long-term by providing their parents with the tools they need to achieve social and economic self-sufficiency.

HOW YOU CAN HELP AS A VOLUNTEER.

We are in need of patient, dependable individuals to volunteer as Playspace Activity Leaders with children living in area homeless shelters.

Specifically, you would be responsible for preparing and leading activities, games and projects with a group of 1-5 children.

A commitment of 2 hours per week, for a minimum of 6 months, and attendance at our 6-hour training session is required. Shelters are located in more than 16 communities in the Greater Boston area. Day and evening times are available.

The second color, dark green, highlights important information, making it stand out from the rest of the text.

TAKE THE FIRST STEP.

For more information on volunteering, or for a Playspace Activity Leader application, please call 1.800.560.7702 or visit The Horizons Initiative website at www.horizonsinitiative.org today.

Logo repeated for coherence.

VOLUNTEER FOR

The Horizons Initiative
Helping Hands For Homeless Children
Call 1.800.560.7702 to volunteer

Courtesy of The Horizons Initiative, Dorchester, Massachusetts.

26 Résumés and Letters of Application

Communication in the work world frequently revolves around technology: telephones, faxes, computers, e-mail, presentational software, and spreadsheets. In business, knowing how to prepare documents for the screen and the page is a valuable skill whether you are applying for a job or communicating with colleagues and clients.

26a How to write a résumé

Résumés can be delivered on paper, on the Web, or via e-mail. Designs differ, and no one format works for everyone. However, in all formats, you need to convey to a prospective employer what you have accomplished and when, providing details of your education, work experience, honors or awards, interests, and special skills. Above all, you need to show that your qualifications and experience make you suitable for the job you are applying for.

KEY POINTS

Writing a Résumé

1. Decide how to present your résumé, or follow a prospective employer's instructions: on paper, on the Web, in the body of an e-mail message, as an e-mail attachment—or all of these. Start with a paper version and save it as .rtf or .doc, which you can easily convert to HTML.

2. For a hard-copy version, print on standard-size paper of good quality, white or off-white.

3. Use headings to indicate the main sections.

4. For a hard-copy version, highlight section headings and important information with boldface, italics, bullets, indentation, or different fonts. Use a clear, simple design. Do not use overly elaborate fonts, colors, or design features.

5. Keep a print résumé to one page, if possible. Do not include extraneous information to add length, but do not cram by using single-spacing between sections, a small font, or a tiny margin.

6. Include information and experience relevant to the job you are applying for. Use reverse chronological order (begin with your most recent work experience and education).

7. Proofread your résumé several times, and ask someone else to examine it carefully as well. Make sure it contains no errors. Avoid howlers such as "rabid typist" and "responsible for ruining a five-store chain."

8. Accompany your print résumé with a cover letter (**26e**), also carefully checked to avoid an error such as "Thank you for considering me. I look forward to hearing from you shorty."

Note: Microsoft Word provides résumé templates that set up headings for you—a useful guide.

26b Sample print or Web page résumé

Notice how Aurelia Gomez organized her résumé into clear divisions, using bold headings and a space between sections. This résumé presents the most recent job experience and education first and works backward.*

225 West 70th Street
New York, NY 10023
Phone: 212-555-3821
E-mail: agomez@nyu.edu

Aurelia Gomez

Objective:	Entry-level staff accounting position with a public accounting firm	
Experience:	Summer 2003	**Accounting Intern:** Coopers & Lybrand, NYC • Assisted in preparing corporate tax returns • Attended meetings with clients • Conducted research in corporate tax library and wrote research reports
	Nov. 1999– Aug. 2002	**Payroll Specialist:** City of New York • Worked in a full-time civil service position in the Department of Administration • Used payroll and other accounting software on both DEC 1034 minicomputer and Pentium III • Represented 28-person work unit on the department's management-labor committee • Left job to pursue college degree full-time
Education:	Jan. 1998– Present	Pursuing a 5-year bachelor of business administration degree (major in accounting) from NYU • Expected graduation date: June 2004 • Attended part-time from 1999 until 2002 while holding down a full-time job • Have financed 100% of all college expenses through savings, work, and student loans • Plan to sit for the CPA exam in May 2005
Personal Data:		• Helped start the Minority Business Student Association at NYU and served as program director for two years; secured the publisher of *Black Enterprise* magazine as a banquet speaker • Have traveled extensively throughout South America • Am a member of the Accounting Society • Am willing to relocate
References:	Available on request	

Provides specific enough objective to be useful

Places work experience before education because applicant considers it to be her stronger qualification

Uses action words such as *assisted* and *conducted;* uses incomplete sentences to emphasize the action words and to conserve space

Provides degree, institution, major, and graduation date

Makes the major section headings parallel in format and in wording

Formats the side headings for the dates in a column for ease of reading

Provides additional data to enhance her credentials

Omits actual names and addresses of references

*Sample documents in **26b–27e** are adapted from Scot Ober's *Contemporary Business Communication*, 5th ed. (Boston: Houghton, 2003). Used with permission.

26c An electronic résumé

Companies often scan the print résumés they receive, in order to establish a database of prospective employees. They can then use a keyword search to find suitable candidates from those in the database. You may also need to e-mail your résumé to a prospective employer. In either case, you need to be able to adapt a print résumé to make it easy for users to read and scan. You do not need to limit the length of either a scannable or an e-mail résumé.

KEY POINTS

Preparing a Scannable or an E-mail Résumé

- Check any prospective employer's Web site to find its emphasis and important keywords.

- Use nouns as résumé keywords to enable prospective employers to do effective keyword searches (use "educational programmer," for example, rather than "designed educational programs").

- Use a standard typeface (Times New Roman or Arial), 10- to 12-point, and for an e-mail document use "text-only" or ASCII (a file name with a .txt extension).

- Avoid italics, underlining, and graphics.

- Avoid marked lists, or change bullets to + (plus signs) or to * (asterisks).

- Begin each major heading line at the left margin.

- Do not include any decorative vertical or horizontal lines or borders.

- Consult the Web site for the division of employment and training in your state.

- E-mail yourself or a friend a copy of your résumé (both as an attachment and within the body of a message) before you send, so that you can verify the formatting.

- If you feel it is necessary, attach a note saying that a formatted version is available in hard copy, and send one as a backup.

- For further advice and examples of online résumés, consult <http://jobsearchtech.about.com>.

26d Sample electronic résumé

Here is Aurelia Gomez's résumé adapted for e-mailing.

Runs longer than one page (acceptable for electronic résumés)

Includes notice of availability of a fully formatted version

Begins with name at the top, followed immediately by addresses

Emphasizes, where possible, nouns as keywords

Uses only ASCII characters; all text is one size with no special formatting; no rules, graphics, columns, tables, and the like are used

Uses vertical line spaces (Enter key) and horizontal spacing (space bar) to show relationship of parts

Formats lists with asterisks instead of bullets

```
PERSONAL DATA
     * Helped start the Minority Business Student
       Association at New York University and served as
       program director for two years; secured the
       publisher of BLACK ENTERPRISE magazine as a banquet
       speaker
     * Have traveled extensively throughout South America
     * Am a member of the Accounting Society
     * Am willing to relocate

REFERENCES
     Available upon request

NOTE
     An attractive and fully formatted hard-copy version
     of this resume is available upon request.
```

```
AURELIA GOMEZ

    225 West 70 Street
    New York, NY 10023
    Phone: 212-555-3821
    E-mail:agomez@nyu.edu

OBJECTIVE
    Entry-level staff accounting position with a public
    accounting firm

EXPERIENCE
    Summer 2003
    Accounting Intern: Coopers & Lybrand, NYC
    * Assisted in preparing corporate tax returns
    * Attended meetings with clients
    * Conducted research in corporate tax library and
      wrote research reports

    Nov. 1999-Aug. 2002
    Payroll Specialist: City of New York
    * Full-time civil service position in the Department of
      Administration
    * Proficiency in payroll and other accounting
      software on DEC 1034 minicomputer and Pentium III
    * Representative for a 28-person work unit on the
      department's management-labor committee
    * Reason for leaving job: To pursue college degree
      full-time

EDUCATION
    Jan. 1998-Present
    Pursuing a 5-year bachelor of business
    administration degree (major in accounting) from NYU
    * Expected graduation date: June 2004
    * Attended part-time from 1999 until 2002 while
      holding down a full-time job
    * Have financed 100% of all college expenses through
      savings, work, and student loans
    * Plan to sit for the CPA exam in May 2005
```

26e Cover letter and sample

Accompany your print or e-mail résumé with a cover letter that explains what position you are applying for and why you are a good candidate. Find out as much as you can about the potential employer and type of work; then, in your letter, emphasize the connections between your experience and the job requirements. (Here is an example of a solicited application letter; it accompanies the résumé on

February 13, 2004

Mr. David Norman, Partner
Ross, Russell & Weston
452 Fifth Avenue
New York, NY 10018

Dear Mr. Norman:

Subject: EDP Specialist Position (Reference No. 103-G)

My varied work experience in accounting and payroll services, coupled with my accounting degree, has prepared me for the position of EDP specialist that you advertised in the February 9 *New York Times*.

In addition to taking required courses in accounting and management information systems as part of my accounting major at New York University, I took an elective course in EDP auditing and control. The training I received in this course in applications, software, systems, and service-center records would enable me to immediately become a productive member of your EDP consulting staff.

My college training has been supplemented by an internship in a large accounting firm. In addition, my two and one-half years of experience as a payroll specialist for the city of New York have given me firsthand knowledge of the operation and needs of nonprofit agencies. This experience should help me to contribute to your large consulting practice with governmental agencies.

After you have reviewed my enclosed résumé, I would appreciate having the opportunity to discuss with you why I believe I have the right qualifications and personality to serve you and your clients. I can be reached by phone after 3 p.m. daily.

Sincerely,

Aurelia Gomez

Aurelia Gomez
225 West 70 Street
New York, NY 10023
Phone: 212-555-3821
E-mail: agomez@nyu.edu

Enclosure

Side annotations:

Identifies the job position and source of advertising

Emphasizes a qualification that might distinguish her from other applicants

Relates her work experience to the specific needs of the employer

Provides a telephone number (may be done either in the body of the letter or in the last line of the address block)

page 257). Let the employer see that you understand the type of person he or she is looking for. State when, where, and how you can be contacted. As with the résumé itself, proofread the letter carefully.

Once you have had an interview, write a short note to thank the interviewer and emphasize your interest in the position.

27 Business Letters and Memos

27a Features of a business letter

A good business letter usually has the following qualities:

1. It is brief.

2. It clearly conveys to the reader information and expectations for action or response.

3. It lets the reader know how he or she will benefit from or be affected by the proposal or suggestion.

4. It is polite.

5. It is written in relatively formal language.

6. It contains no errors.

LANGUAGE AND CULTURE
Business Letters across Cultures

Basic features of business letters vary from culture to culture. Business letters in English avoid both flowery language and references to religion, elements that are viewed favorably in some other cultures. Do not assume that there are universal conventions. When writing cross-cultural business letters, follow these suggestions:

1. Use a formal style; address correspondents by title and family name.

2. If possible, learn about the writing conventions of your correspondent's culture.

3. Use clear language and summary to get your point across.

4. Avoid humor; it may fall flat and could offend.

27b   Sample business letter

The sample letter uses a block format, with all parts aligned at the left. This format is commonly used with business stationery.

November 1, 2003 ↓ 4

> The arrows indicate how many lines to space down before typing the next part. For example, ↓ *4* after the date means to press Enter four times before typing the recipient's name.

Ms. Ella Shore, Professor
Department of Journalism
Burlington College
North Canyon Drive
South Burlington, VT 05403 ↓ 2

Dear Ms. Shore: ↓ 2

Subject: Newspaper Advertising

Thank you for thinking of Ben & Jerry's when you were planning the advertising for the back-to-school edition of your campus newspaper at Burlington College. We appreciate the wide acceptance your students and faculty give our products, and we are proud to be represented in the *Mountain Lark*. We are happy to purchase a quarter-page ad, as follows.

- The ad should include our standard logo and the words "Welcome to Ben & Jerry's." Please note the use of the ampersand instead of the word "and" in our name. Note also that "Jerry's" contains an apostrophe.

- We would prefer that our ad appear in the top right corner of a right-facing page, if possible.

Our logo is enclosed for you to duplicate. I am also enclosing a check for $375 to cover the cost of the ad. Best wishes as you publish this special edition of your newspaper. ↓ 2

Sincerely, ↓ 4

Joseph W. Dye

Joseph W. Dye
Sales Manager ↓ 2

rmt
Enclosures
c: Advertising Supervisor

> **Reference initials:**   initials of the person who typed the letter (if other than the signer)
> **Notations:**   indications of items being enclosed with the letter, copies of the letter being sent to another person, special-delivery instructions, and the like

30 Community Drive • South Burlington, Vermont • 05403-6828 • Tel: 802/846-1500 • www.benjerry.com

27c Technical requirements of a business letter

Paper and page numbering   Use $8^1/_2'' \times 11''$ white unlined paper. If your letter is longer than one page, number the pages beginning with page 2 in the top right margin.

Spacing   Type single-spaced, on one side of the page only, and double-space between paragraphs. Double-space below the date, the inside address, and the salutation. Double-space between the last line of the letter and the closing. Quadruple-space between the closing and the typed name of the writer, and then double-space to *Enclosure* (or *Enc.*) or *c:* (indicating that you are enclosing materials or are sending a copy to another person).

Left and right margins   The sample letter in **27b** uses a block format: the return address, inside address, salutation, paragraphs, closing, and signature begin at the left margin. The right margin should not be justified; it should be ragged (with lines of unequal length) to avoid awkward gaps in the spacing between words. A modified block format places the return address and date, closing, and signature on the right.

Return address   If you are not using business letterhead, give your address as the return address, followed by the date. Do not include your name with the address. (If you are using business letterhead on which an address is printed, you do not have to write a return address.)

Inside address   The inside address gives the name, title, and complete address of the person you are writing to. With a word processing program and certain printers, you can use this part of the letter for addressing the envelope.

Salutation   In the salutation, mention the recipient's name if you know it, with the appropriate title (*Dr., Professor, Mr., Ms.*), or just the recipient's title (*Dear Sales Manager*). If you are writing to a company or institution, use a more general term of address (*Dear Sir or Madam*) or the name of the company or institution (*Dear Gateway 2000*). Use a colon after the salutation in a business letter.

Closing phrase and signature   Capitalize only the first word of a closing phrase, such as *Yours truly* or *Sincerely yours.* Type your name four lines below the closing phrase (omitting *Mr.* or *Ms.*). If you have a title (*Supervisor, Manager*), type it underneath your name. Between the closing phrase and your typed name, sign your name in ink.

Other information   Indicate whether you have enclosed materials with the letter (*Enclosure* or *Enc.*) and to whom you have sent copies (*cc: Ms. Amy Ray*). The abbreviation *cc:* used to refer to *carbon copy* but now refers to *courtesy copy* or *computer copy.* You may, however, use a single *c:* followed by a name or names, to indicate who besides your addressee is receiving the letter.

The envelope   Choose an envelope that fits your letter folded from bottom to top in thirds. Use your computer's addressing capability to place the name, title, and full address of the recipient in the middle of the envelope, and your own name and address in the top left-hand corner. Remember to include ZIP codes. Word processing programs include a function (Tools) that allows you to create labels for envelopes.

27d Basic features of a memo

A memo (from the Latin *memorandum,* meaning "to be remembered") is a message from one person to someone else within an organization. It can be sent on paper or by e-mail. A memo usually reports briefly on an action, raises a question, or asks permission to follow a course of action. It addresses a specific question or issue in a quick, focused way, conveying information in clear paragraphs or numbered points.

Begin a memo with headings such as *To, From, Date,* and *Subject;* such headings are frequently capitalized and in boldface type. In the first sentence, tell readers what your point is. Then briefly explain, giving reasons or details. Single-space the memo. If your message is long, divide it into short paragraphs, or include numbered or bulleted lists and headings (see **20d** and **20e**) to organize and draw attention to essential points. Many computer programs provide a standard template for memo format. The design and headings are provided; you just fill in what you want to say.

27e Sample memo

Barnes & Noble Inc.
Booksellers Since 1873
122 Fifth Avenue New York, NY 10011
(212) 633-3300

→ TAB

Heading

MEMO TO: Max Dillon, Sales Manager ↓ 2

FROM: Andrea J. Hayes ↓ 2 *ajh*

DATE: February 25, 2003 ↓ 2

SUBJECT: New-Venture Proposal ↓ 3

The arrows indicate how many lines to space down before typing the next part. For example, ↓ 2 after the date means to press Enter twice before typing the recipient's name.

Body

I propose the purchase or lease of a van to be used as a mobile bookstore. We could then use this van to generate sales in the outlying towns and villages throughout the state.

We have been aware for quite some time that many small towns around the state do not have adequate bookstore facilities, but the economics of the situation are such that we would not be able to open a comprehensive branch and operate it profitably. However, we could afford to stock a van with books and operate it for a few days at a time in various small towns throughout the state. As you are probably aware, the laws of this state would permit us to acquire a statewide business license fairly easily and inexpensively.

With the proper advance advertising (see attached sample), we should be able to generate much interest in this endeavor. It seems to me that this idea has much merit because of the flexibility it offers us. For example, we could tailor the length of our stay to the size of the town and the amount of business generated. Also, we could customize our inventory to the needs and interests of the particular locales.

The driver of the van would act as the salesperson, and we would, of course, have copies of our complete catalog so that mail orders could be taken as well. Please let me have your reactions to this proposal. If you wish, I can explore the matter further and generate cost and sales estimates in time for your next manager's meeting. ↓ 2

Reference initials
Attachment notation

jmc
Attachments

Barnes & Noble Bookstores ■ B. Dalton Bookseller ■ Doubleday Book Shops ■ Scribner's Bookstores ■ Bookstop

28   Oral and Multimedia Presentations

You may be asked to give oral presentations in writing courses, in other college courses, and in the business world. Usually you will do some writing as you prepare your talk, and you will deliver your oral report either from notes or from a manuscript text written especially for oral presentation.

28a   Preparing an oral presentation

Consider the background and expectations of your audience. Jot down what you know about your listeners and what stance and tone will best convince them of the validity of your views. For example, what effect do you want to have on the members of your audience? Do you want to inform, persuade, move, or entertain them? What do you know about your listeners' age, gender, background, education, occupation, political affiliation, beliefs, and knowledge of your subject? What do listeners need to know? In a college class, your audience will be your classmates and instructor. It is often desirable to build a sense of community with your audience by asking questions and using the inclusive pronoun *we*.

Making an effective oral presentation is largely a matter of having control over your material, deciding what you want to say, and knowing your subject matter well. Preparation and planning are essential.

KEY POINTS

Tips for Preparing an Oral Presentation

1. Select a topic you are committed to, and decide on a clear focus. If you are assigned a topic, concentrate on its key points.

2. Make a few strong points. Back them up with specific details. Have a few points that you can expand on and develop with interesting examples, quotations, and stories.

3. Include signposts and signal phrases to help your audience follow your ideas (*first, next, finally; the most important point is . . .*).

4. Structure your report clearly. Present the organizational framework of your talk along with illustrative materials in handouts, overhead transparencies, PowerPoint slides (**28e**), posters, charts, or other visuals (**21**).

(Continued)

(Continued)

5. Use short sentences, accessible words, memorable phrases, and natural language. In writing, you can use long sentences with one clause embedded in another, but these are difficult for listeners to follow.

6. You can effectively use repetition much more in an oral report than in a written report. Your audience will appreciate being reminded of the structure of the talk and of points you referred to previously.

7. Meet the requirements set for the presentation in terms of time available for preparation, length of presentation, and possible questions from the audience.

8. Prepare a strong ending that will have an impact on the audience. Make sure that you conclude. Do not simply stop or trail off.

28b Speaking from notes or manuscript

Speaking from notes Speaking from notes allows you to be more spontaneous and to look your audience in the eye. Think of your presentation as a conversation. For this method, notes or a key-word outline must be clear and organized, so that you feel secure about which points you will discuss and in what order. Here are a speaker's notes for a presentation of her views on paternity leave.

Paternity Leave
1. Children's needs
   Benefits
   Bonding
2. Issue of equity
   Equal treatment for men and women
   Cost

Your notes or outline should make reference to specific illustrations and quotations and contain structural signals so that the audience knows when you begin to address a new point. You can also use either slides prepared with your word processor or PowerPoint slides to guide the direction and structure of your presentation (**28e**). For a short presentation on a topic that you know very well, use notes with or without the visual aid of slides. Do not read aloud, though, especially in front of a small audience.

Speaking from a manuscript Writing out a complete speech may be necessary for a long formal presentation. Still, even if you do this, you should practice and prepare so that you do not have to labor over every word. Remember, too, to build in places to pause and make spontaneous comments. The advantages of speaking from a prepared manuscript are that you can time the presentation exactly and that you will never dry up and wonder what to say next. The disadvantage is that you have to read the text, and reading aloud is not easy, especially if you want to maintain eye contact with your audience. If you prefer to speak from a complete manuscript text, prepare the text for oral presentation as follows:

- Triple-space your text and use a large font.

- When you reach the bottom of a page, begin a new sentence on the next page. Do not start a sentence on one page and finish it on the next.

- Highlight key words in each paragraph so that you will be able to spot them easily.

- Underline words and phrases that you want to stress.

- Use slash marks (/ or //) to remind yourself to pause. Read in sense groups (parts of a sentence that are read as a unit—a phrase or clause, for example—often indicated by a pause when spoken and by punctuation when written). Mark your text at the end of a sense group.

- Number your pages so that you can keep them in the proper sequence.

28c Practicing and presenting

Whether you speak from notes or from a manuscript, practice is essential.

- Practice not just once, but many times. Try tape-recording yourself, listening to the tape, and asking a friend for comments.

- Speak at a normal speed and at a good volume. Speaking too quickly and too softly is a common mistake.

- Imagine a full audience; use gestures, and practice looking up to make eye contact with people in the audience.

- Beware of filler words and phrases like *OK, well, you know,* and *like.* Such repeated verbal tics annoy and distract an audience.
- Do not punctuate pauses with "er" or "uhm."

It is natural to feel some anxiety before the actual presentation, but most people find that their jitters disappear as soon as they begin talking, especially when they are well prepared.

Look frequently at your listeners. Work the room so that you gaze directly at people in all sections of the audience. In *Secrets of Successful Speakers,* Lilly Walters points out that when you look at one person, all the people in a V behind that person will think you are looking at them. Bear in mind that no matter how well prepared a report is, listeners will not respond well if the presenter reads it too rapidly or in a monotone or without looking up and engaging the audience. If your topic is lighthearted, remember to smile.

28d Using presentation aids and multimedia

If you use visual aids to outline your talk and provide essential information, check your equipment and practice with it. With an overhead projector or PowerPoint slides (see **28e**), the font size must be large enough for people at the back of the room to read, and the colors you choose should be clear—black or blue on white is best. Use headings (**20d**) and bulleted lists (**20e**) to make your material clear. When you speak, remember to face the audience, not the projector or screen. Do not provide lengthy or complicated visual aids, or your audience will be reading them instead of listening to you.

28e Using PowerPoint

Using a tool like PowerPoint to prepare a presentation gives you access to organizing tools. As the name suggests, PowerPoint forces you to think of your main points and organize them. Preparing slides that illustrate the format and logic of your talk helps you separate the main points from the supporting details and examples, and the slides keep you focused as you give your presentation. Your audience follows your ideas not only because you have established a clear principle of organization, but also because the slide on the presentation screen is a reminder of where you are in your talk, what point you are addressing, and how that points fits into your total scheme. Presentation software also allows you to include sound, music, and movie clips to illustrate and drive home the points you want to make. It is possible to insert a graph, clip art, and animation effects, such as a text line dropping in from the top, flying in, appearing one letter at a time, flashing, or sliding across from one side (but do not overdo these effects). You can also import material from Word and Excel into a PowerPoint slide. To help with all these features, PowerPoint provides a self-paced tutorial.

The slides you prepare can be used as a basis for overhead transparencies or 35mm slides, as handouts, or as outlines for the audience or yourself. But the best use of the slides is direct projection from the computer onto a large screen.

Once you have prepared, sorted, and saved your slides, you can access them with a click. A slide can diagram the structure of your talk or provide material to support the points you make.

A PowerPoint specialist has advised, "If you have something to show, use PowerPoint." *Show* is the important word. Do not expect your audience to read a lot of text. PowerPoint is not for writing paragraphs and essays for readers to digest. It's for getting and keeping the audience's attention with the main points and illustrative details. Outlines, bulleted lists, tables, pie charts, and graphs are what PowerPoint does well. See also **20a** and **20b**.

28f A student's PowerPoint slides

The PowerPoint slides shown here were prepared by student Emily Luo for a project in a course called "Empirical Research Using the Internet." The assignment was to find public-opinion data and documents to present a "fact-based and balanced summary of the public debate" surrounding an issue. The students each wrote a paper to be posted on the course Web site, with links to all sources. Each student also prepared a classroom presentation of his or her research, using PowerPoint slides. Luo chose the assigned topic "Genetic Engineering" and narrowed the focus to "Genetically Modified Crops." For her presentation, she prepared nine slides: an outline slide (shown here), one slide for each of the first four topics listed in the outline (two shown here), three slides showing public-opinion data (one shown here), and a conclusion. She prepared the bar charts herself with Microsoft Word, using data from the three polling organizations.

The Debate over Genetically Modified Crops

- An Overview
- Governmental Agencies
- The Proponents
- The Opponents
- Public Opinions

Presenter: Emily Luo

Governmental Agencies

A. The United States Department of Agriculture (USDA)
-What is safe to grow?
-Regulates through a permit system
-Environmental assessment

B. The Environmental Protection Agency (EPA)
-What is safe for the environment?
-Regulates pesticides produced for genetically modified plants

C. The Food and Drug Administration (FDA)
-What is safe for the consumers?
-1992 "Statement of Policy: Foods Derived from New Plant Varieties"

The Opponents

A. The Concerned Environmental and Advocacy Organizations:
Greenpeace USA

B. Arguments
-Not a natural extension of traditional breeding methods
-Potential harms to health
-Potential environmental harms
-Governmental failure to conduct long-term testing in food and
environment
-Failure to label

Public Opinions

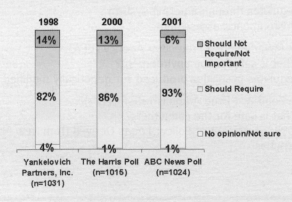

Whether Genetically Engineered Food Should Be Labeled

Style

PART 6   Style

THE FIVE C'S OF STYLE

STYLE IN ACTION

What is style? William Strunk, Jr., and E. B. White in their classic book *The Elements of Style,* 4th edition, define it as the sound "words make on paper." That sound is important to readers. It affects their response to a piece of writing and influences their willingness to continue reading. Sometimes, even when ideas are well organized, readers can suffer from the so-called MEGO reaction to a piece of writing—"My Eyes Glaze Over." Readers are bored by wordiness, flatness, inappropriate word choice, clichés, and sentences constructed without interesting variations. Working on sentence structure and style can help prevent that glazing over.

With acknowledgment to Joseph Williams's *Style: Ten Lessons in Clarity and Grace,* 7th edition, sections **29–33** examine five anti-MEGO strategies, called here the "Five C's of Style": cut, check for action, connect, commit, and choose your words. Sections **34–36** focus on developing sentence variety and offer stylistic options, a sample of a passage revised for style, and tips for writers.

THE FIVE C'S OF STYLE

29 The First C: Cut

You can improve most of your writing if you focus on stating your ideas succinctly. Examine your writing for unnecessary ideas, sentences, phrases, and individual words. Do not be tempted to pad your work to fill an assigned number of pages.

29a Cut repetition and wordiness.

Say something only once and in the best place.

▶ The Lilly Library ~~contains many rare books. The books in~~

~~the library are~~ carefully preserved~~,~~ ⟨s⟩ ~~The library also houses~~
many rare books and manuscripts
~~a manuscript collection.~~
∧

director of
▶ Steven Spielberg, ~~who has directed~~ the movie ~~that has been~~ described as the best war movie ever made, ~~is someone who~~ knows many politicians.

▶ California residents voted to abolish bilingual education~~/~~
~~The main reason for their voting to abolish bilingual~~

because
~~education was that~~ many children were being placed
^

indiscriminately into programs and kept there too long.

If your draft says something like "As the first paragraph states" or "As previously stated," beware. Such phrases probably indicate that you have repeated yourself.

29b Cut formulaic phrases.

Writers sometimes use formulaic phrases in a first draft to keep the writing process going. In revision, these wordy phrases should come out or be replaced with shorter or more concise expressions.

FORMULAIC	CONCISE
at the present time	now
at this point in time	
in this day and age	
in today's society	
because of the fact that	because
due to the fact that	
are of the opinion that	believe
have the ability to	can
in spite of the fact that	although, despite
last but not least	finally
prior to	before
concerning the matter of	about

In *The Elements of Style,* Strunk and White rail against any use of the phrase "the fact that," seeing it as "especially debilitating." Their advice? Cut it out.

▶ Few people realize ~~the fact~~ that the computer controlling the *Eagle* lunar module in 1969 had less memory than a cheap wristwatch does today.

29c As appropriate, cut references to your intentions.

In writing for the social sciences or sciences, the main goal is usually to provide information. State, therefore, how you intend to structure your argument, and then summarize that structure again at the end of the essay—that is, present a plan of your organization at both the beginning and the end of the essay.

In the humanities, readers want to read about your topic and usually are not interested in explanations of your thinking process and plan of organization. Eliminate references to the organization of your text and your own planning, such as *In this essay, I intend to prove . . .* or *In the next few paragraphs, I hope to show . . .* or *In conclusion, I have demonstrated . . .* or *What I want to say here is. . . .* Don't announce it. Just do it.

29d Cut redundant words and phrases.

Trim words that simply repeat an idea expressed by another word in the same phrase: *basic* essentials, *true* facts, circle *around*, cooperate *together*, *final* completion, return *again*, refer *back*, *advance* planning, consensus of *opinion*, *completely* unanimous, *free* gift. Also edit redundant pairs: *various and sundry, hopes and desires, each and every.*

▶ The task took ~~diligence and~~ perseverance.

▶ His surgeon ^has^ ~~is a doctor with~~ a great deal of clinical experience.

▶ ^Ninety-seven^ ~~A total of 97~~ students completed the survey.

30 The Second C: Check for Action

The parts of a sentence that carry the weight of the meaning are the subject and the verb. Don't waste them. As a general rule, write vigorous sentences with vivid, expressive verbs. Avoid overusing the verb *be* (*be, am, is, are, was, were, being, been*), and let the subject of your sentence perform the action.

30a Ask "Who's doing what?" about subject and verb.

The subject (*approval*) and verb (*was*) in the following sentence tell readers very little:

WORDY   **The mayor's approval of the new law was due to voters' suspicion of the concealment of campaign funds by his deputy.**

This dull thud of a sentence revolves around the verb *was*. It contains three abstract nouns (*approval, suspicion,* and *concealment*) formed from verbs (*approve, suspect,* and *conceal*), as well as five prepositional phrases: *of the new law, due to voters' suspicion, of the concealment, of campaign funds,* and *by his deputy.*

WHO'S DOING WHAT?

SUBJECT	VERB
the mayor	approved
the voters	suspected
his deputy	had concealed

Always put verbs to work to make a stronger sentence.

REVISED   **The mayor approved the new law because voters suspected that his deputy had concealed campaign funds.**

30b Use caution in beginning a sentence with *there* or *it.*

For a lean, direct style, rewrite sentences in which *there* or *it* occupies the subject position (as in *there is, there were, it is, it was*). Revise by using verbs that describe an action and subjects that perform the action.

WORDY   **There was a discussion of the health care system by the politicians.**   [Who's doing what?]

REVISED   **The politicians discussed the health care system.**

WORDY   **There is a big gate guarding the entrance to the park.**

REVISED   **A big gate guards the entrance to the park.**

WORDY   **It is a fact that Arnold is proudly displaying a new tattoo.**

REVISED   **Arnold is proudly displaying a new tattoo.**

Use the Search function of your computer to find all instances in your draft of *it is, there is,* and *there are* in the initial position in a clause. If you find a filler subject with little purpose, revise.

30c Avoid unnecessary passive voice constructions.

The *passive voice* tells what is done to the grammatical subject of a clause ("The turkey *was cooked* too long"). Extensive use of the passive voice makes your style dull and wordy. When you can, replace it with active voice verbs, especially when you mention the doer of the action.

PASSIVE	The problem will be discussed thoroughly by the committee.
ACTIVE	The committee will discuss the problem thoroughly.

If you are studying in the social sciences or sciences, where readers are primarily interested in procedures and results, not in who developed or produced them, the frequent use of passive voice constructions may seem natural—for example, in lab reports and experiments, you will read *The rats were fed* instead of *The researchers fed the rats.* For other acceptable uses of the passive voice, see **31a** and **42**.

31 The Third C: Connect

In coherent pieces of writing, information that has been mentioned before is linked to new information in a smooth flow, not in a series of grasshopper-like jumps.

31a Use consistent subjects and topic chains for coherence.

Readers expect to be able to connect the ideas beginning a sentence with what they have already read. From one sentence to the next, avoid jarring and unnecessary shifts from one subject to another. Let your subjects form a topic chain.

JARRING SHIFT	*Memoirs* are becoming increasingly popular. *Readers* of all ages are finding them appealing.
TOPIC CHAIN	*Memoirs* are becoming increasingly popular. *They* appeal to readers of all ages.

In the revised version, the subject of the second sentence, *they,* refers to the subject of the previous sentence, *memoirs;* the new information about "readers of all ages" comes at the end, where it receives more emphasis (**31b**).

Examine your writing for awkward topic switches. Note that preserving a topic chain may mean using the passive voice, as in the last sentence of the next revision (see also **42d**).

FREQUENT TOPIC SWITCHES	*I* have lived all my life in Brooklyn, New York. *Park Slope* is a neighborhood that has many different ethnic cultures. *Harmony* exists among the people, even though it does not in many other Brooklyn neighborhoods. *Many articles in the press* have praised the Slope for its ethnic variety.

REVISED
WITH TOPIC
CHAIN
> *Many different ethnic cultures* **flourish in Park Slope, Brooklyn, where I have lived all my life.** *These different cultures* **live together harmoniously, even though they do not in many other Brooklyn neighborhoods. In fact,** *the ethnic variety* **of the Slope has often been praised in the press.**

31b Put new information at the end of a sentence for emphasis.

If you form a topic chain of old information, new information will come at the end of a sentence. Make your sentences end on a strong and interesting note, one that you want to emphasize. This technique helps keep the flow of your ideas moving smoothly. Don't let a sentence trail off weakly.

WEAK
ENDING
> **Women often feel silenced by men, according to one researcher.**

REVISED
> **According to one researcher, women often feel silenced by men.**

31c Explore options for connecting ideas: coordination, subordination, and transitions.

When you write sentences containing two or more clauses (**34c**), consider where you want to place the emphasis.

Coordination   You give two or more clauses equal emphasis when you connect them with one of the following coordinating conjunctions: *and, but, or, nor, so, for,* or *yet.* (For more on clauses, see **34c** and **37d**.)

▶ **The bus trip was long. The seats seemed more uncomfortable with every mile.**

┌─── independent clause ───┐   ┌─── independent clause ───┐
▶ **The bus trip was long, and the seats seemed more**

─────────────────────────────────────
uncomfortable with every mile.

Subordination   When you use subordinating conjunctions such as *when, if,* or *because* to connect clauses, you give one idea more importance by putting it in the independent clause (**34c** and **38b**).

▶ **We cannot now end our differences. At least we can help make the world safe for diversity.** [Two sentences with equal importance]

┌─────── dependent clause ───────┐ ┌──────────────
▶ **If we cannot now end our differences, at least we can help**
┌─────── independent clause ───────┐
make the world safe for diversity.   —John F. Kennedy

[Two clauses connected by *if*; emphasis on the independent clause at the end of the sentence]

Transitional expressions   Use words such as *however, therefore,* and *nevertheless* (known as *conjunctive adverbs*) and phrases such as *as a result, in addition,* and *on the other hand* to signal the logical connection between independent clauses (for a list of transitional expressions, see **2d**). A transitional expression can move around in its own clause—yet another stylistic option for you to consider.

▶ **He made a lot of money; however, his humble roots were always evident.**

▶ **He made a lot of money; his humble roots, however, were always evident.**

KEY POINTS

Options for Connecting Clauses

COORDINATING CONJUNCTION	TRANSITIONAL EXPRESSION	SUBORDINATING CONJUNCTION
and (addition)	also, further, furthermore, moreover, in addition	
but, yet (contrast)	however, nevertheless, on the other hand	although, even though, whereas, while
or, nor (alternative)	instead, otherwise, alternatively	unless
so, for (result)	therefore, as a result, hence, consequently, thus, accordingly, then	because, as, since, so/such . . . that, now that, once

---

The following examples illustrate some options.

▶ **Brillo pads work well. I don't give them as gifts.**

▶ **Brillo pads work well, but I don't give them as gifts.**

▶ **Although Brillo pads work well, I don't give them as gifts.**

▶ Brillo pads work well; however, I don't give them as gifts.

▶ Brillo pads work well; I, however, don't give them as gifts.

Make your choice by deciding what you want to emphasize and seeing what structures you used in nearby sentences. If, for example, you used *however* in the immediately preceding sentence, choose some other option for expressing contrasting ideas. Notice how subordinating a different idea can change your meaning and emphasis.

▶ Although I don't give Brillo pads as gifts, they work well.

Avoiding excessive coordination or subordination   Too much of any one stylistic feature will become tedious to readers.

Excessive Coordination with *And*	I grew up in a large family, and we lived on a small farm, and every day I had to get up early and do farm work, and I would spend a lot of time cleaning out the stables, and then I would be exhausted in the evening, and I never had the energy to read.
Revised	Because I grew up in a large family on a small farm, every day I had to get up early to do farm work, mostly cleaning out the stables. I would be so exhausted in the evening that I never had the energy to read.
Excessive Subordination	Because the report was weak and poorly written, our boss, who wanted to impress the company president by showing her how efficient his division was, to gain prestige in the company, decided, despite the fact that work projects were piling up, that he would rewrite the report over the weekend.
Revised	Because the report was weak and poorly written, our boss decided to rewrite it over the weekend, even though work projects were piling up. He wanted to impress the company president by showing her how efficient his division was; that was his way of gaining prestige.

31d   Perhaps begin a sentence with *and* or *but*.

Occasionally, writers choose to start a sentence with *and* or *but*, either for stylistic effect or to make a close connection to a previous, already long sentence:

▶ **You can have wealth concentrated in the hands of a few, or democracy. But you cannot have both.** —Justice Louis Brandeis

People who consider *and* and *but* conjunctions to be used to join two or more independent clauses within a sentence may frown when they see these words starting a sentence. Nevertheless, examples of this usage can be found in literature from the tenth century onward. As with any other stylistic device, it is wise not to use *and* or *but* too often to begin a sentence. And, given the difference of opinion on this usage, check with your instructor, too.

31e Connect paragraphs.

Just as readers appreciate a smooth flow of information from sentence to sentence, they also look for transitions—word bridges—to move them from paragraph to paragraph. A new paragraph signals a shift in topic, but careful readers will look for transitional words and phrases that tell them *how* a new paragraph relates to the paragraph that precedes it. Provide your readers with steppingstones; don't ask them to leap over chasms.

KEY POINTS

A Checklist for Connecting Paragraphs

1. Read your draft aloud. When you finish a paragraph, make a note of the point you made in the paragraph. Then, check your notes for the flow of ideas and logic.

2. Refer to the main idea of the previous paragraph as you begin a new paragraph. After a paragraph on retirement, the next paragraph could begin like this, moving from the idea of retirement to saving: *Retirement is not the only reason for saving. Saving also provides a nest egg for the unexpected and the pleasurable.*

3. Use adjectives like *this* and *these* to provide a link. After a paragraph discussing urban planning proposals, the next paragraph might begin like this: *These proposals will help. However, . . .*

4. Use transitions such as *also, too, in addition, however, therefore,* and *as a result* to signal the logical connection between ideas (**2d**).

32   The Fourth C: Commit

According to E. B. White, William Strunk, Jr., "scorned the vague, the tame, the colorless, the irresolute. He felt it was worse to be irresolute than to be wrong." This section focuses on ways to be detailed, colorful, bold, and resolute.

32a   Commit to including a personal presence.

Academic writing is certainly not the same as personal accounts of feelings, events, and opinions. But it is not writing from which you as the writer should fade from sight. The best academic writing reveals personal engagement with the topic, details of what the writer has observed and read, an unmistakable *you*. Always ask yourself: Where am I in this draft? What picture of me and my world do readers get from my piece of writing? Do they see clearly what I base my opinions on? If you use sources, readers should be able to perceive you in conversation with your sources; they should see not just a listing of what sources say, but your responses to and comments on those sources.

Showing a personal presence does not necessarily mean always using "I" or repeatedly saying "In my opinion." It means writing so that readers see you in what you write.

32b   Commit to an appropriate and consistent tone.

Readers will expect the tone of your document to fit its purpose. The tone of your piece of writing reflects your attitude to your subject matter and is closely connected to your audience's expectations and your purpose in writing. If you were, for example, writing about a topic such as compensation for posttraumatic stress disorder suffered by families of victims of the September 11, 2001, World Trade Center attack, a serious, respectful tone would be appropriate.

For most academic writing, commit resolutely to an objective, serious tone. Avoid sarcasm, colloquial language, name-calling, or pedantic words and structures, even in the name of variety. Make sure you dedicate a special reading of a draft to examining your tone; if you are reading along and a word or sentence strikes you as unexpected and out of place, flag it for later correction. In formal college essays, watch out especially for sudden switches to a chatty and conversational tone, as in "Nutrition plays a large part in whether people *hang on to* their own teeth as they age." (You would revise *hang on to*, changing it to *retain*.) Since tone is really a function of how you anticipate your readers' expectations, ask a tutor or friend to read your document and note any lapses in consistency of tone.

32c Commit to a confident stance.

Your background reading, critical thinking, and drafting will help you discover and decide upon a perspective and thesis that seem correct to you (**1e**). Once you have made those decisions, commit to that point of view. When you are trying to persuade readers to accept your point of view, avoid the ambivalence and indecisiveness evident in words and phrases like *maybe, perhaps, it could be, it might seem,* and *it would appear.*

Hedging will not heighten readers' confidence in you:

▶ Tough economic times did not stop me from bidding on eBay, ~~but others might have had different experiences.~~

Aim for language that reflects accountability and commitment: *as a result, consequently, of course, believe, need, demand, should, must.* Use the language of commitment, however, only after thoroughly researching your topic and satisfying yourself that the evidence is convincing.

In addition, convey to readers an attitude of confidence in your own abilities and judgment. Make an ethical appeal to readers by stressing your expertise (**4f**). Avoid apologies. One student ended a first draft this way:

Too
APOLOGETIC
I hope I have conveyed something about our cultural differences. I would like my reader to note that this is just my view, even if a unique one. Room for errors and prejudices should be provided. The lack of a total overview, which would take more time and expertise, should also be taken into account.

If you really have not done an adequate job of making and supporting a point, try to gather more information to improve the draft instead of adding apologetic notes. The writer revised the ending after reading **2e** on conclusions.

REVISED
VERSION

> **The stories I have told and the examples I have given come from my own experience; however, my multicultural background has emphasized that cultural differences do not have to separate people but can bring them closer together. A diverse, multicultural society holds many potential benefits for all its members.**

33 The Fifth C: Choose Your Words

Word choice, or *diction*, contributes a great deal to the effect your writing has on your readers. Do not give readers puzzles to solve.

33a Word choice checklist

KEY POINTS

Word Choice: A Checklist for Revision

1. Underline words whose meaning or spelling you want to check and words that you might want to replace. Then spend some time with a dictionary and a thesaurus. (**33b**)

2. Look for words that might not convey exactly what you mean (*thrifty* vs. *stingy*, for example), and look for vague words. (**33c**)

3. Check figurative language for appropriateness, think about where a simile (a comparison) might help convey your meaning, and find original substitutes for any clichés. (**33e**, **33g**)

4. Check for level of formality and for the appropriateness of any colloquial, regional, ethnic, or specialized work terms. (**33d**)

5. Check for gender bias in your use of *he* and *she* and other words that show gender. (**33f**)

6. Look for language that might exclude or offend (such as *normal* to mean people similar to you). Build community with your readers by eliminating disrespectful or stereotyping terms referring to race, place, age, politics, religion, abilities, or sexual orientation. (**33f**)

33b Use a dictionary and a thesaurus.

A good dictionary contains a wealth of information—spelling and definitions, syllable breaks, pronunciation, grammatical functions and features, word forms, etymology (word origins and historical development), usage, synonyms (words of similar meaning), and antonyms (words of opposite meaning). The following dictionary entry from *The American Heritage Dictionary of the English Language,* 4th edition, shows how much information is available. A "Usage Note" after this entry endorses using "She graduated from Yale in 1998" but notes that "She graduated Yale in 1998" was unacceptable to 77 percent of a usage panel.

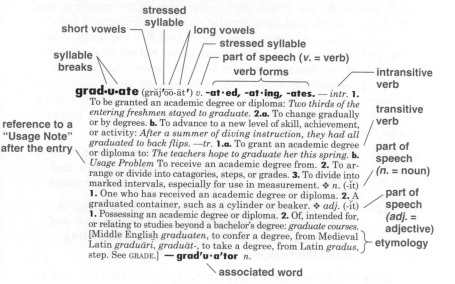

Use a dictionary to learn or confirm the *denotation*—the basic meaning—of a word. Some words that appear similar are not interchangeable. For example, *respectable* has a meaning very different from *respectful; emigrant* and *immigrant* have different meanings; and so do *defuse* and *diffuse, uninterested* and *disinterested,* and *principal* and *principle.*

A thesaurus is useful when you want to find alternatives to words that you know. Exercise caution, however, to make sure that the word you choose fits your context. Suppose you use the word *privacy* a few times and want an alternative in the sentence "She values the privacy of her own home." You could consult a thesaurus but might find words such as *aloofness, seclusion,* and *isolation* listed.

The word *aloofness* would not work as a replacement for *privacy* in the example sentence, and the others do not capture the idea of *privacy*. You might, in the end, want to use two words to convey your meaning: *She values the* safety *and* seclusion *of her own home,* or you might stick with *privacy.*

Thesaurus programs attached to word processing programs typically offer lists of synonyms but little guidance on *connotation*—the meaning associated with a word beyond its literal definition. Always check a word in a dictionary.

33c Use exact words and connotations.

When you write, use words that convey exactly the meaning you intend. Two words that have similar dictionary definitions (*denotation*) can also have additional positive or negative implications and emotional overtones (*connotation*). Readers will not get the impression you intend if you describe a person as *lazy* when you mean *relaxed*.

Select words with appropriate connotations. Hurricanes *devastate* neighborhoods; construction workers *demolish* buildings. Writing "Construction workers devastated the building" would be inappropriate. Note how word choice can affect meaning:

VERSION 1   **The crowd consisted of young couples holding their children's hands, students in well-worn clothes, and activist politicians, all voicing support of their cause.**

VERSION 2   **The mob consisted of hard-faced workers dragging children by the hand, students in leather jackets and ragged jeans, and militant politicians, all howling about their cause.**

Some words do little more than fill space because they are so vague. Words such as the following signal the need for revision: *area, aspect, certain, circumstance, factor, kind, manner, nature, seem, situation, thing.*

VAGUE   **Our perceptions of women's roles differ as we enter new *areas*. The girl in Kincaid's story did many *things* that are commonly seen as women's work.**

REVISED   **Our perceptions of women's roles differ as we learn more from what we *see, hear, read, and experience*. The girl in Kincaid's story did many *household chores* that are commonly seen as women's work. She washed the clothes, cooked, swept the floor, and set the table.**

Some words are abstract and general; other words are concrete and specific. Notice the increasing concreteness and specificity in this list: *tool, cutting instrument, knife, penknife.* If you do not move away from the general and abstract, you will give readers too much imaginative leeway. "Her grandmother was shocked by the clothing she bought" leaves a great deal to readers' imaginations. What kind of clothing do you mean: a low-necked dress, high-heeled platform shoes, and black fishnet stockings, or a conservative navy blue wool suit? Choose words that convey exact images and precise information.

33d Monitor the language of speech, region, and workplace.

The language of speech   In a formal college essay, avoid colloquial language and slang unless you are quoting someone's words. Do not enclose a slang expression in quotation marks to signal to readers that you know it is inappropriate. Instead, revise to reach an appropriate level of formality.

> disgusting
> ▶ The working conditions were ~~"gross."~~

> difficulty
> ▶ Organic farmers have ~~a rough time~~ protecting their crops.

> defendant
> ▶ The jury returned the verdict that the ~~guy~~ was guilty.

In formal writing, avoid colloquial words and expressions, such as *folks, guy, OK, okay, pretty good, hassle, kind of interesting/nice, too big of a deal, a lot of, lots of, a ways away, no-brainer.*

Note that the synonyms of the italicized words listed below convey different attitudes and different degrees of formality:

child: kid, offspring, progeny

friend: pal, buddy, chum, mate, brother/sister, comrade

jail: slammer, cooler, prison, correctional institution

angry: ticked off, furious, mad, fuming, wrathful

computer expert: geek, hacker, techie, programmer

threatening: spooky, scary, eerie, menacing

fine: cool, first-rate, excellent, superior

Some of these words—*kid, pal, slammer, ticked off, geek, spooky*—are so informal that they would rarely if ever be appropriate in formal academic writing or business letters, though they would raise no eyebrows in journalism, advertising, or e-mail. Overuse of the formal words—*progeny, comrade, wrathful*—on the other hand, could produce a tone that suggests a stuffy, pedantic attitude (see **33g**).

Regional and ethnic language   Use regional and ethnic dialects in your writing only when you are quoting someone directly (*"Your car needs fixed," the mechanic grunted.*) or you know that readers will understand why you are using a nonstandard phrase.

myself
▶ I bought ~~me~~ a camcorder.

any attention
▶ He vowed that he wouldn't pay them ~~no never mind~~.

have been
▶ They'~~re~~ here three years already.

be able to
▶ She used to ~~could~~ run two miles, but now she's out of shape.

The language of the workplace   People engaged in most areas of specialized work and study use technical words that outsiders perceive as jargon. A sportswriter writing about baseball will refer to *balks, twinight double-headers, ERAs, brushbacks,* and *crooked numbers.* A linguist writing about language for an audience of linguists will use terms like *phonemics, sociolinguistics, semantics, kinesics,* and *suprasegmentals.* If you know that your audience is familiar with the technical vocabulary of a field, specialized language is acceptable. Try to avoid jargon when writing for a more general audience; if you must use technical terms, provide definitions that will make sense to your audience.

33e   Use figurative language for effect, but use it sparingly.

Figures of speech can enhance your writing and add to imaginative descriptions. Particularly useful are similes and metaphors. A simile is a comparison in which both sides are stated explicitly and linked by the words *like* or *as.* A metaphor is an implied comparison in which the two sides are indirectly compared. When figurative language is overused, however, it becomes tedious and contrived.

Simile: an explicit comparison with both sides stated

▶ America is *not like a blanket*—one piece of unbroken cloth, the same color, the same texture, the same size. America is more *like a quilt*—many pieces, many colors, many sizes, all woven and held together by a common thread.

—Rev. Jesse Jackson

▶ He was reading, leaning so far back in the chair that it was balanced on its two hind legs *like a dancing dog*.

—Barbara Kingsolver

Metaphor: an implied comparison, without *like* or *as*

▶ A foolish consistency is the hobgoblin of little minds.

—Ralph Waldo Emerson

▶ Some television programs are so much chewing gum for the eyes.

—John Mason Brown

Mixed metaphors   Take care not to mix metaphors.

▶ As she walked onto the tennis court, she was ready to sink or swim. [Swimming on a tennis court?]

▶ He is a snake in the grass with his head in the clouds.

[The two metaphors clash.]

▶ He was a whirlwind of activity, trumpeting defiance whenever anyone crossed swords with any of his ideas.

[The three metaphors—*whirlwind, trumpet, crossed swords*—obscure rather than illuminate.]

For more on figurative language in literature, see **5b**.

33f   Avoid biased and exclusionary language.

You cannot avoid writing from perspectives and backgrounds that you know about, but you can avoid divisive terms that reinforce stereotypes or belittle other people. Be sensitive to differences. Consider the feelings of members of the opposite sex, minorities (now sometimes called "world majorities"), and special-interest groups. Do not emphasize differences by separating society into *we* (people like you) and *they* or *these people* (people different from you). Use *we* only to be truly inclusive of yourself and all your readers. Be aware, too, of terms that are likely to offend. You don't have to be excessive in your zeal to be PC ("politically correct"), using *underachieve* for *fail,* or *vertically challenged* for *short,* but do your best to avoid alienating readers.

Gender   The writer of the following sentence edited to avoid gender bias in the perception of women's roles and achievements.

> Andrea
> ▶ ~~Mrs. John~~ Harrison, ~~married to a real estate tycoon and herself the bubbly, blonde~~ chief executive of a successful computer company, has expanded the business overseas.

Choice of words can reveal gender bias, too.

AVOID	USE
actress	actor
chairman	chairperson
female astronaut	astronaut
forefathers	ancestors
foreman	supervisor
mailman	mail carrier
male nurse	nurse
man, mankind (meaning any human being)	person, people, our species, human beings, humanity
manmade	synthetic
policeman, policewoman	police officer
salesman	sales representative, salesclerk
veterans and their wives	veterans and their spouses

When using pronouns, too, avoid the stereotyping that occurs by assigning gender roles to professions. See **44e.**

> or she
> ▶ Before a surgeon can operate, he‸must know every detail of the patient's history.

Often it is best to avoid the *he-or-she* issue by recasting the sentence or using plural nouns and pronouns.

> ▶ Before operating, a surgeon must know every detail of the patient's history.

> ▶ Before surgeons can operate, they must know every detail of the patient's history.

At times when the singular form is preferable, consider using *he* in one section of your manuscript and *she* in another, as long as you do not alternate within a paragraph. See **44e** for more on pronouns, gender, and the use of *he or she.*

Race   Mention a person's race only when it is relevant. If you write "Attending the meeting were three doctors and an Asian computer programmer," you reveal more about your own stereotypes than you do about the meeting. In general, use the names that people prefer for their racial or ethnic affiliation. *The Columbia Guide to Standard American English* advises: "It is good manners (and therefore good usage) to call people only by the names they wish to be called." Consider, for example, that *black* and *African American* are preferred terms; *Native American* is preferred to *American Indian; Asian* is preferred to *Oriental.*

Place   Avoid stereotyping people according to where they come from. Some British people may be stiff and formal, but not all are. Not all Germans eat sausage and drink beer; not all North Americans carry cameras and wear plaid shorts.

Be careful, too, with the way you refer to countries and continents. The Americas include both North and South America, so you need to make the distinction. England, Scotland, Wales, and Northern Ireland make up Great Britain, or the United Kingdom. In addition, shifts in world politics and national borders have resulted in the renaming of many countries: *Ceylon* became *Sri Lanka; Rhodesia* is now *Zimbabwe; Czechoslovakia* has been divided into the *Czech Republic* and *Slovakia.* Check a current atlas or almanac.

Age and condition   Avoid derogatory or condescending terms associated with age. Refer to a person's age or condition neutrally, if at all: not "a well-preserved little old lady" but "a woman in her eighties"; not "an immature sixteen-year-old" but simply "a teenager."

Politics   Words referring to politics are full of connotations. Consider, for instance, the positive and negative connotations of *liberal* and *conservative* in various election campaigns. Take care when you use words like *radical, left-wing, right-wing,* and *moderate.* How do you want readers to interpret them? Are you identifying with one group and implicitly criticizing other groups?

Religion   An old edition of an encyclopedia referred to "devout Catholics" and "fanatical Muslims." The new edition refers to both Catholics and Muslims as "devout," thus eliminating biased language. Examine your use of the following: words that sound derogatory or exclusionary, such as *cult* or *fundamentalist*; expressions, such as *these people*, that emphasize difference; and even the word *we* when it implies that all your readers share your beliefs.

Health and abilities Avoid expressions such as *confined to a wheelchair* and *AIDS victim*, so as not to focus on difference and disability. Instead, write *someone who uses a wheelchair* and *person with AIDS*, but only if the context makes it necessary to include that information. Do not unnecessarily draw attention to a disability or an illness.

Sexual orientation Mention a person's sexual orientation only if the information is relevant in context. To write that someone accused of stock market fraud was "defended by a homosexual lawyer" would be to provide gratuitous information. The sexual orientation of the attorney might be more relevant in a case involving discrimination against homosexuals. Since you may not know the sexual orientation of your readers, do not assume it is the same as your own.

The word *normal* Be especially careful about using the word *normal* when referring to your own health, ability, or sexual orientation. Some readers might justifiably find that usage offensive.

33g Avoid tired expressions (clichés) and pretentious language.

Avoid clichés. *Clichés* are tired, overly familiar expressions, those anyone can complete: as cool as a _____. Common clichés are *hit the nail on the head, crystal clear, better late than never,* and *easier said than done*. They never contribute anything fresh or original. Avoid or eliminate them as you revise your early drafts.

▶ ~~Last but not least,~~ the article recommends the TeleZapper.
     Finally

▶ My main ambition in life is not to make a fortune, since I
                  having money does not guarantee a good life.
know that/~~as they say, "money is the root of all evil."~~

▶ For Baldwin, the problem never ~~reared its ugly head~~ until
                                       arose
one dreadful night in New Jersey.

Distinguish the formal from the stuffy. Formal does not mean stuffy and pretentious. Writing in a formal situation does not require you to use obscure words and long sentences. Clear, direct expression can be formal. Pretentious language makes reading difficult, as the following example shows:

> ▶ When a female of the species ascertains that a male with whom she is acquainted exhibits considerable desire to extend their acquaintance, that female customarily will first engage in protracted discussion with her close confidantes.

Simplify your writing if you find sentences like that in your draft. Here are some words to watch out for:

STUFFY	DIRECT	STUFFY	DIRECT
ascertain	find out	optimal	best
commence	begin	prior to	before
deceased	dead	purchase	buy
endeavor	try	reside	live
finalize	finish	terminate	end
implement	carry out	utilize	use

Avoid euphemisms. *Euphemisms* are expressions that try to conceal a forthright meaning and make the concept seem more delicate, such as *change of life* for *menopause* or *downsized* for *fired*. Because euphemisms often sound evasive or are unclear, avoid them in favor of direct language. Similarly, avoid *doublespeak* (evasive expressions that seek to conceal the truth, such as *incendiary device* for *firebomb, combat situation* for *battle,* and *collateral damage* for *civilian casualties*). Examples of such language are easy to find in advertising, business, politics, and especially in war reporting. Do not equate formality with these indirect expressions.

> ▶ The building's owners offered the inspectors many
>   bribes
>   ~~financial incentives~~ to overlook code violations.

STYLE IN ACTION

The more you write, the more you will strive for variety, rhythm, and specific effects. The next two sections focus on using a variety of sentences and revising your work to improve style and sentence variety. In the concluding section are some tips to help you actively review your drafts for style.

34   Sentence Variety

34a   Sentence length

Readers appreciate variety, so aim for a mix of long and short sentences. If your editing program can print out your text in a series of single numbered sentences, you will easily be able to examine the length and structure of each. Academic writing need not consist solely of long, heavyweight sentences. Short sentences interspersed among longer ones can have a dramatic effect.

This passage from a student memoir demonstrates the use of short sentences to great effect:

> When I started high school and Afros became the rage, I immediately decided to get one. Now at that time, I had a head full of long, thick, kinky hair, which my mother had cultivated for years. When she said to me, "Cut it or perm it," she never for one minute believed I would do either. I cut it. She fainted.
>
> ——Denise Dejean, student

34b   Using statements, questions, commands, and exclamations

Declarative sentences make statements, *interrogative* sentences ask questions, *imperative* sentences give commands, and *exclamatory* sentences express surprise or some other strong emotion. Most of the sentences in your college writing will be declarative.

▶ **Winsor McCay's surrealist comic strip *Little Nemo in Slumberland* ran intermittently in newspapers from 1905 to 1927. It remains famous for its extraordinary beauty and artistry.**

34c   Types of sentences

Vary the structure of your sentences throughout any piece of writing. Aim for a mix of simple, compound, complex, and compound-complex sentences.

A *simple sentence* contains one independent clause.

▶ **Kara raised her hand.**

A *compound sentence* contains two or more independent clauses connected with one or more coordinating conjunctions (*and, but, or, nor, so, for, yet*), or with a semicolon alone, or with a semicolon and a transitional expression (**2d**).

┌─ independent clause ─┐   ┌──────── independent clause ────────┐
▶ **She raised her hand, and the whole class was surprised.**

┌─ independent clause ─┐   ┌──── independent clause ────┐
▶ **She raised her hand, but nobody else responded.**

┌─ independent clause ─┐   ┌──── independent clause ────┐
▶ **She raised her hand; the whole class was surprised.**

┌─ independent clause ─┐   ┌──────── independent clause ────────┐
▶ **She raised her hand; as a result, the whole class was surprised.**

A *complex sentence* contains an independent clause and one or more dependent clauses.

┌──── dependent clause ────┐   ┌──── independent clause ────┐
▶ **When she raised her hand, the whole class was surprised.**

┌──── independent clause ────┐   ┌──── dependent clause ────┐
▶ **The whole class was surprised when she raised her hand.**

A *compound-complex sentence* contains at least two independent clauses and at least one dependent clause.

┌──── dependent clause ────┐   ┌──── independent clause ────┐
▶ **When she raised her hand, the whole class was surprised,**

┌──── independent clause ────┐   ┌── dependent clause ──┐
and the professor waited eagerly as she began to speak.

34d Inverted word order

Sometimes, inverted word order (switching from the usual subject + verb order to verb + subject) will help you achieve coherence, consistent subjects, emphasis, or a smooth transition:

           V   ┌──── S ────┐
▶ **Next to the river runs a superhighway.**

        V S V
▶ **Never have I been so tired.**

      V ┌─ S ─┐   V
▶ **Not only does the novel entertain, but it also raises our awareness of poverty.**

       V S
▶ **So eager was I to win that I set off before the starter's gun.**

     V ┌─S─┐   V
▶ **Rarely has a poem achieved such a grasp on the times.**

34e Sentence beginnings

Consider using some of these variations to begin a sentence, but remember that beginning with the subject will always be clear and direct for readers. Any of the following beginnings repeated too often will seem like a stylistic tic and will annoy or bore readers.

Begin with a dependent clause or a condensed clause.

```
┌──────────────────── dependent clause ────────────────────┐
```
▶ **While my friends were waiting for the movie to begin, they ate three tubs of popcorn.**

```
┌────── clause condensed to a phrase ──────┐
```
▶ **While waiting for the movie to begin, my friends ate three tubs of popcorn.**

Begin with a participle or an adjective. A sentence can begin with a participle or an adjective if the word is in a phrase that refers to the subject of the independent clause. (See **38a, 40c**.)

-ing participle
▶ **Waiting for the movie to begin, my friends ate popcorn.**

past participle
▶ **Forced to work late, they ordered a pepperoni pizza.**

adjective
▶ **Aware of the problems, they nevertheless decided to continue.**

Begin with a prepositional phrase.

```
┌─prepositional phrase ─┐
```
▶ **With immense joy, we watched our team win the pennant.**

You can also occasionally use inverted word order after a prepositional phrase (**34d, 43d**).

```
┌─── prepositional phrase ───┐   verb   ┌──── subject ────┐
```
▶ **At the end of my block stands a deserted building.**

35 Revising for Style: A Student's Drafts

Mariana Gonzalez was asked in class to write a paragraph on the issue of banning smoking in bars as well as in restaurants. She produced this first draft.

I think smoking is not a good idea in bars and restaurants, so it should be banned in New York. Some people may disagree with this, but it is not fair to people that they should have to breathe in the smoke that other people breathe out. Bars and restaurants are public places. They are crowded and there are always some people among all the people there who smoke and do not go outside to smoke. I think those people should be made to go outside. If they stay inside they should not be allowed to smoke. All people should be allowed to be healthy. Smoking can kill you, even if you are not doing the smoking yourself, and should be banned.

Extensive discussion of style ensued in a peer group discussion in her class, during which her group members read and discussed her paragraph. Then they wrote the following feedback:

> You make a point, but I wonder if you need to make it so often. There's a lot of repetition.
>
> Remember what the prof said about cutting.
>
> It is all a bit general. I don't get any sense that you have a real place in mind. Could you tell about a restaurant or bar that *you* go to? Include real people, too, if you can.
>
> Play up the point about secondhand smoke.
>
> Are there too many instances of "should" and "I think"?
>
> Try to paint a picture of a place. I can't see a time, a place, or you here anywhere.
>
> Remember what the book says about being confident. I'd cut out "Some people may disagree with this."

Gonzalez took the comments home and produced the following:

The Corner Bistro on West 4th Street in Manhattan is a crowded neighborhood bar and restaurant, where Greenwich Village customers have been enjoying burgers and mugs of beer since the 1960s. They also used to enjoy, or suffer, what the Zagat Survey calls "side orders of cigarette smoke." It is a cleaner, safer environment since smoking has been banned in all Manhattan restaurants and bars. Some of the locals there, however, are outraged. One of them, shouting hoarsely above the noise, gestures with nicotine-stained fingers toward an unnamed enemy: "Who do they think they are, telling me I can't smoke in here? Soon they will be telling me I can't eat and drink in here. They talk about freedom *from* smoke. What about my freedom *to* smoke?" He storms outside to light up. The issue, though, is not just freedom. The issue is the proven danger of secondhand smoke. Out there he will no longer endanger the health of his fellow customers or of the restaurant employees.

36   Style Tips

As you write and revise, keep in mind the five C's of style, and aim for sentence variety. For a final quick review of your style, read your draft aloud and use these tips.

1. *Be adaptable.* Consider the style your readers will expect. Don't work on developing a figurative style for short stories and then continue to use it in business communications or e-mail. Choose a style as you choose your clothes: the right outfit for the occasion.

2. *When in doubt, favor a plain style.* Be clear and straightforward. Don't search for the big words or the obscure turn of phrase. The following sentences, part of an e-mail message to the author of this book from a technical adviser in response to a question about sending an e-mail message, are decidedly overdressed and stuffed with bureaucratic nothings: "It has been a pleasure assisting you. It is my hope that the information provided would be of great help with regards to your concern."

3. *Less is often better.* Details and descriptions are interesting, but don't overload your writing with adjectives and adverbs: *The perky little redheaded twin sat languidly in the comfortable overstuffed green-striped armchair and bit enthusiastically into a red and yellow fleshy, overripe peach.* Such prose is as overripe as the peach. Also avoid intensifying adverbs such as *very, really, extremely, terribly,* and *enormously.* Find a stronger word to use in place of the two words, such as *terrified* in place of *extremely scared.*

4. *Place your emphasis.* Use to best advantage the parts of a sentence that carry the most weight: the subject, the verb, the ending.

NOT **Speed is a feature of the new Jaguar manufactured in Germany.**

BUT **The new Jaguar manufactured in Germany roars past other cars.**

5. *Focus on rhythm, not rules.* Heed the advice of *The New York Times Manual of Style and Usage:* "One measure of skill is exceptions, not rules." And keep in mind this remark by novelist Ford Madox Ford: "Carefully examined, a good—an interesting—style will be found to consist in a constant succession of tiny, unobservable surprises." Ask yourself how you can provide pleasant surprises for your readers.

PART 7

Common Sentence Problems

37   Troublespots and Terms

37a Students' frequently asked questions—and where to find answers

Questions	Short Answer	More Information
Can I begin a sentence with *and* or *but*?	Yes	31d
Can I begin a sentence with *because*?	Yes	38b

Questions	Short Answer	More Information
How do I know whether to use *I* or *me* with *and*?	Use the "Drop the noun in the *and* phrase" test.	**44a**
What is the difference between *who* and *whom*?	Use *whom* in formal writing as an object form.	**44i, 46a**
When do I use *who*, *which*, or *that*?	Ask: person or thing? Consider *restrictive* vs. *nonrestrictive*.	**46a, 46d**
When is it OK to use the phrase *he or she*?	To refer to a singular noun phrase—but limit the use, or use plural throughout.	**44e**
Can I interchange *but* and *however*?	No. Meanings are similar; usage and punctuation differ.	**39, 47e**
When do I use *good* or *well, bad* or *badly*?	*Good* and *bad* modify nouns, not verbs, but can follow linking verbs.	**45b, 45c**
What is the difference between		
a. *its* and *it's*?	*It's* stands for *it is* or *it has*.	**48f**
b. *whose* and *who's*?	*Who's* stands for *who is* or *who has*.	Glossary of Usage
c. *lie* and *lay*?	Use *lay* with a direct object. Learn all the forms.	**41b**

37b Teachers' top ten sentence problems

Here are the problems that teachers often find and mark in their students' writing. Try to find these in your own writing before your instructor does. If you cannot immediately identify and explain an error in the middle column, read the section listed in the right column for more explanation and examples.

Type of Error	Example of Error	More details and examples
1. Fragment	She had an ambitious dream. *To become a CEO.*	**38**
2. Run-on sentence or comma splice	The city is *lively the clubs* are open late. The city is *lively, the clubs* are open late.	**39**
3. Fuzzy syntax	In the essay "Notes of a Native Son" by James Baldwin discusses his feelings about his father.	**40a**
4. Wrong verb form or tense	They have never *drank* Coke.	**41a, 41d**
5. Tense shift	Foote *wrote* about Shiloh and *describes* its aftermath.	**41h**
6. Lack of subject-verb agreement	The *owner have* gone bankrupt.	**43**
7. Pronoun error	The coach rebuked my teammates and *I.* Nobody knows *whom* will be fired.	**44a, 44i**
8. Unclear pronoun reference	When I crossed the border, *they* searched my backpack.	**44c**
9. Adjective/adverb confusion	The Diamondbacks played *good* in spring training.	**45a–45c**
10. Double negative	They *don't* have *no* luck.	**45f**

Pages 516 and 517 show you the editing and correction marks that your instructor is likely to use.

37c What Is Standard English?

Science fiction writer and editor Teresa Neilson Hayden, in *Making Book*, characterizes English as "a generous, expansive, and flexible language" but adds, "a less charitable description would characterize it as

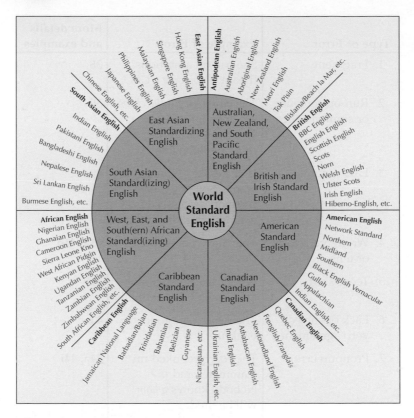

The Circle of World English (used with permission)

drunk and disorderly." The task of editing, she claims, is to try to impose "a degree of regularity on something that is inherently irregular." What can help you move away from irregularities that appear in your writing is a set of conventions referred to as Standard English.

The American Heritage Dictionary, 4th edition, defines Standard English as "the variety of English that is generally acknowledged as the model for the speech and writing of educated speakers." A Usage Note in the AHD, however, continues, "A form that is considered standard in one region may be nonstandard in another" and points out that *standard* and *nonstandard* are relative terms, depending largely on context.

In short, the concept of Standard English is complex. It is inextricably entwined with the region, race, class, education, and gender of both the speaker (or writer) and the listener (or reader). Standard English is far from monolithic (see the Circle of World English above). It is constantly being supplemented and challenged by other ways of writing, such as those coming from technology, the rap movement, the worlds of gender and sexual politics, popular culture, and conventions in use in different parts of the English-speaking world.

Nevertheless, Standard English, with all its quirks, irregularities, rules, and exceptions, is politically and sociologically branded as the language of those in power in society; its practices are what most readers expect in the academic and business worlds. However insightful and original your ideas may be, readers will soon become impatient if those ideas are not expressed in sentences that follow conventions determined by the history of the language and the prescriptive power of its educated users.

To meet readers' expectations, use Standard English in all academic and business writing.

37d What are the terms for the parts of a sentence?

To think about and discuss how sentences work, a shared vocabulary is useful. Here are some of the basic terms covering the parts of speech and the parts of a sentence. The Glossary of Grammatical Terms on page 470 provides further definitions and examples.

Parts of speech Words are traditionally classified into eight categories called *parts of speech*. Note that the part of speech refers not to the word itself but to its function in a sentence. Some words can function as different parts of speech.

▶ They re*verb*spect the orchestra manager.

▶ Re*noun*spect is a large part of a business relationship.

NOUNS Words that name a person, place, thing, or concept—*teacher, valley, furniture, Hinduism*—are called nouns. When you use a noun, determine the following: Is it a proper noun, requiring a capital letter? Does it have a plural form? If so, are you using the singular or plural form? See **53b** and **60a** ESL.

PRONOUNS A pronoun represents a noun or a noun phrase. In writing, a pronoun refers to its antecedent—that is, a noun or noun phrase appearing just before it in the text.

▶ My sister loves *her* new car, but *she* dented *it* last week.

Pronouns fall into seven types: personal (**44a**), possessive (**43j**, **44b**), demonstrative (**43i**), intensive or reflexive (**44h**), relative (**46a**), interrogative (**44i**), and indefinite (**43h**). When you use a pronoun, determine the following: What word or words in the sentence does the pronoun refer to? Does the pronoun refer to a noun or pronoun that is singular or plural?

VERBS Words that tell what a person, place, thing, or concept does or is—*smile, throw, think, seem, become, be*—are called verbs. Verbs change form, so when you use a verb, determine the following: What time does the verb refer to? What auxiliary or modal verbs are needed for an appropriate tense? Is the subject of the verb singular or plural? Is the verb in the active voice or passive voice? What are the five forms of the verb (*sing, sings, singing, sang, sung*), and are you using the correct form?

Main verbs often need auxiliary verbs (*be, do, have*) or modal auxiliaries (*will, would, can, could, shall, should, may, might, must*) to complete the meaning. For more on verbs, see **41**, **42**, and **43**.

ADJECTIVES Words that describe nouns—*purple, beautiful, big*—are called adjectives. An adjective can precede a noun or follow a linking verb:

▶ She is wearing *purple* boots.

▶ Her boots are *purple.*

Descriptive adjectives have comparative and superlative forms: *short, shorter, shortest* (**45g**). Also functioning as adjectives (before a noun) are *a, an,* and *the,* as well as possessives and demonstratives: *a* cabbage, *an* allegory, *their* poems, *this* book. For more on adjectives, see **45**.

ADVERBS Words that provide information about verbs, adjectives, adverbs, or clauses are called adverbs. Many but not all adverbs end in *-ly: quickly, efficiently.* Adverbs also provide information about how or when: *very, well, sometimes, often, soon, never.* Adverbs modify verbs, adjectives, other adverbs, or clauses.

modifies verb   modifies adverb

▶ He dunked brilliantly. He played spectacularly well.

modifies adjective   modifies whole clause

▶ He is a very energetic player. Undoubtedly, he is a genius.

Conjunctive adverbs—such as *however, therefore, furthermore*—make connections between independent clauses. For more on adverbs, see **2d** and **45**.

CONJUNCTIONS Words that connect words, phrases, and clauses are called conjunctions.

▶ She loves ham *and* eggs.

▶ We bought a red table, a blue chair, *and* a gold mirror.

▶ The magazine was published, *and* his article won acclaim.

Coordinating conjunctions—*and, but, or, nor, so, for, yet*—connect ideas of equal importance. Subordinating conjunctions—*because, if, when, although,* for instance (see **38b** for a list)—make one clause dependent on another. Consider the meaning before using a conjunction. See **31c.**

PREPOSITIONS Words used before nouns and pronouns to form phrases that usually do the work of an adjective or adverb are called prepositions.

                preposition   preposition
▶ A bird with a red crest flew onto the feeder.

Some common prepositions are *against, around, at, behind, between, except, for, from, in, into, like, on, over, regarding, to,* and *without.* Prepositional phrases are often idiomatic: *on occasion, in love.* To understand their use and meaning, consult a good dictionary. See also **63 ESL.**

INTERJECTIONS Words that express emotion and can stand alone—*Ha! Wow! Ugh! Ouch! Say!*—are called interjections. Use them only in informal writing or when representing direct speech.

Parts of a sentence

SUBJECT AND PREDICATE A sentence consists of a *subject* (the person or thing doing or receiving the action) and a *predicate* (a comment or assertion about the subject). A predicate must contain a complete *verb*, expressing action or state.

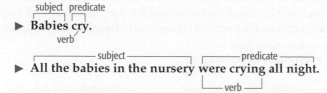

        subject predicate
▶ Babies cry.
        verb

        ────────── subject ──────────   ────── predicate ──────
▶ All the babies in the nursery were crying all night.
                                          └── verb ──┘

DIRECT AND INDIRECT OBJECT Some verbs are followed by a direct object.

direct object
▶ Many people wear glasses.

[A verb that is followed by a direct object is known as a *transitive verb*. *Intransitive verbs* such as *sit, happen, occur,* and *rise* are never followed by a direct object.]

Verbs such as *give, send,* and *offer* can be followed by both a direct and an indirect object.

┌── indirect object ──┐ ┌── direct object ──┐
▶ He gave his leading lady one exquisite rose.

See **62c** ESL.

COMPLEMENT Verbs such as *be, seem, look,* and *appear* are not action verbs but *linking verbs*. They are followed by a *subject complement*.

subject complement
▶ The singers in the choir look happy.

An *object complement* renames or describes the direct object.

direct object
┌──────┐ ┌──────── object complement ────────┐
▶ We appointed a student the chairperson of the committee.

PHRASE A *phrase* is a group of words that lacks a subject, a verb, or both. A phrase is only a part of a sentence. It cannot be punctuated as a sentence.

    an elegant evening gown

    singing in the rain

    on the corner

    worried by the news

    with her thoughts in turmoil

    to travel around the world

See **38a** for more on phrase fragments.

CLAUSE Clauses can be independent or dependent. A sentence must contain an *independent clause*, one that can stand alone. A clause introduced by a word such as *because, when, if,* or *although* is a *dependent clause*. Every independent clause and dependent clause needs a subject and predicate.

┌──────── independent clause ────────┐
▶ Her eyesight is deteriorating.

┌──── dependent (subordinate) clause ────┐ ┌─ independent clause ─┐
▶ Because her eyesight is deteriorating, she wears glasses.

Dependent clauses can function as adverbs, adjectives, or nouns.

▶ *When the sun shines,* **the strawberries ripen.**

[Adverb clause expressing time]

▶ **The berries** *that we picked yesterday* **were delicious.**

[Adjective clause modifying *berries*]

▶ **The farmers know** *what they should do.*

[Noun clause functioning as a direct object]

See **38b** for more on dependent clause fragments.

38 Sentence Fragments

A fragment is a group of words incorrectly punctuated as if it were a complete sentence.

KEY POINTS

The Requirements of a Sentence

To be complete, a sentence must contain the following:

1. A subject

                  They were arguing

▶ **They drove for six days.** ~~Arguing~~ **all the way.**

2. A predicate that includes a complete verb

                    ┌── predicate ──┐

            ┌── subject ── *were*

▶ **We watched the rehearsal. The jugglers practicing for**

  ┌──────────┐

  four hours.

3. An independent clause (a clause that can stand alone)

               because

▶ **The spectators shrieked,** ~~Because~~ **the race was so close.**

[A clause introduced by *because* is a dependent, not an independent, clause.]

A command has an understood *you* subject: [You] Arrive early.

Advertisers and writers occasionally use fragments deliberately for a crisp, immediate effect: "What a luxury should be." "Sleek lines." "Efficient in rain, sleet, and snow." "A magnificent film." However, you should identify and correct them in your formal writing.

38a Identifying and correcting a phrase fragment

A phrase is a group of words that lacks a subject, a complete verb, or both. Do not punctuate a phrase as a complete sentence.

┌────── phrase fragment ──────┐
▶ He wanted to make a point. To prove his competence.

Methods of correcting a phrase fragment

1. Attach the phrase to a nearby independent clause. Remove the period and the capital letter.

   to
   ▶ He wanted to make a point, ~~To~~ prove his competence.

   on
   ▶ The officer parked illegally, ~~On~~ the corner, right in front of a hydrant.

   the
   ▶ A prize was awarded to Ed, ~~The~~ best worker in the company.

   [Use a comma before an appositive phrase.]

2. Change the phrase to an independent clause with its own subject and verb.

   She is just
   ▶ Althea works every evening. ~~Just~~ trying to keep up with her boss's demands.

   he valued
   ▶ Nature held many attractions for Thoreau. First, the solitude.

3. Rewrite the passage.

   was so *elated* *that he talked for hours.*
   ▶ Ralph ~~talked for hours. Elated~~ by the company's success.

38b Identifying and correcting a dependent clause fragment

A dependent clause begins with a word that makes the clause subordinate. Unable to stand alone, a subordinate clause must be attached to an independent clause. Here are the words that introduce subordinate adverb clauses:

SUBORDINATING CONJUNCTIONS

time: when, whenever, until, till, before, after, while, once, as
  soon as, as long as

place: where, wherever

cause: because, as, since

condition: if, even if, unless, provided that

contrast: although, though, even though, whereas, while

comparison: than, as, as if, as though

purpose: so that, in order that

result: so . . . that, such . . . that

Words introducing dependent (adjective or noun) clauses include
who, whom, whose, which, that, what, when, and *whoever.*

▶ Lars wants to be a stand-up comic. — fragment — Because he likes to make
people laugh.

Methods of correcting a dependent clause fragment

1. Connect the dependent clause to an independent clause.

▶ Lars wants to be a stand-up comic, ~~Because~~ because he likes to make
people laugh.

▶ The family set out for a new country, ~~In~~ in which they could
practice their culture and religion.

▶ She made many promises to her family, ~~That~~ that she would
write to them every day.

2. Delete the subordinating conjunction. The dependent clause then
becomes an independent clause, which can stand alone.

▶ Lars wants to be a stand-up comic. ~~Because he~~ He likes to
make people laugh.

Note: A subordinating conjunction at the beginning of a sentence does
not always signal a fragment. A correctly punctuated sentence may
begin with a subordinating conjunction introducing a dependent
clause, as long as the sentence also contains an independent clause.

subordinating conjunction   comma   independent
     — dependent clause — || — clause —

▶ Because Lars likes to make people laugh, he wants to be a

stand-up comic.

38c Identifying and correcting a fragment with a missing verb or verb part

Every sentence must contain a complete verb in an independent clause. A word group that is punctuated like a sentence but lacks a verb or has an incomplete verb is a fragment. A complete verb is a verb that shows tense (see **41a, 41c**).

┌──── fragment: incomplete verb ────
▶ **Overcrowding is a problem. Too many people living in**

└────┐
one area.

┌─ fragment: missing verb ─
▶ **The candidate explained his proposal. A plan for off-street**

└────┐
parking.

Methods of correcting Supply all necessary verb forms, connect the fragment to the sentence before or after, or recast the sentence.

                are
▶ **Overcrowding is a problem. Too many people living in**
one area.

             with too
▶ **Overcrowding is a problem. Too many people living in**
one area.

▶ **The candidate explained his ~~proposal. A~~ plan for off-street**
parking.

               He emphasized a
▶ **The candidate explained his proposal. A plan for off-street**
parking.

38d Identifying and correcting a fragment with a missing subject

Unless it is a command with the implied subject *you*, a word group appearing without a subject is never a complete clause.

┌──── fragment ────
▶ **After an hour, the dancers changed partners. And adapted to**

└────────────┐
a different type of music.

Methods of correcting

1. Correct the fragment by removing the period and capital letter.

   > *and*
   > ▶ After an hour, the dancers changed partners. ~~And~~ adapted to
   > a different type of music.   [This forms what is known as a
   > *compound predicate.*]

2. Include an appropriate subject to form an independent clause.

   > *They*
   > ▶ After an hour, the dancers changed partners. ~~And~~ adapted
   > to a different type of music.

3. Turn the fragment into an *-ing* participle phrase, and attach it to
   the independent clause.

   > *adapting*
   > ▶ After an hour, the dancers changed partners. ~~And adapted~~
   > to a different type of music.

38e Using fragments intentionally

Fragments are used frequently in advertisements to keep the text short.
In academic writing, writers sometimes use a fragment intentionally for
emphasis after a question, as an exclamation, or at a point of transition.

> ▶ Is this unease what Kincaid intends? Maybe.

When you are writing academic papers in college, use intentional
fragments sparingly, if at all. Readers of your academic writing might
not realize when a fragment is intentional.

39   Run-ons and Comma Splices

39a Identifying run-on (or *fused*) sentences and
comma splices

If you run two independent clauses together without punctuation or
a coordinating conjunction between them, readers may find it hard to
determine where one idea ends and the next one begins.

RUN-ON ERROR

▶ The lion cubs were <mark>fighting the</mark> elephants were snoozing.

If you use only a comma to separate independent clauses, the meaning may be clearer, but the sentence has a comma splice error. A comma cannot do the work of a period or semicolon.

COMMA SPLICE ERROR

▶ The lion cubs were <mark>fighting, the</mark> elephants were snoozing.

Here a reader seeing the comma might anticipate a series: *The lion cubs were fighting, the elephants were snoozing, and the seals were splashing.*

Note: As with fragments, you will find comma splices and run-ons used in advertising and other writing for stylistic effect.

comma splice for stylistic effect

▶ **It's not that I'm afraid to die, I just don't want to be there when it happens.** —Woody Allen, *Without Feathers*

However, in formal academic writing, use more conventional punctuation.

39b Correcting run-on sentences and comma splices

You can correct run-ons and comma splices in the following five ways. Select the one that works best for the sentence you are editing.

Method 1 Separate the independent clauses into individual sentences with a period (or question mark or exclamation point, if required).

▶ The lion cubs were fighting ~~the~~ The elephants were snoozing.

Method 2 Separate the independent clauses with a semicolon if their ideas are closely related.

▶ The lion cubs were fighting; the elephants were snoozing.

▶ The hummingbird is amazing; its wings beat fifty to seventy-five times per second.

Method 3   Separate the independent clauses with a comma and a coordinating conjunction (*and, but, or, nor, so, for, yet*).

▶ The lion cubs were fighting␣the elephants were snoozing.
   , and

▶ Woodpeckers look for insects in trees␣they do not intentionally destroy live trees.
   but

Method 4   Make one clause dependent by adding a subordinating conjunction (see the list on p. 313).

▶ ~~The~~ lion cubs were fighting, the elephants were snoozing.
   While

▶ The scenery flashed by␣the train picked up speed.
   when

Method 5   Recast the sentence.

▶ ~~The~~ lion cubs ~~were~~ fighting, the elephants were ~~snoozing~~.
   With the   *still able to snooze.*

▶ Salmon swim upstream, ~~they leap~~ over huge dams to reach their destination.
   leaping

39c Correcting run-ons and comma splices formed by transitional expressions

Run-ons and comma splices often occur with transitional expressions such as *in addition, however, therefore, for example,* and *moreover* (see the list in **2d**). When one of these expressions precedes the subject of its own clause, end the previous sentence with a period or a semicolon. Put a comma after the transitional expression, not before it.

CORRECTED RUN-ON ERROR	Margaret cleaned her closets ⊙~~in~~ addition␣she reorganized the kitchen. *In* ,
CORRECTED COMMA SPLICE ERROR	The doctor prescribed some medicine␣however␣she did not alert the patient to the side effects. ; ,

Note: You can use the coordinating conjunctions *and, but,* and *so* after a comma to connect two independent clauses, but *in addition, however,* and *therefore* do not follow the same pattern.

▶ The stock market was rising, so he decided to invest most of his savings.

▶ The stock market was rising; therefore, he decided to invest most of his savings.

Commas should both precede and follow a transitional expression that does not appear at the beginning of its own clause:

▶ The doctor prescribed some medicine. She did not,

however, alert the patient to the side effects.

40   Sentence Snarls

Snarls, tangles, and knots are as difficult to deal with on a bad writing day as on a bad hair day, though they may not be as painful. Sentences with structural inconsistencies give readers trouble. They make readers work to untangle the meaning. This section points out how to avoid or edit common sentence snarls.

40a   Avoid fuzzy syntax.

Revise sentences that begin in one way and then veer off the track, departing from the original structure. When you mix constructions, make faulty comparisons, or tangle your syntax (sentence structure), you confuse readers. Pay special attention to sentences beginning with *with, by -ing,* or *when -ing.*

Some

▶ ~~With some~~ professors who never give grades like to write comments.   [Who are the people who "like to write comments"? The prepositional phrase *with some professors* cannot serve as the subject of the sentence.]

MIXED   **When wanting to take on a greater role in business**
CONSTRUCTION **might lead a woman to adopt new personality traits.**
           [The reader gets to the verb *might lead* without knowing what the subject is.]

POSSIBLE REVISIONS	**When wanting to take on a greater role in business, a woman might adopt new personality traits.**

[This version provides a grammatical subject—*woman*—for the independent clause.]

Wanting to take on a greater role in business might lead a woman to adopt new personality traits.

[This version deletes the preposition *by* and eliminates the prepositional phrase; now the *-ing* phrase functions as the subject of *might lead*.]

When you make comparisons, be sure to tell readers clearly what you are comparing to what. See also **44a**, **44b**, and **45h**.

FAULTY COMPARISON	**Like Wallace Stevens, her job strikes readers as unexpected for a poet.** [It is not her job that is like the poet Wallace Stevens; her job is like his job.]

REVISED	**Like Wallace Stevens, she holds a job that strikes readers as unexpected for a poet.**

Revise sentences that ramble on to such an extent that they become tangled. Make sure your sentences have clear subjects and verbs, and use coordination or subordination effectively. Cut and check for action (**29, 30**).

TANGLED	**The way I feel about getting what you want is that when there is a particular position or item that you want to try to get to do your best and not give up because if you give up you have probably missed your chance of succeeding.**

POSSIBLE REVISION	**To get what you want, keep trying.**

40b Position modifiers appropriately.

A modifier is a word or phrase that describes or limits another word or phrase. Keep single words, phrases, and clauses next to or close to the sentence elements that they modify.

Take care with words such as *only*.   Place *only, even, just, nearly, merely,* or *simply* immediately before the word it modifies.

> ▶ She ~~only~~ likes ^only^ Tom.   [Tom is the only one she likes.]

The meaning of a sentence changes significantly as the position of *only* changes, so careful placement is important.

▶ *Only* the journalist began to investigate the forgery.
[and nobody else]

▶ The journalist *only* began to investigate the forgery.
[but did not finish]

▶ The journalist began to investigate *only* the forgery.
[and nothing else]

Place a phrase or clause close to the word it modifies.

MISPLACED   Sidel argues that young women's dreams will not always come true in her essay.

[Will the dreams come true in Sidel's essay or does Sidel argue in her essay?]

REVISED   In her essay, Sidel argues that young women's dreams will not always come true.

Consider the case for splitting an infinitive.   You split an infinitive when you place a word or phrase between *to* and the verb. *The New Oxford Dictionary of English* finds the use of split infinitives "both normal and useful," as in "To boldly go where no man has gone before…" (*Star Trek*). However, such splitting may irritate readers, especially when a clumsy sentence is the result, as in the following:

┌─────────── clumsy split infinitive *(to inform)* ───────────┐
▶ We want to sincerely, honestly, and in confidence inform you of our plans for expansion.

40c Avoid dangling modifiers.

A modifier that is not grammatically linked to the noun or phrase it is intended to describe is said to be dangling. An *-ing* or *-ed* modifier at the beginning of a sentence must provide information about the subject of the sentence.

DANGLING   Walking into the house, the telephone rang.
[The sentence says the telephone was walking.]

DANGLING   **Delighted with the team's victory, the parade route was decorated by the fans.**

[The sentence says the parade route was delighted.]

You can fix a dangling modifier in the following ways:

Method 1   Retain the modifier, but make the subject of the independent clause the person or thing modified.

REVISED   **Walking into the house, we heard the telephone ring.**

REVISED   **Delighted with the team's victory, the fans decorated the parade route.**

Method 2   Change the modifier phrase into a clause with its own subject and verb.

REVISED   **While we were walking into the house, the telephone rang.**

REVISED   **Because the fans were delighted with the team's victory, they decorated the parade route.**

40d   Avoid shifts: From statements to commands, from indirect to direct quotation, and in point of view.

Sudden shifts in your sentences can disconcert readers. (See also **41h** on avoiding unnecessary shifts in verb tense.)

Do not shift abruptly from statements to commands.

▶ The students in this university should do more to keep the
                                              They should pick
place clean. ~~Pick~~ up the litter and treat the dorms like home.

Do not shift a verb phrase from indirect to direct quotation.   (See **41h** and **62d** ESL for more on tenses in indirect quotations.)

SHIFT   **The client told us that he wanted to sign the lease and would we prepare the papers.**

REVISED   **The client told us that he wanted to sign the lease and asked us to prepare the papers.**

SHIFT   She wanted to find out whether any interest had accumulated on her account and was she receiving any money.

REVISED   She wanted to find out whether any interest had accumulated on her account and whether she was receiving any money.

Do not shift point of view.   Be consistent in using first, second, or third person pronouns. For example, if you begin by referring to *one*, do not switch to *you* or *we*. Also avoid shifting unnecessarily between third person singular and plural forms.

SHIFT   *One* needs a high salary to live in a city because *you* have to spend so much on rent and transportation.

POSSIBLE   *One* needs a high salary to live in a city because *one*
REVISIONS has to spend so much on rent and transportation.

          People need a high salary to live in a city because *they* have to spend so much on rent and transportation.

          A high salary is necessary in a city because rent and transportation cost so much.

40e Make the subject and predicate match.

To avoid confusing readers, never use a subject and predicate that do not make logical sense together. This error is known as *faulty predication*.

                    Building
▶ ~~The decision to build~~ an elaborate extension onto the train station made all the trains arrive late.
[It was not the decision that delayed the trains, but the building of the extension.]

          Finding the
▶ ~~The~~ solution to the problem is a hard task.
[A solution is not a task.]

40f Avoid "is when" with definitions and "is because" with reasons.

When you write a definition of a term, use parallel structures on either side of the verb *be*. In formal writing, avoid defining a term by using *is when* or *is where* (or *was when, was where*).

FAULTY   A tiebreaker in tennis *is where* they play one final game to decide the set.

REVISED   A tiebreaker in tennis is the final deciding game of a tied set.

Writing about reasons, like writing definitions, has pitfalls. Avoid *the reason is because* in Standard English. Grammatically, an adverb clause beginning with *because* cannot follow the verb *be*. Instead, use *the reason is that*, or recast the sentence.

FAULTY   *The reason* Kournikova lost *is because* her opponent was serving so well.

POSSIBLE REVISIONS   *The reason* Kournikova lost *is that* her opponent was serving so well.

           Kournikova lost *because* her opponent was serving so well.

Note that Standard English requires *the reason that* and not *the reason why*.

▶ The TV commentator explained the reason ~~why~~ ^{that} Kournikova lost.

[Another possibility here is to omit *that*.]

40g   Avoid using an adverb clause as the subject of a sentence.

A dependent adverb clause (**37d**) cannot function as the subject of a sentence.

▶ ~~Just because she swims~~ ^{Swimming} every day does not mean she is healthy.

[The subject is now a noun phrase, *Swimming every day,* instead of a clause, *Because she swims every day.*]

▶ When people eat too much fat_^ increases^{, they} their cholesterol.

[The dependent clause *When people eat too much fat* is now attached to an independent clause with its own subject, *they*.]

40h Include all necessary words and apostrophes.

Include necessary words in compound structures. If you omit a verb form from a compound verb, the main verb form must fit into each part of the compound; otherwise, you must use the complete verb form (see **40j** on parallelism).

> tried
> ► He has always ^ and will always try to preserve his father's good name in the community. [*Try* fits only with *will*, not with *has*.]

Include necessary words in comparisons. (See also **45h**.)

> as
> ► The volleyball captain is as competitive ^ or even more competitive than her teammates.
> [The comparative structures are *as competitive as* and *more competitive than*. Do not merge them.]

If you omit the verb in the second part of a comparison, ambiguity may occur.

> did
> ► He liked baseball more than his son ^. [Omitting *did* implies that he liked baseball more than he liked his son.]

Include apostrophes with words that need them.

> 's
> ► My mother's expectations differed from Jing-Mei's mother. ^

See also **45h** and **48c**.

40i State the grammatical subject only once.

Even when a phrase or clause separates the subject and main verb of a sentence, do not restate the subject in pronoun form. (See also **62f** ESL.)

> restated subject
> ► The nurse who took care of my father for many years ~~she~~ gave him comfort and advice.

When the subject is a whole clause, do not add an *it* subject.

▶ **What may seem moral to some ~~it~~ is immoral to others.**

40j Keep structures parallel.

The use of parallel structures helps produce cohesion and coherence in a text. Aim for parallelism in sentences and in longer passages. The structures can be clauses or phrases, as shown in the following passages from "Maintenance" by Naomi Shihab Nye.

PARALLEL STRUCTURES: CLAUSES

We saw one house *where walls and windows had been sheathed in various patterns of gloomy brocade.* We visited another *where the kitchen had been removed* because the owners only ate in restaurants.

PARALLEL STRUCTURES: VERB PHRASES

Sometimes I'd come home to find her *lounging* in the bamboo chair on the back porch, *eating* melon, or *lying* on the couch with a bowl of half-melted ice cream balanced on her chest.

Sentences become confusing when you string together phrases or clauses that lack parallelism.

NOT PARALLEL   **He wants a new girlfriend, to get a house, and find a good job.**

PARALLEL   **He wants a new girlfriend, a house, and a good job.**

Parallel structures with paired (correlative) conjunctions When your sentence contains correlative conjunctions, pairs such as *either ... or, neither ... nor, not only ... but also, both ... and, whether ... or,* and *as ... as,* the structure after the second part of the pair should be exactly parallel in form to the structure after the first part.

▶ **He made up his mind *either* to paint the van *or*ˬ sell it to** to
   another buyer. [*To paint* follows *either*; therefore, *to sell* should follow *or*.]

▶ **She loves *both* swimming competitively *and* ~~to play~~ golf.** playing
   [An *-ing* form follows *both*; therefore, an *-ing* form should also follow *and*.]

▶ **The drive to Cuernavaca was *not only* too expensive *but also***
   ~~was~~ too tiring to do alone. [*Too expensive* follows *not only*; therefore, *too tiring* should follow *but also*.]

Parallel structures in comparisons When making comparisons with *as* or *than*, use parallel structures.

> To drive
> ▶ ~~Driving~~ to Cuernavaca is *as* expensive *as* to take the bus.
> ˄

> Taking
> ▶ ~~To take~~ the bus is less comfortable *than* driving.
> ˄

41 Verbs

A verb will fit into one or more of the following sentences:

a. They want to ———————. It is going to ———————.
b. They will ———————. It will ———————.

Identify a verb by checking that the *base form* (that is, the form listed as a dictionary entry) fits these sentences.

41a Verb forms in Standard English

Although you might use a variety of verb forms when you speak, readers generally expect formal writing to conform to Standard English usage. All verbs except *be* have five forms.

Regular verbs The five forms of *regular verbs* follow a predictable pattern. Once you know the base form, you can construct all the others:

1. base form: the form listed in a dictionary (*paint, help*)

2. *-s* form: the third person singular form of the present tense (*paints, helps*)

3. *-ing* form (the *present participle*): needs auxiliary verbs to function as a complete verb; can appear in a verbal phrase and as a noun (gerund) (*painting, helping*)

4. past tense form: functions as a complete verb, without auxiliary verbs (*painted, helped*)

5. past participle: sometimes called the *-ed* form; needs auxiliary verbs to function as a complete verb (*has painted, was helped*); can appear in a phrase (*the painted wall*)

Irregular verbs *Irregular verbs* do not use *-ed* to form the past tense and the past participle. Here are the forms of some common irregular verbs.

IRREGULAR VERBS

BASE FORM	PAST TENSE	PAST PARTICIPLE
arise	arose	arisen
bear	bore	born
beat	beat	beaten
become	became	become
begin	began	begun
bend	bent	bent
bet	bet	bet, betted
bind	bound	bound
bite	bit	bitten
bleed	bled	bled
blow	blew	blown
break	broke	broken
bring	brought	brought
build	built	built
burst	burst	burst
buy	bought	bought
catch	caught	caught
choose	chose	chosen
cling	clung	clung
come	came	come
cost	cost	cost
creep	crept	crept
cut	cut	cut
deal	dealt	dealt
dig	dug	dug
do	did	done
draw	drew	drawn
drink	drank	drunk
drive	drove	driven
eat	ate	eaten
fall	fell	fallen
feed	fed	fed
feel	felt	felt
fight	fought	fought
find	found	found
flee	fled	fled
fly	flew	flown
forbid	forbad(e)	forbidden
forget	forgot	forgotten
forgive	forgave	forgiven
freeze	froze	frozen

BASE FORM	PAST TENSE	PAST PARTICIPLE
get	got	gotten, got
give	gave	given
go	went	gone
grind	ground	ground
grow	grew	grown
hang*	hung	hung
have	had	had
hear	heard	heard
hide	hid	hidden
hit	hit	hit
hold	held	held
hurt	hurt	hurt
keep	kept	kept
know	knew	known
lay	laid	laid (**41b**)
lead	led	led
leave	left	left
lend	lent	lent
let	let	let
lie	lay	lain (**41b**)
light	lit, lighted	lit, lighted
lose	lost	lost
make	made	made
mean	meant	meant
meet	met	met
put	put	put
quit	quit	quit
read	read	read
ride	rode	ridden
ring	rang	rung
rise	rose	risen (**41b**)
run	ran	run
say	said	said
see	saw	seen
seek	sought	sought
sell	sold	sold
send	sent	sent
set	set	set (**41b**)
shake	shook	shaken
shine	shone	shone
shoot	shot	shot

Hang meaning "put to death" is regular: *hang, hanged, hanged.*

BASE FORM	PAST TENSE	PAST PARTICIPLE
shrink	shrank	shrunk
shut	shut	shut
sing	sang	sung
sink	sank	sunk
sit	sat	sat (**41b**)
sleep	slept	slept
slide	slid	slid
slit	slit	slit
speak	spoke	spoken
spend	spent	spent
spin	spun	spun
spit	spit, spat	spit
split	split	split
spread	spread	spread
spring	sprang	sprung
stand	stood	stood
steal	stole	stolen
stick	stuck	stuck
sting	stung	stung
stink	stank, stunk	stunk
strike	struck	struck, stricken
swear	swore	sworn
sweep	swept	swept
swim	swam	swum
swing	swung	swung
take	took	taken
teach	taught	taught
tear	tore	torn
tell	told	told
think	thought	thought
throw	threw	thrown
tread	trod	trodden, trod
understand	understood	understood
upset	upset	upset
wake	woke	waked, woken
wear	wore	worn
weave	wove	woven
weep	wept	wept
win	won	won
wind	wound	wound
wring	wrung	wrung
write	wrote	written

41b Verbs commonly confused

Give special attention to verbs that are similar in form but differ in meaning. Some of them can take a direct object; these are called *transitive verbs*. Others never take a direct object; these are called *intransitive verbs*. (See **62c** ESL.)

1. *rise:* to get up, to ascend (intransitive; irregular)

   raise: to lift, to cause to rise (transitive; regular)

BASE	–s	–ing	PAST TENSE	PAST PARTICIPLE
rise	rises	rising	rose	risen
raise	raises	raising	raised	raised

   ▶ The sun *rose* at 5:55 a.m. today.

   ▶ She *raised* the blind and peeked out.

2. *sit:* to occupy a seat (intransitive; irregular)

   set: to put or place (transitive; irregular)

BASE	–s	–ing	PAST TENSE	PAST PARTICIPLE
sit	sits	sitting	sat	sat
set	sets	setting	set	set

   ▶ He *sat* on the wooden chair.

   ▶ She *set* the vase on the middle shelf.

3. *lie:* to recline (intransitive; irregular)

   lay: to put or place (transitive; regular)

BASE	–s	–ing	PAST TENSE	PAST PARTICIPLE
lie	lies	lying	lay	lain
lay	lays	laying	laid	laid

        lay
   ▶ I ~~laid~~ down for half an hour.

          lying
   ▶ I was ~~laying~~ down when you called.

        Lay
   ▶ ~~Lie~~ the map on the floor.

In addition, note the verb *lie* ("to say something untrue"), which is intransitive and regular.

BASE	–s	–ing	PAST TENSE	PAST PARTICIPLE
lie	lies	lying	lied	lied

▶ He *lied* when he said he had won three trophies.

41c Auxiliary verbs

An auxiliary verb is used with a main verb and sometimes with other auxiliaries. The auxiliary verbs are *be, do, have,* and the nine modal verbs are *will, would, can, could, shall, should, may, might,* and *must* (**61b ESL**). Note the irregular forms of *be, do,* and *have*.

BASE	PRESENT TENSE FORMS	–ing	PAST	PAST PARTICIPLE
be	am, is, are	being	was, were	been
do	do, does	doing	did	done
have	have, has	having	had	had

See **43a** for agreement with present tense forms of *be, do,* and *have*.

LANGUAGE AND CULTURE
Language and Dialect Variation with *Be*

In some languages (Chinese and Russian, for example), forms of *be* used as an auxiliary ("She *is* singing") or as a linking verb ("He *is* happy") can be omitted. In some spoken dialects of English (African American Vernacular, for example), subtle linguistic distinctions not possible in Standard English can be achieved: the omission of a form of *be* and the use of the base form in place of an inflected form (a form that shows number, person, mood, or tense) signal entirely different meanings.

VERNACULAR		STANDARD
He busy.	(temporarily)	He is busy now.
She be busy.	(habitually)	She is busy all the time.

Standard English always requires the inclusion of a form of *be*.

　　　　　are
▶ Latecomers ⌄always at a disadvantage.

Auxiliary verbs can be used in combination. Whatever the combination, the form of the main verb is determined by the auxiliary that precedes it, as in the following examples.

What to use after forms of *be*

1. After *be, am, is, are, was, were,* and *been,* use the *-ing* form for active voice verbs. To form a complete verb, you must use a *be* form with *-ing* (**61a** ESL).

> ▶ She *is taking* her driving test.   ▶ You *were watching.*

> ▶ He might have *been driving.*   ▶ They could *be jogging.*

2. After *be, am, is, are, was, were, been,* and *being,* use the past participle for passive voice (see **42**).

> ▶ They *were taken* to a tropical island for their anniversary.

> ▶ The faucet should *be fixed.*

> ▶ The pie might have *been eaten.*

> ▶ The suspects are *being watched.*

 ESL NOTE   *Be, Been,* and *Being*

Be requires a modal auxiliary before it to form a complete verb (*could be jogging; will be closed*). *Been* requires *have, has,* or *had* (*have been driving; has been eaten*). *Being* must be preceded by *am, is, are, was,* or *were* to form a complete verb and must be followed by an adjective or a past participle: *You are being silly. He was being followed.* ∎

What to use after *do* and modal auxiliaries

After *do, does, did,* and the nine modal auxiliaries, use the base form immediately after the first auxiliary.

> ▶ *Did* she *leave*?

> ▶ He *should stay.*

> ▶ He *must have* seen that play.

What to use after *have*

After *has, have,* and *had,* use the past participle.

> ▶ It *has snowed.*

> ▶ They *had eaten* when I arrived.

> ▶ They should *have gone.*
>
> [*not* They should *have went.*]

In informal speech, we run sounds together, and the pronunciation may be mistakenly carried over into writing.

> have
> ▶ She should ~~of~~ left that job last year.

The pronunciation of the contraction *should've* is probably responsible for the nonstandard form *should of*. Edit carefully for the appearance of the word *of* in place of *have* in verb phrases.

41d Verb tenses

Tenses indicate time as perceived by the speaker or writer. The following examples show active voice verbs referring to past, present, and future time. For passive voice verbs, see **42**.

PAST TIME

Simple past	They *arrived* yesterday./They *did* not *arrive* today.
Past progressive	They *were leaving* when the phone rang.
Past perfect	Everyone *had left* when I called.
Past perfect progressive	We *had been sleeping* for an hour before you arrived.

PRESENT TIME

Simple present	He *eats* Wheaties every morning./He *does* not *eat* eggs.
Present progressive	They *are working* today.
Present perfect	She *has* never *read* Melville.
Present perfect progressive	He *has been living* here for five years.

FUTURE TIME (USING *WILL*)

Simple future	She *will arrive* soon.
Future progressive	They *will be playing* baseball at noon tomorrow.
Future perfect	He *will have finished* the project by Friday.
Future perfect progressive	By the year 2009, they *will have been running* the company for twenty-five years.

Other modal auxiliaries can substitute for *will* and thus change the meaning: *must arrive, might be playing, may have finished, should have been running*. (See **61b** ESL.)

ESL Note Verbs Not Followed by *—ing* Forms

Use simple tenses but not progressive forms with verbs expressing mental activity referring to the senses, preference, or thought, as well as with verbs of possession, appearance, and inclusion (for example, *smell, prefer, understand, own, seem, contain*).

> smells
> ▶ The fish in the showcase ~~is smelling~~ bad.

> possess
> ▶ They ~~are possessing~~ different behavior patterns. ■

41e Present tenses

Simple present   Use the simple present tense for the following purposes:

1. To make a generalization

   ▶ Babies *sleep* a lot.

2. To indicate an activity that happens habitually or repeatedly

   ▶ He *works* for Sony.

   ▶ We *turn* the clocks ahead every April.

3. To discuss literature and the arts even if the work was written in the past or the author is no longer alive

   ▶ In *Zami*, Audre Lorde *describes* how a librarian *introduces* her to the joys of reading.

When used in this way, the present tense is called the *literary present*. However, when you write a narrative of your own, use past tenses to tell about past actions.

> walked   kissed
> ▶ Then the candidate ~~walks~~ up to the crowd and ~~kisses~~ all the babies.

 ESL Note   No *Will* in Time Clause

In a dependent clause beginning with a conjunction such as *if, when, before, after, until,* or *as soon as,* do not use *will* to express future time. Use *will* only in the independent clause. Use the simple present in the subordinate clause.

> ▶ When they ~~will~~ arrive, the meeting will begin. ■

Present progressive Use the present progressive to indicate an action in progress at the moment of speaking or writing.

▶ He *is playing* pool with his nephew.

Present perfect and present perfect progressive Use the present perfect in the following instances:

1. To indicate that an action occurring at some unstated time in the past is related to present time

▶ They *have worked* in New Mexico, so they know its laws.

2. To indicate that an action beginning in the past continues to the present

▶ She *has worked* for the same company since I *have known* her.

If you state the exact time when something occurred, use the simple past tense, not the present perfect.

worked
▶ They ~~have worked~~ in Arizona three years ago.

Use the present perfect progressive when you indicate the length of time an action has been in progress up to the present time.

▶ They *have been dancing* for three hours.

[This implies that they are still dancing.]

41f Past tenses

Use past tenses consistently. Do not switch to present or future for no reason (see **41h**).

Simple past Use the simple past tense when you specify a past time or event.

▶ World War I soldiers *suffered* in the trenches.

When the sequence of past events is indicated with words like *before* or *after*, use the simple past for both events.

▶ She *knew* how to write her name before she *went* to school.

Past progressive Use the past progressive for an activity in progress over time or at a specified point in the past.

▶ They *were working* all day yesterday.

▶ He *was lifting* weights when I called.

Past perfect Use the past perfect or the past perfect progressive only when one past event was completed before another past event or stated past time.

▶ Ben *had cooked* the whole meal by the time Sam arrived.

[Two events occurred: Ben cooked the meal; then Sam arrived.]

▶ He *had been cooking* for three hours when his sister finally offered to help.

[An event in progress—cooking—was interrupted in the past.]

Make sure that the past tense form you choose expresses your exact meaning.

▶ When the student protesters marched into the building at noon, the administrators *were leaving.* [The administrators were in the process of leaving. They began to leave at, say, 11:57 a.m.]

▶ When the student protesters marched into the building at noon, the administrators *had left.*

[There was no sign of the administrators. They had left at 11 a.m.]

▶ When the student protesters marched into the building at noon, the administrators *left.*

[The administrators saw the protesters and then left at 12:01 p.m.]

41g *-ed* endings: Past tense and past participle forms

Both the past tense form and the past participle of regular verbs end in *-ed*. This ending causes writers trouble because in speech the ending is often dropped—particularly when it blends into the next sound.

▶ They wash~ed~ two baskets of laundry last night.

Standard English requires the *-ed* ending in the following instances.

1. To form the past tense of a regular verb

▶ He ask~ed~ to leave early.

2. To form the expression *used to*, indicating past habit

▶ They use~d~ to smoke.

3. To form the past participle of a regular verb after the auxiliary *has*, *have*, or *had* in the active voice or after forms of *be* (*am, is, are, was, were, be, being, been*) in the passive voice (see **42**)

► She has work~~ed~~ there for a long time. [Active]

► The work will be finish~~ed~~ tomorrow. [Passive]

4. To form a past participle for use as an adjective

► Put in some chop~~ped~~ meat.   ► The frighten~~ed~~ boy ran away.

Note: The following *-ed* forms are used with *be* or *get*: *concerned, confused, depressed, divorced, embarrassed, married, prejudiced, satisfied, scared, supposed (to), surprised, used (to), worried.* Do not omit the *-d* ending.

► I was surprise~~d~~ to see how many awards he had won.

► The general was suppose~~d~~ to be in charge.

► Parents get worr~~ied~~ when their children are depress~~ed~~.

Do not confuse the past tense form and the past participle of an irregular verb. A past tense form stands alone as a complete verb, but a past participle does not.

► He ~~drunk~~ drank too much last night.   ► You could have ~~went~~ gone alone.

► She ~~done~~ did her best.   ► The bell was ~~rang~~ rung five times.

41h Unnecessary tense shifts

If you use tenses consistently throughout a piece of writing, you help readers understand what is happening and when. Check that your verbs consistently express present or past time, both within a sentence and from one sentence to the next. Avoid unnecessary tense shifts.

TENSE SHIFTS   Selecting a jury *was* very difficult. The lawyers *ask* many questions to discover bias and prejudice; sometimes the prospective jurors *had* the idea they *are acting* in a play.

REVISED   Selecting a jury *was* very difficult. The lawyers *asked* many questions to discover bias and prejudice; sometimes the prospective jurors *had* the idea they *were acting* in a play.

When you write about events or ideas presented by another writer, use the literary present consistently (see **41e**).

► The author ~~illustrated~~ *illustrates* the images of women in two ways, using advertisements and dramas on TV. One way shows women who advance~~d~~ their careers by themselves, and the other shows those who use~~d~~ beauty to gain recognition.

Tense shifts are appropriate in the following instances:

1. When you signal a time change with a time word or phrase

signal for switch from past to present

► Harold *was* my late grandfather's name, and *now* it *is* mine.

2. When you follow a generalization (present tense) with a specific example of a past incident

┌─────────── generalization ───────────┐
► Some bilingual schools *offer* intensive instruction in English.

┌─────────── specific example ───────────┐
My sister, for example, *went* to a bilingual school where she *studied* English for two hours every day.

41i Tenses in indirect quotations

An indirect quotation reports what someone said. It does not use quotation marks, and it follows the tense of the introductory verb. For example, when the verb introducing an indirect quotation is in a present tense, the indirect quotation should preserve the tense of the original direct quotation. See also **62d** ESL.

DIRECT   "The client *has signed* the contract."

present   ┌─────── indirect quotation ───────┐
INDIRECT   ► The lawyer *says* that the client *has signed* the contract.

When the introductory verb is in a past tense, use forms that express past time in the indirect quotation.

DIRECT   "The meetings *are* over and the buyer *has signed* the contract."

past   ┌─────── indirect quotation ───────┐
INDIRECT   ► The lawyer *said* that the meetings *were* over and the buyer *had signed* the contract.

In a passage of more than one sentence, preserve the sequence of tenses showing past time throughout the whole passage.

▶ Our lawyer, Larraine, told us that the meetings *were* over and the buyer *had signed* the contract. Larraine's firm *had reassigned* her to another case, so she *was leaving* the next day.

Note: Use a present tense after a past tense introductory verb only if the statement is a general statement that holds true in present time.

▶ Our lawyer *told* us she *is* happy with the progress of the case.

41j Verbs in conditional sentences, wishes, requests, demands, and recommendations

Conditions When *if* or *unless* is used to introduce a dependent clause, the sentence expresses a condition. Four types of conditional sentences are used: two refer to actual or possible situations, and two refer to speculative or hypothetical situations.

KEY POINTS

Verb Tenses in Conditional Sentences

MEANING EXPRESSED	*IF* CLAUSE	INDEPENDENT CLAUSE
1. Fact	Simple present	Simple present

▶ **If people *earn* more, they *spend* more.**

2. Prediction/ possibility	Simple present	*will, can, should, might* + base form

▶ **If you *turn* left here, you *will end up* in Mississippi.**

3. Speculation about present or future	Simple past *or* subjunctive *were*	*would, could, should, might* + base form

▶ **If he *had* a cell phone, he *would use* it.**
   [But he does not have one.]

▶ **If she *were* my lawyer, I *might win* the case.**
   [But she is not.]

(Continued)

(Continued)

MEANING EXPRESSED	*IF* CLAUSE	INDEPENDENT CLAUSE
4. Speculation about past	Past perfect (*had* + past participle)	*would have* *could have* *should have* *might have* } + past participle

▶ If they *had saved* the diaries, they *could have sold* them.

[But they did not save them.]

USE OF SUBJUNCTIVE *WERE* IN PLACE OF *WAS* With speculative conditions about the present and future using the verb *be, were* is used in place of *was* in the dependent *if* clause. This use of *were* to indicate hypothetical situations involves what is called the *subjunctive mood*.

▶ If my aunt *were* sixty-five, she *could get* a discount air fare.

[My aunt is sixty.]

BLENDING Some blending of time and tenses can occur, as in the case of a condition that speculates about the past in relation to the effect on the present.

▶ If I *had bought* a new car instead of this old wreck, I *would feel* a lot safer today.

USE OF *WOULD* When writing Standard English, use *would* only in the independent clause, not in the conditional clause. However, *would* occurs frequently in the conditional clause in speech and in informal writing.

showed
▶ If the fish fry committee ~~would show~~ more initiative, people might attend their events more regularly.

had
▶ If the driver ~~would have~~ heard what the pedestrian said, he would have been angry.

WOULD, COULD, AND MIGHT WITH CONDITIONAL CLAUSE UNDERSTOOD *Would, could,* and *might* are used in independent clauses when no conditional clause is present. These are situations that are contrary to fact, and the conditional clause is understood.

▶ I *would* never *advise* her to leave college without a degree. She *might come back* later and blame me for her lack of direction.

Wishes   Like some conditions, wishes deal with speculation. For a present wish—about something that has not happened and is therefore hypothetical and imaginary—use the past tense or subjunctive *were* in the dependent clause. For a wish about the past, use the past perfect: *had* + past participle.

A WISH ABOUT THE PRESENT

▶ I wish I *had* your attitude.

▶ I wish that Shakespeare *were* still alive.

A WISH ABOUT THE PAST

▶ Some union members wish that the strike *had* never *occurred*.

▶ He wishes that he *had bought* a lottery ticket.

Requests, demands, and recommendations   The subjunctive also appears after certain verbs, such as *request, command, insist, demand, move* (meaning "propose"), *propose,* and *urge.* In these cases, the verb in the dependent clause is the base form, regardless of the person and number of the subject.

▶ The dean suggested that students *be* allowed to vote.

▶ He insisted that she *submit* the report.

▶ I move that the treasurer *revise* the budget.

Some idiomatic expressions preserve the subjunctive in standard English—for example, *far* be *it from me, if need* be, *as it* were.

---

42   Passive Voice

In the active voice, the grammatical subject is the doer of the action, and the sentence tells "who's doing what." The passive voice tells what *is done to* the subject of the sentence. The person or thing doing the action may or may not be mentioned but is always implied: "My car was repaired" (by somebody at the garage).

ACTIVE

   ┌— subject —┐ active voice verb ┌— direct object —┐
▶ **Alice Walker**   **wrote**   *The Color Purple.*

PASSIVE

                      passive voice
  ┌——— subject ———┐ ┌— verb —┐ ┌— doer or agent —┐
▶ *The Color Purple* **was written** by Alice Walker.

42a Know when to use the passive voice.

Use the passive voice sparingly. A general rule is to use the passive voice only when the doer or agent in your sentence (the person or thing acting) is unknown or is unimportant (see **42c**) or when you want to connect the topics of two clauses (see **31a** and **42d**).

▶ The pandas are rare. Two of them *will be returned* to the wild.

 ESL NOTE Passive Voice with Transitive Verbs

Use the passive voice only with verbs that are transitive in English. Intransitive verbs such as *happen, occur,* and *try (to)* are not used in the passive voice.

▶ The accident ~~was~~ happened yesterday.

▶ Morality is an issue that ~~was~~ ^{have} tried to explain ~~by~~ <u>many philosophers</u>.

42b Know how to form the passive voice.

The complete verb of a passive voice sentence consists of a form of the verb *be* followed by a past participle.

```
          receiver        verb: be +
       ── as subject ──   past participle   doer omitted or named after by
```
▶ The windows are cleaned [by someone] every month.

▶ The windows *were being cleaned* yesterday afternoon.

▶ The windows *will have been cleaned* by the end of the workday.

Auxiliaries such as *would, can, could, should, may, might,* and *must* can also replace *will* when the meaning demands it.

▶ The windows *might be cleaned* next month.

42c Use passive voice when the doer or agent is unknown or unimportant.

▶ He had a lot of people working for him, maybe sixty, and most of them liked him most of the time. Three of them *will be* seriously *considered* for his job.

—Ellen Goodman, "The Company Man"

In scientific writing, the passive voice is often preferred to indicate objective procedures. Scientists and engineers are interested in analyzing data and in performing studies that other researchers can replicate. The individual doing the experiment is therefore relatively unimportant and usually is not the subject of the sentence.

▶ The experiment *was conducted* in a classroom. Participants *were instructed* to remove their watches prior to the experiment.

If you are writing in the humanities, however, question each use of the passive voice, and ask yourself whether you need it.

42d Use the passive voice to connect the subject of a sentence to what has gone before.

Notice how the passive voice preserves the topic chain of *I* subjects in the following passage (see also **31a**):

▶ I remember to start with that day in Sacramento . . . when I first entered a classroom, able to understand some fifty stray English words. The third of four children, I *had been preceded* to a Roman Catholic school by an older brother and sister.
—Richard Rodriguez, *Hunger of Memory*

42e Do not overuse the passive voice.

Generally your writing will be clearer and stronger if you name the subject and use verbs in the active voice to explain who is doing what. If you overuse the passive voice, the effect will be heavy and impersonal (see **30a**).

UNNECESSARY PASSIVE	He *was alerted* to the danger of drugs by his doctor and *was persuaded* by her to enroll in a treatment program.
REVISED	His doctor alerted him to the danger of drugs and persuaded him to enroll in a treatment program.

---

43 Subject-Verb Agreement

In Standard English, a third person singular subject takes a singular verb (with -*s*), and a plural subject takes a plural verb (with no -*s*).

SINGULAR SUBJECT	PLURAL SUBJECT
A baby *cries*.	Babies *cry*.
He *loses*.	They *lose*.
His brother *plays* baseball.	His brothers *play* baseball.

43a Basic principles of subject-verb agreement

When you use the present tense, subject and verb must agree in person (first, second, or third) and number (singular or plural). In English, the ending -s is added to both nouns and verbs, but for very different reasons.

1. An -s ending on a noun is a plural signal: *her brothers* (more than one).

2. An -s ending on a verb is a singular signal; -s is added to a third person singular verb in the present tense: *Her plumber wears gold jewelry.*

KEY POINTS

Two Key Points about Agreement

1. Follow the "one -s rule." Generally, you can put an -s on a noun to make it plural, or you can put an -s on a verb to make it singular. (But see the irregular forms *is* and *has*, on p. 345.) An -s on both subject and verb is not Standard English.

   FAULTY AGREEMENT   **My friends comes over every Saturday.**
   [Violates the "one -s rule"]

   POSSIBLE REVISIONS   **My friend comes over every Saturday.**

   My friends come over every Saturday.

2. Do not omit a necessary -s.

   ▶ His supervisor want̬ him to work the night shift.

   ▶ The book̬ on my desk describe life in Tahiti.

   ▶ She *uses* her experience, *speaks* to the crowds, and *win̬* their confidence.

Most simple present verbs show agreement with an -s ending. The verb *be*, however, has three instead of two present tense forms. In addition, *be* is the only verb to show agreement in the past tense, where it has two forms: *were* and the third person singular *was*.

SUBJECT-VERB AGREEMENT

BASE FORM	like	have	be	do
SIMPLE PRESENT: SINGULAR				
First person: I	like	have	am	do
Second person: you	like	have	are	do
Third person: he, she, it	likes	has	is	does
SIMPLE PRESENT: PLURAL				
First person: we	like	have	are	do
Second person: you	like	have	are	do
Third person: they	like	have	are	do

LANGUAGE AND CULTURE
Issues of Subject-Verb Agreement

Many languages make no change in the verb form to indicate number and person, and several spoken versions of English, such as African American Vernacular (AAV), Caribbean Creole, and London Cockney do not observe the standard rules of agreement.

▶ AAV: She *have* a lot of work experience.

▶ Cockney: He *don't* never wear that brown whistle.

[The standard form is *doesn't*; other nonstandard forms in this sentence are *don't never* (a double negative) and *whistle*— short for *whistle and flute*, rhyming slang for *suit*.]

Use authentic forms like these when quoting direct speech; for your formal academic writing, though, follow the subject-verb agreement conventions of Standard English.

 ESL NOTE Base Form after a Modal

Never add an -*s* ending to a modal, and always use a base form after a modal: I *can sing*; she *should go*; he *might be* leaving; she *will have* been promoted (**61b** ESL). ■

43b Words between the subject and verb

When words separate the subject and verb, find the verb and ask "Who?" or "What?" about it to determine the subject. Ignore the intervening words.

▶ The general discussing the attacks looks tired.

[Who looks tired? The subject, *general*, is singular.]

▶ Her collection of baseball cards is valuable.

[What is valuable? The subject, *collection*, is singular.]

▶ The government's proposals about preserving the

environment cause controversy.

[What things cause controversy? The subject, *proposals*, is plural.]

Do not be confused by intervening words ending in *-s*, such as *always* and *sometimes*. The *-s* ending still must appear on a present tense verb if the subject is singular.

▶ His assistant always make^s mistakes.

Phrases introduced by *as well as, along with*, and *in addition to* that come between the subject and the verb do not change the number of the verb.

▶ His daughter, as well as his two sons, want^s him to move nearby.

43c Agreement with linking verb and complement

Linking verbs such as *be, seem, look,* and *appear* are followed by a complement, and a subject complement should not be confused with a subject (see **37d**). Make the verb agree with the subject stated before the linking verb, not with the noun complement that follows the verb.

| plural subject | singular complement | singular subject | plural complement |

▶ Rare books *are* her passion. ▶ Her passion *is* rare books.

plural verb   singular verb

▶ My favorite part of city life *is* the parties.

▶ Parties *are* my favorite part of city life.

43d Subject after verb

When the subject follows the verb in the sentence, make the subject and verb agree.

1. Questions   In a question, the auxiliary verb agrees with the subject.

singular
┌─ subject ─┐
▶ *Does* the editor agree to the changes?

┌──────────── plural subject ────────────┐
▶ *Do* the editor and the production manager agree to them?

2. Initial *here* or *there*   When a sentence begins with *here* or *there*, the verb agrees with the subject.

singular
┌ subject ┐
▶ There *is* a reason to rejoice.

┌ plural subject ┐
▶ There *are* many reasons to rejoice.

However, avoid excessive use of initial *there* (see **30b**): *We have a reason to rejoice.*

 ESL Note   Singular Verb after *It*

It does not follow the same pattern as *here* and *there*. The verb attached to an *it* subject is always singular.

▶ It *is* hundreds of miles away.   ■

3. Inverted word order   When a sentence begins not with the subject but with a phrase preceding the verb, the verb still agrees with the subject (see also **34d**).

plural
┌─ prepositional phrase ─┐ verb ┌─ plural subject ─┐
▶ In front of the library sit two stone lions.

[Who or what performs the action of the verb? Two stone lions do.]

43e Tricky subjects with singular verbs

1. *Each* and *every*   *Each* and *every* may seem to indicate more than one, but grammatically they are singular words, used with a singular verb, even if they are parts of a compound subject joined by *and* or *or*.

▶ Each of the cakes *has* a different frosting.

▶ Every change in procedures *causes* problems.

▶ Every toy and game *has* to be put away.

▶ Each plate and glass *looks* new.

2. *-ing* or infinitive form as subject   With a subject beginning with the *-ing* verb form (called a *gerund*) or with an infinitive, always use a singular verb form.

singular
subject

▶ Playing the piano in front of a crowd *causes* anxiety.

▶ To keep our air clean *takes* careful planning.

3. Singular nouns ending in *-s*   Some nouns that end in *-s* (*news, economics, physics, politics, mathematics, statistics*) are not plural. Use them with a singular verb.

▶ The news *has* been bad lately.   ▶ Politics *is* dirty business.

4. Phrases of time, money, and weight   When the subject is regarded as one unit, use a singular verb.

▶ Five hundred dollars *seems* too much to pay.

▶ Seven years *was* a long time to spend at college.

5. Uncountable nouns   An uncountable noun (*furniture, jewelry, equipment, advice, happiness, honesty, information, knowledge*) encompasses all the items in its class. An uncountable noun does not have a plural form and is always followed by a singular verb (**60b** ESL).

▶ That advice *makes* me nervous.

▶ The information found in the press *is* not always accurate.

6. One of   *One of* is followed by a plural noun (the object of the preposition *of*) and a singular verb form.

▶ *One* of her friends *loves* to tango.

▶ *One* of the reasons for his difficulties *is* that he spends too much money.

For agreement with *one of* and *the only one of* followed by a relative clause, see **46c**.

7. The number of/a number of The phrase *the number of* is followed by a plural noun (the object of the preposition *of*) and a singular verb form.

▶ The number of reasons *is* growing.

With *a number of,* meaning "several," use a plural verb.

▶ A number of reasons *are* listed in the letter.

8. The title of a long work or a word referred to as the word itself
Use a singular verb with the title of a long, whole work or a word referred to as the word itself. Use a singular verb even if the title or word is plural in form. See also **52a** and **52c**.

▶ <u>Cats</u> *was* based on a poem by T. S. Eliot.

▶ In her story, the word <u>dudes</u> *appears* five times.

43f Collective nouns

Generally, use a singular verb with a collective noun (*class, government, family, jury, committee, group, couple, team*) if you are referring to the group as a whole.

▶ My family *goes* on vacation every year.

Use a plural verb if you wish to emphasize differences among individuals or if members of the group are thought of as individuals.

▶ His family *are* mostly artists and musicians.

▶ The jury *are* from every walk of life.

If that usage seems awkward, revise the sentence.

▶ His close relatives *are* mostly artists and musicians.

▶ The members of the jury *are* from every walk of life.

Some collective nouns, such as *police, poor, elderly,* and *young,* always take plural verbs.

► **The elderly *deserve* our respect.**

43g Subjects with *and, or,* or *nor*

With *and*   When a subject consists of two or more parts joined by *and*, treat the subject as plural and use a plural verb.

┌────── plural subject ──────→ plural verb
► **His instructor and his advisor *want* him to change his major.**

However, if the parts of the compound subject refer to a single person or thing, use a singular verb.

┌────── singular subject (one person) ──────→ singular verb
► **The restaurant's chef and owner *makes* good fajitas.**

┌singular subject ┌→ singular verb
► **Fish and chips *is* a popular dish in England, but it is no longer served wrapped in newspaper.**

With *or* or *nor*   When the parts of a compound subject are joined by *or* or *nor*, the verb agrees with the part nearer to it.

► **Her sister or her parents *plan* to visit her next week.**

► **Neither her parents nor her sister *drives* a station wagon.**

43h Indefinite pronouns and quantity words

Words (indefinite pronouns) that refer to nonspecific people or things and words and phrases that refer to quantity can be tricky. Some take a singular verb; some take a plural verb; and some take a singular or a plural verb, depending on what they refer to. Some are used alone as a pronoun; others are used with a countable or uncountable noun in a noun phrase (for more on this, see **60a** and **60b** ESL). In addition, usage may differ in speech and writing.

Indefinite pronouns used with a singular verb

anybody	everyone	nothing
anyone	everything	somebody
anything	nobody	someone
everybody	no one	something

▶ Nobody *knows* the answer.

▶ Someone *has* been sitting on my chair.

▶ Everyone *agrees* on the author's intention.

▶ Everything about the results *was* questioned in the review.

Quantity words referring to a countable noun and used with a singular verb

another	every
each	neither (see pp. 352–353)
either	none (see p. 352)

▶ Another company *has* bought the land.

▶ Each of the chairs *costs* more than $300.

▶ Of the two options, neither *was* acceptable.

▶ Every poem *contains* a stark image.

Quantity words referring to an uncountable noun and used with a singular verb

a(n) _____ amount (of)	(a) little
a great deal (of)	much (of)
less (see p. 353)	

▶ Less *has* been accomplished than we expected.

▶ A great deal of information *is* being released.

▶ Much of the machinery *needs* to be repaired.

▶ An enormous amount of equipment *was* needed to clean up the spilled oil.

Quantity words referring to a plural countable noun and used with a plural verb

both	many
a couple/number of	other/others
(a) few (see **64c** ESL)	several
fewer (see p. 353)	

▶ She has written two novels. Both *receive* praise.

▶ Many *have* gained from the recent stock market rise.

▶ Few of his fans *are* buying his recent book.

▶ A number of articles *refer* to the same statistics.

Quantity words used with a plural verb to refer to a plural count-able noun or with a singular verb to refer to an uncountable noun

all	half	most	some
any	more	no	

▶ All the students *look* healthy.

[The plural countable noun *students* takes a plural verb.]

▶ All the furniture *looks* old.

[The uncountable noun *furniture* takes a singular verb.]

▶ You gave me some information. More *is* necessary.

[*More* refers to the uncountable noun *information*.]

▶ You gave me some facts. More *are* needed.

[*More* refers to the countable noun *facts*.]

▶ Some of the jewelry *was* recovered.

[The uncountable noun *jewelry* takes a singular verb.]

▶ Some of the windows *were* open.

[The plural countable noun *windows* takes a plural verb.]

A note on *none, neither, less,* and *fewer*

NONE Some writers prefer to use a singular verb after *none (of)*, because *none* means "not one": *None of the contestants has smiled.* However, as *The American Heritage Dictionary* (4th ed.) points out about *none,* "The word has been used as both a singular and a plural noun from old English onward." In formal academic writing, a singular or a plural verb is therefore technically acceptable: *None of the authorities has* (or *have*) *greater tolerance on this point than H. W. Fowler.* As with many issues of usage, however, readers form preferences. Check to see if your instructor prefers the literal singular usage.

NEITHER The pronoun *neither* is, like *none,* technically singular: *The partners have made a decision; neither wants to change the product.* In informal writing, however, you will see it used with a plural verb, especially when it is followed by an *of* phrase: *Neither of the novels* reveal *a polished style.* Ask your instructor about his or her preferences.

LESS AND FEWER Technically, *less* refers to a singular uncountable noun *(less spinach)*, *fewer* to a plural countable noun *(fewer beans)*. In journalism and advertising, and especially on supermarket signs *(12 items or less)*, *less* is often used in place of *fewer.* In formal writing, however, use *fewer* to refer to a plural word: *In the last decade, fewer Olympic medalists have been using steroids.*

For agreement with *one of,* see page 348–349. For agreement with *one of* and *the only one of* followed by a relative clause, see **46c**.

43i Demonstrative pronouns and adjectives *(this, that, these, those)*

A demonstrative adjective must agree in number with the noun it modifies: *this solution, these solutions; that problem, those problems.*

SINGULAR	PLURAL
this	these
that	those

A demonstrative pronoun must agree in number with its antecedent (see **44d**).

► The mayor is planning changes. These will be controversial.

43j Possessive pronoun as subject

The antecedent of a possessive pronoun standing alone determines whether the verb is singular or plural. Possessive pronouns such as *mine, his, hers, ours, yours,* and *theirs* can refer to both singular and plural antecedents (see **44d**).

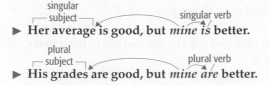

► Her average is good, but *mine is* better.

► His grades are good, but *mine are* better.

43k Subject clauses beginning with *what* or other question words

When a clause introduced by *what* or other question words, such as *how, who,* and *why,* functions as the subject of an independent clause, use a third person singular verb in the independent clause.

> ┌────── subject ──────┐
> ▶ **What they are proposing** *concerns* **us all.**

> ┌────── subject ──────┐
> ▶ **How the players train** *makes* **all the difference.**

When the verb is followed by the linking verb *be* and a plural complement, some writers use a plural verb. However, some readers may object.

> ▶ **What I need** *are* **black pants and an orange shirt.**

You can avoid the issue by revising the sentence to eliminate the *what* clause.

> ▶ **I need black pants and an orange shirt.**

44 Pronouns

A pronoun is a word that substitutes for a noun, a noun phrase, or another pronoun (see **37d**).

> ▶ **Jack's hair is so long that** *it* **hangs over** *his* **collar.**

44a Use the correct forms of personal pronouns.

Personal pronouns change form to indicate person (first, second, or third), number (singular or plural), and function in a clause.

In a compound subject or compound object with *and: I* or *me; he* or *him?* To decide which pronoun form to use with a compound subject or compound object, mentally recast the sentence with only the pronoun in the subject or object position.

> ┌───── subject ─────┐   ┌───── object ─────┐
> ▶ **He and his sister invited my cousin and me to their party.**
>
> [He invited me.]

KEY POINTS

Summary of Forms of Personal Pronouns

PERSON	SUBJECT	OBJECT	POSSESSIVE (+ NOUN)	POSSESSIVE (STANDS ALONE)	INTENSIVE AND REFLEXIVE
First person singular	I	me	my	mine	myself
Second person singular and plural	you	you	your	yours	yourself/ yourselves
Third person singular	he she it	him her it	his her its	his hers its [rare]	himself herself itself
First person plural	we	us	our	ours	ourselves
Third person plural	they	them	their	theirs	themselves

I
▶ Jenny and ~~me~~ went to the movies.

[If *Jenny* is dropped, you would say *I went to the movies*, not *me went to the movies*. Here you need the subject form, *I*.]

Sometimes people who are not sure of the use of *I* or *me* in the subject position get anxious and correct from *me* to *I* in the object position—and make another error.

me
▶ They told my brother and ~~I~~ to wait in line.

[If *my brother* is dropped, you would say *They told me to wait in line*. Here you need the object form, *me*.]

After a preposition   After a preposition, you need an object form.

▶ **I started off rapping for people just like myself, people who were in awe of wealth and flash. It was a conversation** *between me* **and** *them.*   —Ice-T, *Observer,* 27 Oct. 1991

He   me
▶ ~~Him~~ **and his brother waved to my colleague and** ~~I~~.

[He waved to my colleague. They waved to me.]

               me
▶ **Between you and** ~~I~~, **the company is in serious trouble.**

After a linking verb   In formal academic writing, use the subject form of a personal pronoun after a linking verb, such as *be, seem, look,* or *appear.*

▶ **Was that Sharon Stone? It was** *she.*

[Informal: "It was her."]

▶ **It was** *she* **who sent the flowers.**

[Many writers would revise this sentence to sound less formal: "She was the one who sent the flowers."]

After a verb and before an infinitive   Use the object form of a personal pronoun after a verb and before an infinitive. When a sentence has only one object, this principle is easy to apply.

▶ **The dean wanted** *him* **to lead the procession.**

Difficulties occur with compound objects.

                     him and me
▶ **The dean wanted** ~~he and I~~ **to lead the procession.**

In appositive phrases and with *we* **or** *us* **before a noun**   When using a personal pronoun in an appositive phrase (a phrase that gives additional information about a preceding noun), determine whether the noun that the pronoun refers to functions as subject or as object in its own clause.

                  — direct object ◄—   appositive phrase
▶ **The supervisor praised only two employees, Ramon and me.**

       — subject ◄—   appositive phrase
▶ **Only two employees, Ramon and I, received a bonus.**

Similarly, when you consider whether to use *we* or *us* before a noun, use *us* when the pronoun is the direct object of a verb or preposition, *we* when it is the subject.

object of preposition
▶ LL Cool J waved to us fans.

subject
▶ We fans have decided to form a club.

In comparisons When writing comparisons with *than* and *as,* decide on the subject or object form of the personal pronoun by mentally completing the meaning of the comparison. (See also **45h**.)

▶ She is certainly not more intelligent than I. [. . . than I am]

▶ Jack and Sally work in the same office; Jack criticizes his boss more than she. [. . . more than Sally does.]

▶ Jack and Sally work in the same office; Jack criticizes his boss more than her. [. . . more than he criticizes Sally.]

44b Use appropriate possessive forms of pronouns.

Distinguish between the adjective form of the possessive personal pronoun and the pronoun itself, standing alone.

▶ The large room with three windows is *her* office.
[*Her* is an adjective.]

▶ The office is *hers.*
[*Hers*, the possessive pronoun, can stand alone.]

Note: The word *mine* does not follow the pattern of *hers, theirs, yours,* and *ours.* The form *mines* is not Standard English.

▶ The little room on the left is *mine.*

When a possessive pronoun functions as a subject, its antecedent determines singular or plural agreement for the verb. (See **43j**.)

▶ My shirt is cotton; hers *is* silk.   [Singular antecedent and singular verb]

▶ My gloves are black; hers *are* yellow.   [Plural antecedent and plural verb]

Possessive pronoun before an *-ing* form   Generally, use a possessive personal pronoun before an *-ing* verb form used as a noun.

▶ We would appreciate *your* participating in the auction.

▶ We were surprised at *their* winning the marathon.

   Sometimes the *-ing* form is a participle functioning as an adjective. In that case, the pronoun preceding the *-ing* form should be the object form.

▶ We saw *them* giving the runners foil wraps.

No apostrophe with possessive personal pronouns   Even though possessive in meaning, the pronouns *yours, ours, theirs, his,* and *hers* should never be spelled with an apostrophe. Use an apostrophe only with the possessive form of a noun.

▶ That coat is *Maria's*.   ▶ These books are the *twins'*. (48c)

▶ That is *her* coat.   ▶ These are *their* books.

▶ That coat is *hers*.   ▶ These books are *theirs*.

No apostrophe with *its* as a possessive pronoun   The word *it's* is not a pronoun; it is the contraction of *it is* or *it has*. An apostrophe is never used with *its*, the possessive form of the pronoun *it* (see also **48f**).

▶ The paint has lost *its* gloss.

▶ *It's* not as glossy as it used to be.   [It is not as glossy…]

Comparisons using possessive forms   Note how using *them* in place of *theirs* in the following sentence would change the meaning by comparing suitcases to roommates, not suitcases to suitcases.

▶ It's really hard to be roommates with people if your suitcases are much better than *theirs*.   —J. D. Salinger, *The Catcher in the Rye*

Forgetting to use the appropriate possessive form in the next example, too, could create a misunderstanding: are you comparing a house to a person, or his house to her house?

▶ I like his house more than I like her._^^s

44c   Make a pronoun refer to a clear antecedent.

A pronoun substitutes for a noun, a noun phrase, or a pronoun already mentioned. The word or phrase that a pronoun refers to is known as the pronoun's *antecedent*. Antecedents should always be clear and explicit.

▶ Although the Canadian skater practiced daily with *her* trainers,

she didn't win the championship.

State a specific antecedent. Be sure to give a pronoun such as *they* or *it* an explicit antecedent.

NO SPECIFIC ANTECEDENT | When Mr. Rivera applied for a loan, they outlined the procedures for him.

[The pronoun *they* lacks an explicit antecedent.]

REVISED | When Mr. Rivera applied to bank officials for a loan, *they* outlined the procedures for him.

When you use a pronoun, make sure it does not refer to a possessive noun or to a noun within a prepositional phrase.

George Orwell
▶ In ~~George Orwell's~~ "Shooting an Elephant," ~~he~~ reports an incident that shows the evil effects of imperialism.

[The pronoun *he* cannot refer to the possessive noun *Orwell's*.]

Lance Morrow's essay
▶ ~~In the essay by Lance Morrow, it~~ points out the problems of choosing a name.

[*It* refers to *essay*, which functions as the object of the preposition *in* and therefore cannot function as an antecedent.]

Avoid ambiguous pronoun reference. Readers should never wonder what your pronouns refer to.

AMBIGUOUS | My husband told my father that he should choose the baby's name. [Does *he* refer to *husband* or *father*?]

REVISED | My husband told my father to choose the baby's name.

REVISED | My husband wanted to choose the baby's name and told my father so.

AMBIGUOUS | He had to decide whether to move to

California. This was not what he wanted to do.

[Does *This* refer to making the decision or to moving to California?]

REVISED   **He had to decide whether to move to California. The decision was not one he wanted to make.**

REVISED   **He had to decide whether to move to California. Moving there was not something he wanted to do.**

44d Make a pronoun agree in number with its antecedent.

A plural antecedent needs a plural pronoun; a singular antecedent needs a singular pronoun.

Make a demonstrative pronoun agree with its antecedent. The demonstrative pronouns *this* and *that* refer to singular nouns; *these* and *those* refer to plural nouns: *this/that house, these/those houses* (**43i**).

singular antecedent

▶ **He published his autobiography two years ago. This was his first book.**

plural antecedent

▶ **One reviewer praised his honesty and directness. Those were qualities he had worked hard to develop.**

Make a pronoun agree with a generalized (generic) antecedent. Generic nouns name a class or type of person or object, such as *a student* meaning "all students" or *a company* meaning "any company" or "all companies." Do not use *they* to refer to a singular generic noun.

singular antecedent   plural pronoun

FAULTY   **When a student is educated, they can go far in**
AGREEMENT   **the world.**

singular antecedent   singular pronoun

REVISED   **When a student is educated, he or she can go far in the world.**

plural antecedent   plural pronoun

REVISED   **When students are educated, they can go far in the world.**

Increasingly, you see in advertising, journalism, and informal writing a plural pronoun referring to a singular antecedent, as in the following station wagon advertisement:

▶ One day *your child* turns sixteen and you let *them* borrow the keys to the wagon.

However, in formal academic writing, many readers may still expect a pronoun to agree with its antecedent. Often the best solution is to make the antecedent plural.

▶ We should judge ~~a person~~ people by who they are, not by the color of their skin.

Make a pronoun agree with an indefinite pronoun or quantity word. Indefinite pronouns, such as *everyone, somebody,* and *nothing* (pp. 350–351), are singular in form and used with a singular verb. Some quantity words, such as *each, either, every,* and *neither,* are also singular in form (p. 351). A singular antecedent needs a singular pronoun to refer to it. But which singular pronoun should be used—*he, she,* or both? To avoid gender bias (**33f** and **44e**) and possible clumsiness, some writers use the plural *they* to refer to a singular indefinite pronoun. Some readers, however, may object to this usage, so revising the sentence is a good idea.

SINGULAR PRONOUN WITH GENDER BIAS
Everyone picked up *his* marbles and ran home to do *his* homework.

REVISED BUT CLUMSY
Everyone picked up *his or her* marbles and ran home to do *his or her* homework.

REVISED BUT INFORMAL
Everyone picked up *their* marbles and ran home to do *their* homework.

[The plural pronoun *their* refers to a singular antecedent.]

PROBABLY BEST
The *children* all picked up *their* marbles and ran home to do *their* homework.

Make a pronoun agree with the nearer antecedent when the parts of a compound antecedent are joined by *or* or *nor*. When the elements of a compound antecedent are connected by *or* or *nor*, a pronoun agrees with the element that is nearer to it. If one part of the compound is singular and the other part is plural, put the plural antecedent closer to the pronoun and have the pronoun agree with it.

▶ Either my friend or my brother has left *his* bag in the hall.

▶ Neither Bill nor the campers could find *their* soap.

Make a pronoun agree with a collective noun. Use a singular pronoun to refer to a collective noun (*class, family, jury, committee, couple, team*) if you are referring to the group as a whole.

▶ The class revised *its* examination schedule.

▶ The committee has not yet completed *its* report.

Use a plural pronoun if members of the group named by the collective noun are considered to be acting individually.

▶ The committee began to cast *their* ballots in a formal vote.

44e Avoid gender bias in pronouns.

Personal pronouns For many years, the pronoun *he* was used routinely in generic references to unspecified individuals in certain roles or professions, such as student, teacher, doctor, lawyer, and banker; and *she* was used routinely in generic references to individuals in roles such as nurse, secretary, or typist. This usage is now considered biased language.

Not
APPROPRIATE

When an accountant learns a foreign language, *he* gains access to an expanded job market.

To revise such sentences that make general statements about people, roles, and professions, use one of the following methods:

1. Use a plural antecedent plus *they* (see also **33f** and **44d**).

   ▶ When accountants learn a foreign language, *they* gain access to an expanded job market.

2. Rewrite the sentence to eliminate the pronoun.

   ▶ An accountant who learns a foreign language gains access to an expanded job market.

3. Use a singular antecedent and the phrase *he or she*.

   ▶ When an accountant learns a foreign language, *he or she* gains access to an expanded job market.

The problem with option 3 is that awkward and repetitive structures can result when such a sentence is continued.

▶ When an accountant learns a foreign language, *he or she* gains access to an expanded job market once *he or she* has decided on *his or her* specialty.

Use the *he or she* option only when a sentence is relatively short and does not repeat the pronouns.

See also agreement with indefinite pronouns (**43h** and **44d**).

44f Be consistent in your point of view.

Keep the point of view from which you are writing consistent through the careful use of pronouns.

INCONSISTENT **We** are all born with some of *our* personality already established in *us.* However, *I* believe that experiences also help shape who *you* are.

REVISED **We** are all born with some of *our* personality already established in *us.* However, experiences also help shape who *we* are.

44g Use the pronoun *you* appropriately.

In formal writing, do not use the pronoun *you* when you mean "people generally." Use *you* only to address readers directly and to give instructions.

NOT **Credit card companies should educate students about**
APPROPRIATE **how to handle credit.** *You* **should not have to find out the problems the hard way.**

[This usage assumes readers are all students and addresses them directly. Some readers will not feel included in the group addressed as "you." A reader addressed directly in this way might think, "Who, me? I don't need to be educated about credit and I have no problems."]

APPROPRIATE **Turn to the next page, where** *you* **will find an excerpt from Edith Wharton's novel that will help** *you* **appreciate the accuracy of the details in this film.**

Edit uses of *you* if you are making a generalization about a group or if using *you* entails a switch from the third person.

teenagers their
▶ While growing up, ~~you~~ face arguments with ~~your~~ parents.

> It doesn't matter if young professionals are avid music

admirers or comedy fans; ~~you~~ ^{they} can find anything ~~you~~ ^{they} want

in the city.

44h   Use standard forms of intensive and reflexive pronouns.

Intensive pronouns emphasize a previously mentioned noun or pronoun. Reflexive pronouns identify a previously mentioned noun or pronoun as the person or thing receiving the action. See the Key Points box in **44a**.

INTENSIVE   **The president *himself* appeared at the gates.**

REFLEXIVE   **He introduced *himself*.**

Do not use an intensive pronoun in place of a personal pronoun in a compound subject:

> Joe and ~~myself~~ ^I will design the brochure.

Forms such as *hisself, theirself,* and *theirselves* occur in spoken dialects but are not Standard English.

44i   Use *who* and *whom* and *whoever* and *whomever* correctly.

In all formal writing situations, distinguish between the subject and object forms of the pronouns used to form questions (interrogative pronouns) or to introduce a dependent noun clause.

SUBJECT	OBJECT
who	whom (or, informally, who)
whoever	whomever

In questions   In a question, ask yourself whether the pronoun is the subject of its clause or the object of the verb. Test the pronoun's function by rephrasing the question as a statement, substituting a personal pronoun for *who* or *whom*.

> **Who wrote that enthusiastic letter?**
> [*He* wrote that enthusiastic letter. Subject: use *who*.]

▶ **Whoever could have written it?**
[*She* could have written it. Subject: use *whoever*.]

▶ **Who[m] were they describing?**
[*They* were describing *him*. Object: *whom* (formal), though *who* is common in such contexts both in speech and in writing.]

In noun clauses When introducing a dependent clause with a pronoun, determine whether to use the subject or object form by examining the pronoun's function in the clause. Ignore expressions such as *I think* or *I know* when they follow the pronoun; they have no effect on the form of the pronoun.

subject of clause
▶ **They want to know who runs the business.**

subject of clause (who runs the business)
▶ **They want to know who I think runs the business.**

object of *to* [the manager reports to him or her]
▶ **They want to know whom the manager reports to.**

subject of clause
▶ **I will hire whoever is qualified.**

object of *recommends*
▶ **I will hire whomever my boss recommends.**

For uses of *who* and *whom* in relative clauses, see **46a**.

45 Adjectives and Adverbs

Adjectives describe, or modify, nouns or pronouns. They do not add *-s* or change form to reflect number or gender. For the order of adjectives, see **62g** ESL.

▶ **Analysts acknowledge the *beneficial* effects of TV.**

▶ **He tried a *different* approach.**

▶ **The depiction of rural life is *accurate*.**

▶ **She keeps her desk *tidy*.**

ESL NOTE No Plural Form for Adjectives

Do not add *-s* to an adjective that modifies a plural noun.

▶ **He tried three *differents* approaches.** ■

Adverbs modify verbs, adjectives, and other adverbs, as well as whole clauses.

▶ She settled down *comfortably*.

▶ The patient is demanding a *theoretically* impossible treatment.

▶ *Apparently*, the experiment was a success.

45a Use correct forms of adjectives and adverbs.

No single rule indicates the correct form of all adjectives and adverbs.

Adverb: adjective + -ly Many adverbs are formed by adding *-ly* to an adjective: *soft/softly; intelligent/intelligently*. Sometimes when *-ly* is added, a spelling change occurs: *easy/easily; terrible/terribly*.

Adjectives ending in -ic To form an adverb from an adjective ending in *-ic*, add *-ally (basic/basically; artistic/artistically)*, except for *public*, whose adverb form is *publicly*.

Adjectives ending in -ly Some adjectives, such as *friendly, lovely, timely*, and *masterly*, already end in *-ly* and have no distinctive adverb form.

adjective
▶ She is a friendly person. ┌─ adverbial phrase ─┐
▶ She spoke to me in a friendly way.

Irregular adverb forms Certain adjectives do not add *-ly* to form an adverb:

ADJECTIVE	ADVERB
good	well
fast	fast
hard	hard

adjective
▶ He is a good cook.   adverb
▶ He cooks well.

adjective
▶ She is a hard worker.   adverb
▶ She works hard.

[*Hardly* is not the adverb form of *hard*. Rather, it means "barely," "scarcely," or "almost not at all": *I could* hardly *breathe in that stuffy room*.]

Note: Well can also function as an adjective, meaning "healthy" or "satisfactory": *A* well *baby smiles often. She feels* well.

45b Know when to use adjectives and adverbs.

In speech, adjectives (particularly *good, bad*, and *real*) are often used to modify verbs, adjectives, or adverbs. This is nonstandard usage. Use an adverb to modify a verb or an adverb.

▶ They fixed the latch ~~good~~.   ▶ I sing ~~real good~~.

         well   really well

▶ She speaks very ~~clear~~.   ▶ They sing ~~bad~~.

        clearly   badly

45c Use adjectives after linking verbs.

After linking verbs (*be, seem, appear, become*), use an adjective to modify the subject. (See **37d** and **44a** on subject complements.)

▶ That steak is good.

▶ Her new coat seems tight.

▶ She feels bad because she sings so badly.

Some verbs (*appear, look, feel, smell, taste*) are sometimes used as linking verbs, sometimes as action verbs. If the modifier tells about the subject, use an adjective. If the modifier tells about the action of the verb, use an adverb.

ADJECTIVE   She looks *confident* in her new job.

ADVERB   She looks *confidently* at all the assembled partners.

ADJECTIVE   The waiter feels *bad.*

                 The steak smells *bad.*

ADVERB   The chef smelled the lobster *appreciatively.*

45d Use correct forms for compound adjectives.

A compound adjective consists of two or more words used as a unit to describe a noun. Many compound adjectives contain the past participle *-ed* verb form: *flat-footed, barrel-chested, broad-shouldered,* *old-fashioned, well-dressed, left-handed.* Note the forms when a compound adjective is used before a noun: hyphens, past participle (*-ed*) forms where necessary, and no noun plural (*-s*) endings.

▶ **They have a** *five-year-old* **daughter.** [Their daughter is five years old.]

▶ **She gave me a** *five-dollar* **bill.** [She gave me five dollars.]

▶ **He is a** *left-handed* **pitcher.** [He pitches with his left hand.]

For more on hyphenation, see **56b**.

45e **Know where to position adverbs.**

An adverb can be placed in various positions in a sentence.

▶ *Enthusiastically,* **she ate the sushi.**

▶ **She** *enthusiastically* **ate the sushi.**

▶ **She ate the sushi** *enthusiastically.*

ESL NOTE Adverb Placement

Do not place an adverb between a verb and a short direct object (**62b** ESL).

▶ **She ate** *enthusiastically* the sushi. ■

Put adverbs that show frequency (*always, usually, frequently, often, sometimes, seldom, rarely, never*) in one of four positions:

1. At the beginning of a sentence

   ▶ *Sometimes* **I just sit and daydream instead of writing.**

   When *never, seldom,* or *rarely* occurs at the beginning of the sentence, word order is inverted (see also **34d** and **43d**).

   ▶ *Never will* **I let that happen.**

2. Between the subject and the main verb

   ▶ **They** *always* **arrive half an hour late.**

3. After a form of *be* or any auxiliary verb (such as *do, have, can, will, must*)

   ▶ **They are** *always* **unpunctual.**

   ▶ **She is** *seldom* **depressed.**

   ▶ **He has** *never* **lost a game.**

4. In the final position

▶ He goes to the movies *frequently*.

Note: Never place the adverb *never* in the final position.

45f Avoid double negatives.

Adverbs like *hardly*, *scarcely*, and *barely* are considered negatives, and the contraction *-n't* stands for the adverb *not*. Some languages and dialects allow the use of more than one negative to emphasize an idea, but Standard English allows only one negative in a clause. Avoid double negatives.

| DOUBLE NEGATIVE | We do*n't* have *no* excuses. |
| REVISED | We do*n't* have *any* excuses. [or] We have *no* excuses. |

| DOUBLE NEGATIVE | She did*n't* say *nothing*. |
| REVISED | She did*n't* say *anything*. [or] She said *nothing*. |

| DOUBLE NEGATIVE | They ca*n't hardly* pay the rent. |
| REVISED | They can *hardly* pay the rent. |

45g Know the comparative and superlative forms of adjectives and adverbs.

The *comparative* and *superlative* forms of adjectives and adverbs are used for comparisons. Use the comparative form to compare two people, places, things, or ideas; use the superlative to compare more than two.

Regular forms Add the ending *-er* to form the comparative and *-est* to form the superlative of both short adjectives (those that have one syllable or those that have two syllables and end in *-y* or *-le*) and one-syllable adverbs. (Change *-y* to *-i* if *-y* is preceded by a consonant: *icy, icier, iciest.*) Generally, a superlative form is preceded by *the* (*the shortest distance*).

	COMPARATIVE (COMPARING TWO)	SUPERLATIVE (COMPARING MORE THAN TWO)
short	shorter	shortest
pretty	prettier	prettiest
simple	simpler	simplest
fast	faster	fastest

With longer adjectives and with adverbs ending in *-ly*, use *more* (for the comparative) and *most* (for the superlative). Note that *less* (comparative) and *least* (superlative) are used with adjectives of any length (*less bright, least bright; less effective, least effective*).

	COMPARATIVE	SUPERLATIVE
intelligent	more intelligent	most intelligent
carefully	more carefully	most carefully
dangerous	less dangerous	least dangerous

If you cannot decide whether to use *-er/-est* or *more/most*, consult a dictionary. If there is an *-er/-est* form, the dictionary will say so.

Note: Do not use the *-er* form with *more* or the *-est* form with *most*.

▶ The first poem was ~~more~~ better than the second.

▶ Boris is the ~~most~~ fittest person I know.

Irregular forms The following common adjectives and adverbs have irregular comparative and superlative forms:

	COMPARATIVE	SUPERLATIVE
good	better	best
bad	worse	worst
much/many	more	most
little	less	least
well	better	best
badly	worse	worst

Using *than* with comparative forms To compare two people, places, things, or ideas, use the comparative form and the word *than*. If you use a comparative form in your sentence, you need *than* to let readers know what you are comparing with what.

than the previous one

▶ This course of action is more efficient.

Comparative forms are also used without *than* in an idiomatic way.

▶ The *harder* he tries, the *more satisfied* he feels.

▶ The *more*, the *merrier*.

45h Avoid faulty or incomplete comparisons.

Make sure that you state clearly what items you are comparing. Some faulty comparisons can give readers the wrong idea. See **40h, 44a, 44b**.

INCOMPLETE   **He likes the parrot better than his wife.**

To avoid suggesting that he prefers the parrot to his wife, clarify the comparison by completing the second clause.

REVISED   **He likes the parrot better *than his wife does.***

Edit sentences like the following:

▶ **My essay got a higher grade than Maria.** ʼs

[Compare the two essays, not your essay and Maria.]

▶ **Williams's poem gives a more objective depiction of the**

painting than Auden. ʼs

[To compare Williams's poem with Auden's poem, you need to include an apostrophe; otherwise, you compare a poem to the poet W. H. Auden.]

Comparisons must also be complete. If you say that something is "more efficient," your reader wonders, "More efficient than what?"

▶ **Didion shows us a home that makes her feel more tied to her**

than her home in Los Angeles does
roots. [Include the other part of the comparison.]

46   Relative Clauses and Relative Pronouns

Relative clauses are introduced by relative pronouns: *who, whom, whose, which,* and *that.* Relative clauses are also called *adjective clauses* because they modify nouns and noun phrases as adjectives do.

┌ relative clause ┐
▶ **The girl *who* can't dance says the band can't play.**

—Yiddish proverb

46a   Use an appropriate relative pronoun.

The forms of relative pronouns vary in speech and writing and in informal and formal usage. In academic writing, use the formal pronouns unless your instructor indicates that informal ones are acceptable.

Human antecedents

RELATIVE PRONOUNS: HUMAN ANTECEDENTS

SUBJECT	OBJECT	POSSESSIVE
who	whom (often omitted)	whose
that (informal)	that (often omitted)	

The form of the relative pronoun depends on the pronoun's grammatical function in its own clause. To identify the correct form, restate the clause, using a personal pronoun.

subject of clause

▶ The teachers who challenge us are the ones we remember.

[*They* challenge us.]

object of clause

▶ The teachers whom the students honored felt proud.

[The students honored *them*. *Whom* (or *who* in more informal writing) is more commonly omitted.]

possessive

▶ The teachers whose student evaluations were high won an award. [*Their* student evaluations were high.]

Phrases such as *I know, he thinks,* and *they realize* inserted into a relative clause do not affect the form of the pronoun.

subject of clause

▶ We should help children who we realize cannot defend

themselves. [*They* cannot defend themselves.]

Nonhuman antecedents: animals, things, and concepts Standard English, unlike languages such as Spanish, Arabic, and Thai, uses different relative pronouns for human and for nonhuman antecedents. Use *that* or *which* to refer to nonhuman antecedents. Never use *which* to refer to a human antecedent. See **46d** and **46g** for the use of *that* and *which* in restrictive and nonrestrictive clauses.

who

▶ The teacher ~~which~~ taught me math in high school was strict.

RELATIVE PRONOUNS: NONHUMAN ANTECEDENTS		
SUBJECT	OBJECT	POSSESSIVE
that	that (often	of which (formal)
which	omitted)	whose (informal)
	which (often	
	omitted)	

Use the relative pronoun *that* to refer to an antecedent naming an animal, a thing, or a concept (such as *success* or *information*). When the relative pronoun *that* functions as the direct object in its clause, it is usually omitted.

▶ They stayed at a hotel *that* had two pools and a sauna.

[*That* is the subject of the relative clause.]

▶ They stayed at a hotel *that* their friends had recommended.

[*That* is the direct object in the relative clause.]

▶ They stayed at a hotel their friends had recommended.

[*That* as direct object in the relative clause can be omitted.]

▶ They stayed at a hotel the name *of which* I can't remember.

[Formal]

▶ They stayed at a hotel *whose* name I can't remember.

[Informal]

46b Make the verb agree with the antecedent of a subject relative pronoun.

Determine subject-verb agreement within a relative clause by asking whether the antecedent of a subject relative pronoun is singular or plural.

─── relative clause ───────

▶ The book that *is* at the top of the bestseller list gives advice about health.   [The singular noun *book* is the antecedent of *that*, the subject of the singular verb *is* in the relative clause.]

─── relative clause ───────

▶ The books that *are* at the top of the bestseller list give advice about health, success, and making money.

[The plural noun *books* is the antecedent of *that*, the subject of the plural verb *are* in the relative clause.]

46c Check agreement in relative clauses after *one of* and *the only one of*.

The phrase *one of* is followed by a plural noun phrase. However, the verb can be singular or plural, depending on the meaning.

▶ Juan is one of the employees who *work* long hours.

[Several employees work long hours. Juan is one of them. The plural word *employees* is the antecedent of *who*, the subject of the plural verb *work* in the relative clause.]

┌ antecedent ┐   singular verb
▶ Juan is the only one of the employees who *works* long hours.

[Only Juan works long hours.]

46d Distinguish between restrictive and nonrestrictive relative clauses.

The two types of relative clauses, restrictive and nonrestrictive, fulfill different functions and need different punctuation (**47d**).

RESTRICTIVE   **The people *who live in the apartment above mine* make a lot of noise at night.**

NONRESTRICTIVE **The Sullivans, *who live in the apartment above mine*, make a lot of noise at night.**

Restrictive relative clause   A restrictive relative clause provides information essential for identifying the antecedent and restricting its scope.

FEATURES

1. The clause is not set off with commas.

2. An object relative pronoun can be omitted.

3. *That* (rather than *which*) is preferred for reference to nonhuman antecedents.

   ▶ **The teachers *who challenge us* are the ones we remember.**

   [The independent clause—"The teachers are the ones"—leads us to ask, "Which teachers?" The relative clause provides information that is essential to completing the meaning of the subject; it restricts the meaning from "all teachers" to "the teachers who challenge us."]

▶ **The book [*that*] *you gave me* was fascinating.**

[The relative pronoun *that* is the direct object in its clause ("You gave me the book") and can be omitted.]

Nonrestrictive relative clause A nonrestrictive relative clause provides information that is not essential for understanding the antecedent. It refers to and describes a proper noun (which names a specific person, place, or thing and begins with a capital letter) or a noun that is identified and unique.

FEATURES

1. The antecedent is a unique, designated person or thing.

2. The clause is set off by commas.

3. *Which* (not *that*) is used to refer to a nonhuman antecedent.

4. An object relative pronoun cannot be omitted.

▶ **The book *War and Peace*, which you gave me, was fascinating.**

[The independent clause—"The book *War and Peace* was fascinating"—does not promote further questions, such as "Which book?" The information in the relative clause ("which you gave me") is almost an aside and not essential for understanding the independent clause.]

46e Check relative clauses beginning with quantity words *(most of, some of, one of)*.

Relative clauses beginning with a quantity word such as *some, none, many, much, most*, or *one* followed by *of which* or *of whom* are always nonrestrictive.

▶ **They selected five candidates, *one of whom* would get the job.**

▶ **The report mentioned five names, *none of which* I recognized.**

ESL NOTE Relative vs. Personal Pronouns

You need only the relative pronoun, not a personal pronoun in addition.

> *most of whom*
> ► I tutored some students, ~~which most of them~~ were my classmates. ■

46f Take care when a relative clause contains a preposition.

When a relative clause contains a relative pronoun within a prepositional phrase, do not omit the preposition. Keep in mind these three points:

1. Directly after the preposition, use *whom* or *which*, never *that*.

> ┌────── relative clause ──────┐
> ► The man *for whom* we worked last year has just retired.

2. If you place the preposition after the verb, use *that* (or you can omit *that*), but do not use *whom* or *which*.

> [*that*]
> ► The man ~~whom~~ we worked for was efficient.

3. Do not add an extra personal pronoun object after the preposition at the end of the relative clause.

> ► The company [*that*] I worked for ~~it~~ last summer has gone bankrupt.

46g Know when to use *that* as a relative pronoun.

When to use *that* In Standard English, for a nonhuman antecedent, use *that* rather than *which* in the subject position and use *that* (or omit *that*) as an object in a restrictive relative clause. Never use *what* as if it were a relative pronoun.

> *that*
> ► The book ~~which~~ won the prize is a love story.

> [*that*]
> ► The deal ~~what~~ she was trying to make fell through.

> [*that*]
> ► Everything ~~which~~ she does for United Way is appreciated.

Use *that* rather than *who* when referring to groups of people.

               that
▶ The class ~~who~~ meets here is late.

When not to use *that*   In the following instances, use *which* or *whom* instead of *that*.

1. In nonrestrictive clauses supplying extra information (see **46d**)

▶ **Ellsvere Shopping Center, *which* was sold last month, has changed the whole area.**

2. Directly following a preposition

▶ **The woman to *whom* I was talking is a famous physicist.**

In informal contexts, however, the preposition is likely to occur at the end of the clause; in this case, *that* can be used or omitted.

▶ **The woman [that] I was talking to is a famous physicist.**

46h   Position a relative clause close to its antecedent.

To avoid ambiguity, place a relative clause as close as possible to its antecedent. (See also **40b** on misplaced modifiers.)

Ambiguous   **He searched for the notebook all over the house that his friend had forgotten.** [Had his friend forgotten the house?]

Revised   **He searched all over the house for the notebook that his friend had forgotten.**

46i   Avoid using a pronoun after a relative clause to rename the antecedent.

Although a pronoun may sometimes rename the antecedent in informal speech and in many languages, avoid it in formal writing (**62f** ESL).

▶ **My colleague who moved to Italy three years ago and has his own apartment in Milan ~~he~~ has a good life.**

46j Use *where* and *when* as relative pronouns when appropriate.

When you refer to actual or metaphoric places and times, you can use *where* to replace *in which, at which,* or *to which,* and you can use *when* to replace *at which, in which,* or *on which.* Do not use a preposition with *where* or *when.*

► The morning on which she graduated was warm and sunny.

► The morning *when* she graduated was warm and sunny.

► The village in which he was born honored him last year.

► The village *where* he was born honored him last year.

Use *where* or *when* only if actual time or physical location is involved.

► The influence of the Sapir-Whorf hypothesis, ~~where~~ *according to which* behavior is regarded as influenced by language, has declined.

Punctuation, Mechanics, and Spelling

PART 8   Punctuation, Mechanics, and Spelling

When you think about how many ways you can say "That's great" to convey different meanings, you will realize the importance of intonation to speech. In writing, punctuation replaces intonation. It is much more than a set of obscure rules, much more than a few marks to split up sentences. Punctuation serves to regulate the flow of information through a sentence, showing readers how to read your ideas. The following headline from the *New York Times*, "Stock Fraud Is Easier, and Easier to Spot," says that stock fraud is not only easy to engage in but also easy to detect. Without the comma, however, the sentence would send a different message: it would say that detecting stock fraud is becoming increasingly easy.

Keep in mind that there is no ideal model of punctuation, no prescribed length for a sentence. Where a sentence ends and divides depends on its meaning and your style. The writer Ernest Hemingway advised writers to keep punctuation conventional:

"The game of golf would lose a good deal if croquet mallets and billiard cues were allowed on the putting green. You ought to be able to show that you can do it a good deal better than anyone else with the regular tools before you have a license to bring in your own improvements."

47 Commas

A comma separates parts of a sentence; a comma alone does not separate one sentence from another. When readers see a comma, they think, "These parts of the sentence are being separated for a reason." When you can't decide whether to use commas, follow this general guideline: "When in doubt, leave them out." Readers find excessive use of commas more distracting than a few missing ones.

47a Two checklists—comma: yes, comma: no

The two checklists provide general rules of thumb. Details and more examples of each rule follow in the rest of section **47**. Note that in the sample sentences in section **47**, yellow shading means, "No comma here."

KEY POINTS

Comma: Yes

1. Before a coordinating conjunction (*and, but, or, nor, so, for, yet*) to connect independent clauses, including commands, but optional if the clauses are short (**47b**)

   ▶ He frowned, but she did not understand why he was worried.

2. After most introductory words, phrases, or clauses (**47c**)

   ▶ After the noisy party, the neighbors complained.

3. To set off extra (nonrestrictive) information included in a sentence ("extra commas with extra information") (**47d**)

   ▶ My father, a computer programmer, works late at night.

(Continued)

(Continued)

4. To set off a transitional expression (**47e**)

   ▶ The ending, however, is disappointing.

5. To separate three or more items in a series (**47f**)

   ▶ The fans applauded, cheered, and whistled.

6. Between coordinate adjectives (**47g**)

   ▶ We ate a delicious, well-prepared, and inexpensive meal.

7. After a verb that introduces a quotation (**47h**)

   ▶ She gasped, "We haven't a moment to lose!"

KEY POINTS

Comma: No (see 47i)

1. Not between subject and verb

   ▶ The man in the baggy blue jeans is her English teacher.

   However, use two commas to set off any extra information inserted between subject and verb (see **47d**).

2. Not before part of a compound structure that is not an independent clause

   ▶ She won the trophy and accepted it graciously.

3. Not *after* a coordinating conjunction connecting two independent clauses, but *before* it

   ▶ The movie tried to be engaging, but it failed miserably.

4. Not between two independent clauses without a coordinating conjunction (use either a period and a capital letter or a semicolon instead)

   ▶ He won; she was delighted.

5. Not between an independent clause and a following dependent clause introduced by *after, before, because, if, since, unless, until,* or *when* (neither before nor after the subordinating conjunction)

   ▶ She will continue working for the city until she has saved enough for graduate school.

(Continued)

(Continued)

6. Not before a clause beginning with *that*

▶ **They warned us that the meeting would be difficult.**

7. Not before and after essential, restrictive information

▶ **The player who scored the goal became a hero.**

8. Not between a verb and its object or complement

▶ **The best gifts are food and clothes.**

9. Not after *such as*

▶ **Popular fast food items, such as hamburgers and hot dogs, tend to be high in fat.**

47b Use a comma before a coordinating conjunction to connect independent clauses.

When you connect independent clauses with a coordinating conjunction (*and, but, or, nor, so, for, yet*), place a comma before the conjunction.

▶ **The managers are efficient, but personnel turnover is high.**

▶ **The juggler juggled seven plates, and we all cheered.**

When the clauses are short, the comma is often omitted.

▶ **He offered to help and he meant it.**

47c Use a comma after most introductory phrases and clauses.

The comma signals to readers that the phrase or clause has conveyed an idea, and that the introductory part has ended. It says, in effect, "Now wait for the independent clause."

▶ **If you blow out all the candles, your wishes will come true.**

▶ **More than sixteen years ago, Burma was renamed Myanmar.**

After one word or a short phrase, the comma is sometimes omitted:
Immediately the fun began.

Often a comma is essential to prevent misreading.

MISREADING
POSSIBLE
When active viruses can spread easily.

REVISED
When active, viruses can spread easily.

The comma after the introductory material tells readers to expect the subject and verb of the independent clause.

47d Use commas to set off an extra (nonrestrictive) phrase or clause.

When a phrase or clause provides extra information that could be omitted without changing the meaning of the independent clause, the phrase or clause is said to be *nonrestrictive*. Use commas to set off a nonrestrictive element. Doing so signals that the extra information it presents does not limit the meaning of the independent clause. A phrase or clause that limits or restricts the meaning of the independent clause is said to be *restrictive*. Do not use commas with restrictive information.

NONRESTRICTIVE
We'll attend, even though we'd rather not.
[We will definitely attend. The *even though* clause does not restrict the meaning.]

RESTRICTIVE
We'll attend if we have time.
[We will attend only if circumstances permit. The *if* clause restricts the meaning.]

Commas around appositive phrases Use commas to set off an appositive phrase (a phrase that renames or gives additional information about a prior noun or pronoun). If the phrase were omitted, readers might lose some interesting details but would still be able to understand the message.

appositive
phrase
▶ **She loves her car, a red Toyota.**

appositive phrase
▶ **His dog, a big Labrador retriever, is afraid of mice.**

▶ **Salinger's first novel,** *The Catcher in the Rye,* **captures the language and thoughts of teenagers.**

[The commas are used because the title provides supplementary information about the first novel, not information that identifies which novel the writer means. See also **47i**, item 8.]

Commas around nonrestrictive participle phrases Nonrestrictive participle phrases add extra descriptive, but not essential, information.

▶ **My boss, wearing a red tie and a green shirt, radiated the holiday spirit.**

[The participle phrase does not restrict the meaning of *boss* by distinguishing one boss from another.]

Commas around extra information in nonrestrictive relative clauses When you give nonessential information in a relative clause introduced by *who, whom,* or *which* (never *that*), set the clause off with commas.

▶ **My boss, who wears bright colors, is a cheerful person.**

[The independent clause "My boss is a cheerful person" does not lead readers to ask "Which boss?" The relative clause does not restrict the meaning of *boss*.]

▶ **His recent paintings, which are hanging in our local restaurant, show dogs in various disguises.**   [The relative clause, introduced by *which*, merely provides the additional fact that his recent paintings are on display in the restaurant.]

Do not use commas to set off essential, restrictive information (**46d** and **47i**).

           ⌜restricts *people* to a subgroup⌝
▶ **People who wear bright colors send an optimistic message.**

[The relative clause, beginning with *who*, restricts "people" to a subgroup: not all people send an optimistic message; those who wear bright colors do.]

47e Use commas to set off transitional expressions and explanatory insertions.

Transitional expressions and conjunctive adverbs connect or weave together the ideas in your writing and act as signposts for readers. See **2d** for a list of these expressions. Use commas to set off a transitional expression from the rest of the sentence.

▶ **Most Labrador retrievers, however, are courageous.**

Note: When you use a transitional expression such as *however, therefore, nevertheless, above all, of course,* or *in fact* at the beginning of an independent clause, end the previous clause with a period or a semicolon. Then place a comma after the transitional expression.

▶ **The party was a success. In fact, it was still going on at 2 a.m.**

You may sometimes choose to insert a phrase or a clause to make a comment, offer an explanation, drive a point home, or to point out a contrast. Insertions used for these purposes are set off by commas.

▶ **The consequences will be dire, I think.**

▶ **The best, if not the only, solution is to apologize and start over.**

▶ **Seasonal allergies, such as those caused by ragweed, are common.**

▶ **Unlike SUVs, compact cars do not guzzle gas.**

47f Use commas to separate three or more items in a series.

Readers see the commas between items in a series and think, "This is a list." If you said the sentence aloud, you would pause between items; in writing, you use commas to separate them. Journalists and British writers often omit a comma before *and*.

▶ **Searching through the drawer, the detective found a key, a stamp, three coins, and a photograph.**

See also **50a** for when to use semicolons in place of commas in a list.

47g Use commas to separate coordinate adjectives.

Adjectives are *coordinate* when their order can be reversed and the word *and* can be inserted between them without any change in meaning. Coordinate adjectives (*beautiful, delicious, exciting, noisy*) make subjective and evaluative judgments rather than providing objectively verifiable information about, for instance, size, shape, color, or nationality. Separate coordinate adjectives with commas.

▶ **He hires people who are energetic, efficient, and polite.**

Do not, however, put a comma between the final adjective of a series and the noun it modifies.

▶ **Energetic, efficient, and polite salespeople are in demand.**

Note that no comma is necessary to separate adjectives that are cumulative, modifying the whole noun phrase that follows (**62g** ESL).

▶ **Entering the little old stone house brought back memories of her childhood.**

47h Use a comma between a direct quotation and the clause introducing it.

The verb may come either before or after the quotation.

▶ **When asked what she wanted to be later in life, she replied, "An Olympic swimmer."**

▶ **"I want to be an Olympic swimmer," she announced confidently.**   [The comma is inside the quotation marks.]

47i When not to use commas: Ten rules of thumb

1. Do not use a comma to separate a verb from its subject.

▶ **The gifts she received from her colleagues made her realize her value to the company.**

▶ **Interviewing so many women in the United States helped the researcher understand the "American dream."**

Between a subject and verb, you may need to put two commas around inserted material, but never use just one comma.

```
        ┌────── subject ──────┐
```
▶ **The engraved plaque, given to her by her colleagues on her**

                verb
last day of work, made her feel proud.

2. Do not use a comma when the second part of a compound structure is not an independent clause.

▶ **Amy Tan has written novels and adapted them for the screen.**

▶ **Tan has written about her mother and the rest of her family.**

3. Do not use a comma *after* a coordinating conjunction that connects two sentences. The comma goes *before* the conjunction, not *after* it.

▶ *The Joy Luck Club* is supposed to be good, but ▮ I missed it when it came to my local movie theater.

4. Do not use a comma to connect two independent clauses when no coordinating conjunction is present. Instead, end the first clause with a period and make the second clause a new sentence, or insert a semicolon between the clauses. Use a comma only if you connect the clauses with a coordinating conjunction. See **39** for ways to correct a comma splice, the error that results when two independent clauses are incorrectly connected with a comma.

▶ Amy Tan has written novels; ▮ they have been adapted for the screen.

5. Do not use a comma to separate an independent clause from a following dependent clause introduced by *after, before, because, if, since, unless, until,* or *when*.

▶ The test results were good ▮ because all the students had studied in groups.

6. Do not use a comma after *although*.

▶ Although ▮ the oboist had a cold, she performed well.

7. Do not use a comma to separate a clause beginning with *that* from the rest of the sentence.

▶ The girl in Tan's story tried to convey to her mother ▮ that she did not have to be a child prodigy.

Note: A comma can appear before a *that* clause when it is the second comma of a pair before and after extra information inserted as a non-restrictive phrase.

▶ He skates so fast, ▮ despite his size, ▮ that he will probably break the world record.

8. Do not use commas around a phrase or clause that provides essential, restrictive information.

▶ Alice Walker's essay ▮ "Beauty: When the Other Dancer Is the Self" ▮ discusses coping with a physical disfigurement.

[Walker has written more than one essay. The title restricts the noun *essay* to one specific essay.]

Similarly, a restrictive relative clause introduced by *who, whom, whose, which,* or *that* is never set off by commas. The clause provides essential, identifying information (see **46d** and **47d**).

▶ **The teachers praised the children who finished on time.**

[The teachers didn't praise all the children; they praised only the ones who finished on time.]

9. Do not use a comma to separate a verb from its object or complement.

▶ **The qualities required for the job are punctuality, efficiency, and the ability to work long hours.**

10. Do not use a comma after *such as.*

▶ **They bought kitchen supplies such as detergent, paper towels, and garbage bags.**

47j Special uses of commas

To prevent misreading Use a comma to separate elements in a sentence that may otherwise be confusing.

▶ **He who can, does. He who cannot, teaches.**
  —George Bernard Shaw, *Man and Superman*

[Usually a comma is not used to separate a subject from the verb. Here the comma is necessary to prevent confusion.]

With an absolute phrase Use a comma to set off a phrase that modifies the whole sentence (an absolute phrase).

┌──────── absolute phrase ────────┐
▶ **The audience looking on in amusement, the valedictorian blew kisses to all her favorite instructors.**

With a date Use a comma to separate the day from the year in a date.

▶ **On May 14, 1998, the legendary singer Frank Sinatra died.**
  [Do not use a comma before the year when the day precedes the month: 14 May 1998.]

With numbers Use a comma (never a period) to divide numbers into thousands.

▶ **1,200**   ▶ **515,000**   ▶ **34,000,000**

No commas are necessary in years (*2002*), numbers in addresses (*3501 East 10th Street*), or page numbers (*page 1008*).

With titles   Use commas around a person's title or degree.

▶ Stephen L. Carter, Ph.D., gave the commencement speech.

With the parts of an address

▶ Alice Walker was born in Eatonton, Georgia, in 1944.

However, do not use a comma before a ZIP code: Newton, MA 02159.

With a conversational tag or tag question

▶ Yes, Salinger's daughter, like others before her, has produced a memoir.

▶ She has not won a Pulitzer prize, has she?

With a direct address or salutation

▶ Whatever you build here, Mr. Trump, will cause controversy.

---

48   Apostrophes

An apostrophe indicates ownership or possession: *Fred's books; the government's plans; a year's pay* (the books belonging to Fred; the plans of the government; the pay for a year). It can also signal omitted letters (*who's, can't*).

 Two checklists—Apostrophe: yes, apostrophe: no

 KEY POINTS

Apostrophe: Yes

1. Use -'s for the possessive form of all nouns except plural nouns that end with -s: *the hero's misfortune, the actress's Academy Award.*

2. Use an apostrophe alone for the possessive form of plural nouns that end with -s: *many politicians' lives, the heroes' misfortunes.*

(Continued)

(Continued)

3. Use an apostrophe to indicate the omission of letters in contracted forms such as *didn't, they're,* and *let's.*

4. Use *it's* only for "it is" or "it has": *It's a good idea; it's been a long time.* (The possessive form of the pronoun *it* is spelled with no apostrophe: *The house lost* its *roof.*)

KEY POINTS

Apostrophe: No

1. Generally, do not use an apostrophe to form the plurals of nouns. (See **48e** for rare exceptions.)

2. Never use an apostrophe before an *-s* ending on a verb. Note that *let's* is a contracted form for *let us*; the *-s* is not a verb ending.

3. Do not write possessive pronouns *(hers, its, ours, yours, theirs)* with an apostrophe.

4. Do not use an apostrophe to form the plural of names: *the Browns.*

5. Do not use an apostrophe to indicate possession by inanimate objects such as buildings and items of furniture; instead, use *of: the roof of the hotel, the back of the desk.*

48b Use -'s to signal possession.

As a general rule, to signal possession, use -'s with singular nouns, with indefinite pronouns, and with plural nouns that do not form the plural with -s.

the child's books   anybody's opinion
the children's toys   today's world
this month's budget   Mr. Jackson's voice
someone else's idea   their money's worth

Individual and joint ownership   To indicate individual ownership, make each owner possessive.

▶ Updike's and Roth's recent works received glowing reviews.

To show joint ownership, make only the last owner possessive: *Sam, Sue, and Pat's house.*

Compound nouns Add -'s to the last word in a compound noun.

▶ my brother-in-law's car

Singular nouns ending in -s When a singular noun ends in -s, add -'s as usual for the possessive.

▶ Thomas's toys ▶ my boss's instructions

However, when a singular noun ending in -s is a long word or ends with a z or *eez* sound, an apostrophe alone is sometimes used: *Charles' theories, Erasmus' rhetoric, Euripides' dramas.*

48c Use only an apostrophe to signal possession in plural nouns already ending in -s.

Add only an apostrophe when a plural noun already ends in -s.

▶ the students' suggestions ▶ my friends' ambitions
[more than one student] [more than one friend]

Remember to include an apostrophe in comparisons with a noun understood (**40h** and **45h**):

▶ His views are different from other professors'.
[... from other professors' views]

48d Use an apostrophe in contractions.

In a contraction (*shouldn't, don't, haven't*), the apostrophe appears where letters have been omitted. To test whether an apostrophe is in the correct place, mentally replace the missing letters. The replacement test, however, will not help with the following:

won't   will not

Note: Some readers object to contractions in formal academic writing because they view them as colloquial and informal. It is safer not to use contractions unless you know your readers' preferences.

can't	cannot	they'd	they had *or* they would
didn't	did not	they're	they are
he's	he is *or* he has	it's	it is *or* it has
's	is, has, *or* does (How's it taste?)	let's	let us (Let's go.)

Never place an apostrophe before the *-s* ending of a verb:

▶ **The author let's his characters take over.**

An apostrophe can also take the place of the first part of a year or decade.

▶ **the greed of the '80s**   ▶ **the Spirit of '76**

[the 1980s]   [the year 1776]

Note: Fixed forms spelled with an apostrophe, such as *o'clock* and the poetic *o'er,* are contractions ("of the clock," "over").

48e Use *-'s* for plurals only in two instances.

A general rule is never to use an apostrophe to form a plural. However, in the following instances an apostrophe is commonly used.

1. Use *-'s* for the plural form of letters of the alphabet. Italicize only the letter, not the plural ending (**52c**).

▶ **Maria picked all the *M*'s out of her alphabet soup.**

▶ **Georges Perec's novel called *A Void* has no *e*'s in it at all.**

2. Use *-'s* for the plural form of a word referred to as the word itself.   Italicize the word named as a word, but do not italicize the *-'s* ending (**52c**).

▶ **You have too many *but*'s in that sentence.**

MLA and APA prefer no apostrophe in the plural form of numbers, acronyms, and abbreviations (**54f**).

   the 1900s   CDs   FAQs   BAs

However, you will frequently see such plurals spelled with *-'s.* In all cases, be consistent in your usage.

   Never use an apostrophe to signal the plural of common nouns or personal names: *big bargains, the Jacksons.*

48f Distinguish between *it's* and *its.*

When deciding whether to use *its* or *it's,* think about meaning. *It's* is a contraction meaning "it is" or "it has." *Its* is the possessive form of the pronoun *it* and means "belonging to it." See also **44b**.

▶ **It's a good idea.**   ▶ **The committee took its time.**

49 Quotation Marks

In American English, double quotation marks indicate where someone's exact words begin and end. However, for long quotations, see **49f**.

Guidelines for using quotation marks

KEY POINTS

Quotation Marks: Basic Guidelines

1. Quote exactly the words used by the original speaker or writer.
2. Pair opening quotation marks with closing quotation marks to indicate where the quotation ends and your ideas begin.
3. Use correct punctuation to introduce and end a quotation, and place other marks of punctuation carefully in relation to the quotation marks.
4. Enclose the titles of articles, short stories, songs, and poems in quotation marks.
5. Enclose any added or changed material in square brackets (**51e**); indicate omitted material with ellipsis dots (**51g**).

49b Punctuation introducing and ending a quotation

After an introductory verb, such as *say*, *state*, or *write*, use a comma followed by a capital letter to introduce a direct quotation.

> ▶ It was Erma Bombeck who said, "Families aren't dying. They're merging into conglomerates."
>
> — "Empty Fridge, Empty Nest"

Use a colon after a complete sentence introducing a quotation, and begin the quotation with a capital letter.

> ▶ Woody Allen always tries to make us laugh even about serious issues like wealth and poverty: "Money is better than poverty, if only for financial reasons." —*Without Feathers*

When a quotation is integrated into the structure of your own sentence, use no special introductory punctuation other than the quotation marks.

► Phyllis Grosskurth comments that "anxiety over money was driving him [Byron] over the brink."   —*Byron*

Put periods and commas inside quotation marks, even if these punctuation marks do not appear in the original quotation.

► When Henry Rosovsky characterizes Bloom's ideas as "mind-boggling," he is not offering praise.   —*The University*

In a documented paper, when you use parenthetical citations after a short quotation at the end of a sentence, put the period at the end of the citation, not within the quotation. See **49f** for long quotations.

► Geoffrey Wolff observes that when his father died, there was nothing to indicate "that he had ever known another human being" (11).   —*The Duke of Deception*

Put question marks and exclamation points inside the quotation marks if they are part of the original source, with no additional period.   When your sentence is a statement, do not use a comma or period in addition to a question mark or exclamation point.

► She asked, "Where's my mama?"

Put a question mark, exclamation point, semicolon, or colon outside the closing quotation marks.   If your sentence contains punctuation that is your own, not part of the original quotation, do not include it within the quotation marks.

► The chapter focuses on this question: Who are "the new American dreamers"?

49c Quotation marks in dialogue

Do not add closing quotation marks until the speaker changes or you interrupt the quotation. Begin each new speaker's words with a new paragraph.

                                        interruption
                                     ┌ of quotation ┐
►   "I'm not going to work today," he announced. "Why should I? I worked all weekend. My boss is away on vacation. And I have a headache."

── change of speaker ──
"Honey, your boss is on the phone," his wife called from the bedroom.

If a quotation from one speaker continues for more than one paragraph, place *closing* quotation marks at the end of only the *final* paragraph of the quotation. However, place *opening* quotation marks at the beginning of every paragraph, so readers realize that the quotation is continuing.

49d A quotation within a quotation

Enclose quotations in double quotation marks. Use single quotation marks to enclose a quotation or a title of a short work within a quotation. (British usage is different.)

▶ Margaret announced, "I have read 'The Lottery' already."

▶ The comedian Steven Wright once said, "I have an existential map. It has 'You are here' written all over it."

49e Quotation marks with titles, definitions, and translations

KEY POINTS

Titles: Quotation Marks or Italics/Underlining?

1. Quotation marks with the title of an article, short story, poem, song, or chapter: "Kubla Khan"; "Lucy in the Sky with Diamonds"; "The Yellow Wallpaper"; "America: The Multinational Society."

2. Italics or underlining with the title of a book, journal, magazine, newspaper, film, play, long poem published alone: The Lovely Bones , *Newsweek, The Hours,* Beowulf (**52a**).

3. No quotation marks and no italics or underlining with the title of your own essay (**49f**): Why Telemarketing Is a Real Job.

For more on capital letters with titles, see **53d**.

For a translation or definition, use quotation marks:

▶ The abbreviation *p.m.* means "after midday."

49f When not to use quotation marks

Note that in the sample sentences, yellow shading means "no quotation marks here."

Do not put quotation marks around indirect quotations.

▶ One woman I interviewed said that her husband argued like a lawyer.

Do not put quotation marks around clichés, slang, or trite expressions. Instead, revise to eliminate the cliché, slang, or trite expression. See also **33d** and **33g**.

involvement.
▶ All they want is ~~"a piece of the action."~~

Do not put quotation marks at the beginning and end of long indented quotations. When you use MLA style to quote more than three lines of poetry or four typed lines of prose, indent the whole passage one inch (or ten spaces) from the left margin. Do not enclose the quoted passage in quotation marks, but retain any internal quotation marks. See **10f** for an illustration.

On the title page of your own paper, do not put quotation marks around your essay title. Use quotation marks in your title only when your title contains a quotation or the title of a short work.

▶ Charles Baxter's "Gryphon" as an Educational Warning

50 Semicolons and Colons

A colon (:) may look like a semicolon (;). A colon is two dots; the semicolon, a dot above a comma. However, they are used in different ways, and they are not interchangeable. Note the use of the semicolon and colon in the following passage discussing the musical number "Cheek to Cheek" in the Astaire and Rogers film *Top Hat:*

[Ginger] Rogers is perhaps never more beautiful than when she's just listening; she never takes her eyes off him and throughout this scene I don't think she changes her expression once. The modesty of the effect makes her look like an angel: such a compliant, unasking attitude, handsome beyond expectation in such a fierce woman.

—Arlene Croce,
The Fred Astaire and Ginger Rogers Book

Ginger Rogers and Fred Astaire

50a Two checklists—semicolon: yes, semicolon: no

A period separates independent clauses with finality; a semicolon, such as the one you have just seen in this sentence, provides a less distinct separation and indicates that an additional related thought or item will follow immediately. As essayist Lewis Thomas comments in "Notes on Punctuation": "The period tells you that that is that; if you didn't get all the meaning you wanted or expected, anyway you got all the writer intended to parcel out and now you have to move along. But with a semicolon there you get a pleasant little feeling of expectancy; there is more to come."

KEY POINTS

Semicolon: Yes

1. Between closely connected independent clauses when no coordinating conjunction (*and, but, or, nor, so, for, yet*) is used

   ▶ **Biography tells us about the subject; biographers also tell us about themselves.**

   (Do not overuse semicolons in this way.) A comma between the two independent clauses would produce a comma splice, and no punctuation at all would produce a run-on sentence (see **39**). Do not use a capital letter to begin a clause after a semicolon.

   (Continued)

(Continued)

2. Between independent clauses connected with a transitional expression like *however, moreover, in fact, nevertheless, above all,* or *therefore* (see the list in **2d**)

▶ **The results of the study support the hypothesis; however, further research with a variety of tasks is necessary.**

(If the transitional expression is in the middle or at the end of its clause, the semicolon still appears between the clauses: *The results support the hypothesis; further research, however, is necessary.*)

3. To separate items in a list containing internal commas (see also **47f**)

▶ **When I cleaned out the refrigerator, I found a chocolate cake, half-eaten; some canned tomato paste, which had a blue fungus growing on the top; and some possibly edible meat loaf.**

KEY POINTS

Semicolon: No

1. Not in place of a colon to introduce a list or an explanation

▶ **Kelly has produced a variety of works of art; drawings, paintings, prints, and sculptures.**

2. Not after an introductory phrase or dependent clause, even if the phrase or clause is long. Using a semicolon would produce a fragment. Use a comma instead.

▶ **Because the training period was so long and arduous for all the players; the manager allowed one visit by family and friends.**

3. Not before an appositive phrase

▶ **The audience cheered the Oscar winner; Jack Nicholson.**

4. Not in place of a comma before *and, but, or, nor, so, for,* or *yet* joining independent clauses

▶ **The thrift shop in the church basement needed a name; and the volunteers chose Attic Treasures.**

50b Two checklists—colon: yes, colon: no

A colon signals anticipation. It follows an independent clause and introduces information that readers will need. A colon tells readers, "What comes next will define, illustrate, or explain what you have just read." Use one space after a colon. Note that in the sample sentences, yellow shading means "no colon here."

KEY POINTS

Colon: Yes

1. After an independent clause to introduce a list

   ▶ The students included three pieces of writing in their portfolios: a narrative, an argument, and a documented paper.

2. After an independent clause to introduce an explanation, expansion, or elaboration

   ▶ After an alarming cancer diagnosis and years of treatment, Lance Armstrong was victorious: he won the Tour de France five times.

   Some writers prefer to use a capital letter after a colon introducing an independent clause. Whatever you choose to do, be consistent in your usage.

3. To introduce a rule or principle, which may begin with a capital letter

   ▶ The main principle of public speaking is simple: Look at the audience.

4. To introduce a quotation not integrated into your sentence and not introduced by a verb such as *say*

   ▶ Emily Post has provided an alternative to attempting to outdo others: "To do *exactly as your neighbors do* is the only sensible rule."

   A colon also introduces a long quotation set off from your text (**10f**).

(Continued)

(Continued)

5. In salutations, precise time notations, titles, and biblical citations

► **Dear Chancellor Witkin:**

► **To: The Chancellor**

► **7:20 p.m.**

► *Backlash: The Undeclared War against American Women*

► **Genesis 37:31–35** [Here, a period could be used in place of the colon.]

KEY POINTS

Colon: No

1. Not directly after a verb (such as a form of *be* or *include*)

► **The two main effects were the improvement of registration and an increase in the numbers of advisers.**

► **The book includes a preface, an introduction, an appendix, and an index.**

2. Not after a preposition (such as *of, except,* and *regarding*) or the phrase *such as.*

► **The essay consisted of a clear beginning, middle, and end.**

► **The novel will please many readers except linguists and lawyers.**

► **They packed many different items for the picnic, such as taco chips, salsa, bean salad, pita bread, and egg rolls.**

3. Not after *for example, especially,* or *including*

► **His varied taste is shown by his living room furnishings, including antiques, modern art, and art deco lighting fixtures.**

51 Other Punctuation Marks

51a Periods

In British English, a period is referred to as a "full stop." The stop at the end of a sentence is indeed full—more of a stop than a comma provides. Periods are also used with abbreviations, decimals, and amounts of money, as in items 3 and 4.

1. Use a period to end a sentence that makes a statement or gives a command.

▶ The interviewer asked the manager about the company's finances.

The Modern Language Association (MLA), in its list of Frequently Asked Questions at <http://www.mla.org>, recommends leaving one space after a punctuation mark at the end of a sentence, but sees "nothing wrong with using two spaces after concluding punctuation marks." Ask your instructor for her or his preference.

For periods used with sentences within parentheses, see **53a**.

2. Use a period, not a question mark, to end a sentence concluding with an indirect question.

▶ The interviewer asked the manager how much the company made last year.

[See also **40d**, **4li**, and **62d** ESL.]

3. Use a period to signal an abbreviation:

Mr.   Mrs.   Dr.   Rev.   Tues.   etc.

Use only one space after the period: Mr. Lomax.
Some abbreviations contain internal periods:

e.g.   i.e.   a.m.   p.m.   (or A.M.   P.M.)

Note: For some abbreviations with capital letters, you can use periods or not. Just be consistent.

A.M. or AM   P.M. or PM   U.S.A. or USA

When ending a sentence with an abbreviation, do not add an extra period: The plane left at 7 a.m.

Initials of names of government agencies (HUD) or other organizations (ACLU), acronyms (abbreviations pronounced as words: NASA, AIDS), Internet abbreviations (URL), abbreviations for states (CA, NJ), or common time indicators (BC, AD), all occur without periods (**54b**).

4. Use a period with decimals and with amounts of money over a dollar: 3.7, $7.50

51b Question marks and exclamation points

Question marks (?) A question mark at the end of a sentence signals a direct question. Do not use a period in addition to a question mark.

▶ **What is he writing?**

After an indirect question, use a period (**51a**).

▶ **I wonder what he is writing.**

Questions are useful devices to engage readers' attention. You ask a question and then provide an answer.

▶ **Many cooks nowadays are making healthier dishes. How do they do this? For the most part, they use unsaturated oil.**

A question mark can be used to express uncertainty in a sentence that is a statement.

▶ **"She jumped in?" he wondered.**

▶ **Plato (427?–347 BC) founded the Academy at Athens.**

Exclamation points (!) An exclamation point at the end of a sentence indicates that the writer considers the statement amazing, surprising, or extraordinary. As novelist F. Scott Fitzgerald said, "An exclamation point is like laughing at your own joke." Let your words and ideas carry the force of any emphasis you want to communicate. Never accompany an exclamation point with a period, comma, or question mark.

51c Dashes

A dash (—) alerts readers to an explanation, to something unexpected, or to an interruption. Form a dash by typing two hyphens, putting no extra space before, between, or after them. Recent software will transform the two hyphens into one continuous dash. A dash should be followed by a phrase, not a clause.

▶ **Armed with one weapon—his wit—he faced the crowd.**

▶ **The accused gasped, "But I never—" and fainted.**

▶ **In America there are two classes of travel—first class and with children.** —Robert Benchley, in Robert E. Drennan, *The Algonquin Wits*

Commas can be used to set off an appositive phrase, but a pair of dashes is preferable when appositive phrases appear in a list containing commas.

▶ **The contents of his closet—torn jeans, frayed jackets, and suits shiny on the seat and elbows—made him reassess his priorities.**

Overusing the dash may produce a staccato effect. Use it sparingly.

51d Parentheses

Use parentheses to mark an aside or provide additional information.

▶ **Everyone admired Chuck Yeager's feat (breaking the sound barrier).**

Also use parentheses to enclose citations in a documented paper and to enclose numbers or letters preceding items in a list.

▶ **(3) A journalist reports that in the course of many interviews, he met very few people who were cynical about the future of the country (Lamb 5).**

At the end of a sentence, place the period inside the last parenthesis only when a separate new sentence is enclosed (see also **53a**).

▶ **Chuck Yeager's feat led to more competition in the space industry. (He broke the sound barrier.)**

51e Brackets

Square brackets ([ ]) When you insert words or comments or make changes to words within a quotation, enclose the inserted or changed material in square brackets. Be careful to insert only words that help the quotation fit into your sentence grammatically or that offer necessary explanation. Do not insert words that substantially change the meaning.

► According to Ridley, "the key to both of these features of life [the ability to reproduce and to create order] is information."

On occasion, you may need to use brackets to insert the Latin word *sic* (meaning "thus") into a quoted passage in which an error occurs. Using *sic* tells readers that the word or words that it follows were present in the original source and are not your own.

► Richard Lederer tells of a man who did "exercises to strengthen his abominable [sic] muscles."

Square brackets can also be used in MLA style around ellipsis dots that you add to signal an omission (**51g**).

Angle brackets (< >) Use angle brackets to enclose e-mail addresses and URLs, particularly in an MLA-style works-cited list. See **12e** and **57a**.

51f Slashes

Use a slash (/) to separate two or three lines of poetry quoted within your own text. For quoting more than three lines of poetry, see **10f**.

► Philip Larkin asks a question that many of us relate to: "Why should I let the toad *work* / Squat on my life?"

Slashes are also used in expressions such as *and/or* and *he/she* to indicate options. Be careful not to overuse these expressions.

51g Ellipsis dots

When you omit material from a quotation, indicate the omission—the ellipsis—by using spaced dots (. . .). In MLA style, use square brackets around ellipsis dots if the passage you quote itself contains an ellipsis. The following passage by Ruth Sidel, on page 27 of *On Her Own*, is used in the examples that follow.

> These women have a commitment to career, to material well-being, to success, and to independence. To many of them, an affluent lifestyle is central to their dreams; they often describe their goals in terms of cars, homes, travel to Europe. In short, they want their piece of the American Dream.

Words omitted from the middle of a quotation   Use three ellipsis dots when you omit material from the middle of a quotation.

▶ Ruth Sidel reports that the women in her interviews "have a commitment to career . . . and to independence" (27).

Words omitted at the end of your sentence   When you omit part of a quotation and the omission occurs at the end of your own sentence, insert ellipsis dots after the sentence period, followed by the closing quotation marks, making four dots in all.

▶ Ruth Sidel presents interesting findings about jobs and money: "These women have a commitment to career, to material well-being. . . ."

When a parenthetical reference follows the quoted passage, put the final sentence period after the parenthetical reference:

▶ Ruth Sidel presents interesting findings about jobs and money: "These women have a commitment to career, to material well-being . . ." (27).

Complete sentence omitted   When you omit a complete sentence or more, insert three ellipsis dots.

▶ Sidel tells us how "an affluent life-style is central to their dreams; . . . they want their piece of the American dream" (27).

Line of poetry omitted   When you omit one or more lines of poetry from a long, indented quotation, indicate the omission with a line of dots.

▶ This poem is for the hunger of my mother
. . . .
who read the Blackwell's catalogue
like a menu of delights
and when we moved from Puerto Rico to the States
we packed 100 boxes of books and 40 of everything else.
—Aurora Levins Morales, *Class Poem*

When not to use ellipsis dots   Do not use ellipsis dots when you quote only a word or a phrase because it will be obvious that material has been omitted:

▶ The women Sidel interviewed see an "affluent life-style" in their future.

Note: Use three dots to indicate a pause in speech or an interruption.

▶ **The doctor said, "The good news is . . . " and then turned to take a phone call.**

52 Italics and Underlining

Use italic type or underlining to highlight a word, phrase, or title in your own writing. Word processing programs offer italic type. Usually, though, in manuscript form, underlining is more distinctive and therefore preferred, particularly in MLA bibliographical lists and in material to be graded or typeset. Ask your instructor which to use. For underlining when writing online, see **57b**.

52a Italicize or underline titles of long, whole works.

In the body of an essay, italicize or underline the titles of books, journals, magazines, newspapers, plays, films, TV series, long poems, musical compositions, Web sites, online databases, and works of art.

▶ <u>The Sun Also Rises</u>   ▶ *Survivor*   ▶ <u>Newsweek</u>

▶ *The English Patient*   ▶ <u>Mona Lisa</u>   ▶ *InfoTrac*

Do not italicize or underline the names of sacred works such as the Bible, books of the Bible (Genesis, Psalms), and the Koran (Qur'an). Also do not italicize or underline the titles of documents and laws, such as the Declaration of Independence, the Constitution, and the Americans with Disabilities Act.

Do not italicize or underline the titles of short works, such as poems, short stories, essays, and articles; use quotation marks (**49e**). Do not italicize or underline the title of your own essays (**49e**).

52b Italicize or underline names of specific ships, trains, airplanes, and spacecraft.

▶ <u>Mayflower</u>   ▶ *Silver Meteor*   ▶ *Mir*   ▶ <u>Columbia</u>

Do not underline or italicize the abbreviations sometimes preceding them: USS *Constitution.*

52c Italicize or underline letters, numerals, and words referring to the items themselves, not to what they represent.

▶ The sign had a large <u>P</u> in black marker and a <u>3</u> in red.

▶ *Zarf* is a useful word for some board games.

52d Italicize or underline words from other languages.

Expressions not commonly used in English should be italicized or underlined. Do not overuse such expressions because they tend to sound pretentious.

▶ The author's *Weltanschauung* promotes gloom.

Do not italicize common expressions: et al., croissant, film noir, etc.

52e Do not use italics or underlining for emphasis.

                          hair-raising.
▶ The climb was ~~so scary~~.

Select a word that conveys the emphasis you want to express.

53 Capitalization

53a Capitalize *I* and the first word of a sentence

Always use a capital letter for the pronoun *I.* E-mail correspondence without capitalized *I* may annoy some readers. Do not use a capital letter for the first word after a semicolon. In addition, use no capital letter if you insert a complete sentence into another sentence, using parentheses:

▶ The Web site provides further historical information (just click on the icon).

But use a capital letter if the sentence within parentheses stands alone:

▶ **The Web site provides further historical information. (Just click on the icon.)**

Note also the placing of the periods in the examples above (**51d**).

53b Capitalize proper nouns and proper adjectives.

Begin the names of specific people, places, and things with a capital letter.

TYPES OF PROPER NOUNS AND ADJECTIVES	EXAMPLES
People	Albert Einstein, T. S. Eliot, Bill Gates (but bell hooks)
Nations, continents, planets, stars, and galaxies	Hungary, Asia, Mercury, the North Star, the Milky Way
Mountains, rivers, and oceans	Mount Everest, the Thames, the Pacific Ocean
Public places and regions	Golden Gate Park, the Great Plains, the Midwest
Streets, buildings, and monuments	Rodeo Drive, the Empire State Building, the Roosevelt Memorial
Cities, states, and provinces	Toledo, Kansas, Nova Scotia
Days of the week and months	Wednesday, March
Holidays	Labor Day, the Fourth of July
Organizations, companies, and search engines	the Red Cross, Microsoft Corporation, AltaVista, eBay (internal capital)
Institutions (including colleges, departments, schools, government offices, and courts of law)	University of Texas, Department of English, School of Business, Defense Department, Florida Supreme Court
Historical events, named periods, and documents	the Civil War, the Renaissance, the Roaring Twenties, the Declaration of Independence
Religions, deities, revered persons, and sacred texts	Buddhism, Islam, Muslim, Baptist, Jehovah, Mohammed, the Torah, the Koran (Qur'an)

TYPES OF PROPER NOUNS
AND ADJECTIVES   EXAMPLES

Races, tribes, nations, nationalities, and languages	the Navajo, Greece, Greek, Spain, Spanish, Syrian, Farsi
Registered trademarks	Kleenex, Apple, Bic, Nike, Xerox
Names of ships, planes, and spacecraft	the USS *Kearsage*, the *Spirit of St. Louis*, the *Challenger*
Titles of courses	English Composition, Introduction to Sociology

Note: Do not capitalize nouns naming general classes or types of people, places, things, or ideas: *government, jury, mall, prairie, utopia, traffic court, the twentieth century, goodness, reason.* Also, do not capitalize the names of seasons (*next spring*) or subjects of study, except for languages (*She is interested in geology and Spanish.*). For the use of capital letters in online writing, see **57c**.

53c Capitalize a title before a person's name.

▶ The reporter interviewed Senator Thompson.

▶ The residents cheered Grandma Jones.

Do not use a capital letter when a title is not attached to a person's name.

▶ Each state elects two senators.

▶ My grandmother is ninety years old.

When a title substitutes for the name of a known person, a capital letter is often used.

▶ Have you spoken with the Senator [senator] yet?

53d Capitalize major words in titles.

In titles of published books, journals, magazines, essays, articles, films, poems, and songs, use a capital letter at the beginning of all words except articles (*the, a, an*), coordinating conjunctions (*and, but, or, nor, so, for, yet*), *to* in an infinitive (*to stay*), and prepositions unless they begin or end a title or subtitle.

▶ "With a Little Help from My Friends"

▶ *Reflections from the Keyboard: The World of the Concert Pianist*

For more on titles, see the Key Points box in **49e**.

53e Guidelines for using a capital or lowercase letter after a colon or at the beginning of a quotation

Should a capital letter be used at the beginning of a clause after a colon? Usage varies. Usually a capital letter is used if the clause states a rule or principle (**50b**). Make your usage consistent.

Should a capital letter be used at the beginning of a quotation? Capitalize the first word of a quoted sentence if it is capitalized in the original passage.

▶ Quindlen says, "This is a story about a name," and thus tells us the topic of her article.

Do not capitalize when you quote part of a sentence.

▶ When Quindlen says that she is writing "a story about a name," she is telling us the topic of her article.

54 Abbreviations

For abbreviations commonly used in online writing, see **57e**.

54a Abbreviate titles used with people's names.

Use an abbreviation, followed by a period, for titles before or after names. The following abbreviated titles precede names: *Mr., Mrs., Ms., Prof., Dr., Gen.,* and *Sen.* The following abbreviated titles follow names: *Sr., Jr., PhD, MD, BA,* and *DDS.* Do not use a title both before and after a name: *Dr. Benjamin Spock* or *Benjamin Spock, MD.* Do not abbreviate a title if it is not attached to a specific name.

                doctor
▶ He went to the ~~dr.~~ twice last week.

54b Abbreviate the names of familiar institutions, countries, tests, diseases, diplomas, individuals, and objects.

Use capitalized abbreviations of the names of well-known institutions (*UCLA, YWCA, FBI, UN*), countries (*USA* or *U.S.A.*), tests and diplomas (*SAT, GED*), diseases (MS, HIV), individuals (*FDR*), TV and radio stations (PBS, WQXR), and objects (*DVD*). If you use a specialized abbreviation, first use the term in full followed by the abbreviation in parentheses; then use the abbreviation.

▶ **The Graduate Record Examination (GRE) is required by many graduate schools. GRE preparation is therefore big business.**

54c Abbreviate terms used with numbers.

Use the abbreviations such as *BC, AD, a.m., p.m., $, mph, wpm, mg, kg,* and other units of measure only when they occur with specific numbers.

▶ **35 BC** [meaning "before Christ," now often replaced with BCE, "before the Common Era"]

▶ **AD 1776** [*anno domini*, "in the year of the Lord," now often replaced with *CE*, "Common Era," used after the date: 1776 CE]

▶ **2:00 a.m./p.m.** [*ante* or *post meridiem*, Latin for "before or after midday"] Alternatives are A.M./P.M. or AM/PM. Be consistent.

Do not use these abbreviations and other units of measure when no number is attached to them.

▶ **His family gave him a wallet full of $ to spend on vacation.**
                                                       money

▶ **They arrived late in the p.m.**
                              afternoon.

54d Abbreviate common Latin terms.

In notes, parentheses, and source citations, use abbreviations for common Latin terms. In the body of your text, use the English meaning.

ABBREVIATION	LATIN	ENGLISH MEANING
etc.	et cetera	and so on
i.e.	id est	that is
e.g.	exempli gratia	for example
cf.	confer	compare
NB	nota bene	note well
et al.	et alii	and others

54e Do not abbreviate words to save time and space.

In formal writing, write in full expressions such as the following:

&	and
bros.	brothers [Use "Bros." only if it is part of the official name of a business.]
chap.	chapter
Mon.	Monday
nite	night
NJ	New Jersey [Abbreviate the name of a state only in an address, a note, or a reference.]
no.	number [Use the abbreviation only with a specific number: "No. 17 on the list was deleted."]
Oct.	October [Write names of days and months in full, except in some works-cited lists.]
soc.	sociology [Write names of academic subjects in full.]
thru	through
w/	with

54f Use -*s* (not -'*s*) for the plural form of an abbreviation.

Do not use an apostrophe to make an abbreviation plural (**48e**).

▶ **She has over a thousand CDs.**   ▶ **Both his VCRs are broken.**

55   Numbers

Conventions for using numerals (actual figures) or words vary across the disciplines.

55a Use the conventions of the discipline in which you are writing.

In the humanities and in business letters

Use words for numbers expressible in one or two words and for fractions (*nineteen, fifty-six, two hundred, one-half*).

Use numerals for longer numbers *(326; 5,625; 7,642,000).*

Use a combination of words and numerals for whole millions, billions, and so on *(45 million, 1 billion).*

In scientific and technical writing

Use numerals for all numbers above nine.

Use numerals for numbers below ten only when they show precise measurement, as when they are grouped and compared with other larger numbers *(5 of the 39 participants),* or when they precede a unit of measurement *(6 cm),* indicate a mathematical function *(8%; 0.4),* or represent a specific time, date, age, score, or number in a series.

Use words for fractions: *two-thirds.*

55b Spell out numbers that begin a sentence.

▶ **One hundred twenty-five members voted for the new bylaws.**

▶ **Six thousand fans have already bought tickets.**

ESL NOTE Number before *Hundred, Thousand,* and *Million*

Even after plural numbers, use the singular form of *hundred, thousand,* and *million.* Add *-s* only when there is no preceding number.

▶ **Five *hundred* books were damaged in the flood.**

▶ ***Hundreds* of books were damaged in the flood.** ■

55c Use numerals for giving the time and dates and in other special instances.

In nonscientific writing, use numerals for the following:

Time and dates	6 p.m. on 31 May 1995
Decimals	20.89
Statistics	median score 35
Addresses	16 East 93rd Street
Chapter, page, scene, and line numbers	chapter 5, page 97

Quantities appearing with abbreviations or symbols	6°C (for temperature Celsius), $21, 6'7"
Scores	The Knicks won 89–85.

For percentages and money, numerals and the symbol (*75%*, *$24.67*) are usually acceptable, or you can spell out the expression if it is fewer than four words (*seventy-five percent, twenty-four dollars*).

55d Use -*s* (not -*'s*) for the plural form of numerals.

▶ in the 1980s   ▶ They scored in the 700s in the SATs.

56   Hyphens

Use hyphens to divide a word or to form a compound. For the use of hyphens online, see **57d**.

56a   Hyphens with prefixes

Many words with prefixes are spelled without hyphens: *cooperate, nonrestrictive, unnatural*. Others are hyphenated: *all-inclusive, anti-intellectual*. Always use a hyphen when the main word is a number or a proper noun: *all-American, post-1990*. If you are unsure about whether to insert a hyphen after a prefix, check a dictionary.

56b   Hyphens in compound words

Some compound nouns are written as one word (*toothbrush*), others as two words (*coffee shop*), and still others with one or more hyphens (*role-playing, father-in-law*). Always check an up-to-date dictionary.

Similarly, check a dictionary for compound verbs (*cross-examine, overemphasize*).

Hyphenate compound adjectives preceding a noun: *a well-organized party, a law-abiding citizen, a ten-page essay*. When the modifier follows the noun, no hyphen is necessary: *The party was well organized. Most citizens try to be law abiding. The essay was ten pages long.*

Do not insert a hyphen between an -*ly* adverb and an adjective or after an adjective in its comparative (-*er*) or superlative (-*est*) form: *a tightly fitting suit, a sweeter sounding melody.*

56c Hyphens in spelled-out numbers

Use hyphens when spelling out two-word numbers from twenty-one to ninety-nine. (See **55** for more on spelling out numbers.)

▶ **Twenty-two applicants arrived early in the morning.**

Also use a hyphen in spelled-out fractions: *two-thirds of a cup.*

56d End-of-line hyphens

Most word processors either automatically hyphenate words or automatically wrap words around to the next line. Choose the latter option to avoid the strange and unacceptable word division that sometimes appears with automatic hyphenation.

57 Online Guidelines

57a Punctuation in URLs

Punctuation marks communicate essential information in Web site addresses—uniform resource locators (URLs)—and in e-mail addresses. Be sure to include all marks when you write an address, and if you need to spread a URL over more than one line, split it after a slash (MLA style) or before a punctuation mark. Do not split the protocol (<http://>). In a print source, use angle brackets to enclose e-mail and Web addresses.

▶ **The Modern Language Association, whose Web site is at <http://www.mla.org>, provides examples of documenting Web sources.**

Do not include any additional punctuation within the angle brackets (**57d**).

57b Underlining and italics online

In an online source, URLs are hyperlinked and therefore underlined. When you write for publication on the Web, use italics to indicate titles and other usually underlined expressions.

57c Capital letters online

Lowercase and capital (uppercase) letters are often significant (the technical term is *case-sensitive*) in e-mail addresses and URLs, so keep careful records of which are used. If you make a mistake, you will be unable to make a connection. Similarly, the names of many search engines and online organizations have specialized capitalization (WebCrawler, AltaVista, eBay).

Avoid using capitalized text (the whole text, not just initial letters) in e-mail communications and electronic discussion groups. In both places, the prolonged use of capital letters is regarded as "shouting" and may offend readers. See also **22a**.

57d Hyphens online

Some e-mail addresses include hyphens, so never add a hyphen to indicate that you have split an address between lines. When an e-mail address includes a hyphen, do not break the line at a hyphen because readers will not know whether the hyphen is part of the address.

Technological vocabulary changes quickly. We already have new combined words such as *online* and *download.* You will find both *e-mail* and *email.* The MLA prefers the hyphenated spelling, *e-mail*, but the tendency is for common words like this to move toward closing up. Whichever form you use, use it consistently.

57e Asterisks and abbreviations online

Asterisks (*) Some plain text e-mail providers do not support text features such as italics or underlining. In such cases, use asterisks before and after a word or phrase for emphasis.

▶ They were *decidedly* antagonistic.

Abbreviations Many abbreviations in the electronic world have become standard fare: *CD-ROM, RAM, PIN*, and more. In addition, the informal world of online communication leads to informal abbreviations, at least in personal e-mail messages. Abbreviations such as *BTW* ("by the way") and *TTYTT* ("to tell you the truth") are used in e-mail, but you should avoid them in more formal written communication.

58 Spelling

Get into the habit of using a dictionary and a word processor with a spelling-check program. Even if you check your spelling with computer software, you still need to proofread. A program will not alert you to a correctly spelled word used in the wrong place (such as *cite* used in place of *sight* or *site*). However, you may be called upon to write spontaneously without access to a spelling program or a dictionary, so learn the basic rules in **58a–58e**.

58a Plurals of nouns

Regular plural forms   The regular plural of nouns is formed by adding -*s* or -*es* to the singular word.

essay, essays   match, matches

To form the plural of a compound noun, attach the -*s* to the main noun in the phrase.

mothers-in-law   passersby

Proofread carefully for plural forms that form the plural with -*s* but make other changes, too, such as the following:

-*f* OR -*fe* ⟶ -*ves*	(*Exceptions:* beliefs, roofs, chiefs)
thief, thieves	
wife, wives	

-*o* ⟶ -*oes*	-*o* ⟶ -*os*
potato, potatoes	hero (sandwich), heros
tomato, tomatoes	photo, photos
hero (human), heroes	piano, pianos

CONSONANT + -*y* ⟶ -*ies*	VOWEL + -*y* ⟶ -*ys*
family, families	toy, toys
party, parties	monkey, monkeys

Irregular plural forms (no -*s* ending)

man, men	foot, feet
woman, women	tooth, teeth
child, children	mouse, mice

Plural forms borrowed from other languages Words borrowed from other languages, particularly Greek and Latin words, frequently borrow the plural form of the language, too.

basis, bases	nucleus, nuclei
thesis, theses	vertebra, vertebrae
hypothesis, hypotheses	alumnus (m.), alumni
criterion, criteria	alumna (f.), alumnae

Plural forms with no change Some words have the same form in singular and plural: *moose, deer, sheep, fish.*

58b Doubling consonants

Doubled consonants form a link between spelling and pronunciation because the doubling of a consonant signals a short vowel sound.

Double the consonant when the verb stem contains one vowel plus one consonant in one syllable.

slip, slipping, slipped   hop, hopping, hopped

The doubled consonant preserves the short vowel sound. Compare the pronunciation of *hop, hopping, hopped* with *hope, hoping, hoped.* Compare the vowel sounds in *write, writing,* and *written.*

Double the consonant when the verb stem contains two or more syllables with one vowel plus one consonant in the final stressed syllable.

refer, referring, referred   control, controlling, controlled

Compare *traveling* and *traveled* with the stress on the first syllable. (British English usage, however, is *travelling* and *travelled.*)

Double the consonant when the suffix *-er* or *-est* is added to one-syllable adjectives ending in one vowel plus one consonant.

big, bigger, biggest   hot, hotter, hottest

Double the *l* when adding *-ly* to an adjective that ends in one *-l.*

careful, carefully   successful, successfully

58c Spelling with *-y* or *-i*

VERB ENDS IN CONSONANT + *-y*	*-ies*	*-ying*	*-ied*
cry	cries	crying	cried
study	studies	studying	studied

VERB ENDS IN VOWEL + *-y*	*-ys*	*-ying*	*-yed*
play	plays	playing	played

Exceptions: pay/paid, say/said, lay/laid

VERB ENDS IN VOWEL + *-e*	*-ies*	*-ying*	*-ied*
die	dies	dying	died

TWO-SYLLABLE ADJECTIVE ENDS IN *-y*	*-i* WITH A SUFFIX	
happy	happier, happily, happiness	

TWO-SYLLABLE ADJECTIVE ENDS IN *-ly*	*-lier*	*-liest*
friendly	friendlier	friendliest

58d Internal *ie* or *ei*

This traditional rhyme helps with the decision about whether to use *ie* or *ei*: "I before *e*/ Except after *c*/Or when sounded like *ay*/As in *neighbor* and *weigh*."

The following examples illustrate those guidelines:

i BEFORE *e*	*e* BEFORE *i* AFTER *c*	*e* BEFORE *i* WHEN SOUNDED LIKE *ay*
believe	receive	vein
relief	ceiling	reign
niece	deceive	sleigh

Exceptions:

i BEFORE *e* EVEN AFTER *c*	*e* BEFORE *i*, NOT AFTER *c*	
conscience	height	seize
science	either/neither	foreign
species	leisure	weird

58e Adding a suffix

Keep a silent *-e* before an *-ly* suffix.

immediate, immediately   sure, surely

Exceptions: true, truly; whole, wholly; due, duly

Keep a silent -e before a suffix beginning with a consonant.

state, statement   force, forceful   rude, rudeness

Exceptions: acknowledge, acknowledgment; judge, judgment; argue, argument

Drop a silent -e before a suffix beginning with a vowel.

hope, hoping   observe, observant
write, writing   remove, removable

Exceptions: enforce, enforceable; change, changeable. Retaining the -e preserves the soft sound of the preceding consonant.

With adjectives ending in -le, drop the -le when adding -ly.

sensible, sensibly

With adjectives ending in -ic, add -ally to form the adverb.

basic, basically   characteristic, characteristically

Exception: public, publicly

Pay attention to the suffixes -able, -ible, -ant, -ent, -ify, and -efy.   More words end in *-able* than in *-ible*. Here are some of the most common *-ible* words:

eligible   incredible   irresistible   legible
permissible   responsible   terrible   visible

Unfortunately there are no rules of thumb to help you decide whether to use the suffix *-ant* or *-ent*. Learn common words with these suffixes, and have your dictionary handy for others.

-ANT	-ENT
defiant	confident
observant	convenient
relevant	existent
reluctant	imminent
resistant	independent

The suffix *-ify* is more common than *-efy*. Learn the four *-efy* words:

liquefy   putrefy   rarefy   stupefy

58f   Accents, umlauts, tildes, and cedillas

Words and names in languages other than English may be spelled with special marks over or under a letter, such as an accent (é or è), an umlaut or dieresis (ö), a tilde (ñ), or a cedilla (ç). Your word processing program probably provides these characters (in Microsoft Word, go to Insert/Symbol/Font). If it does not, insert them by hand.

PART 9

For Multilingual/
ESL Writers

With the increased frequency of travel and the rapid growth of instantaneous communication on the Internet, many parts of everyday life are becoming less insular and more global. Movies, radio, TV, telephones, Web communication, and e-mail allow many people in many parts of the world to be in constant touch with news, personalities, cultures, and customs many miles from where they live. Learning to write well often means learning to write for readers of many different linguistic and cultural backgrounds; it may also mean writing in more than one language and even in more than one local version of a language. This section focuses on the type of English commonly expected in academic settings in North America and known as *Standard English* (**37c**).

59 Culture, Language, and Writing

59a English and Englishes

At the same time as we are becoming more aware of diversity and other countries' languages and cultures, we are also experiencing a spread in the use of English. More than 350 million people speak English as their first language, and more than a billion use English as a common language for special communicative, educational, and business purposes within their own communities. However, languages are not fixed and static, and the users of English in their various locations adapt the language for their own use (see the Circle of World English in **37c**). The concept of one English or a "standard" language is thus becoming more fluid, focused more on the context and the language users than on one set of rules. Consequently, the English regarded as standard in North America is not necessarily standard in Australia, the United Kingdom, Hong Kong, Singapore, Indonesia, India, or Pakistan. Scholars see Englishes—varieties of English—in place of a monolithic English with an immutable set of rules.

Varieties of English spoken in different geographical locations even have their own names: Spanglish (Spanish English), Singlish (Singaporean English), and Taglish (Tagalog English, spoken in the Philippines) are just a few examples of language varieties that have developed. English is thus being reinvented around the world, sometimes to the dismay of academics and government officials, sometimes with the approval of citizens who see the adaptation as an act of freedom, even rebellion. The Filipino poet Gemino Abad has claimed: "The English language is now ours. We have colonized it."

Nevertheless, to reach the expectations of the largest number of academic readers, a sense of a standard vocabulary, syntax, and grammar still prevails across boundaries.

59b ESL—difference, not deficit

Students in colleges in North America who grew up speaking another language are often called students of English as a Second Language (ESL), and the abbreviation is commonly used in college curricula, professional literature, and the press. However, the term is not broad enough. Many so-called second-language students speak three or four languages, depending on their life and educational circumstances and the languages spoken at home. Along with being bilingual or multilingual, ESL students frequently are multicultural, equipped with all the knowledge and experience that those terms imply.

If your first language is not English, you may not yet be totally fluent in English, but as you learn, it is a good idea to see your knowledge of language and culture as an advantage rather than a problem. Unlike many monolingual writers (individuals who know only one language), you are able to know different cultures in depth and to switch at will among varied linguistic and rhetorical codes. Rather than having only one language, one culture, and one culturally bound type of writing, you have a broader perspective—more to think about, more to write about, more resources to draw on as you write, and far more comparisons to make among languages, writers, writing, and culture. You bring your culture with you into your writing, and as you do so, you help shape and reshape the culture of North America. The questions in the Key Points box will help you examine your unique situation.

KEY POINTS

Cultural, Rhetorical, and Linguistic Differences

Consider the following questions. Discuss them with members of your family or with friends who share your cultural background.

1. What three features of your home culture stand out for you as significantly different from features of North American culture? List them.

   (These features might relate to customs, holidays, religion, relationships, the structure of family life and responsibility, growing up and adolescence, work and entertainment, or educational practices.)
   (Continued)

(Continued)

2. How have these three cultural issues affected you as a student and as a writer?

3. When you read articles, essays, and letters in your first language and in English, do you notice any differences in approach to the topic and in style? How would you characterize those differences?

4. How does your culture view references to classic texts and to the work of others? Does every reference to another writer's ideas have to be documented? Why or why not? (See **9a** for more on Western views of plagiarism.)

5. Write a paragraph in your first language about your experiences as a writer. What considerations occupied you as you wrote (for example, content, organization, grammar, punctuation)? Are they different from or similar to the considerations you have when you write in English?

6. List five linguistic features of English that cause you trouble when you write—problem areas where you may make mistakes in sentence structure or grammar. Decide why you make mistakes in these areas: Are mistakes caused by the influence of your first language? Or do mistakes occur when you construct a hypothesis about English that turns out to be false? (**59c**)

7. For each of the five problem areas you have isolated, write down the corresponding usage in your first language. Does the comparison show why these particular features of English cause you problems?

8. When you first began to learn English, what variety of English did you learn? Have you noticed anything about it that might make it different from other varieties of English?

59c Learning from errors

Even for learners who have been learning a new language or the conventions of a standard dialect for a while, errors are inevitable. They are not a sign of laziness or stupidity. Welcome and embrace your errors; study them; learn from them. Errors show language learning in progress. If you make no errors while you are learning to speak or write a new language, perhaps you are being too careful and using only what you know is correct. Be willing to take risks and try new words, new expressions, new combinations. That is the way to expand your repertoire.

TechNote ESL Web Sites

The Web sites listed here are particularly useful to multilingual students.

- ESL Resources, Handouts, and Exercises from Purdue University's Online Writing Lab at <http://owl.english.purdue.edu/handouts/esl/index.html>.
- Guide to Grammar and Writing at <http://www.ccc.commnet.edu/grammar/index.htm>.

This is a Capital Community College site for students whose first language is not English. You will find information and quizzes on words, paragraphs, and essays. In addition, you can send in a question to "Ask Grammar" and someone will answer it. The Grammar Logs contain people's questions and answers and thus cover interesting points. ▪

When you make an error, make a note of it. Consider why you made the error—was it, for example, transfer from your first language, a guess, a careless mistake? Or was it the employment of an erroneous hypothesis about English (such as "Many verbs form the past tense with *-ed*; therefore, the past tense form of *swear* is probably *sweared"*— but it is actually *swore*)? Analyzing the causes of errors will help you understand how to edit them and avoid them in the future.

59d Language guide to transfer errors

Errors in writing in a new language can occur when you are grappling with new subject matter and difficult subjects. You concentrate on ideas and clarity, but because no writer can do everything at once, you fail to concentrate on editing.

The language guide on pages 429–433 identifies several problem areas for multilingual/ESL writers. It shows grammatical features (column 1) of specific languages (column 2), features that lead to an error when transferred to English (column 3). An edited Standard English version appears in column 4. Of course, the guide covers neither all linguistic problem areas nor all languages. Rather, it lists a selection, with the goal of being useful and practical. Also included in the guide are references to Caribbean Creole (listed simply as "Creole"), a variety of English with features differing from Standard English. Use the guide to raise your awareness about your own and other languages.

 If you think of a feature or a language that should be included in the guide, please write to the author at the publisher's address or send a message at the publisher's Web site at <http://college .hmco.com/keys.html>. This Web site also provides links to sites specifically designed for multilingual students.

LANGUAGE FEATURES	LANGUAGES	SAMPLE TRANSFER ERRORS IN ENGLISH	EDITED VERSION
ARTICLES (60c–60f)			
No articles	Chinese, Japanese, Russian, Swahili, Thai, Urdu	*Sun is hot.* *I bought book.* *Computer has changed our lives.*	*The sun is hot.* *I bought a book.* *The computer has changed our lives.*
No indefinite article with profession	Arabic, Creole, French, Japanese, Korean, Vietnamese	*He is student.* *She lawyer.*	*He is a student.* *She is a lawyer.*
Definite article with days, months, places, idioms	Arabic	*She is in the bed.* *He lives in the Peru.*	*She is in bed.* *He lives in Peru.*
Definite article used for generalization	Farsi, French, German, Greek, Portuguese, Spanish	*The photography is an art.* *The books are more expensive than the disks.*	*Photography is an art.* *Books are more expensive than disks.*
No article for generalization with singular noun	Creole	*Dog can be blind person's eyes.*	*A dog can be a blind person's eyes.*
Definite article used with proper noun	French, German, Portuguese, Spanish	*The Professor Brackert teaches in Frankfurt.*	*Professor Brackert teaches in Frankfurt.*
No definite article	Hindi, Turkish	*Store on corner is closed.*	*The store on the corner is closed.*
No indefinite article	Korean (uses *one* for *a*; depends on context)	*He ran into one tree.*	*He ran into a tree.*
VERBS AND VERBALS (61)			
Be can be omitted.	Arabic, Chinese, Greek, Russian	*India hotter than Britain.* *She working now.* *He cheerful.*	*India is hotter than Britain.* *She is working now.* *He is cheerful.*

LANGUAGE FEATURES	LANGUAGES	SAMPLE TRANSFER ERRORS IN ENGLISH	EDITED VERSION
No progressive forms	French, German, Greek, Russian	*They still discuss the problem.*	*They are still discussing the problem.*
		When I walked in, she slept.	*When I walked in, she was sleeping.*
No tense inflections	Creole, Chinese, Thai, Vietnamese	*He arrive yesterday.*	*He arrived yesterday.*
		When I was little, I always walk to school.	*When I was little, I always walked to school.*
No inflections for person and number	Creole, Chinese, Japanese, Korean, Russian, Thai	*The singer have a big band.*	*The singer has a big band.*
		She work hard.	*She works hard.*
Past perfect formed with *be*	Arabic	*They were arrived when I called.*	*They had arrived when I called.*
Different tense boundaries from English	Arabic, Chinese, Creole, Farsi, French	*I study here for a year.*	*I have been studying here for a year.*
		He has left yesterday.	*He left yesterday.*
Different limits for passive voice	Creole, Japanese, Korean, Russian, Thai, Vietnamese	*They were stolen their luggage.*	*Their luggage was stolen.*
		My name base on Chinese characters.	*My name is based on Chinese characters.*
		The mess clean up quick.	*The mess was cleaned up quickly.*
		A miracle was happened.	*A miracle (has) happened.*
No -*ing* (gerund) /infinitive distinction	Arabic, Chinese, Farsi, French, Greek, Portuguese, Spanish, Vietnamese	*She avoids to go.*	*She avoids going.*
		I enjoy to play tennis.	*I enjoy playing tennis.*
Infinitive not used to express purpose	Korean	*People exercise for losing weight.*	*People exercise to lose weight.*
Overuse of progressive forms	Hindi, Urdu	*I am wanting to leave now.*	*I want to leave now.*

LANGUAGE FEATURES	LANGUAGES	SAMPLE TRANSFER ERRORS IN ENGLISH	EDITED VERSION
WORD ORDER AND SENTENCE STRUCTURE (62)			
Verb precedes subject	Arabic, Hebrew, Russian, Spanish (optional), Tagalog	*Good grades received every student in the class.*	*Every student in the class received good grades.*
Verb-subject order in dependent clause	French	*I knew what would propose the committee.*	*I knew what the committee would propose.*
Verb after subject and object	Bengali, German (in dependent clause), Hindi, Japanese, Korean, Turkish	*. . . (when) the teacher the money collected.*	*. . . (when) the teacher collected the money.*
Coordination favored over subordination	Arabic	Frequent use of *and* and *so*	
Relative clause or restrictive phrase precedes noun it modifies	Chinese, Japanese, Korean, Russian	*The enrolled in college student . . .* *A nine-meter-high impressive monument . . .* *He gave me a too difficult for me book.*	*The student (who was) enrolled in college . . .* *An impressive monument that is nine meters high . . .* *He gave me a book that was too difficult for me.*
Adverb can occur between verb and object or before verb	French, Spanish, Urdu (before verb)	*I like very much clam chowder.* *They efficiently organized the work.*	*I like clam chowder very much.* *They organized the work efficiently.*
That clause rather than an infinitive	Arabic, French, Hindi, Russian, Spanish	*I want that you stay.* *I want that they try harder.*	*I want you to stay.* *I want them to try harder.*
Inversion of subject and verb rare	Chinese	*She is leaving and so I am.*	*She is leaving, and so am I.*

LANGUAGE FEATURES	LANGUAGES	SAMPLE TRANSFER ERRORS IN ENGLISH	EDITED VERSION
Conjunctions occur in pairs	Chinese, Farsi, Vietnamese	*Although she is rich, but she wears simple clothes.*	*Although she is rich, she wears simple clothes.*
		Even if I had money, I would also not buy that car.	*Even if I had money, I would not buy that car.*
Subject (especially pronoun) can be omitted	Chinese, Italian, Japanese, Spanish, Thai	*Is raining.*	*It is raining.*
Commas set off a dependent clause	German, Russian	*He knows, that we are right.*	*He knows that we are right.*
No exact equivalent of *there is/ there are*	Japanese, Korean, Portuguese, Russian, Thai (adverb of place and *have*)	*This article says four reasons to eat beans.*	*This article says [that] there are four reasons to eat beans.*
		In the garden has many trees.	*There are many trees in the garden.*

NOUNS, PRONOUNS, ADJECTIVES, ADVERBS (60a, 60b, 44, 45)

Personal pronouns restate subject	Arabic, Gujarati, Spanish (optional)	*My father he lives in California.*	*My father lives in California.*
No human/ nonhuman distinction for relative pronoun (*who/which*)	Arabic, Farsi, French, Russian, Spanish, Thai	*Here is the student which you met her last week.*	*Here is the student [whom] you met last week.*
		The people which arrived . . .	*The people who arrived . . .*
Pronoun object included in relative clause	Arabic, Chinese, Farsi, Hebrew	*The house that I used to live in it is big.*	*The house [that] I used to live in is big.*
No distinction between subject and object forms of some pronouns	Chinese, Gujarati, Korean, Thai	*I gave the forms to she.*	*I gave the forms to her.* Or *I gave her the forms.*

LANGUAGE FEATURES	LANGUAGES	SAMPLE TRANSFER ERRORS IN ENGLISH	EDITED VERSION
Nouns and adjectives have same form.	Chinese, Japanese	*She is beauty woman.* *They felt very safety on the train.*	*She is a beautiful woman.* *They felt very safe on the train.*
No distinction between *he* and *she*, *his* and *her*	Bengali, Farsi, Gujarati, Spanish (*his* and *her* only), Thai	*My sister dropped his purse.*	*My sister dropped her purse.*
No plural form after a number	Creole, Farsi	*He has two dog.*	*He has two dogs.*
No plural (or optional) forms of nouns	Chinese, Japanese, Korean, Thai	*Several good book . . .*	*Several good books . . .*
No relative pronouns	Korean	*The book is on the table is mine.*	*The book that is on the table is mine.*
Different perception of countable/uncountable	Japanese, Spanish	*I bought three furnitures.* *He has five chalk.*	*I bought three pieces of furniture. Or I bought three chairs.* *He has five sticks of chalk.*
Adjectives show number.	Spanish	*I have helpfuls friends.*	*I have helpful friends.*
Negative before verb	Spanish	*Jack no like meat.*	*Jack does not like meat.*
Double negatives used routinely	Spanish	*They don't know nothing.*	*They don't know anything. Or They know nothing.*

59e False friends (confusing cognates)

Turning to what you already know as you grapple with writing in English can often be helpful, especially if your first language bears close similarities to English. But while the close linguistic connection may be helpful, you also have to be wary of "false friends," words and structures that seem to translate directly from your first language but do not have the same meaning or connotation at all.

Speakers of Spanish and Portuguese report being embarrassed when they told a North American doctor in English that they were suffering from constipation, only to realize that they were thinking of the word *constipado*, which in their language means "congestion from a cold." These false friends are numerous in several languages, especially European ones. Some common false friends in several languages are listed in the Key Points box, but the list is far from complete. Keep your own list or add to this one as you come across other examples.

KEY POINTS

False Friends

LANGUAGE	MEANING	ENGLISH COGNATE (FALSE FRIEND)	MEANING IN ENGLISH
Spanish			
asistir	attend	assist	help
compromiso	commitment	compromise	settlement, concession
embarazado	pregnant	embarassed	self-conscious
librería	bookstore	library	place storing and lending books
pariente	relative	parent	mother or father
suburbio	slum	suburb	residential area close to a city
Portuguese			
entender	understand	intend	plan
pretender	intend	pretend	assume falsely
tenente	lieutenant	tenant	occupant, rent payer
usar	wear	use	employ for a purpose

(Continued)

(Continued)

LANGUAGE	MEANING	ENGLISH COGNATE (FALSE FRIEND)	MEANING IN ENGLISH
French			
actuellement	now, currently	actually	really
decevoir	disappoint	deceive	trick
demander	ask, request	demand	insist
large	wide	large	big
phrase	sentence	phrase	part of a sentence
sympathique	nice, friendly	sympathetic	understanding others' feelings
German			
also	therefore, well	also	too, in addition
bekommen	get, obtain	become	develop to be
Greek			
agenda	notebook	agenda	plan, program for a meeting
cabaret	bar	cabaret	live entertainment, floor show
idiotic	private	idiotic	stupid
Russian			
salyut	show of fireworks	salute	gesture of respect
simpatichniy	nice, friendly	sympathetic	understanding others' feelings
Japanese			
konsento	electric outlet	consent	agreement, approval

Sources: Information from Hunter College ESL students, supplemented by *Learner English* by Michael Swan and Bernard Smith (Cambridge: Cambridge University Press, 1991) and advice from Ted Johnston, El Paso Community College, and Carlos Hortas, Hunter College.

60 Nouns and Articles

60a Categories of nouns

Nouns in English fall into various categories. A *proper noun* names a unique person, place, or thing and begins with a capital letter: *Walt Whitman, Lake Superior, Grand Canyon, Vietnam Veterans Memorial, Tuesday* (**53b, 60f**). A *common noun* names a general class of persons, places, or things and begins with a lowercase letter: *bicycle, furniture, plan, daughter, home, happiness.* Common nouns can be further categorized as countable and uncountable.

A *countable noun* can have a number before it (*one, two,* and so on) and has a plural form. Countable nouns frequently add *-s* to indicate the plural: *picture, pictures; plan, plans.*

An *uncountable noun* cannot be directly counted. It has no plural form: *furniture, advice, information.*

COMMON NOUNS

COUNTABLE	UNCOUNTABLE
tool, hammer (tools, hammers)	equipment
chair, desk (chairs, desks)	furniture
necklace, earring (necklaces, earrings)	jewelry
view, scene (views, scenes)	scenery
tip, suggestion (tips, suggestions)	advice

The concept of countability varies across languages. Japanese, for example, makes no distinction between countable and uncountable nouns. In French, Spanish, and Chinese, the word for *furniture* is a countable noun; in English, it is not.

60b Uncountable nouns

Some nouns are invariably uncountable in English and are commonly listed as such in a language learners' dictionary such as *The American Heritage ESL Dictionary.* Learn the most common uncountable nouns, and note the ones that end in *-s* but are nevertheless singular:

> *A mass made up of parts:* clothing, equipment, furniture, garbage, homework, information, jewelry, luggage, machinery, money, scenery, traffic, transportation
>
> *Abstract concepts:* advice, courage, education, fun, happiness, health, honesty, information, knowledge

Natural substances: air, blood, cotton, heat, ice, sunshine, water, wood, wool

Diseases: diabetes, influenza, measles

Games: checkers, chess, soccer, tennis

Subjects of study: biology, economics, history, physics

Note the following features of uncountable nouns.

1. An uncountable noun has no plural form:

> ► She gave me s̶e̶v̶e̶r̶a̶l̶ informations̶.
>
>   some

KEY POINTS

What to Use before an Uncountable Noun

Use

The zero article (generalization)	Furniture is expensive.
The (specific reference)	*The* furniture she bought is hideous.
This, that	*This* furniture is tacky.
A possessive pronoun: *my, his, their,* etc.	*Their* furniture is modern.
A quantity word: *some, any, much, less, more, most, a little, a great deal (of), all, other*	She has bought *some* new furniture.

Do not use

A/an (except in phrases *a little* or *a great deal of*)	The room needs a̶ new furniture.
A singular quantity word: *each, every, another*	All furniture E̶v̶e̶r̶y̶ f̶u̶r̶n̶i̶t̶u̶r̶e̶ should be practical.
These, those	That furniture is T̶h̶o̶s̶e̶ f̶u̶r̶n̶i̶t̶u̶r̶e̶s̶ a̶r̶e̶ elegant.
Numerals: *one, two, three,* etc.	two pieces of furniture They bought t̶w̶o̶ f̶u̶r̶n̶i̶t̶u̶r̶e̶s̶.
A plural quantity word: *several, many, a few*	a little furniture She took only a̶ f̶e̶w̶ f̶u̶r̶n̶i̶t̶u̶r̶e̶ with her to her new apartment.

2. An uncountable noun subject is always followed by a singular verb:

>   is
> ▶ **Their advice ~~are~~ useful.**

3. You can give an uncountable noun a countable sense—that is, indicate a quantity of it—by adding a word or phrase that indicates quantity. The noun itself will always remain singular: three pieces of *furniture,* two items of *information,* many pieces of *advice.*

4. Some nouns can be countable in one context and uncountable in another.

GENERAL CLASS (UNCOUNTABLE)

He loves *chocolate.* [all chocolate, in whatever form]

Time flies.

He has red *hair.*

A COUNTABLE ITEM OR ITEMS

She gave him *a chocolate.* [one piece of candy from a box of many chocolates]

They are having *a good time.*

There is *a long grey hair* on her pillow.

60c Basic rules for articles (*a, an,* and *the*)

1. Use *the* whenever a reference to a common noun is specific and unique for writer and reader (see **60d**).

>   the
> ▶ **He loves house that she bought.**
>   ^

2. Do not use *a* or *an* with a plural countable noun.

> ▶ **They cited ̶a̶ reliable surveys.**

3. Do not use *a* or *an* with an uncountable noun.

> ▶ **He gave ̶a̶ helpful advice.**

4. Use *a* before a consonant sound: *a bird, a house, a unicorn.* Use *an* before a vowel sound: *an egg, an ostrich, an hour, an ugly vase.* Take special care with the sounds associated with the letters *h* and *u,* which can have either a consonant or a vowel sound: *a housing project, an honest man.*

5. To make a generalization about a countable noun, do one of the following:

- Use the plural form: *Lions are majestic.*
- Use the singular with *a* or *an*: *A lion is a majestic animal.*
- Use the singular with *the* to denote a classification: *The lion is a majestic animal.*

6. A countable singular noun can never stand alone, so make sure that a countable singular noun is preceded by an article or by a demonstrative pronoun (*this, that*), a number, a singular word expressing quantity, or a possessive.

> A (Every, That, One, Her) nurse
> ▶ ~~Nurse~~ has a difficult job.
>   ^

7. In general, though there are many exceptions, use no article with a singular proper noun (*Mount Everest*), and use *the* with a plural proper noun (*the Himalayas*). See **60f**.

60d *The* for a specific reference

When you write a common noun that both you and your readers know refers to one or more specific persons, places, things, or concepts, use the article *the*. The reference can be specific in two ways: outside the text or inside it.

Specific reference outside the text

▶ I study *the* earth, *the* sun, and *the* moon. [the ones in our solar system]

▶ She closed *the* door. [of the room she was in]

▶ Her husband took *the* dog out for a walk. [the dog belonging to the couple]

Specific reference inside the text

▶ *The* kitten that her daughter brought home had a distinctive black patch above one eye. [a specific kitten—one that was brought home]

▶ Her daughter found *a* kitten. When they were writing a lost-and-found ad that night, they realized that *the* kitten had a distinctive black patch above one eye. [The second mention is of a specific kitten identified earlier—the one her daughter found.]

▶ He bought *the most expensive* bicycle in the store.
[A superlative makes a reference to one specific item.]

60e Which article? Four basic questions

Multilingual writers often have difficulty choosing among the articles *a, an,* and *the* and the *zero article* (no article at all). Languages vary greatly in their representation of the concepts conveyed by English articles (see the Language Guide to Transfer Errors in **59d**).

The Key Points box lists four questions to ask about a noun to decide whether to use an article and, if so, which article to use.

KEY POINTS

Articles at a Glance: Four Basic Questions about a Noun

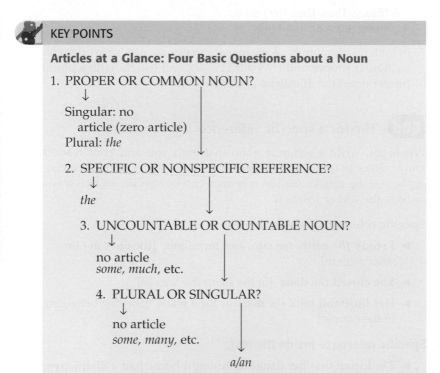

1. PROPER OR COMMON NOUN?
   ↓
   Singular: no
      article (zero article)
   Plural: *the*

2. SPECIFIC OR NONSPECIFIC REFERENCE?
   ↓
   the

3. UNCOUNTABLE OR COUNTABLE NOUN?
   ↓
   no article
   some, much, etc.

4. PLURAL OR SINGULAR?
   ↓
   no article
   some, many, etc.

   a/an

You can use the questions to decide which article, if any, to use with the noun *poem* as you consider the following sentence:

▶ Milton wrote ___?___ moving poem about the blindness that afflicted him before he wrote some of his greatest works.

1. Is the noun a proper noun or a common noun?

   COMMON **Go to question 2.**

2. Does the common noun refer to a specific person, place, thing, or idea known to both writer and reader as unique or is the reference nonspecific?

   NON-SPECIFIC [*Poem* is not identified to the reader in the same way that *blindness* is. We know the reference is to the blindness that afflicted Milton before he wrote some of his greatest works. However, there is more than one "moving poem" in literature. The reference would be specific for readers only if the poem had been previously discussed.] **Go to question 3.**

3. Is the noun uncountable or countable?

   COUNTABLE [We can say *one poem, two poems.*] **Go to question 4.**

4. Is the noun plural or singular?

   SINGULAR [The first letter in the noun phrase *moving poem* is *m,* a consonant sound.] **Use *a* as the article.**

   ▶ **Milton wrote *a* moving poem about the blindness that afflicted him before he wrote some of his greatest works.**

60f Proper nouns and articles

Singular proper nouns: Use with no article Examples are *Stephen King, General Powell, Central America, Italy, Islam, Golden Gate Park, Hollywood Boulevard, Cornell University, Lake Temagami, Mount St. Helens, Thursday, July.* There are, however, many exceptions.

EXCEPTIONS: SINGULAR PROPER NOUNS WITH *THE*

Proper nouns with a common noun and *of* as part of the name: *the University of Texas, the Fourth of July, the Museum of Modern Art, the Statue of Liberty*

Highways: *the New Jersey Turnpike, the Long Island Expressway*

Buildings: *the Eiffel Tower, the Prudential Building*

Bridges: *the Golden Gate Bridge*

Hotels and museums: *the Hilton Hotel, the Guggenheim Museum*

Countries named with a phrase: *the United Kingdom, the Dominican Republic*

Parts of the globe: *the North Pole, the West, the East*

Seas, oceans, gulfs, rivers, and deserts: *the Dead Sea, the Atlantic Ocean, the Persian Gulf, the Yangtze River, the Mojave Desert*

Historical periods and events: *the Enlightenment, the October Revolution*

Plural proper nouns: Use with *the* Examples are *the United States, the Great Lakes, the Himalayas, the Philippines, the Chinese* (people) (**53b**).

61 Verbs and Verbals

A clause needs a complete verb consisting of one of the five verb forms (**41a**) and any necessary auxiliaries. A verbal cannot serve as the verb of a clause. It is a form derived from a verb: an -*ing* form, a past participle (ending in -*ed* for a regular verb), or an infinitive (*to* + base form). Because readers get so much information from verbs and verbals, they have a relatively low level of tolerance for error, so make sure you edit with care.

61a The *be* auxiliary

Inclusion (See also **41c**.) The *be* auxiliary must be included in a verb phrase in English, though in languages such as Chinese, Russian, and Arabic it can be omitted.

> are
> ► They ˄ studying this evening.

> been
> ► They have ˄ studying since dinner.

Sequence (See also **41c**.) What comes after a *be* auxiliary?

- The -*ing* form follows a verb in the active voice: He *is sweeping* the floor.

- The past participle follows a verb in the passive voice: The floor *was swept* yesterday.

61b Modal auxiliary verbs: Form and meaning

The modal auxiliary verbs (*will, would, can, could, shall, should, may, might,* and *must*) do not change form, never add an -*s* ending, and are always followed by a base form without *to*: *could* go, *should* ask, *must* arrive, *might have* seen, *would be* sleeping. (See also **41c**.)

	MEANINGS OF MODAL VERBS	
MEANING	PRESENT AND FUTURE	PAST

1. Intention   *will, shall*   *would*

▶ **She *will* explain.**   ▶ **She said that she *would* explain.**

Shall is used mostly in questions: *Shall I buy that big green ceramic horse?*

2. Ability   *can (am/is/are*   *could (was/were*
                      able to)   *able to)*

▶ **He *can* cook well.** [He is able to cook well.]

▶ **He *could* not read until he was eight.** [He was not able to read until he was eight.]

Do not use *can* and *able to* together:
    am not
▶ **I ~~cannot~~ able to give you that information.**
     ^

3. Permission   *may, might, can, could*   *could, might*

▶ ***May* I open the window?** [*Might* or *could* is more tentative.]

▶ **She said I *could* leave early.**

4. Polite question   *would, could*

▶ ***Would* you please pass the carrots?**

▶ ***Could* you possibly help me?**

5. Speculation   *would (could, might)*   *would (could, might)*
                                           + *have* + past
                                           participle

▶ **If I had time, I *would* bake a cake.**

▶ **If I had studied, I *might have* passed the test.**

(See also **41j**.)

6. Advisability   *should*   *should* + *have*
                                           + past participle

▶ **You *should* go home and rest.**

▶ **You *should have* taken your medication.**
[Implied here is "But you did not."]

	MEANINGS OF MODAL VERBS	
MEANING	PRESENT AND FUTURE	PAST

7. Necessity *must* (or *have to*) *had to* + base form
(stronger than
should)

▶ He *must* apply for a driver's license.

▶ She *had to* apply last month.

8. Prohibition *must* + *not*

▶ You *must not* leave until we tell you to.

9. Expectation *should* *should* + *have*
+ past participle

▶ You *should* receive the check soon.

▶ You *should have* received the check a week ago.

10. Possibility *may, might* *might* + *have*
+ past participle

▶ They *might* be at home now.

▶ She *might have* gone to the movies.

11. Logical *must* *must* + *have*
assumption + past participle

▶ She's late; she *must* be stuck in traffic.

▶ She *must have* taken the wrong route.

12. Repeated past *would* (or *used to*)
action + base form

▶ When I was a child, I *would* spend hours drawing.

61c Verbs followed by an infinitive

Some verbs are followed by an infinitive (*to* + base form).

             V   ┌─Inf─┐
▶ His father *wanted to rule* the family.

These verbs are commonly followed by an infinitive (*to* + base form):

agree	choose	fail	offer	refuse
ask	claim	hope	plan	venture
beg	decide	manage	pretend	want
bother	expect	need	promise	wish

Note any differences between English and your own language. For example, the Spanish word for *refuse* is followed by the equivalent of an *-ing* form.

 to criticize
▶ He refused ~~criticizing~~ the system.

Position of a negative　In a verb + infinitive pattern, the position of the negative affects meaning. Note the difference in meaning that the position of a negative (*not, never*) can create.

▶ He did *not* decide to buy a new car. His wife did.

▶ He decided *not* to buy a new car. His wife was disappointed.

Verb + noun or pronoun + infinitive　Some verbs are followed by a noun or pronoun and then an infinitive. See also **44a** for pronouns before an infinitive.

　　　　　　　　　V　　　　pron.　┌ inf ┐
▶ The librarian *advised them to use* a better database.

Verbs that follow this pattern are *advise, allow, ask, cause, command, convince, encourage, expect, force, help, need, order, persuade, remind, require, tell, urge, want, warn*.

　　Spanish and Russian use a *that* clause after verbs like *want*. In English, however, *want* is followed by an infinitive.

　　　　　　　　　　　　　　　to
▶ Rose wanted ~~that~~ her son ~~would~~ become a doctor.
　　　　　　　　　　　　　　^

Make, let, and have　After these verbs, use a noun or pronoun and a base form of the verb (without *to*).

▶ He *made his son practice* for an hour.

▶ They *let us leave* early.

▶ She *had her daughter wash* the car.

Note the corresponding passive voice structure with *have*:

▶ We *have the car washed* once a month.

61d Verbs followed by an *-ing* verb form used as a noun

▶ I can't help *laughing* at Jon Stewart.

The *-ing* form of a verb used as a noun is known as a *gerund*. The verbs that are systematically followed by an *-ing* form make up a relatively short and learnable list.

admit	consider	enjoy	miss	resist
appreciate	delay	finish	postpone	risk
avoid	deny	imagine	practice	suggest
be worth	discuss	keep	recall	tolerate
can't help	dislike			

inviting
▶ We considered ~~to invite~~ his parents.
              ^

hearing
▶ Most people dislike ~~to hear~~ cell phones at concerts.
                 ^

Note that a negation comes between the verb and the *-ing* form:

▶ During their vacation, they enjoy *not* getting up early every day.

61e Verbs followed by an infinitive or an *-ing* verb form

Some verbs can be followed by either an infinitive or an *-ing* verb form (a gerund) with almost no discernible difference in meaning: *begin, continue, hate, like, love, start.*

▶ She loves *cooking.*   ▶ She loves *to cook.*

The infinitive and the *-ing* form of a few verbs, however *(forget, remember, try, stop)*, signal different meanings:

▶ He remembered *to mail* the letter. [an intention]

▶ He remembered *mailing* the letter. [a past act]

61f *-ing* and *-ed* verb forms used as adjectives

Both the present participle (*-ing* verb form) and the past participle (ending in *-ed* in regular verbs) can function as adjectives (see **41a** and **41g**). Each form has a different meaning: the *-ing* adjective indicates that the word modified produces an effect; the past participle adjective indicates that the word modified has an effect produced on it.

▶ The *boring* cook served baked beans yet again.

[The cook produces boredom. Everyone is tired of baked beans.]

▶ The *bored* cook yawned as she scrambled eggs.

[The cook felt the emotion of boredom as she did the cooking, but the eggs could still be appreciated.]

PRODUCES AN EFFECT	HAS AN EFFECT PRODUCED ON IT
amazing	amazed
amusing	amused
annoying	annoyed
confusing	confused
depressing	depressed
disappointing	disappointed
embarrassing	embarrassed
exciting	excited
interesting	interested
satisfying	satisfied
shocking	shocked
surprising	surprised
worrying	worried

Note: Do not drop the *-ed* ending from a past participle. Sometimes in speech it blends with a following *t* or *d* sound, but in writing the *-ed* ending must be included.

▶ I was surprise͜d to see her wild outfit.

▶ The researchers were ~~worry~~ worried that the results were contaminated.

62 Word Order and Sentence Structure

62a Inclusion of a subject

In some languages, a subject can be omitted. In English, you must include a subject in every clause, even just a filler subject such as *there* or *it*.

>   *there*
> ▶ The director's business partners lost money, and ₐwere immediate effects on the share prices.

>   *it*
> ▶ He went bankrupt because ₐwas too easy to borrow money.

Do not use *it* to point to a long subject that follows.

> ▶ We can say that ~~it~~ |does not matter| the historical period of
>
> the society|.

62b Order of elements

Order of subject, verb, object   Languages vary in their basic word order for the sentence elements of subject (S), verb (V), and direct object (DO). In English, the most commonly occurring sentence pattern is S + V + DO ("Children like candy"). See also **37d**.

>   *Every*   *received good grades*
> ▶ ~~Good grades received every~~ student in the class.ₐ

Expressions of time and place   Put adverbs and adverb phrases of time and place at the beginning or end of a clause, not between the verb and its direct object.

> ▶ The quiz show host congratulated |many times| the winner|.

Descriptive adjective phrases   Put a descriptive adjective phrase after, not before, the noun it modifies.

> ▶ I would go to |known only to me| places|.

62c Direct and indirect objects

Some verbs—such as *give, send, show, tell, teach, find, sell, ask, offer, pay, pass,* and *hand*—can be followed by both a direct object and an indirect object. The indirect object is the person or thing to whom or to which, or for whom or for which, something is done. It follows the verb and precedes the direct object (**37d**).

$\overset{\text{IO}}{\overbrace{\qquad}} \overset{\text{DO}}{\overbrace{\qquad}}$

▶ He gave his mother some flowers.

$\overset{\text{IO}}{\overbrace{\qquad}} \overset{\text{DO}}{\overbrace{\qquad}}$

▶ He gave her some flowers.

An indirect object can be replaced with a prepositional phrase that *follows* the direct object:

$\overset{\text{DO}}{\overbrace{\qquad}} \overset{\text{prepositional phrase}}{\overbrace{\qquad}}$

▶ He gave some flowers to his mother.

Some verbs—such as *explain, describe, say, mention,* and *open*—are never followed by an indirect object. However, they can be followed by a direct object and a prepositional phrase with *to* or *for*:

> to me
▶ She explained ~~me~~ the election process.

> to us
▶ He described ~~us~~ the menu.

Note that *tell*, but not *say*, can take an indirect object.

> told
▶ She ~~said~~ him the secret.

62d Direct and indirect quotations and questions

In a direct quotation or direct question, the exact words used by the speaker are enclosed in quotation marks. In an indirect quotation or indirect question, the writer reports what the speaker said, and quotation marks are not used. Changes also occur in pronouns, time expressions, and verb tenses (**41i**).

$\overbrace{\qquad\text{direct quotation}\qquad}$

▶ He said, "I have lost my notebook."

$\overbrace{\qquad\text{indirect quotation}\qquad}$

▶ He said that he had lost his notebook.

$\overbrace{\quad\text{direct question}\quad}$

▶ He asked, "Have you seen it?"

$\overbrace{\text{indirect question}}$

▶ He asked if we had seen it.

Direct and indirect quotations Usually you must make several changes when you rewrite a direct quotation as an indirect quotation. You will do this often when you write college papers and report the views of others. Avoid shifts from direct to indirect quotations (**40d**).

TYPE OF QUOTATION	EXAMPLE
1. *Direct quotation* with quotation marks and present tense	The young couple said, "The price *is* too high."
Indirect quotation: no quotation marks; tense change (**41i**)	The young couple said that the price *was* too high.
2. *Direct quotation* with first person pronoun and present tense	He insisted, "*I understand* the figures."
Indirect quotation: change to third person pronoun; tense change (**41i**)	He insisted that *he understood* the figures.
3. *Direct quotation* of a command	"Cancel the payment," her husband said.
Indirect quotation: verb + *to*	Her husband *said* [told her] *to* cancel the payment.
4. *Direct quotation* with expressions of time and place	The bankers said that, "*We will* work on this deal *tomorrow.*"
Indirect quotation: expressions of time and place not related to speaker's perspective; tense change (**41i**); change to third person pronoun	The bankers said *that they would* work on *that* deal *the next day.*
5. *Direct quotation* of spoken words and phrases	The clients said, "Well, no thanks; *we won't* wait."
Indirect quotation: spoken words and phrases omitted or rephrased; tense change (**41i**)	The clients thanked the bankers but said *that they would not* wait.

Direct and indirect questions When a direct question is reported indirectly, it loses the word order of a question and also loses the question mark. Sometimes changes in tense are necessary (see **41i**).

DIRECT
QUESTION

                    V   S

The buyer asked, "*Are* the goods ready to be shipped?"

INDIRECT
QUESTION

                          S   V

The buyer asked if the goods *were* ready to be shipped.

DIRECT
QUESTION
    V   S
    The boss asked, "What *are* they doing?"

INDIRECT
QUESTION
    S   V
    The boss asked what they *were* doing.

Use only a question word or *if* or *whether* to introduce an indirect question. Do not use *that* as well.

▶ Her secretary asked ~~that~~ why they sent a letter instead of a fax.

62e Dependent clauses with *although* and *because*

In some languages, a subordinating conjunction (such as *although* or *because*) can be used along with a coordinating conjunction (*but, so*) or a transitional expression (*however, therefore*) in the same sentence. In English, only one is used.

FAULTY
    Although he loved his father, *but* he did not have much opportunity to spend time with him.

POSSIBLE
REVISIONS
    Although he loved his father, he did not have much opportunity to spend time with him.

    He loved his father, *but* he did not have much opportunity to spend time with him.

FAULTY
    Because she had been trained in the church, *therefore* she was sensitive to the idea of audience.

POSSIBLE
REVISIONS
    Because she had been trained in the church, she was sensitive to the idea of audience.

    She had been trained in the church, *so* she was sensitive to the idea of audience.

    She had been trained in the church; *therefore,* she was sensitive to the idea of audience.

See **47e** for the punctuation of transitional expressions.

62f Unnecessary pronouns

Do not restate the simple subject of a sentence as a pronoun. See also **40i**.

▶ Visitors to the Statue of Liberty ~~they~~ have worn the steps down.

▶ The counselor who told me about dyslexia ~~he~~ is a man I will never forget.

In a relative clause introduced by *whom, which,* or *that*, do not include a pronoun that the relative pronoun has replaced. See also **46f**.

▶ The house that I lived in ~~it~~ for ten years has been sold.

62g Order of adjectives

When you use cumulative adjectives (the word *and* cannot be inserted between them as each modifies the whole noun phrase that follows it), follow the conventional sequence before the head noun: (1) size, (2) shape, (3) age, (4) color, (5) geographical origin, (6) architectural style or religion, (7) material, (8) noun used as adjective to modify the head noun.

```
        1    3     5      7      head noun
```
▶ the big old Italian stone house

```
         2         4       6        8       head noun
```
▶ our rectangular green Art Deco storage chest

Do not use commas between cumulative adjectives. For punctuation with other (coordinate) adjectives, see **47g**.

63 Prepositions in Idiomatic Expressions

Prepositions appear in phrases with nouns and pronouns, and they also combine with adjectives and verbs in various ways. Learn the idioms one by one, as you come across them.

63a Expressions with three common prepositions

Learn the uses of prepositions by writing them down in lists when you come across them in your reading. Here is a start:

IN

in July, in 2004, in the morning, in the drawer, in the closet, in Ohio, in Milwaukee, in the cookie jar, in the library stacks, singing in the rain, in the United States, in his pocket, in bed, in school, in class, in Spanish, in time (to participate in an activity), in love, the letter in the envelope

ON

on the menu, on the library shelf, on Saturday, on 9 September 1999, on Union Street, on the weekend, on the roof, a ring on her finger, an article on education, on the moon, on earth, on occasion, on time (punctual), on foot, on the couch, knock on the door, the address on the envelope

AT

at 8 o'clock, at home, at a party, at night, at work

63b Adjective + preposition

When you are writing, use a dictionary to check the specific prepositions used with an adjective.

▶ He is *afraid of* spiders.   ▶ She was *interested in* bees.

Some idiomatic adjective + preposition combinations are *afraid of, ashamed of, aware of, fond of, full of, jealous of, proud of, suspicious of, tired of, interested in, grateful to* (someone), *grateful for* (something), *responsible to* (someone), *responsible for* (something), *anxious about, content with,* and *satisfied with.*

63c Verb + preposition

Some idiomatic verb + preposition combinations are *concentrate on, congratulate* (someone) *on* (success or good fortune), *depend on, insist on, rely on, consist of, take care of, apologize to* (someone) *for* (an offense or error), *blame* (someone) *for* (an offense or error), *thank* (someone) *for* (a gift or favor), *complain about, worry about, laugh at, smile at, explain* (facts) *to* (someone), *throw* (an object) *to* (someone waiting to catch it), *throw* (an object) *at* (someone not expecting it), *arrive in* (a country or city), and *arrive at* (a building or an event). Keep a list of others you notice.

63d Phrasal verbs

Prepositions and a few adverbs (such as *away* and *forward*) can combine with verbs in such a way that they no longer function as prepositions or ordinary adverbs. They are then known as *particles*. Only a few languages other than English—Dutch, German, and Swedish, for example—have this verb-plus-particle (preposition or adverb) combination, which is called a *phrasal verb*. Examples of English phrasal verbs are *put off* and *put up with*.

The meaning of a phrasal verb is entirely different from the meaning of the verb alone. Note the idiomatic meanings of some common phrasal verbs.

break down [stop functioning]	run across [meet unexpectedly]
get over [recover from]	run out [become used up]
look into [examine]	take after [resemble]

Always check the meanings of such verbs in a specialized dictionary such as *The American Heritage English as a Second Language Dictionary*.

A particle can be followed by a preposition to make a three-word combination:

▶ She *gets along with* everybody. [She is friendly toward everybody.]

Other three-word verb combinations are

catch up with [draw level with]	look up to [admire]
look down on [despise]	put up with [endure]
look forward to [anticipate]	stand up for [defend]

Position of direct objects with two-word phrasal verbs Some two-word transitive phrasal verbs are separable. The direct object of these verbs can come between the verb and the accompanying particle.

▶ She *put off* her dinner party.   [She postponed her dinner party.]

▶ She *put* her dinner party *off*.

When the direct object is a pronoun, however, always place the pronoun between the verb and the particle.

▶ She *put* it *off*.

Some commonly used phrasal verbs that follow that principle are listed here. They can be separated by a noun as a direct object; they must be separated when the direct object is a pronoun.

call off [cancel]	give up [surrender]	make up [invent]
fill out [complete]	leave out [omit]	turn down [reject]
find out [discover]	look up [locate]	turn off [stop]

Most dictionaries list phrasal verbs that are associated with a particular verb, along with their meanings and examples. Develop your own list of such verbs from your reading.

63e Preposition + *-ing* verb form used as a noun

The *-ing* verb form that functions as a noun (the *gerund*) frequently occurs after a preposition.

▶ They congratulated him *on winning* the prize.

▶ Sue expressed interest *in participating* in the fundraiser.

▶ He ran three miles *without stopping.*

▶ The cheese is the right consistency *for spreading.*

Note: Take care not to confuse *to* as a preposition with *to* used in an infinitive. When *to* is a preposition, it is followed by a noun, a pronoun, a noun phrase, or an *-ing* form, not by the base form of a verb.

⌐infinitive ⌐
▶ They want *to adopt* a child.

preposition + *-ing* form (gerund)
▶ They are looking forward *to adopting* a child.

Check which to use by testing a noun replacement:

▶ They are looking forward to parenthood.

Note also *be devoted to, be/get used to* (see **63f**).

63f The difference between *get used to* and *used to*

For multilingual writers of English, the distinction between *used to* + base form and *be/get used to* + *-ing* (gerund) is difficult.

▶ He *used to work* long hours.

[He did in the past but doesn't anymore. The infinitive form follows *used* in this sense.]

▶ Air traffic controllers *are used to dealing* with emergencies.

[They are accustomed to it. The *-ing* form follows *be/get used to.*]

64 Frequently Asked ESL Editing Questions

64a When do I use *no* and *not*?

Not is an adverb that negates a verb, an adjective, or another adverb. *No* is an adjective and therefore modifies a noun.

▶ She is *not* wealthy. ▶ She is *not* really poor.

▶ The author does *not* intend to deceive the reader.

▶ The author has *no* intention of deceiving the reader.

64b What is the difference between *too* and *very*?

Both *too* and *very* intensify an adjective or adverb, but they are not interchangeable. *Too* indicates excess. *Very* indicates degree, meaning "extremely."

▶ It was *very* hot.

▶ It was *too* hot to sit outside. [*Too* occurs frequently in the pattern *too* + adjective or adverb + *to* + base form of verb.]

▶ The Volvo was *very* expensive, but he bought it anyway.

▶ The Volvo was *too* expensive, so he bought a Ford instead.

64c Does *few* mean the same as *a few*?

A few is the equivalent of *some*. *Few* is the equivalent of *hardly any*; it has more negative connotations than *a few*. Both expressions are used with countable plural nouns. Although *a* is not generally used with plural nouns, the expression *a few* is an exception.

some

▶ She feels fortunate because she has *a few* helpful colleagues.

hardly any

▶ She feels depressed because she has *few* helpful colleagues.

You might prefer to use only the more common *a few* and use *hardly any* in sentences where the context demands *few*. Similar expressions used with uncountable nouns are *little* and *a little*.

▸ She has *a little* time to spend on work-related projects.

⌈ some ⌉

hardly any

▸ She has *little* time to spend on recreation.

64d How do I distinguish *most, most of,* and *the most*?

Most expresses a generalization, meaning "nearly all."

▸ *Most* Americans like ice cream.

When a word like *the, this, these, that,* or *those* or a possessive prono (such as *my, their*) precedes the noun to make it specific, *most* used. The meaning is "nearly all of."

▸ I did *most of* this needlework.

▸ *Most of* his colleagues work long hours.

The most is used to compare more than two people or iter

▸ Bill is *the most* efficient of all the technicians.

64e What structures are used with *easy, har* and *difficult*?

The adjectives *easy, hard,* and *difficult* cause problems f Japanese and Chinese. All of the following patterns ar English.

▸ It is *easy* for me to change a fuse.

▸ It is *easy* to change a fuse.

▸ To change a fuse is *easy* for me.

▸ To change a fuse is *easy*.

▸ Changing a fuse is *easy* for me.

▸ Changing a fuse is *easy*.

▸ I find it *easy* to change a fuse.

However, a sentence like the following needs to

into one of the patterns listed above or as follow

think it is

▸ I ~~am~~ *easy* to change a fuse.
   ^

64f How do I use *it* and *there* to begin a sentence?

Use *there* to indicate that something exists (or existed) or happens (or happened). See also **30b**.

> There
> ► I̶t̶ was a royal wedding in my country two years ago.

> There
> ► I̶t̶ is a tree on the corner of my block.

Use *it* for weather, distance, time, and surroundings.

> ► It is a long way to Tipperary. ► It is hot.

Use *it* also in expressions such as *it is important, it is necessary,* and *it is obvious,* emphasizing the details that come next. See also **30b**.

> ► It is essential for all of you to sign your application forms.

> *It* or *there* cannot be omitted as a filler subject.

> it
> ► As you can see, is dark out already.
>   ^

g Which possessive pronoun do I use: *his* or *her*?

ne languages, the form of the pronoun used to indicate posses-
anges according to the gender of the noun that follows it, not
ng to the pronoun's antecedent. In French, for instance, *son* or
s "his" or "her," and in Spanish *su* means *his* or *her*, the form
termined by the noun the pronoun modifies.

> e et sa mère   [Marie and her mother]

> et sa mère   [Pierre and his mother]

> son père   [Pierre and his father]

In Engl
always d ever, the gender of a possessive (*his, her,* or *its*) is
ed by the antecedent.

> ► I met M
>   and her mother. ► I met Pierre and his mother.

PART 10

Glossaries and Index

65 Glossary of Usage

Listed in this glossary are words that are often confused (*affect/effect, elicit/illicit*) or misspelled (*alright, it's/its*). Also listed are nonstandard words (*irregardless, theirself*) and colloquial expressions (*a lot, OK*) that should be avoided in formal writing.

a, an Use *an* before words that begin with a vowel sound (the vowels are *a, e, i, o,* and *u*): *an apple, an hour* (silent *h*). Use *a* before words that begin with a consonant sound: *a planet, a yam, a ukelele, a house* (pronounced *h*).

accept, except, expect *Accept* is a verb: *She accepted the salary offer. Except* is usually a preposition: *Everyone has gone home except my boss. Expect* is a verb: *They expect to visit New Mexico on vacation.*

adapt, adopt *Adapt* means "to adjust" and is used with the preposition *to: It takes people some time to adapt to the work routine after college. Adopt* means "to take into a family" or "to take up and follow": *The couple adopted a three-year-old child. The company adopted a more aggressive policy.*

advice, advise *Advice* is a noun: *Take my advice and don't start smoking. Advise* is a verb: *He advised his brother to stop smoking.*

affect, effect In their most common uses, *affect* is a verb, and *effect* is a noun. To *affect* is to have an *effect* on something: *Pesticides can affect health. Pesticides have a bad effect on health. Effect,* however, can be used as a verb meaning "to bring about": *The administration hopes to effect new health care legislation. Affect* can also be used as a noun in psychology, meaning "a feeling or emotion."

all ready, already *All ready* means "totally prepared": *The students were all ready for their final examination. Already* is an adverb meaning "by this time": *He has already written the report.*

all right, alright *All right* is standard. *Alright* is nonstandard.

all together, altogether *All together* is used to describe acting simultaneously: *As soon as the boss had presented the plan, the managers spoke up all together. Altogether* is an adverb meaning "totally," often used before an adjective: *His presentation was altogether impressive.*

allude, elude *Allude* means "to refer to": *She alluded to his height. Elude* means "to avoid": *He eluded her criticism by leaving the room.*

allusion, illusion The noun *allusion* means "reference to": *Her allusion to his height made him uncomfortable.* The noun *illusion* means "false idea": *He had no illusions about being Mr. Universe.*

almost, most Do not use *most* to mean *almost: Almost* [not *Most*] *all my friends are computer literate.*

alot, a lot of, lots of　*Alot* is nonstandard. *A lot of* and *lots of* are regarded by some as informal for *many* or *a great deal of: They have performed many research studies.*

ambiguous, ambivalent　*Ambiguous* is used to describe a phrase or act with more than one meaning: *The ending of the movie is ambiguous; we don't know if the butler really committed the murder. Ambivalent* describes uncertainty and the coexistence of opposing attitudes and feelings: *The committee is ambivalent about the proposal for restructuring the company.*

among, between　Use *between* for two items, *among* for three or more: *I couldn't decide between red or blue. I couldn't decide among red, blue, or green.*

amount, number　*Amount* is used with uncountable expressions: *a large amount of money, work, or effort. Number* is used with countable plural expressions: *a large number of people, a number of attempts.* See **60b** ESL.

an　See *a.*

anyone, any one　*Anyone* is a singular indefinite pronoun meaning "anybody": *Can anyone help me? Any one* refers to one from a group and is usually followed by *of* + plural noun: *Any one* [as opposed to any two] *of the suggestions will be considered acceptable.*

anyplace　The standard *anywhere* is preferable.

anyway, anywhere, nowhere; anyways, anywheres, nowheres　*Anyway, anywhere,* and *nowhere* are standard forms. The others, ending in *-s,* are not.

apart, a part　*Apart* is an adverb: *The old book fell apart. A part* is a noun phrase: *I'd like to be a part of that project.*

as, as if, like　See *like.*

as regards, in regard to　See *in regard to.*

awful　Avoid using *awful* to mean "bad" or "extremely": <u>not</u> *He's awful late* <u>but</u> *He's extremely late.*

a while, awhile　*A while* is a noun phrase: *a while ago; for a while. Awhile* is an adverb meaning "for some time": *They lived awhile in the wilderness.*

bad, badly　*Bad* is an adjective, *badly* an adverb. Use *bad* after linking verbs (such as *am, is, become, seem*): *They felt bad after losing the match.* Use *badly* to modify a verb: *They played badly.*

because, because of　*Because* is a subordinating conjunction used to introduce a dependent clause: *Because it was raining, we left early. Because of* is a two-word preposition: *We left early because of the rain.*

being as, being that　Avoid. Use *because* instead: *Because* [not *Being as*] *I was tired, I didn't go to class.*

belief, believe *Belief* is a noun: *She has radical beliefs. Believe* is a verb: *He believes in an afterlife.*

beside, besides *Beside* is a preposition meaning "next to": *Sit beside me. Besides* is a preposition meaning "except for": *He has no assistants besides us. Besides* is also an adverb meaning "in addition": *I hate horror movies. Besides, there's a long line.*

better See *had better.*

between See *among.*

breath, breathe The first word is a noun, the second a verb: *Take three deep breaths. Breathe in deeply.*

can't hardly This expression is nonstandard. See *hardly.*

cite, site, sight *Cite* means "to quote or mention"; *site* is a noun meaning "location"; *sight* is a noun meaning "view": *She cited the page number in her paper. They visited the original site of the abbey. The sight of the skyline from the plane produced applause from the passengers.*

complement, compliment As verbs, *complement* means "to complete or add to something," and *compliment* means "to make a flattering comment about someone or something": *The wine complemented the meal. The guests complimented the hostess on the fine dinner.* As nouns, the words have meanings associated with the verbs: *The wine was a fine complement to the meal. The guests paid the hostess a compliment.*

compose, comprise *Compose* means "to make up"; *comprise* means "to include." *The conference center is composed of twenty-five rooms. The conference center comprises twenty-five rooms.*

conscience, conscious *Conscience* is a noun meaning "awareness of right and wrong." *Conscious* is an adjective meaning "awake" or "aware." *Her conscience troubled her after the accident. The victim was still not conscious.*

continual, continuous *Continual* implies repetition; *continuous* implies lack of a pause. *The continual interruptions made the lecturer angry. Continuous rain for two hours stopped play.*

could care less This expression is often used but is regarded by some as nonstandard. In formal English, use it only with a negative: *They could not care less about their work.*

custom, customs, costume All three words are nouns. *Custom* means "habitual practice or tradition": *a family custom. Customs* refers to taxes on imports or to the procedures for inspecting items entering a country: *go through customs at the airport.* A *costume* is "a style of dress": *a Halloween costume.*

dairy, diary The first word is associated with cows and milk, the second with daily journal writing.

decent, descent, dissent *Decent* is an adjective meaning "good" or "respectable": *decent clothes, a decent salary. Descent* is a noun meaning "way down" or "lineage": *She is of Scottish descent. Dissent,* used both as a noun and a verb, refers to disagreement: *The dissent about freedom led to civil war.*

desert, dessert *Desert* can be pronounced two ways and can be a noun with the stress on the first syllable *(the Mojave Desert)* or a verb with the stress on the second syllable: *When did he desert his family?* The noun *desert* means "a dry, often sandy, environment." The verb *desert* means "to abandon." *Dessert* (with stress on the second syllable) is the sweet course at the end of a meal.

different from, different than Standard usage is *different from: She looks different from her sister.* However, *different than* appears frequently in speech and informal writing, particularly when *different from* would require more words: *My writing is different than* [in place of *different from what*] *it was last semester.*

discreet, discrete *Discreet* means "tactful": *Be discreet when you talk about your boss. Discrete* means "separate": *He writes on five discrete topics.*

disinterested, uninterested *Disinterested* means "impartial or unbiased": *The mediator was hired to make a disinterested settlement. Uninterested* means "lacking in interest": *He seemed uninterested in his job.*

dissent, decent, descent See *decent.*

due to the fact that, owing to the fact that Wordy. Use *because* instead: *They stopped the game because* [not *due to the fact that*] *it was raining.*

each, every These are singular pronouns; use them with a singular verb. See also **43h** and **44d.**

each other, one another Use *each other* with two; use *one another* with more than two: *The twins love each other. The triplets all love one another.*

effect See *affect.*

e.g. Use *for example* or *for instance* in place of this Latin abbreviation.

elicit, illicit *Elicit* means "to get or draw out": *The police tried in vain to elicit information from the suspect's accomplice. Illicit* is an adjective meaning "illegal": *Their illicit deals landed them in prison.*

elude See *allude.*

emigrate, immigrate *Emigrate from* means "to leave a country"; *immigrate to* means "to move to another country": *They emigrated from Ukraine and immigrated to the United States.* The noun forms *emigrant* and *immigrant* are derived from the verbs.

eminent, imminent *Eminent* means "well known and noteworthy": *an eminent lawyer. Imminent* means "about to happen": *an imminent disaster.*

etc. This abbreviation for the Latin *et cetera* means "and so on." Do not let a list trail off with *etc.* Rather than *They took a tent, a sleeping bag, etc.,* write *They took a tent, a sleeping bag, cooking utensils, and a stove.*

every, each See *each.*

everyday, every day *Everyday* (one word) is an adjective meaning "usual": *Their everyday routine is to break for lunch at 12:30. Every day* (two words) is an adverbial expression of frequency: *I get up early every day.*

except, expect See *accept.*

explicit, implicit *Explicit* means "direct": *She gave explicit instructions. Implicit* means "implied": *A tax increase is implicit in the proposal.*

farther, further Both words can refer to distance: *She lives farther (further) from the campus than I do. Further* also means "additional" or "additionally": *The management offered further incentives. Further, the union proposed new work rules.*

female, male Use these words as adjectives, not as nouns in place of *man* and *woman: There are only three women* [not *females*] *in my class. We are discussing female conversational traits.*

few, a few For the distinction, see **64c** ESL.

fewer, less Formal usage demands *fewer* with plural countable nouns *(fewer holidays), less* with uncountable nouns *(less sunshine).* However, in informal usage, *less* with plural nouns commonly occurs, especially with *than: less than six items, less than ten miles, fifty words or less.* In formal usage, *fewer* is preferred.

first, firstly Avoid *firstly, secondly,* and so on when listing reasons or examples. Instead, use *first, second.*

flaunt, flout *Flaunt* means "to show [something] off," or "to display in a proud or boastful manner." *Flout* means "to defy or to show scorn for." *When she flaunted her jewels, she flouted good taste.*

get married to, marry These expressions can be used interchangeably: *He will get married to his fiancée next week. She will marry her childhood friend next month.* The noun form is *marriage: Their marriage has lasted thirty years.*

had better Include *had* in Standard English, although it is often omitted in advertising and in speech: *You had better* [not *You better*] *try harder.*

hardly This is a negative word. Do not use it with another negative: <u>not</u> *He couldn't hardly walk* <u>but</u> *He could hardly walk.*

height Note the spelling and pronunciation: not *heighth.*

heroin, heroine Do not confuse these words. *Heroin* is a drug; *heroine* is a brave woman. *Hero* may be used for an admirable person of either sex.

hisself Nonstandard; instead, use *himself*.

hopefully This word is an adverb meaning "in a hopeful manner" or "with a hopeful attitude": *Hopefully, she e-mailed her résumé.* Avoid using *hopefully* in place of *I hope that:* not *Hopefully, she will get the job* but *I hope that she will get the job.*

illicit, elicit See *elicit*.

illusion, allusion See *allusion*.

immigrate, emigrate See *emigrate*.

imminent, eminent See *eminent*.

implicit, explicit See *explicit*.

imply, infer *Imply* means "to suggest in an indirect way": *He implied that further layoffs were unlikely.* *Infer* means "to guess" or "to draw a conclusion": *I inferred that the company was doing well.*

incredible, incredulous *Incredible* means "difficult to believe": *The violence of the storm was incredible.* *Incredulous* means "skeptical, unable to believe": *They were incredulous when he told them about his daring exploits in the whitewater rapids.*

in regard to, as regards Use one or the other. Do not use the nonstandard *in regards to.*

irregardless Nonstandard; instead use *regardless: He selected a major regardless of the preparation it would give him for a career.*

it's, its The apostrophe in *it's* signals not a possessive but a contraction of *it is* or *it has. Its* is the possessive form of the pronoun *it: The city government agency has produced its final report. It's available upon request.* See also **48f.**

kind, sort, type In the singular, use each of these with *this* and a singular noun: *this type of book.* Use in the plural with *these* and a plural noun: *these kinds of books.*

kind of, sort of Do not use these to mean "somewhat" or "a little." *The pace of the baseball game was somewhat* [not *kind of*] *slow.*

knew, new *Knew* is the past tense of the verb *know. New* is an adjective meaning "not old."

lend, loan *Lend* is a verb, and *loan* is ordinarily used as a noun: *Our cousins offered to lend us some money, but we refused the loan.*

less, fewer See *fewer*.

lie, lay Be sure not to confuse these verbs. *Lie* does not take a direct object; *lay* does. See **41b.**

like, as, as if In formal usage, *as* and *as if* are subordinating conjunctions and introduce dependent clauses: *She walks as her father does. She looks as if she could eat a big meal. Like* is a preposition and is followed by a noun or pronoun, not by a clause: *She looks like her father.* In speech, however, and increasingly in writing, *like* is often used where formal usage dictates *as* or *as if: She walks like her father does. He looks like he needs a new suit.*

loan See *lend, loan.*

loose, lose *Loose* is an adjective meaning "not tight": *This jacket is comfortable because it is so loose. Lose* is a verb (the past tense form and past participle are *lost*): *Many people lose their jobs in a recession.*

lots of, alot, a lot of See *alot.*

marital, martial *Marital* is associated with marriage, *martial* with war.

may be, maybe *May be* consists of a modal verb followed by the base form of the verb *be; maybe* is an adverb meaning "perhaps." If you can replace the expression with *perhaps,* make it one word: *They may be there already, or maybe they got caught in traffic.*

most, almost See *almost.*

myself Use only as a reflexive pronoun *(I told them myself)* or as an intensive pronoun *(I myself told them).* Do not use *myself* as a subject pronoun: not *My sister and myself won* but *My sister and I won.*

nowadays All one word. Be sure to include the final *-s.*

nowhere, nowheres See *anyway.*

number, amount See *amount.*

off, off of Use only *off,* not *off of: She drove the car off* [not *off of*] *the road.*

oftentimes Do not use. Prefer *often.*

OK, O.K., okay Reserve these forms for informal speech and writing. Choose another word in a formal context: not *Her performance was OK* but *Her performance was satisfactory.*

one another See *each other.*

owing to the fact that See *due to the fact that.*

passed, past *Passed* is a past tense verb form: *They passed the deli on the way to work. He passed his exam. Past* can be a noun *(in the past),* an adjective *(in past times),* or a preposition *(She walked past the bakery).*

plus Do not use *plus* as a coordinating conjunction or a transitional expression. Use *and* or *moreover* instead: *He was promoted, and* [not *plus*] *he received a bonus.* Use *plus* as a preposition meaning "in addition to": *His salary plus his dividends placed him in a high tax bracket.*

precede, proceed *Precede* means "to go or occur before": *The Roaring Twenties preceded the Great Depression. Proceed* means "to go ahead": *After you pay the fee, proceed to the examination room.*

prejudice, prejudiced   *Prejudice* is a noun. *Prejudice is harmful to society. Prejudiced* is a past participle verb form: *He is prejudiced against ethnic minorities.*

pretty   Avoid using *pretty* as an intensifying adverb. Use *really, very, rather,* or *quite: The stew tastes very* [not *pretty*] *good.* Often, however, the best solution is to avoid using any adverb: *The stew tastes good.*

principal, principle   *Principal* is a noun *(the principal of a school)* or an adjective meaning "main" or "most important": *His principal motive was monetary gain. Principle* is a noun meaning "standard or rule": *He always acts on his principles.*

quite, quiet   Do not confuse the adverb *quite,* meaning "very," with the adjective *quiet* ("still" or "silent"): *We were all quite relieved when the audience became quiet.*

quote, quotation   *Quote* is a verb. Do not use it as a noun; use *quotation: The quotation* [not *quote*] *from Walker tells the reader a great deal.*

real, really   *Real* is an adjective; *really* is an adverb. Do not use *real* as an intensifying adverb: *She acted really* [not *real*] *well.*

reason is because   Avoid *the reason is because.* Instead, use *the reason is that* or rewrite the sentence. See **40f.**

regardless   See *irregardless.*

respectable, respectful, respective   *Respectable* means "presentable, worthy of respect": *Wear some respectable shoes to your interview. Respectful* means "polite or deferential": *Parents want their children to be respectful to adults. Respective* means "particular" or "individual": *The friends of the bride and the groom sat in their respective seats in the church.*

rise, raise   *Rise* is an intransitive verb: *She rises early every day. Raise* is a transitive verb: *We raised alfalfa last summer.* See **41b.**

sale, sell   *Sale* is a noun: *The sale of the house has been postponed. Sell* is a verb: *They are still trying to sell their house.*

should (could, might) of   Nonstandard; instead use *should have: You should have paid.* See **41c,** pp. 332–333.

since   Use this subordinating conjunction only when time or reason is clear: *Since you insist on helping, I'll let you paint this bookcase.* Unclear: *Since he got a new job, he has been happy.*

site, sight, cite   See *cite.*

sometimes, sometime, some time   The adverb *sometimes* means "occasionally": *He sometimes prefers to eat lunch at his desk.* The adverb *sometime* means "at an indefinite time": *I read that book sometime last year.* The noun phrase *some time* consists of the noun *time* modified by the quantity word *some: After working for Honda, I spent some time in Brazil.*

sort, type, kind   See *kind*.

sort of, kind of   See *kind of*.

stationary, stationery   *Stationary* is an adjective meaning "not moving" (*a stationary vehicle*); *stationery* is a noun referring to writing paper.

supposedly   Use this, not *supposably: She is supposedly a great athlete*.

than, then   *Then* is a time word; *than* must be preceded by a comparative form: *bigger than, more interesting than*.

their, there, they're   *Their* is a pronoun indicating possession; *there* indicates place or is used as a filler in the subject position in a sentence; *they're* is the contracted form of *they are: They're over there, guarding their luggage*.

theirself, theirselves, themself   Nonstandard; instead, use *themselves*.

to, too, two   Do not confuse these words. *To* is a sign of the infinitive and a common preposition; *too* is an adverb meaning *also; two* is the number: *She is too smart to agree to report to two bosses*.

undoubtedly   This is the correct word, not *undoubtably*.

uninterested, disinterested   See *disinterested*.

used to, get (become) used to   These expressions share the common form *used to*. But the first, expressing a past habit that no longer exists, is followed by the base form of a verb: *He used to wear his hair long*. (Note that after *not*, the form is *use to: He did not use to have a beard*.) In the expression *get (become) used to, used to* means "accustomed to" and is followed by a noun or an *-ing* form: *She couldn't get used to driving on the left when she was in England*. See also **63f** ESL.

way, ways   Use *way* to mean "distance": *He has a way to go. Ways* in this context is nonstandard.

wear, were, we're   *Wear* is a verb meaning "to have on as covering adornment or protection" (*wearing a helmet*); *were* is a past tense form of *be; we're* is a contraction for *we are*.

weather, whether   *Weather* is a noun; *whether* is a conjunction: *The weather will determine whether we go on the picnic*.

who, whom, which, that   See **46a** and **46g**.

whose, who's   *Whose* is a possessive pronoun: *Whose goal was that? Who's* is a contraction of *who is* or *who has: Who's the player whose pass was caught? Who's got the ball?*

your, you're   *Your* is a pronoun used to show possession. *You're* is a contraction for *you are: You're wearing your new shoes today, aren't you?*

66 **Glossary of Grammatical Terms**

absolute phrase   A phrase consisting of a noun phrase followed by a verbal or a prepositional phrase and modifying an entire sentence: *Flags flapping in the wind,* the stadium looked bleak.

acronym   A pronounceable word formed from the initials of an abbreviation: *NATO, MADD, NOW.* **51a.**

active voice   Attribute of a verb when its grammatical subject performs the action: The dog *ate* the cake. **42.** See also *passive voice.*

adjective   The part of speech that modifies a noun or pronoun: She wears *flamboyant* clothes. His cap is *orange.* **37d, 45, 62g** ESL. See also *comparative; coordinate adjective; cumulative adjective; superlative; parts of speech.*

adjective clause   A dependent clause beginning with a relative pronoun *(who, whom, whose, which,* or *that)* and modifying a noun or pronoun: The writer *who won the prize* was elated. Also called a *relative clause.* **37d, 46.**

adverb   The part of speech that modifies a verb, an adjective, another adverb, or a clause: She ran *quickly.* He is *really* successful. The children were *well* liked. Many adverbs end in *-ly.* **37d, 45.** See also *comparative; conjunctive adverb; frequency adverb; superlative; parts of speech.*

adverb clause   A dependent clause that modifies a verb, an adjective, or an adverb and begins with a subordinating conjunction: He left early *because he was tired.* **37d.**

agent   The person or thing doing the action described by a verb: *His sister* won the marathon. The marathon was won by *his sister.* **42a.**

agreement   The grammatical match in person, number, and gender between a verb and its subject or between a pronoun and its antecedent (the word the pronoun refers to): The *benefits continue; they are* pleasing. The *benefit continues; it is* pleasing. **43, 44d.**

antecedent   The noun that a pronoun refers to: My son who lives nearby found a *kitten. It* was black and white. **44c, 44d, 46a.**

appositive phrase   A phrase occurring next to a noun and used to describe it: His father, *a factory worker,* is running for office. **38a, 44a, 47d.**

article   *A, an* (indefinite articles), or *the* (definite article). Also called a *determiner.* **60c** ESL, **60d** ESL, **60e** ESL.

auxiliary verb   A verb that joins with another verb to form a complete verb. Auxiliary verbs are forms of *do, be,* and *have,* as well as the modal auxiliary verbs. **37d, 41c.** See also *modal auxiliary verb.*

base form   The dictionary form of a verb, used in an infinitive after *to: see, eat, go, be.* **41a.**

clause A group of words that includes a subject and a verb. **37d.** See also *dependent clause; independent clause.*

cliché An overused, predictable expression: *as cool as a cucumber.* **33g.**

collective noun A noun naming a collection of people or things that are regarded as a unit: *team, jury, family.* For agreement with collective nouns, see **43f, 44d.**

comma splice The error that results when two independent clauses are incorrectly joined with only a comma. **39.**

common noun A noun that does not name a unique person, place, or thing. **60 ESL.** See also *proper noun.*

comparative The form of an adjective or adverb used to compare two people or things: *bigger, more interesting.* **45g.** See also *superlative.*

complement A *subject complement* is a word or group of words used after a linking verb to refer to and describe the subject: Harry looks *happy.* An *object complement* is a word or group of words used after a direct object to complete its meaning: They call him a *liar.* **37d, 43c.**

complete verb A verb that shows tense. Some verb forms, such as *-ing* (present) participles and past participles, require auxiliary verbs to make them complete verbs. *Going* and *seen* are not complete verbs; *are going* and *has been seen* are complete. **38c, 41c.**

complex sentence A sentence that has one independent clause and one or more dependent clauses: *He wept when he won the marathon.* **34c.**

compound adjective An adjective formed of two or more words often connected with hyphens: a *well-constructed* house. **45d, 56b.**

compound-complex sentence A sentence that has at least two independent clauses and one or more dependent clauses: *She works in Los Angeles, but her husband works in San Diego, where they both live.* **34c.**

compound noun A noun formed of two or more words: *toothbrush, merry-go-round.* **56b.**

compound predicate A predicate consisting of two or more verbs and their objects, complements, and modifiers: He *whistles and sings in the morning.* **38d, 40h.**

compound sentence A sentence that has two or more independent clauses: *She works in Los Angeles, but her husband works in San Diego.* **34c.**

compound subject A subject consisting of two or more nouns or pronouns and their modifiers: *My uncle and my aunt* are leaving soon. **43g, 44a.**

conditional clause A clause introduced by *if* or *unless,* expressing conditions of fact, prediction, or speculation: *If we earned more,* we would spend more. **41j.**

conjunction   The part of speech used to link words, phrases, or clauses. **37d, 43g.** See also *coordinating conjunction; correlative conjunctions; subordinating conjunction; parts of speech.*

conjunctive adverb   A transitional expression used to link two independent clauses. Some common conjunctive adverbs are *moreover, however,* and *furthermore.* **2d, 37d.**

connotation   The meanings and associations suggested by a word, as distinct from the word's denotation, or dictionary meaning. **33c.**

contraction   The shortened form that results when an apostrophe replaces one or more letters: *can't* (for *cannot*), *he's* (for *he is* or *he has*), *they're* (for *they are*). **48d.**

coordinate adjective   Evaluative adjective modifying a noun. When coordinate adjectives appear in a series, their order can be reversed, and they can be separated by *and.* Commas are used between coordinate adjectives: the *comfortable, expensive car.* **47g.**

coordinating conjunction   The seven coordinating conjunctions are *and, but, or, nor, so, for,* and *yet.* They connect sentence elements that are parallel in structure: He couldn't call, *but* he wrote a letter. **31c, 37d, 47b.**

coordination   The connection of two or more ideas to give each one equal emphasis: *Sue worked after school,* so *she didn't have time to jog.* **31c.**

correlative conjunctions   A pair of conjunctions joining equivalent elements. The most common correlative conjunctions are *either... or, neither... nor, both... and,* and *not only... but also: Neither* my sister *nor* I could find the concert hall. **40j.**

countable noun   A common noun that has a plural form and can be used after a plural quantity word (such as *many* or *three*): one *book,* three *stores,* many *children.* **60a ESL, 60e ESL.**

cumulative adjective   An adjective that modifies a noun and occurs in a conventional order with no comma between adjectives: a *new red plastic* bench. **62g ESL.**

dangling modifier   A modifier that fails to modify the noun or pronoun it is intended to modify: not *Turning the corner,* the lights went out. but *Turning the corner, we* saw the lights go out. **40c.**

demonstrative pronoun   The four demonstrative pronouns are *this, that, these,* and *those: That* is my glass. **43i.**

denotation   A word's dictionary meaning. See also *connotation.* **33b, 33c.**

dependent clause   A clause that cannot stand alone as a complete sentence and needs to be attached to an independent clause. A dependent clause begins with a subordinating word such as *because, if, when, although, who, which,* or *that: When it rains,* we can't take the children outside. **37d, 38b.**

diction   Choice of appropriate words and tone. **33.**

direct object   The person or thing that receives the action of a verb: They ate *cake* and *ice cream*. **37d, 62c** ESL.

direct quotation   A person's words reproduced exactly and placed in quotation marks: *"I won't be home until noon,"* she said. **10f, 40d, 62d** ESL.

double negative   The use of two negative words in the same sentence: He does *not* know *nothing*. This usage is nonstandard and needs to be avoided: *He does not know anything. He knows nothing.* **45f.**

ellipsis   Omission of words from a quotation, indicated by three dots: "I pledge allegiance to the flag . . . and to the republic for which it stands . . ." **51g.**

etymology   The origin of a word. **33b.**

euphemism   A word or phrase used to disguise literal meaning: She *is in the family way* [meaning "pregnant"]. **33g.**

faulty predication   The error that results when subject and verb do not match logically: <u>not</u> The *decrease* in stolen cars *has diminished* in the past year. <u>but</u> The *number* of stolen cars *has decreased* in the past year. **40e.**

figurative language   The use of unusual comparisons or other devices to draw attention to a specific meaning. See *metaphor; simile.* **5b, 33e.**

filler subject   *It* or *there* used in the subject position of a clause, followed by a form of *be*: *There are* two elm trees on the corner. **30b, 43d, 64f** ESL.

first person   The person speaking or writing: *I* or *we*. **44a.**

fragment   A group of words that is punctuated as if it were a sentence but is grammatically incomplete because it lacks a subject or a predicate or begins with a subordinating word: *Because it was a sunny day.* **38.**

frequency adverb   An adverb that expresses time (such as *often, always,* or *sometimes*). It can be the first word in a sentence or be used between the subject and the main verb, after an auxiliary verb, or as the last word in a sentence. **45e.**

fused sentence   See *run-on sentence.*

gender   Classification of a noun or pronoun as masculine *(Uncle John, he)*, feminine *(Ms. Torez, she)*, or neuter *(book, it)*. **44e, 64g** ESL.

generic noun   A noun referring to a general class or type of person or object: A *student* has to write many papers. **44d.**

gerund   The *-ing* verb form used as a noun: *Walking* is good for your health. **43e, 61** ESL, **63e** ESL. See also *verbal.*

helping verb   See *auxiliary verb.*

imperative mood   Verb mood used to give a command: *Follow* me. **34b.**

indefinite pronoun   A pronoun that refers to a nonspecific person or thing: *anybody, something.* **43h, 44d.**

independent clause   A clause that has a subject and predicate and is not introduced by a subordinating word. An independent clause can function as a complete sentence. *Birds sing. The old man was singing a song. Hailing a cab, the woman used a silver whistle.* **31c, 37d.**

indicative mood   Verb mood used to ask questions or make statements. It is the most common mood. **34b.**

indirect object   The person or thing to whom or to which, or for whom or for which, an action is performed. It comes between the verb and the direct object: He gave his *sister* some flowers. **37d, 62c** ESL.

indirect question   A question reported by a speaker or writer, not enclosed in quotation marks: They asked *if we would help them.* **62d** ESL.

indirect quotation   A description or paraphrase of the words of another speaker or writer, integrated into a writer's own sentence and not enclosed in quotation marks: He said *that they were making money.* **40d, 62d** ESL.

infinitive   The base form, or dictionary form, of a verb, preceded by *to: to see, to smile.* **41a, 61c** ESL, **61e** ESL.

infinitive phrase   An infinitive with its objects, complements, or modifiers: *To wait for hours* is unpleasant. He tries hard *to be punctual.* **38a, 43e.**

intensive pronoun   A pronoun ending in *-self* or *-selves* and used to emphasize its antecedent: They *themselves* will not attend. **44h.**

interjection   The part of speech that expresses emotion and is able to stand alone: *Aha! Wow!* Interjections are seldom appropriate in academic writing. **37d.**

interrogative pronoun   A pronoun that introduces a direct or indirect question: *Who* is that? I don't know *what* you want. **43k, 44i.**

intransitive verb   A verb that does not take a direct object: Exciting events *have occurred.* He *fell.* **37d, 42a.** See also *transitive verb.*

inverted word order   The presence of the verb before the subject in a sentence; used in questions or for emphasis: *Do you expect* an award? Not only *does she do* gymnastics, she also wins awards. **30b, 43d.**

irregular verb   A verb that does not form its past tense and past participle with *-ed: sing, sang, sung; grow, grew, grown.* **41a.**

linking verb   A verb connecting a subject to its complement. Typical linking verbs are *be, become, seem,* and *appear:* He *seems* angry. A linking verb is intransitive; it does not take a direct object. **37d, 41c, 44a, 45c.**

mental activity verb   A verb not used in a tense showing progressive aspect: *prefer, want, understand:* <u>not</u> He *is wanting to leave.* <u>but</u> He *wants* to leave. **41d.**

metaphor   A figure of speech implying a comparison but not stating it directly: a *gale* of laughter. **5b, 33e.**

misplaced modifier   An adverb (particularly *only* and *even*) or a descriptive phrase or clause positioned in such a way that it modifies the wrong word or words: She showed the ring to her sister *that her aunt gave her.* **40b.**

mixed structure   A sentence with two or more types of structures that clash grammatically: *By doing* her homework at the last minute *caused* Meg to make many mistakes. **40a, 40e, 40f.**

modal auxiliary verb   The nine modal auxiliaries are *will, would, can, could, shall, should, may, might,* and *must.* They are followed by the base form of a verb: *will go, would believe.* Modal auxiliaries do not change form. **41c, 61b** ESL.

modifier   A word or words that describe another noun, adverb, verb, phrase, or clause: He is a *happy* man. He is smiling *happily.* **45.**

mood   The mood of a verb tells whether the verb states a fact (*indicative:* She *goes* to school); gives a command (*imperative: Come* back soon); or expresses a condition, wish, or request (*subjunctive:* I wish you *were* not leaving). **41j.** See also *imperative mood; indicative mood; subjunctive mood.*

nonrestrictive phrase or clause   A phrase or clause that adds extra or non-essential information to a sentence and is set off with commas: His report, *which he gave to his boss yesterday,* received enthusiastic praise. **46d, 47d.**

noun   The part of speech that names a person, place, thing, or idea. Nouns are proper or common and, if common, countable or uncountable. **37d, 60** ESL. See also *collective noun; common noun; compound noun; countable noun; generic noun; noun clause; parts of speech; proper noun; uncountable noun.*

noun clause   A dependent clause that functions as a noun: I like *what you do. Whoever scores a goal* will be a hero. **37d.**

noun phrase   A noun with its accompanying modifiers and articles: *a brilliant, hard-working student.* **37d.**

number   The indication of a noun or pronoun as singular (one person, place, thing, or idea) or plural (more than one). **43a, 44d.**

object of preposition   The noun or pronoun (along with its modifiers) that follows a preposition: on *the beach.* **37d.**

paragraph   A group of sentences set off in a text, usually on one topic. **2b, 2c.**

parallelism   The use of coordinate structures that have the same grammatical form: She likes *swimming* and *playing* tennis. **40j.**

participle phrase   A phrase beginning with an *-ing* verb form or a past participle: The woman *wearing a green skirt* is my sister. *Baffled by the puzzle,* he gave up. **34e.** See also *verbal.*

particle A word (frequently a preposition or adverb) that combines with a verb to form a phrasal verb, a verb with an idiomatic meaning: get *over,* take *after.* **63d** ESL.

parts of speech Eight traditional categories of words used to form sentences: noun, pronoun, verb, adjective, adverb, conjunction, preposition, and interjection. See **37d** and the listing for each in this glossary.

passive voice Attribute of a verb when its grammatical subject is the receiver of the action that the verb describes: The book *was written* by my professor. **30c, 42**. See also *active voice.*

past participle A verb form that in regular verbs ends with *-ed*. The past participle needs an auxiliary verb to function as the complete verb of a clause: *has chosen, was cleaned, might have been told.* The past participle can function alone as an adjective. **41a, 41c, 41d, 41g, 61f** ESL.

perfect progressive tense forms Verb tenses that show actions in progress up to a specific point in present, past, or future time. For active voice verbs, use forms of the auxiliary *have been* followed by the *-ing* form of the verb: *has/have been living, had been living, will have been living.* **41d**.

perfect tense forms Verb tenses that show actions completed by present, past, or future time. For active voice verbs, use forms of the auxiliary *have* followed by the past participle of the verb: *has/have arrived, had arrived, will have arrived.* **41d**.

person The form of a pronoun or verb that indicates whether the subject is doing the speaking (first person, *I* or *we*); is spoken to (second person, *you*); or is spoken about (third person, *he, she, it,* or *they*). **43a, 44a**.

phrasal verb An idiomatic verb phrase consisting of a verb and a preposition or adverb called a particle: *put off, put up with.* **63d** ESL.

phrase A group of words that lacks a subject or predicate and functions as a noun, verb, adjective, or adverb: *under the tree, has been singing, amazingly simple.* **37d**. See also *absolute phrase; appositive phrase; infinitive phrase; participle phrase; prepositional phrase.*

possessive The form of a noun or pronoun that indicates ownership. Possessive pronouns include *my, his, her, their, theirs,* and *whose: my* boat, *your* socks. The possessive form of a noun is indicated by an apostrophe or an apostrophe and *-s: Mario's* car, the *children's* nanny, the *birds'* nests. **43j, 44b, 48a, 48b**.

predicate The part of a sentence that contains the verb and its modifiers and that comments on or makes an assertion about the subject. To be complete, a sentence needs a subject and a predicate. **37d**.

prefix Letters attached to the beginning of a word that change the word's meaning: *un*necessary, *re*organize, *non*stop. **56a**.

preposition The part of speech used with a noun or pronoun in a phrase to indicate time, space, or some other relationship. **37d, 46f, 63** ESL. The noun or pronoun is the object of the preposition: *on the table, after dinner, to her.* Examples of prepositions:

about	among	between	for	near	past	under
above	around	by	from	of	since	until
across	at	despite	in	off	through	up
after	before	down	inside	on	till	with
against	behind	during	into	out	to	within
along	below	except	like	over	toward	without

prepositional phrase A phrase beginning with a preposition and including the object of the preposition and its modifiers: The head *of the electronics company* was waiting *for an hour.* **37d, 38a, 46f.**

present participle The *-ing* form of a verb, showing an action as being in progress or continuous: They are *sleeping.* Without an auxiliary, the *-ing* form cannot function as a complete verb but can be used as an adjective: *searing* heat. When the *-ing* form is used as a noun, it is called a gerund: *Skiing* can be dangerous. **41a, 43e, 61d** ESL, **61f** ESL. See also *verbal.*

progressive tense forms Verb tenses that show actions in progress at a point or over a period of time in past, present, or future time. They use a form of *be* + the *-ing* form of the verb: They *are working;* he *will be writing.* **41d, 41e, 41f.**

pronoun The part of speech that takes the place of a noun, a noun phrase, or another pronoun. Pronouns are of various types: personal *(I, they);* possessive *(my, mine, their, theirs);* demonstrative *(this, that, these, those);* intensive and reflexive *(myself, herself);* relative *(who, whom, whose, which, that);* interrogative *(who, which, what);* and indefinite *(anyone, something).* **37d, 43i, 43j, 44.** See *parts of speech.*

pronoun reference The connection between a pronoun and its antecedent. Reference should be clear and unambiguous: The *lawyer* picked up *his* hat and left. **44c.**

proper noun The capitalized name of a specific person, place, or thing: *Golden Gate Park, University of Kansas.* **37d, 53b, 60f** ESL. See also *common noun.*

quantity word A word expressing the idea of quantity, such as *each, every, several, many,* and *much.* Subject-verb agreement is tricky with quantity words: *Each* of the students *has* a different assignment. **43h.** See also *agreement.*

reflexive pronoun A pronoun ending in *-self* or *-selves* and referring to the subject of a clause: They incriminated *themselves.* **44h.**

regular verb Verb that ends with *-ed* in its past tense and past participle forms. **41a.**

relative clause See *adjective clause.*

relative pronoun Pronoun that introduces a relative clause: *who, whom, whose, which, that.* **46.**

restrictive phrase or clause A phrase or clause that provides information essential for identifying the word or phrase it modifies. A restrictive phrase or clause is not set off with commas: The book *that is first on the bestseller list* is a memoir. **46d, 47i.**

run-on sentence The error that results when two independent clauses are not separated by a conjunction or by any punctuation: not *The dog ate the meat the cat ate the fish.* but *The dog ate the meat; the cat ate the fish.* Also called a *fused sentence.* **39.**

second person The person addressed: *you.* **44a, 44g.**

shifts Inappropriate switches in grammatical structure, such as from one tense to another or from statement to command or from indirect to direct quotation: not Joan asked *whether I was warm enough* and *did I sleep well* but *Joan asked whether I was warm enough and had slept well.* **40d, 41h.**

simile A figure of speech that makes a direct comparison: She has a laugh *like a fire siren.* **5b, 33e.**

simple tense forms Verb tenses that show present, past, or future time with no perfect or progressive aspects: they *work,* we *worked,* she *will work.* **41d, 41e, 41f.**

split infinitive An infinitive with a word or words separating *to* from the base verb form: *to successfully complete.* This structure has become acceptable. **40b.**

Standard English "The variety of English that is generally acknowledged as the model for the speech and writing of educated speakers." This *American Heritage Dictionary,* 4th edition, definition warns that the use of the term is "highly elastic and variable" and confers no "absolute positive evaluation." **33d, 37c.**

subject The noun or pronoun that performs the action of the verb in an active voice sentence or receives the action of the verb in a passive voice sentence. To be complete, a sentence needs a subject and a verb. **37d, 38d, 40i, 62a** ESL.

subjunctive mood Verb mood used in conditions and in wishes, requests, and demands: I wish he *were* here. She demanded that he *be* present. **41j.**

subordinate clause See *dependent clause.*

subordinating conjunction A conjunction used to introduce a dependent adverb clause: *because, if, when, although, since, while.* **31c, 37d, 38b.**

suffix Letters attached to the end of a word that change the word's function or meaning: gentle*ness,* humor*ist,* slow*er,* sing*ing.* **58e.**

superlative   The form of an adjective or adverb used to compare three or more people or things: *biggest; most unusual; least effectively.* **45g, 60d** ESL. See also *comparative.*

synonym   A word that has the same or nearly the same meaning as another word: *quick, rapid; stanza, verse; walk, stroll; shiny, sparkling.* **33b.**

tense   The form of a verb that indicates time. Verbs change form to distinguish present and past time: he *goes;* he *went.* Various structures are used to express future time, mainly *will* + the base form, or *going to* + the base form. **41d.** See also *perfect progressive tense forms; perfect tense forms; progressive tense forms; simple tense forms.*

third person   The person or thing spoken about: *he, she, it, they,* or nouns. **43a, 44a.**

topic chain   Repetition of key words or related words throughout a passage to aid cohesion. **31a, 42d.**

transitional expression   A word or phrase used to connect two independent clauses. Typical transitional expressions are *for example, however,* and *similarly:* We were able to swim today; *in addition,* we took the canoe out on the river. A semicolon frequently connects the two independent clauses. **2d, 47e, 50a.**

transitive verb   A verb that takes an object—the person or thing that receives the action (in the active voice): Dogs *chase* cats. When transitive verbs are used in the passive voice, the subject receives the action of the verb: Cats *are chased* by dogs. **37d, 41b, 42a, 42b.** See also *intransitive verb.*

uncountable noun   A common noun that cannot follow a plural quantity word (such as *several* or *many*) is never used with *a* or *an,* is used with a singular third person verb, and has no plural form: *furniture, happiness, information.* **43e, 60b** ESL.

verb   The part of speech that expresses action or being and tells (in the active voice) what the subject of the clause is or does. The complete verb in a clause might require auxiliary or modal auxiliary verbs to complete its meaning. **37d, 41, 61** ESL. See also the following entries for more specific information:

active voice	*mental activity verb*	*predicate*
agreement	*modal auxiliary verb*	*present participle*
auxiliary verb	*mood*	*progressive tense forms*
base form	*parts of speech*	*regular verb*
complete verb	*passive voice*	*simple tense forms*
compound predicate	*past participle*	*subjunctive mood*
indicative mood	*perfect progressive*	*tense*
infinitive	*tense forms*	*transitive verb*
intransitive verb	*perfect tense forms*	*verb chain*
irregular verb	*phrasal verb*	*voice*
linking verb		

verbal A form, derived from a verb, that cannot function as the main verb of a clause. The three types of verbals are the infinitive, the *-ing* participle, and the past participle (for example, *to try, singing, stolen*). A verbal can function in a phrase as a noun, adjective, or adverb. **61** ESL, **63e** ESL.

verb chain Combination of an auxiliary verb, a main verb, and verbals: She *might have promised to leave;* they *should deny having helped* him. **61** ESL.

verb phrase A complete verb formed by auxiliaries and the main verb: *should have waited.* **37d.**

voice Transitive verbs (verbs that take an object) can be used in the active voice *(He is painting the door)* or the passive voice *(The door is being painted)*. **42.**

zero article The lack of an article *(a, an,* or *the)* before a noun. Uncountable nouns are used with the zero article when they make no specific reference. **60b** ESL, **60d** ESL, **60e** ESL.

Index

Note: An asterisk (*) refers to a page number in the Glossary of Grammatical Terms.

Text Credits
Part 1 Berlin, Irving. "A Pretty Girl Is Like a Melody." *Ziegfeld Follies of 1919*. Irving Berlin Music Corp.
Braithwaite, Dawn O. "Viewing Persons with Disabilities as a Culture." *Intercultural Communication*.
    6th ed. Ed. Larry A. Samovar and Richard E. Porter. Belmont, CA: Wadsworth, 1991. 36.
Columbia Encyclopedia online. Definition of "life." <http://www.bartleby.com/65/li/life.html>.
    Copyright © Columbia University Press. Used with permission.
Frost, Robert. "Stopping by Woods on a Snowy Evening." *The Poetry of Robert Frost*. Ed. Edward
    Connery Lathem. New York: Henry Holt and Company, Inc., 1979. Copyright © 1951 by Robert
    Frost, copyright © 1969 by Henry Holt and Company, Inc. Reprinted by permission of Henry Holt
    and Company.
Gallop-Goodman, Gerda. "Please Don't Hang Up." *American Demographics* 23.5 (2001): 28. Figure "Do
    Not Disturb" copyright © 2001, Primedia Business Magazines and Media, Inc. All rights reserved.
Gilbert, Mathew. "All Talk, All the Time." *Boston Globe Magazine* 4 June 2000: 9. Reprinted courtesy of
    the Boston Globe.
Hölldobler, Bert, and Edward O. Wilson. *Journey to the Ants*. Cambridge, MA: Harvard University
    Press, 1994. 29.
Mallon, Thomas. *A Book of One's Own: People and Their Diaries*. New York: Ticknor and Fields, 1984. 1.
Nielsen, Jakob. *Designing Web Usability*. Indianapolis: New Riders, 1999. 168.
Reed, Ishmael. "America: The Multinational Society." *Writin' Is Fightin'*. New York: Atheneum, 1990.
    1. Copyright © 1990 by Atheneum.
Reichl, Ruth. *Tender at the Bone: Growing Up at the Table*. New York: Broadway, 1991. 95.
Rose, Phyllis. *Parallel Lives: Five Victorian Marriages*. New York: Knopf, 1986. 106.
Soriano, Joanne L. "KCC Service Learning at the Lyon Arboretum" (reflective journal). Kapi'olani
    Community College. 2 June 1997 <http://leahi.kcc.hawaii.edu/josian/service/jo.html>. Reprinted
    by permission of Joanne L. Soriano.
Tannen, Deborah. *You Just Don't Understand*. New York: Ballantine, 1990. 226.
Toulmin, Stephen. *The Uses of Argument*. 1958. Cambridge: Cambridge University Press, 1964. 101–102.
Ward, Geoffrey C. *The Civil War: An Illustrated History*. New York: Knopf, 1990. 12.
Part 2 City University of New York. Library catalog (CUNY Union Catalog) screen shot for "Hasci,
    Timothy."
EBSCOhost database, City University of New York Libraries, Microsoft Internet Explorer. Screen shots
    showing entry for "Rafilson, Fred M." and search terms "fire fighters" and "recruiting " with three
    results. Copyright © EBSCO Publishing 2004. All rights reserved.
Google search screen shot showing results of search using key words "recruiting women police."
    Copyright © Google, Inc. Used with permission.
Laird, Ellen. "Internet Plagiarism: We All Pay the Price." *Chronicle of Higher Education* 13 July 2001: 5.
    Reprinted by permission of the author. Ellen Laird teaches in the English Department at Hudson
    Valley Community College.
LexisNexis database screen showing top of text article: Baker, Al. "Fire Department Looks to Diversify
    the Ranks." *New York Times*, April 3, 2002. Copyright © 2003 Lexis/Nexis, a division of Reed
    Elsevier, Inc. All rights reserved.
Newcomb, Amelia. "Suspense and Suspension." *Christian Science Monitor*, 2 May 2000: 13. Copyright
    © 2000 by The Christian Science Monitor (www.csmonitor.com). Reproduced with permission. All
    rights reserved.

COMMON EDITING AND PROOFREADING MARKS

Symbol	Example (change marked)	Example (change made)
⌒o	Correct a typu.	Correct a typo.
⌒r⌒/m⌒/⌒o	Corrlect ʌore than one typn.	Correct more than one typo.
t	Insert a leter.	Insert a letter.
or words	Insert a word.	Insert a word or words.
✗	Make a ⌀deletion.	Make a deletion.
⌯	Deleʈe and close up space.	Delete and close up space.
⌒	Close up exʈra space.	Close up extra space.
#	Insertproper spacing.	Insert proper spacing.
#/⌒	Insertsʌpace and close up.	Insert space and close up.
tr	Transpose letters inʈcated.	Transpose letters indicated.
tr	Transpose⌐as words⌐indicated.	Transpose words as indicated.
tr	Reorder shown as words several.	Reorder several words as shown.
⌐	⌐ Move text to left.	Move text to left.
⌐	⌐ Move text to right.	Move text to right.
⌒	⌐Indent for paragraph.	Indent for paragraph.
no ⌒	⌐ No paragraph indent.	No paragraph indent.
run in	Run back turnover⌐ lines.	Run back turnover lines.
⌐	Break line when it runs farʈtoo long.	Break line when it runs far too long.
⊙	Insert period here⌐	Insert period here.
⌃	Commas⌐commas everywhere.	Commas, commas everywhere.
⌄	Its in need of an apostrophe.	It's in need of an apostrophe.
⅋ / ⅋	⌐Add quotation marks⌐he begged.	"Add quotation marks," he begged.
;	Add a semicolon⌐don't hesitate.	Add a semicolon; don't hesitate.
:	She advised⌐"You need a colon."	She advised: "You need a colon."
?	How about a question mark⌐	How about a question mark?
⌐=⌐	Add a hyphen to a bill⌐like receipt.	Add a hyphen to a bill-like receipt.
⟨/⟩	Add parentheses⌐as they say⌐	Add parentheses (as they say).
lc	Sometimes you want ⌀owercase.	Sometimes you want lowercase.
caps	Sometimes you want upperCASE.	Sometimes you want UPPERCASE.
ital	Add italics instantly.	Add italics *instantly*.
rom	But use *roman* in the main.	But use roman in the main.
bf	Add boldface if necessary.	Add **boldface** if necessary.
sp	Spell out all ③ terms.	Spell out all three terms.
stet	Let stand as is.	Let stand as is. (This retracts a change already marked.)

CORRECTION GUIDE

Note: Numbers refer to sections in the book.

Abbreviation	Meaning/Error
ab or abbr	abbreviation, **54, 57e**
adj	adjective, **37d, 45**
adv	adverb, **37d, 45**
agr	agreement, **43, 44d**
apos	apostrophe, **40h, 48**
arg	argument error, **4e–4j**
art	articles, **60**
awk	awkward, **30, 31, 40**
bias	biased or sexist language, **33f, 44e**
ca or case	case, **44a**
cap (t̲om)	use capital letter, **53, 57c, 60f**
coh	coherence, **2d**
comp	comparative, **45g, 45h**
coord	coordination, **31c, 47b**
cs	comma splice, **39**
d	diction, **33**
db neg	double negative, **45f**
dev	development, **2c**
dm	dangling modifier, **40c**
doc	documentation, **11–19**
-ed	error with *-ed* ending, **41g**
exact	exactness, **33c**
frag	sentence fragment, **38**
fs	fused sentence, **39**
gen	gender bias, **33f, 44e**
hyph	hyphenation, **56, 57d**
id	idiom, **63**
inc	incomplete sentence or construction, **40h, 62a**
ind quot	indirect quotation, **41i, 62d**
-ing	error with *-ing* ending, **61**
ital	italics/underlining, **12a, 15a, 18c, 19a, 52, 57b**
jar	jargon, **33d**
lc (M̶e)	use a lowercase letter, **53**
log	logic, **4h, 4i, 4j**

Abbreviation	Meaning/Error
mix or mixed	mixed construction, **40a**
mm	misplaced modifier, **40b**
ms	manuscript form, **3f, 26, 27**
nonst	nonstandard usage, **37c, 38–46**
num	faulty use of numbers, **55**
//	parallelism, **40j**
p	punctuation, **47–51, 57a**
pass	passive voice, **30c, 42**
prep	preposition, **37d, 63**
pron	pronoun, **37d, 44**
quot	quotation, **10f, 49**
ref	pronoun reference, **44c**
rel cl	relative clause, **46**
rep or red	repetitive or redundant, **29a, 29d**
-s	error with *-s* ending, **43**
shift	needless shift, **40d, 41h**
sp	spelling, **58**
s/pl	singular/plural, **43a, 43h, 58a**
sub	subordination, **31c, 62e**
sup	superlative, **45g**
s-v agr	subject-verb agreement, **43**
t	verb tense, **41d**
trans	transition, **2d, 47e**
und	underlining/italics, **12a, 52, 57b**
us	usage, **65**
v or vb	error with verb, **41**
var	[sentence] variety, **34**
w	wordy, **29**
wc	word choice, **33**
wo	word order, **34d, 62b, 62g**
ww	wrong word, **33**

CONTENTS